Lucifer
Rising

LUCIFER RISING

BRITISH INTELLIGENCE AND THE OCCULT IN THE SECOND WORLD WAR

NICHOLAS BOOTH

The
History
Press

For Sarah, with all my love.

First published 2016

The History Press
The Mill, Brimscombe Port
Stroud, Gloucestershire, GL5 2QG
www.thehistorypress.co.uk

© Nicholas Booth, 2016

The right of Nicholas Booth to be identified as the Author
of this work has been asserted in accordance with the
Copyright, Designs and Patents Act 1988.

British Library Cataloguing in Publication Data.
A catalogue record for this book is available from the British Library.

ISBN 978 0 07509 6511 8

Typesetting and origination by The History Press
Printed in Great Britain

CONTENTS

Where facts are lacking, rumours abound
Alberto Moravia

INTRODUCTION

ON HIS SATANIC MAJESTY'S SECRET SERVICE

To the Director of Naval Intelligence   *24 May 1941*
Sir:
If it is true that Herr Hess is much influenced by astrology and Magick, my services
might be of use to the Department in case he should not be willing to do what you
wish. I have the honour to be, Sir,
Your obedient servant
ALEISTER CROWLEY

The only way to describe it is a lair and, in its dimly lit and chintzy ostentation, an evil one at that. When the tall naval officer entered, he tried to keep both an open mind and a straight face. The circumstances might well have portended great dangers for, at face value, this meeting with the self-appointed necromancer who liked to call himself the wickedest man in the world, was one of the most extraordinary that the man from Naval Intelligence would ever experience. And given some of the people Commander Ian Fleming RNVR encountered during his wartime secret service, that is saying something.

With his usual urbane aplomb, the future creator of James Bond took it all in his stride. As the personal assistant to the sometimes acerbic head of Naval Intelligence, Fleming was used to considering strange and bizarre operations. Wartime expediency dictated that no matter how seemingly ridiculous, nothing was beyond their remit. In so many ways, Ian Fleming's meeting with Aleister Crowley lent itself to his later writings with villains defined by their physical repugnance. As several commentators have pointed out, Crowley himself would have made an ideal Bond villain. It was his eyes, and their unwavering hypnotic stare, that captivated the future thriller writer. Their mesmeric aspect informed the hypnotic stare – to wit, 'the whites of his eyes, which showed all around the irises, lending something impassive and doll-like to his gaze' – of his first ever prototypical villain, Le Chiffre.

In the spring of 1941, though, the discussion itself (at face value concerning a generous offer of help) was politely received. In the previous war, Aleister Crowley had, he claimed, been employed by British Intelligence as some sort of propagandist. Now, according to some accounts, this latest meeting was merely a stepping stone to even greater employment. The Beast, as Crowley liked to refer to himself, was extremely impressed by Fleming's 'unalloyed joy in sex, food and thrills'.

'You could well have been an occultist,' Crowley is supposed to have said.

'I consider that I am,' Fleming replied, no doubt stroking a black (or possibly, a white) cat for good measure.

What exactly they discussed and why has been the source of endless – often farcical – speculation over the years. It has fuelled endless conspiracy theories that have become ever more elaborate and byzantine with the passing of time. Some are rooted in tongue-in-cheek mischief-making, others as proof of the supremacy of supernatural forces.

The reality, as this book will show, is much more mundane.

The greater truth is that while many have maintained their wartime meeting smacks of James Bond, in truth, his rendezvous with Aleister Crowley reads more like Austin Powers. According to the dialogue above, courtesy of Amado Crowley who was supposedly the Beast's son (in reality, one of a strange number of fantasists who gathered in his wake) the overarching sense of theatricality had more to do with pantomime.

That it took place on the English Riviera is another surreal aspect to the story.

Torquay is hardly a den of devilish iniquity, yet that was where the wickedest man in the world had washed up. By now in his late 60s, Crowley was a pitiful shadow of his former self, thanks to a heroin addiction fuelled by the debilitating effects of his asthma, made worse by having been bombed out during the Blitz. Far from achieving the acclaim and respect he felt he deserved, Crowley was on his uppers. Throughout his life he had embellished details of his greatness as a chess player, mountaineer, writer, artist and occult magus but was, probably more accurately in the phrase of a grandson of one of his lovers, 'the rottenest son of a bitch I ever met'.

If Aleister Crowley was never quite a lovable eccentric, he had made a certain strain of English strangeness all his own. As the man who claimed to be his son Amado has pointed out, 'his very eccentricity ... was his cover as an agent.' Certainly that seems to have been the case in the First World War and now, in the Second, that a representative of an organisation as staid as Naval Intelligence had even agreed to meet the self-styled Beast may seem very peculiar indeed. Yet Fleming's meeting with Crowley was one of a gathering series of surreal events which would culminate that same late spring of 1941 with perhaps the most bizarre occurrence of all – the arrival of Rudolf Hess in the British Isles a few days earlier.

These surreal events did not occur in isolation and had, at least, some basis in reality. As strange as it may seem to posterity, that same spring of 1941 saw the zenith of some of the most bizarre aspects of secret warfare – astrology, magic, political warfare and black propaganda – which would emanate from a zoo located on the outskirts of London. Far from being a concerted effort to harness the occult, this particular strand of an already surreal story had begun with the rather more mundane desire to understand if Adolf Hitler was being advised by astrologers and ended, with whatever divination of astral significance, with Rudolf Hess's parachute descent over Scotland.

Over the years, these events have prompted many strange rumours and contradictory conspiracies. Ian Fleming's supposed omniscience extends to not only being in league with the Beast, but that he had somehow already placed an astrologer in Hess's immediate circle. This mysterious figure then supposedly briefed an associate of the Deputy Führer, who then advised Hess to fly to Britain as it was written in the stars (or, at least, an unusual conjunction of planets in Taurus). In other words, a very different form of bull was taking place against the backdrop of what one bemused chronicler – a senior intelligence official – later termed a 'period of horoscopes, crystal-gazing and guesswork'.

So what really happened when 666 met the literary father of 007?

That and similar questions which have gathered like urban myths is the purpose of this book. It will examine, reassess and reveal the reality of what actually happened with some of the more peculiar stories of the secret war, how writers embellished many of them and, underlying it, that the only reason the occult was even considered was because of desperation as Britain stood alone against the Third Reich in 1940–1. The ultimate irony is that for all this use of seers – and occultists and prognosticators of various hues – none could predict what the end result might be.

That was not for lack of trying, and some of the characters involved were, as the contemporary records make clear, very, very trying. Their number includes a repressed homosexual Hungarian émigré astrologer with a penchant for dressing up in women's clothes as well as a military uniform that he wasn't entitled to wear; a mysterious agent runner who sometimes paraded around Central London with what appeared to be a dancing bear, whose first wife was rumoured to have died in an occultic ceremony that went hideously wrong; a lord of the realm who was an ornithologist of some note, dabbled in the occult, recruited to carry out secret operations with pigeons and whose mother seems to have thought she was a bird.

As in an early Bond novel where 007 is reminiscing about the good old days – and moral certainties of a war against evil – he wonders, as no doubt readers of this book will at times, if they should be better dismissed as 'all just the stuff of boys' adventure books, but it was all true'?

The answer, incredibly in many cases in this story, is yes.

The occult is defined as secret, hidden knowledge. For those who believe in its power, such concealed wisdom, especially that handed down from the ancients, provides a key to unlocking all the great mysteries of life. Yet so too, in a different sense, do intelligence operatives and spies, who are also trying to unravel secrets and hidden information to provide strategic advantage. Significantly, for this narrative, the occult and espionage are linked, as both concern hidden worlds, replete with concerns about security, consciousness and a sense of righteousness (particularly for those who are cut off from the refuge of their homelands).

When both have been combined together, even greater riddles and stranger rumours have resulted – especially with regard to the Second World War. In the story which follows, an even greater blurring has occurred of almost mythic grandeur: art imitates life; fiction becomes taken as fact, the more lurid the more egregiously so; much evidence has been exaggerated or mangled to become potent fiction; and many urban myths have emerged from the twilight reality of whoever could make the most ridiculous story sound even remotely plausible.

The Second World War was probably the last great battle between obvious good and evil. At some level that stark delineation contrasts truth and lies, informing both magic and propaganda that were truly also black and white.

Ultimately, it is a story of how good won out as British Intelligence prevailed against breathtaking incompetence on the part of its German equivalents. It is an all-too-human story of foolishness, bravery and folly involving bedtime indiscretions, broken promises, curious delusions and bizarre coincidences at the most unlikely times of the fighting.

As the late intelligence historian M.R.D. Foot has correctly diagnosed, many of the operations in the Second World War were 'true to the tradition of English eccentricity; the sort of thing that Captain Hornblower or Mycroft Holmes in fiction [would] have gone in for had they been faced with a similar challenge'. To their roll call should be added newer, equally ingenious gentlemen adventurers like Kimball O'Hara, Sandy Arbuthnott and William Hannay, created by authors who had all served, in some capacity, on their majesty's respective secret service. All blurred the boundaries between fact and fiction, none more significantly than a character which a vaguely amnesiac Russian general recalls in perhaps the finest novel written by Ian Fleming, a man named Bond.

In the story that follows, much remains hidden in plain sight.

As with 007 himself – a supposed secret agent who seemed to be on first-name terms with most of the concierges and barmen in the fanciest hotels around the world – there was a strange paradox. For organisations that were supposedly concealed, much of the British secret services were remarkably visible. There is hardly an organisation in the world which has been publicly examined as much as British Intelligence. It is, and always has been, one of the most unsecret services in the world. And, in the face of an official policy never to comment on many claims made against it, much of what has been written has reached the level of an urban myth. Even in an era of greater government openness with the release of many thousands of hitherto secret files, many of the more peculiar operations during the Second World War have often relied on the invariably bizarre recollections of some equally perplexing characters.

As the incomparable M.R.D. Foot has also written, 'It was only to be expected that hoaxers and fraudsters would take advantage of the public's apparently insatiable appetite for war stories describing episodes of extraordinary courage and adventure.'

Given that many people in this story were writers, it is hardly surprising that the more ridiculous claims have become embedded within the public imagination, dusted off and reprinted over the Internet and other dubious places. Many of the stories veer from the utterly improbable to the extremely inconceivable. Taking many of these stories at face value is set with pitfalls. In all the acres of newsprint and breathless blogs which have followed, particularly when James Bond elevated him to immortality, too much can be read into aspects of Ian Fleming's secret service. Yet as the producer Cubby Broccoli – who was instrumental in putting his creation on the silver screen – noted of one particular script meeting with Roald Dahl, one of Fleming's wartime colleagues, his own recollections were very different to what the writer claimed, 'but then I wasn't the best fairy tale writer in the world'.

In other words, the odd leg-pull was to be expected.

None are so exasperating as those involving spying and the supernatural. 'Many of its protagonists are grail-seekers steeped in the occult,' notes one eminently sensible review, 'who want us to share their belief in magic.' And yet oddly, the truth, as we will see, is far stranger still, a story that actually began at the end of the sixteenth century when the country faced invasion from overseas and also had to consider any means possible in fighting the enemy – and that, supposedly, included the occult.

1

007 and Counting

The creation of real life intelligence operative and old Etonian Ian Fleming, Bond borrowed his 007 title from Dr John Dee. The 16th Century British secret agent used the code for his messages to Queen Elizabeth I. The two zeros meant 'for your eyes only'.

BBC *News*, 22 November 2002

Intelligence work necessarily involves such cheating, lying and betraying, which is why it has so deleterious effect on the character. I never met anyone professionally engaged in it whom I should care to trust in any capacity.

Malcolm Muggeridge, 1972

The first time espionage, deception and the occult came together at the behest of the British government was in the sixteenth century when, by a supposed historical coincidence, the symbol 007 was involved. Or at least that was the claim of someone who has done much to muddy both this and the more recent historical record concerning the supposed omniscience of British Intelligence. After all, it makes for great symbolism that a real-life character – on whom Shakespeare supposedly based Prospero – was a magician who used that same code number, a supposed kabbalistic cipher, in his most secret communications.

It is a matter of record that Dr John Dee was an adviser to the Elizabethan Court on mathematics, geography, astronomy, navigation and philosophy (and the originator of the phrase British Empire). His experiments in alchemy, casting of horoscopes and supposed conversations with angels have eclipsed the certainty with which he was most likely an intelligencer (in effect, a spy for the court) as he travelled around Europe. But in all the acres of academic assessment of Dr Dee's accomplishments, there is no evidence that he ever used the symbol 007.

The writer who made that claim in the sixties, Richard Deacon – whose real name was Donald McCormick – had been employed after the war by Ian Fleming and knew him very well. Like so many others in this story, McCormick enjoyed nothing more than a good, old-fashioned wind up in his writings, bringing to them a certain élan: not many authors in their eightieth year ever manage to publish a connoisseur's guide to erotic literature. For many previous decades, McCormick had spun often similarly outrageous yarns amongst more genuine, easily verifiable information.

When writing a book about the British Secret Service in 1969, McCormick (writing as Deacon) claimed that Dr Dee used the symbol 007. It found a willing, appreciative audience. Spy mania, spearheaded by Ian Fleming's creation, was then at its height. James Bond had become the epitome of cool when, as one witty chronicler has noted, 'it came to pass that Thomas Connery (later Sean) did – as women will tell you – make the word flesh'.

But putting flesh on fraudulent bones would become a greater, ever growing diversion for McCormick and others, too, in the truly cottage industry which places Ian Fleming at the heart of bizarre wartime operations. As the author of a recent, highly amusing appreciation of Fleming's impact – that James Bond was indeed nothing less than the man who saved post-war Great Britain – has written, the author's real wartime record 'relied on individual pluck and initiative and which, while reasonable as part of a genuine policy of total war, were in the end, irrelevant to the war's outcome'.

What is indisputable is that during the reign of Elizabeth I, England was under almost constant threat of invasion thanks to a chasm in the religious divisions between Catholics and Protestants. Worse, a Cold War had developed over Spain's desire for a trade monopoly (which led to an actual outbreak of hostilities in 1585). Against this background, the fomenting and foiling of plots against Her Majesty's government was a constant preoccupation for which her principal secretary – and unofficial spymaster – had to be constantly alert.

In those doom-laden times, Sir Francis Walsingham made it his business to look at all sources of intelligence (especially 'foreign places from whence Mr Secretary Walsingham was wont to receive his advertisements', to quote a contemporary chronicle), no matter how unlikely their source nor exotic their provenance.

Hence his use of the good Dr Dee, who was a curious polymath on the cusp of the renaissance.[1] John Dee was undoubtedly the most colourful agent in the land. Most of Walsingham's informants in foreign courts and within the orbit of both domestic plotting and papist cabals were much less vividly drawn. Nevertheless, Sir Francis would stop at nothing in the name of security. He pioneered covert operations, plausible deniability and encouraged the cracking of codes to reveal the intentions of perfidious foreigners (such as those surrounding Mary Queen of Scots, which would come to include both the Ridolfi and Babington plots).

A wary, melancholic man who was eventually worn down by the very weight of the secrets he was carrying, Walsingham was, in a sense, the first modern spymaster. 'A most subtle searcher of hidden secrets' in the estimation of a contemporary, William Camden, Walsingham could be described as the spiritual forefather for the secret service. In the centuries which followed, espionage became a growing preoccupation for Walsingham's heirs, both spiritual and literal.

With each subsequent threat of invasion, notably following the French Revolution and the rise of Napoleon, England's ambassadors were happy to pay agents and stool pigeons for their news. The king's navy and army had its own spies, too, but it wasn't until the opening years of the twentieth century – with the rise of the kaiser's Germany – that espionage gained the imprimatur of official legitimacy with the formation of the modern secret service.

Then, as now, Britannia had to waive the rules of conventional warfare to face off the threat of an arms race, spy scares and a constant worry about foreign terror campaigns. Such was the case when, as late as 1909, the Committee on Imperial Defence (a quango of senior ministers and military chiefs of staff) came to consider how to stand off the kaiser's warmongering; they were stunned to discover there wasn't, as was usually claimed, actually a British secret service in existence.

They, it was clear, were as much victims of myth as everyone else and decided that they had better do something about it.

When, in the spring of 2015, the most recently appointed Chief of the Secret Intelligence Service, MI6, Alex Younger, made his first public appearance, he took care to discuss some of his own experiences: 'As I speak, there are

SIS officers serving in some of the most dangerous and forbidding places on Earth. I had the honour of leading some of them in Afghanistan.' Adding that he was 'particularly proud' of how their work had saved numerous British and coalition lives, there was, perhaps without his realising it, also an unacknowledged link with why there needed to be a secret service in the first place.

Unsurprisingly, a writer was involved.

Rudyard Kipling's *Kim* is the apotheosis of the Victorian spy novel, wherein unseen agents of the Raj played 'the Great Game that never ceases day and night throughout India' (a phrase which is used thirty-six times in Kipling's story) with its own eerie echoes of today's war on terror and establishing of political supremacy in the Near East. Intrigue, espionage and, at times, secret warfare centred on the mountains of Afghanistan, where Kipling's eponymous hero searched for a Russian and a French spy. And so it continues today with the Taliban and Islamist insurgents.

Kipling's fiction imitated late Victorian life and exaggerated it a little. The actual military intelligence organisation in the Raj at the time was hardly on the scale nor quite as sophisticated as that described in *Kim*. There was no overall intelligence-gathering body in India, though, as a foretaste of things to come, there was much rivalry and jealousy between those which did exist.

Real-life espionage – or rather its deficiencies – soon became more marked at the turn of the century when the Empire was threatened by Afrikaner insurgents. The Boer War saw a handful of guerrillas running rings around the British Army. Many battalions were brought to their knees by the use of unorthodox forces. Unmilitary methods, suggested a brave and resourceful reporter for the *Morning Post*, might be a better answer. Winston Churchill would become an important figure in distilling the need for greater flexibility, more imagination and the use of the unconventional.

Yet in the first years of the new century, the myths remained. While the British Empire was believed to have the best espionage system in the world, it actually had no agents in mainland Europe. Worse, with continuing trouble in South Africa and on the North West Frontier, various foreigners from without and terrorists within – encompassing suffragettes, anarchists and, admittedly, people they just didn't like the look of – threatened the certainties of kingdom. But, even worse, was 'a menace to the rest of the world', as the Foreign Office referred to Germany's militarism and expansionism in 1907.

At the start of the twentieth century, Britain was a naval power with an empire that stretched across a quarter of the globe. With a navy twice the size of any rivals, interlopers could hardly be tolerated. 'If the German fleet becomes superior to ours,' the then First Sea Lord had written at the turn of the century, 'the German army can conquer this country.'

The Kriegsmarine warships were taken as potent symbols of Teutonic power. The accession of Kaiser Wilhelm II saw him declare that the ocean 'is essential to German greatness'. This Germanic desire for naval pre-eminence fuelled an arms race over the new Dreadnought-class ships, which could both outgun and outrun existing vessels. These anxieties would be inflamed by erroneous reports that Berlin was stepping up its building programme. So began the first ever version of mutual assured destruction: that the Germans would invade Britain or else the Royal Navy would do the same in German waters as it had done at Copenhagen in 1807 and sink the new fleet.

No more potent symbol of this Teutonic aggression came in the form of his Imperial Majesty himself. Often appearing in public wearing his naval uniform, Kaiser Bill found glory and a positive fetish in the potential power of battleships. Supported by propaganda, many of his underlings in the German Navy – including Admiral von Tirpitz – had concluded that war with Britain was unavoidable. The kaiser, in conversation with a friend who later, with his permission, published the conversation in a sensational article in 1908, famously declared: 'You English are mad, mad as March hares. What on Earth has come over you that you harbour such suspicions against us?'

Something had to be done – and quickly.

Naval Intelligence, originally a committee looking at information gathered from overseas created in 1882, now concentrated purely on the collection and collation of all available material about the Germany Navy. Officers who worked for the Naval Intelligence Division (NID) now became heirs to that grand Nelsonian tradition with a far greater acuity than all other military intelligence branches (partly because, unofficially at least, it was also relying on Lloyds of London). In time, its officers distributed extensive questionnaires to captains of His Majesty's Ships, later making secret surveys of Kiel Harbour using cameras.

As Germany started to rattle its sabres, a more efficient national intelligence organisation was needed right across the board. That was why, in 1909, the Committee of Imperial Defence came to consider the matter and the need to counteract a gathering virulence that had taken hold of the British public: the inhumanity and ubiquity of the German spy, a notion stirred by the breathtakingly malign genius that was William Tufnell Le Queux.

War correspondent, lecturer, novelist and unashamed fantasist, Le Queux was, almost inevitably, a contributor to the *Daily Mail*, where he was given free rein to play on the great fears that foreigners were plotting the downfall of the Empire. In 1906, a series of his inflamed articles were collected together in book form as *The Invasion of 1910*. The ordinary Londoner would have been hard-pressed to avoid its promotion. With sandwichboarded men parading up and down the busiest streets in Prussian uniforms and spike helmets, his work could hardly fail to draw attention.

In vain, the prime minister dismissed Le Queux as 'a pernicious scavenger',[2] and today, Alan Judd terms his work fantastic, awful and 'bad enough to be enjoyable'. That same year of 1906, he dashed off half a dozen further potboilers. Within a decade, Le Queux had written dozens of similar works, the most famous being *Spies Of The Kaiser* in 1909. Overheated, melodramatic and replete with execrable dialogue, he was a kind of Dan Brown *de nos jours* in claiming that all his stories were based in reality. The public was simply being served what it wanted to hear: legions of German waiters and barbers – potential poisoners and throatcutters numbering their thousands – were waiting to subvert the country into submission.

This, then, was the atmosphere in which the luminaries of the War Department met in the summer of 1909 to consider such febrile claims. And for that, the Committee of Imperial Defence turned to a curiously benign character in his fifties, a passed-over naval officer then paddling around in a backwater, both literal and actual, who, as his most recent heir and inheritor says, was, in every sense of the word, ultimately a hard act to follow, an eccentric and an inspired choice to head up the secret service.

There is white magic and there is black magic, with many subtle variations in between, as with shadings of light and dark: there is illusion and there are hoaxes; there is also legerdemain, a splendid word suggesting deftness of touch with military connotations; there are séances and spiritual happenings, along with esotericism, dualism and gnosticism – ancient religions whose supporters shunned the material world and embraced the spiritual one. Indeed, the very word magic comes from the Persian magi, whose original meaning was 'fire-worshippers'. Most of those fires were seen in the sky, whose portents these high priests found it prudent to discern, such as those which propelled perhaps the most illustrious magi in history towards a stable in Bethlehem.

In other words, the history of magic provides us with the fragments of childhood memory and half-forgotten (or half-remembered) folk stories. The list is long: Arabian nights; carpets which transported their owners to mysterious lands; rings that granted miraculous wishes; ubiquitous genies in bottles; seventh sons of seventh sons; and trees which sprout wonderful fruits. Add to them the grails, quests and dragons of ancient myth, and we can trace a lineage to today's Harry Potter and Philip Pullman's Lyra and Will, which still enthral present-day children – and their parents.

In a wider sense, hidden or secret knowledge has an irresistible appeal.

If the main criticism of the occult is its readiness 'to relate the unrelated', the same, too, could be levelled at the fruit of espionage and intelligence material. The rich spiritual world – of magic, mysticism, astrology and alchemy – all evolve from the notion that the ancients or other civilizations somehow possessed the ultimate wisdom. It doesn't take too great a leap from cracking these hidden codes to creating those employed by agents right under the noses of the enemy.

Occultic revelations may be viewed as the ultimate spiritual need-to-know basis. 'When you are operating as an agent in the field, you never know what's happening behind your back,' said the late Professor Nicholas Goodrick-Clarke of Exeter University, the acknowledged world expert on these matters. 'Even your own people may think you are completely dispensable. That's very similar to the religious situation with the mortal in a gnostic world.'

Even after the age of enlightenment, when superstition was supposedly banished, divining the truth from specialist knowledge that gave an insight into a higher order continued. As a result, various occultic concepts have become curiously intertwined in the popular imagination, though each represent separate tributaries in its long, often surreal history. Illusion, magic and hidden or even forbidden knowledge are all viewed as one and the same. Secrets and secrecy are not restricted to one sphere of human endeavour.

Small wonder that many people who later dabbled in the occult world were also drawn from – and to – the espionage services in the Second World War. Nowhere does the subject have a starker contrast than that between Great Britain and Germany in the first few years of the twentieth century. The fighting to come in the Great War made the careers of many of the secret servants who came to prominence in the Second. Their own loyalties to king and kaiser spilled over into the later conflict. Shadowing it was another far stranger story, involving hidden and often unexplored dimensions, despite the superficial similarities between them.

Wishful thinking, it should be noted, has always been a leitmotif of the secret world. Who needed dull, prosaic facts when fiction was so much more believable. The main reason Edwardian spy scares took hold was because, for all its deficiencies, the fiction captured the public imagination. It is significant that many of the characters in the story which follows were writers, journalists and hacks of one kind or another. Both journalism and espionage have intertwined to create myths of great potency that, as the sometimes acerbic chronicler of espionage history, Philip Knightley, has commented, are nothing less than 'romantic nonsense that thrives in the intellectual twilight of the intelligence world, folk tales on which new recruits are nurtured and trained'.

Certainly, espionage and literature share an ancient lineage. The biblical King David had his own 'emissaries', Odysseus seized (and killed) a spy to reveal information about a bivouac, while Rosencrantz and Guildenstern spied on no less an exalted figure than the Danish Prince himself, Hamlet. Literary links with spies are as old as the novel itself: the Restoration author Apla Behn was involved in espionage, more tragically still was Christopher Marlowe and, in a more pedestrian way, Daniel Defoe. And this literary tradition continues, for no better reason then that writers, after all, are as inquisitive as spies. At some level, journalism and espionage are almost identical in their needs of gathering information that will gain primacy, either on the front page of a newspaper or else in a classified document that will be destined for the prime minister's eyes only.

Given that many of the more remarkable intelligence officers in the Second World War were writers or journalists, myths were inevitable. With writers of the calibre of Graham Greene, Somerset Maugham, Compton Mackenzie, Ian Fleming and Roald Dahl, it could hardly be otherwise.

Exaggeration was in their lifeblood. When asked about the distinction between spying and reporting, one chronicler – who characteristically did a great deal to confuse the two in the seventies – stated outright: 'There is none.' The late William Stevenson, who, as we will see, wrote one of the more misleading books about espionage ever, preferred to use the word 'Spyglass'. 'All through the centuries,' he took care to explain, 'reporters of one kind or another have put the spyglass to events.'

It is notable that many former spooks were pithily dismissive of their earlier careers as it all seemed so wonderfully absurd. As a journalist who had worked for MI6 during the Second World War commented, the shoe was usually on the other foot. 'Diplomats and intelligence agents, in my experience,' the caustic Malcolm Muggeridge would famously lament, 'are even bigger liars than journalists, and the historians who try to reconstruct the past out of their records are, for the most part, dealing in fantasy.'[3]

There are very few people – let alone fictional agents imperilled by fiendish foreigners – who can make the extraordinary claim of cutting off their own leg with a penknife. This often repeated story about Mansfield Cumming, the founding chief of the modern Secret Intelligence Service, is not quite true. Yet it remains part of his enduring legend, its peculiar symbolism inevitably growing 'with the telling and it became part of service mythology' in the words of the SIS's own authorised history.

The current chief, in unveiling a plaque to his extraordinary predecessor, noted with a great deal of satisfaction that Cumming's modern-day heirs use 'guile, creativity – and that thing that he would most certainly recognise – the sheer satisfaction of putting one over on those who mean us harm'. And, in this particular context, his self-inflicted sacrifice comes to define much of the potency of the fables surrounding Mansfield Cumming and why he is still so revered today within the modern MI6.

When the Great War broke out, the 55-year-old Captain Cumming had embarked on a new career as a spymaster without any particular qualification for the job. An agreeable eccentric with a paunch and, it has to be said, a Mr Punch-like physiognomy, he was an inspired choice. Cumming enjoyed all the more entertaining appurtenances of tradecraft – disguises such as toupées, false moustaches and a variety of outfits which he obtained from a theatrical costumiers in Soho – and sometimes disappeared for weeks on end. In some accounts, it is said that he pretended to be a German businessman, travelling through the Balkans, despite the fact that he didn't speak a single word of German.

That his successors still use the first letter of his surname (and, tongue in cheek, Ian Fleming appropriated the other) is a remarkable heritage. 'I am the only person in the Service allowed to write or type in Green ink,' says the latest C – as the chief still signs himself in all official communications – which also reflects Cumming's naval background.

In many ways, it is unfortunate that Mansfield Cumming was born on April Fool's Day (1859). Many accounts of people who worked with the first C have portrayed him as little more than a glorious buffoon: wearing a gold-rimmed monocle, with a penchant for disguises and always referring to his work as 'capital sport' and gleefully relating such escapades to his 'top mates', as he called his closest associates.

Yet he was hardly an upper-class twit. The man born Mansfield George Smith into a comfortable middle-class existence was a career naval officer who was commissioned as a sub-lieutenant after attending Dartmouth Naval College. A later estimation describes him as 'a clever officer with a great taste for electricity'. In time, Cumming developed an unusual attribute for a sailor, suffering from chronic, debilitating seasickness. While routing pirates in the Strait of Malacca in the late 1890s, he had to take extended sick leave. Its annoying recurrence meant that he was declared unfit for active service.

Soon, he was restricted to shore-based commands.

A second marriage followed into the family of a fairly wealthy Scottish landowner, Lady May, a prim, demure lady who remained aloof from her spouse's day job at the family home in Hampshire. Her husband simply added her maternal name Cumming to his own surname. In 1898, he had been seconded to the foreign section of the Naval Intelligence Division, which by now was distributing extensive questionnaires to captains of His Majesty's Ships. It later followed this up by developing a network of volunteer coastal observers all around the world to record shipping movements, not least those of the increasingly belligerent Germany.

Small wonder the Admiralty was terrified of a surprise attack. With this in mind, Cumming was retired on half pay to a houseboat in Bursledon[4] on the Hamble, where his work involved the building up of boom defences on Southampton Water. These were an intricate series of wires, extended and elongated poles and various wooden men-of-war that would easily ensnare any enemy ships trying to break through naval defences. In July 1906, Cumming was 'promoted' to the rank of commander (ret'd), with his work on boom defences described as 'valuable'.

Though it was hardly a front-line posting, his handicap never stopped him in his tracks. Like many other ageing officers who had been invalided out of active service, Mansfield Cumming might well have seen his career fade in the glorious sunset that was Edwardian England. What transformed his fortunes was compounded by the worst spy scares to date – courtesy of two Williams, Le Queux and the kaiser – and resulted in his being summoned up to London to face a committee that wanted to transform British Intelligence into something more than the 'amateur improvisation' which was then in existence.

Some time in the spring of 1908, a failed artist who was subsisting on bread and milk could be found shuffling aimlessly around a variety of Viennese flophouses for a few hours of itinerant rest. With nothing much better to do in the capital of his native Austria, this shambling, anti-social drifter spent most of his days visiting museums, libraries, art galleries and the opera. The young Adolf Hitler was, his apologists have made out, absorbing as much Viennese culture as any self-respecting artist and future leader of the *Deutsches Volk* would be expected to do.[5]

So it came to pass that one day that spring in the Habsburg Treasure House, the suffering artist caught sight of an elongated sword on to which various adornments had been inscribed or written over the subsequent centuries. Shambling around the ornate exhibit case, the young Adolf Hitler first saw its name – the Spear of Destiny – then heard a nearby guide extolling its virtues.

'There is a legend associated with this spear,' the guide said in suitably portentous tones. 'Whoever claims it and solves its secrets, holds the destiny of the world in his hands, for good or evil.'

Adolf Hitler was supposedly electrified. The guide pointed out that the spear could be traced as far back as Emperor Otto the Great in the tenth century AD – if not before. It was, he claimed, supposedly the lance which the Roman soldier Longinus had used to pierce the flesh of Jesus while he was on the cross. Allegedly used by such leaders as Constantine, Justinian and Charlemagne (in no less than forty-seven military campaigns), 'the Spear had passed like the finger of destiny,' one breathless chronicle relates, 'forever creating new patterns of force which had again and again changed the entire history of Europe.'

Whatever its true origins and its current provenance, Adolf Hitler went over to the nearby Hof Library to find out more. There were, it seemed, a whole tranche of spears, all of which were candidates for that which had pierced Jesus on the cross. But the one on display in Vienna seemed to be uniquely possessed of the kind of epoch-making powers which your average fascist dictator-in-the-making and putative tyrant might find useful one day. For three days, Hitler read up on the legends surrounding the spear. On the fourth, he went back to the Treasure House.

'I slowly became aware of a mighty presence around it,' he would later recall. 'The same awesome presence which I had experienced inwardly on those rare occasions in my life when I had sensed that a great destiny awaited me.'

This revelation presented Hitler with an apocalyptic 'window into the future' in which his own importance became abundantly apparent, if not immediately attainable.

The message, though, was simple. He who controlled the Spear of Destiny would control the destiny of the world.

This story is, of course, arrant nonsense, but apologists for the Nazis and the occult have rarely let the facts get in the way of a good story. The notion that Adolf Hitler's ultimate supremacy came from such demonic influences still persists today. Most of the preceding story can be dismissed as entertaining, and indeed overheated, fiction.

'Hitler's rise to power is directly linked to supernatural powers,' wrote the acknowledged expert on the subject, Professor Nicholas Goodrick-Clarke. 'According to this mythology, the appeal of Nazism cannot be explained adequately by secular material or material considerations.'

The flames of fantasy have been further fanned by that unique repository of the weird and wonderful, the World Wide Web. Even a cursory search on the Internet shows how pervasive the myth of the Spear of Destiny has become. In reality, the object which now resides in Vienna's Kunsthistorisches' Museum has been shown (in a metallurgical analysis from 2003) to date from the seventh century AD.

Yet the legend of the Spear of Destiny lives on.

For a mindlessly diverting time, simply do a search for the Spear of Destiny on the Internet. Every kind of site imaginable 'from ultra-religious Catholic to fascist fruitcake and new age cult' provide new wrinkles to the essential kernel of the story outlined above. Certainly, by the time Adolf Hitler came to power, these sorts of accounts suggest he had come to view the Spear of Destiny in much the same way that King Arthur did Excalibur.

The reality of Adolf Hitler's supposed obsession with the Spear of Destiny is less Indiana Jones and more an amateur dramatic production where the cast ham it up mercilessly in the silly-ass theatrical style of *'Allo 'Allo*. Most of the claims for the Spear of Destiny's influence on the Führer are hogwash, spread by a fellow flophouse inhabitant who, despite his subsequent stories, was never even a friend of the young Adolf Hitler. These particular yarns have been elaborated by a former British Commando who had been captured in the Western Desert in 1941 after a raid to assassinate Rommel.

Major Trevor Ravenscroft escaped from captivity three times (but was caught on each occasion) and after the war became a practitioner of white magic. At some point, Ravenscroft met Walter Johannes Stein, who claimed to have met the future Führer in a Viennese flophouse. The truth is Stein never actually knew Adolf Hitler at the time and only ever came across the Spear of Destiny legend years later, supposedly after finding a copy of a book in an occult bookshop which had apparently been owned by Adolf Hitler.

Major Ravenscroft simply collected them together and embellished them to concoct a ludicrously fanciful account of Hitler's supposed obsession with the occult. The result is what Professor Goodrick-Clarke called 'probably the single most influential "Nazi Mysteries" book in the English speaking world'. When *The Spear of Destiny* appeared in 1972, it became a kind of *The Da Vinci Code* of its day. It certainly caused an uproar with its claims that Adolf Hitler took peyote, attended séances, employed both satanic powers and planetary doppelgängers, as well as coming under the direct influence of a social network of occultists in Munich and recruited Aleister Crowley as one of his disciples. Although conspiracy theorists continue to pick over these kinds of stories, another more recent historian has aptly noted, 'books written about Nazi occultism between 1960 and 1975 were typically sensational and under-researched'.

And, for the most part, complete and utter nonsense.

Perhaps the strangest part of this already peculiar story is that Walter Johannes Stein was actually Jewish and fled to Britain in 1933. He liked to make two claims: that Aleister Crowley was a black magician who had influenced Hitler, and that he himself was a 'confidential adviser' to Winston Churchill. There is, bizarrely, some truth in the latter, for according to MI5 files he was an emissary to a nebulous group of anti-Hitler aristocrats to whom he was sent in October 1939 to Belgium. This was part of an an ongoing series of contacts with high-ranking Germans opposed to Hitler via various cutouts and back channels to foment anti-Nazi sentiment which would, as we will see, come to a dramatic denouement.

As to what Stein had done in his earlier years, a pall of mystery descends.

According to Professor Goodrick-Clarke, Ravenscroft may well have met Walter Stein when he was searching for medical treatment, which the latter clearly needed at various points in his life. Stein himself seriously claimed that he was the reincarnation of Charlemagne's confidant, Hugo of Tours. He also believed he could capture lost moments in time through transcendental meditation or what he called 'mind expansion'. The latter, in Trevor Ravenscroft's account, led to the Führer remembering Stein decades later.

To say that both were party to wishful thinking is similar to calling Adolf Hitler a shade impetuous. While there was never any doubt that Trevor Ravenscroft had been an extraordinarily brave man, he was not exactly the most reliable of witnesses. Ravenscroft never took any contemporaneous notes, and neither did Stein. One evening in 1957, Stein supposedly told Ravenscroft that he should write the story of the spear. In a bilious irony, Stein became ill and passed away the very next day.

Two decades later, the major tried to sue the writer James Herbert[6] for supposed plagiarism in *The Spear* – the latter's improbably silly but enjoyable story about neo-Nazi terrorism in England – which Ravenscroft claimed was stolen from his own *The Spear of Destiny*. As they waited at the High Court in March 1979, a weirdly illuminating conversation took place. During a discussion with a QC, Ravenscroft suddenly announced that he and his litigant had met before.

At the crucifixion.

'I was on the right-hand side of Christ and Herbert was on the other,' Ravenscroft said. That particular legal action ended with James Herbert having to pay damages for plagiarism. 'He did so to give his novel a backbone of truth with the least possible labour to himself,' said the judge, before adding his own splenetically vitriolic coda. 'One must not underestimate the commercial attraction of the rubbish I have attempted to describe.'

It is for reasons like this that a powerful urban myth has taken hold about the Führer's time in Vienna. Wandering around soup kitchens, dressing like a tramp, imbibing half-forgotten items of cultural knowledge to fuel his prejudices, the Spear of Destiny supposedly provides a continuous link with all past and future worlds of magic and occultic power, a kind of lucky talisman between the worlds of sense and spirit. Three decades later, after the *Anschluss* which re-annexed his native Austria, the Führer is supposed to have spent as much time with the Spear of Destiny as he could. That was why it was removed and placed beneath the streets of Nuremberg, symbolically and significantly, the spiritual home of Nazism's most Wagnerian excesses.

What we do know is that the Nazis did indeed seize the Hapsburg 'Crown Jewels' – with which the Spear of Destiny was associated – in 1938 and transport them from Vienna to Nuremberg. It was a pattern of plunder to be repeated around Occupied Europe. Today, the Spear resides in Vienna's Kunsthistorisches' Museum[7] and would, like any other mildly interesting military relic, have led a blameless life if it were not for the idiotic claims of modern-day would-be mystics.

By the time that Adolf Hitler had moved into a homeless shelter at the end of 1909 after once more failing to gain entrance to a Viennese art school, the British Secret Service was born out of extreme political expediency. A sub-committee of The Committee of Imperial Defence recommended that a unified, national intelligence service be created, 'just as convinced as any reader of Le Queux's books that large numbers of German spies were at work in Britain' in one academic assessment.

What was originally known as the Secret Service Bureau came into being on 24 July 1909. One half concerned itself with home security, the other keeping a gimlet eye on the foreigners who were believed to be causing all the trouble in the first place. Both organisations would be commanded by officers who had been invalided out of their respective services.

To keep an eye on the enemy within, the government turned to an accomplished linguist, Captain Vernon Kell, who had served in the South Staffordshire Regiment in the Boer Rebellion. Kell had returned home with the terrible asthma that would afflict him for the rest of his life, yet could, in the estimation of one colleague, 'smell a spy like a terrier smells a rat'. Heading up the home section of the Secret Service Bureau, Kell soon exhibited imperturbable steeliness and a propensity for hand-to-hand bureaucratic fighting with the fellow desk-bound officer with whom he now shared an office.

Even though Mansfield Cumming was junior and of a lower rank to Kell, he was hardly respectful. According to the records, Captain Kell and Captain Smith-Cumming spent most of their time bickering over resources, perhaps because they had very little else to do. By the time Cumming took up his post at the start of October, both he and Kell had moved into the War Office and came under the control of Military Operations.[8] 'Went to the office,' Captain Cumming noted in his diary on his first day at work, 'and remained all day, but saw no one, nor was there anything to do there.'

In its first few years of existence, Mansfield Cumming's putative secret service had few agents, little money and was 'frequently frustrated and often overruled and even ignored'. The 'overseas' section was continually eclipsed by Naval Intelligence, which was now well into its second decade of operations. Whereas the navy had a full admiral in charge of its own dedicated intelligence service, Cumming did not even attain the rank of acting captain until 1915. Within weeks of starting his work, he had complained in exasperation to the Director of Naval Intelligence (who had suggested him for the role) that, 'Surely we can not be expected to sit in the office month by month doing nothing?'

His own meeting with agents went some way to relieve the boredom.

Cumming would often arrive by taxi 'as it is almost impossible for the man – if a rascal – to point you out to his friends, who may be waiting with a camera' and was diligent in working hard to develop a network of agents, who were most often businessmen who travelled abroad. 'Agents lay at the heart of Cumming's world as they lie at the heart of ours,' the current chief, Alex Younger, has noted. 'They are our lifeblood. They always have been.' Cumming's diary, as revealed by his biographer, has any number of cryptic annotations referring to agents and people who could provide information.

Within a year, full-time assistants were assigned to both, and soon Cumming was asking for an agent in Copenhagen to report on 'German naval construction and armaments', for it was blindingly obvious who would be the inevitable enemy, a country whose citizens were more likely to invoke magic, superstition and a long occultic heritage.

Magic and the supernatural had exerted a peculiar hold over the various Germanic tribes which was quite unparalleled in Western Europe. In many ways, the occult uniquely defined the German experience. The Holy Roman Empire, for example, burned to death more than 100,000 people for practising witchcraft. In more recent times, there had been a steady flood of membership to secret societies – real or imaginary – such as the Rosicrucians and Freemasons.

The latter, for all the later cheerleading of its evil intent by conspiracy theorists, grew out of the medieval building trade whose lodges for itinerant workers were transformed over the years to become more akin to gentlemen's clubs. Soon, its members were believed to be party to hidden knowledge and the secrets supposedly brought to Scotland by The Knights Templar. Around this same time, the Bavarian branch of the Freemasons was infiltrated by the Illuminati and a whole host of conspiracies were triggered.

Mysticism had also, by the start of the Edwardian era, become hugely popular in Britain, with the birth of the Golden Dawn, a branch of

Rosicrucianism informed by secret knowledge going back to Egyptian times. Many of its members had been recruited from yet another sect — the Theosophical Society — who believed that immortal knowledge had been revealed by the so-called Secret Chiefs. Two of these mysterious figures had revealed themselves to Madame Helena Petrovina Blavatsky, the founder and curious promoter of the theosophical philosophy.

Tall and shapeless, with thick hair 'crinkled to the roots like the fleece of a Cotswold ewe', Madame Blavatsky's head was topped by a fireman's felt hat and a veil. She lived in a house that she shared with a stuffed baboon which had a copy of *On the Origin of Species* under its arm. Her version of the occult — 'with its melange of Egyptian and Buddhist elements', as one reviewer terms it — essentially showed that science couldn't explain everything. Darwin was wrong. Mankind came not from the apes, but spirit beings who had arrived here from Venus, via the Moon.

Madame Blavatsky's own mysterious background in Victorian times added to her lustre. On her various travels, she had met a Tibetan sage, Master Morya, whom only initiates could see: one of many hidden figures who supposedly populated the universe and, in one tart reviewer's later estimation, communicated 'by a kind of interstellar radio, and linking chosen humans [with] the divine hierarchy that rules the cosmos'. In an age of the camera, telephone and the transoceanic cable, telepathic communication hardly seemed out of place.

Madame Blavatsky acted, in effect, as a post office for the Secret Chiefs. Yet when people investigated her claims, it seemed her notebook on which she recorded their wisdom appeared to be filled with childlike graffiti. Both she and the Theosophical Society were soon condemned by the Society for Psychical Research. Other scientists got in on the act, too, wanting, as everybody else did, to find proof of life after death.

From out of her organisation grew the Golden Dawn, dismissed as a self-regarding collection of 'mediums, spells, the Mysterious Orient' by W.H. Auden. Its own rituals were its greatest secrets but by the turn of the century, it had passed through its own golden age, splintering into factionalism. Around the same time, another organisation was created which would come to have a disproportionate effect as 'the world's most dangerous secret society'.

The Order of the Oriental Templars (OTO) had its own leanings towards oriental mysticism — with a certain amount of sexual liberation thrown in for good measure. Formed by a clique of German Freemasons, a wealthy industrialist and an American who had experimented with hallucinogens, the OTO's leading light was Theodor Reuss, who had been engaged as a spy to keep tabs on Karl Marx and his family in Victorian England.

Under his expert tutelage, the OTO expanded across Europe in the first few years of the century, and eventually into the United States. The instrument for this later expansion was a mystic who not only had been a member of the Golden Dawn, but now took on the name Perdurabo: 'The brother who will endure'. Yet as one who examined these tangled origins put it, with his recruitment, the order 'had given birth to its first pseudo messiah'.

His name was Aleister Crowley.

In the run-up to war, the real-life Secret Chief, Mansfield Cumming, dominated his own odd looking-glass world, not least when he moved into Whitehall Court, a large mansion block just round the corner from the War Office wherein nothing was ever quite what it seemed. After climbing six flights of stairs, a visitor found himself wandering through a warren of corridors, coming across mirrors and doors which, when opened, all seemed to lead nowhere. By the time they reached the chief's office, many felt that they had ended up from whence they had started.

C would be awarded no official recognition 'as we were to be dissociated from the authorities entirely', he noted for the record, 'and not recognised secretly'. Captain Cumming soon developed a reputation for toughness – and it is hard to see how an effective spymaster could be otherwise – as well as mystery. Secrecy for its own sake and also obduracy ('Obstinate as a mule,' vividly recalled one colleague, 'with a chin like the cut-water of a battleship.') would cloak much of his work with the aura of great inscrutability. That would become his stock in trade, as it continues today for the modern Secret Intelligence Service. Cumming did his best to keep all his ideas, staff and methods clandestine, 'as secrets shared with anyone else cease to be secrets'.[9]

His own exploits add to the chief's marvellously absurd sense of theatre. On one wall of his office was a photograph of a heavily built man in obvious German clothing. Cumming delighted when people didn't recognise that it was him on one of his own adventures. As well as signing himself C, intriguingly, some of Cumming's first agents were known as M, P and Q in his cryptic diaries.

Cumming's desk, lovingly transported to what today's staff call 'Legoland', the curious post-modern building at Vauxhall Cross, was built from oak hewn from Nelson's *Victory*. His naval logbooks, recounting many of his escapades, are kept in the modern C's office and shown to recruits. Another antique which remains in the chief's office is the solid-oak clock which Cumming built by his own hand, described by those who have seen it as solid as its maker with a square top, an open glass front and oversize Roman numerals. According to some, it still keeps good time, revealing both his mechanical skills and interests.

'Cumming was a surprisingly modern man,' says the current incumbent as C. 'He was not a bureaucrat, he was an innovator fascinated by technology, and the development of new equipment ranging from cars and aeroplanes to secret inks and wireless sets.' As well as his study in Whitehall Court, Cumming spent a lot of time fiddling around in his own workshop, where he would tinker to his heart's content. 'He had a passion for inventions of all sorts,' noted one officer with the unlikely name of Edward Knoblock, 'and being a rich man, he often bought the rights to them, such as strange telescopes, mysterious mechanisms with which to signal in the dark.'

In other words (with apologies to Ian Fleming) C was both M and Q rolled into one. Cumming clearly loved this aspect of his work, which lead to some highly surreal conversations, such as that which resulted from enquiries at London University about invisible inks. Some time later, in October 1915, the deputy head of military intelligence at GHQ France noted that he 'heard from C that the best invisible ink is semen', which did not react to the main methods of detection.

Seminal fluid apparently had the advantage of being readily available.

One colleague recalled C's delight when the Deputy Chief Censor said one day that one of his staff had found out that 'semen would not react to iodine vapour', a great breakthrough at the time. Yet the officer who had identified this novel use had to be moved from his department after becoming the butt of jokes. At least one agent in the field had to be reminded to use only fresh supplies of the 'ink' when correspondents began noticing an unusual smell.

When, in March 2015, the newly appointed chief of MI6, Alex Younger, came to venerate Mansfield Cumming by unveiling a plaque at Whitehall Court, he claimed that Cumming's service was ('as SIS is now', Younger added) 'a small organisation that achieved big things'. As the new chief noted, his first predecessor 'took the service through World War I while incidentally learning to fly a biplane'. The chief was also an early and enthusiastic member of the Royal Automobile Club and the Royal Motor Yacht Club. Despite the accident which later claimed the life of his son, Cumming became a competitive racing driver of some note.

'I know of nothing more enjoyable than skimming along at a cracking pace,' Cumming would write in the RAC journal, 'especially if you are picking up on the next car ahead.' Perhaps this devotion to speed explains why he subsequently drove his Rolls-Royce far too fast for his own good – and let his great niece, aged just 12, steer it down Piccadilly – or else terrified colleagues when he took them to his club. In time, many of his officers gained a reputation for indiscreet, indescribable, unorthodox and utterly unruly behaviour, mainly because the sort of people attracted to espionage were the least likely to keep secrets. Many were businessmen involved in shipping, who reported on what they found on their travels. More often than not, their information was gossip or facts regurgitated from newspapers.

'C always employed scoundrels,' one of his officers would complain, and Cumming himself once termed them 'blackguards'. Some absconded with money, never to be seen again: one agent staged his own suicide, disappearing to the United States with all the secret service funds he could get his hands on; another shot himself when he was asked to explain the whereabouts of £28,000 he had been sent by Captain Cumming's contact. The chief took such escapades in his stride, knowingly referring to some of his agents as 'scallywags' and 'rascals'. On one occasion, Cumming said to one ne'er-do-well he wanted to employ, 'You are just the man we want', claiming he knew all about his past history, which was chequered to say the least.

Mischief was meat and drink to the chief. Returning officers were often thanked and entertained by Cumming in person. The chief's private wealth meant that he could dine at The Savoy and entertained his guests there, where their tales of derring-do were enough to allow entry into Mansfield Cumming's innermost circle, a kind of brotherhood bound by scoundrels and secrets of their own making.

When the Great War broke out, there was no greater scoundrel so far as many in Britain were concerned than the man christened Edward Alexander Crowley, one of the more remarkable fantasists and exotic protagonists in this already peculiar story. Given the nature of many of the characters to come, that is saying something. Aleister (as he styled himself) Crowley was many things: a complex polymath, egotistical, ambitious, possessed of a brilliant mind but also a self-seeking show off who enjoyed operating in full public view. His various obsessions with the occult meant that by the outbreak of the Great War, he had become (in the public prints, at least) something of an enigma.

Pitching himself as something like the diabolical progeny of Russell Brand and Yoko Ono in terms of self-promotion and wilful obscurity, Aleister Crowley was relentless in his need for recognition. By now, Crowley was better known for various theatrical performances and obscure utterances that baffled most of his listeners (and diminishing number of readers). Another writer and recruit to MI6, who worked in Russia in 1917 for Cumming, Somerset Maugham, termed him, with perhaps the greatest and simplest accuracy of all, as 'a fake, but not entirely fake'.

Aleister Crowley casts a curious, baleful influence upon this story. Nothing can ever quite be pinned down, rather like the man himself, with his devotion to sex, drugs and magic (though, to be fair, the man himself claimed it was poetry, mountaineering and magick). The rock and roll, it should be noted, came later, after The Beatles put him on the cover of their *Sergeant Pepper* album, thereby elevating him into the iconography of the sixties counterculture. Throughout his life, Crowley considered himself a prophet rejected in his own land, a fate which he claimed only befell 'most men of distinction'.

His own self-reverential mythology was no less pervasive than those spread by agents of Mansfield Cumming's secret service. His exaggerations created a legend as durable as those of any secret agent. Aleister Crowley termed magic 'the act of communicating without obvious means' and always spelled it with a k, 'to distinguish between mere conjuring and real magic', as he liked to put it. There is even greater smoke and mirrors concerning his supposed involvement in intelligence operations, which are hard to confirm and thus difficult to dispel.

To be fair, Crowley had tried to bring together various esoteric traditions, becoming, as we will see, many things to many people.[10] It was almost inevitable that he would create his own sect, though, as perhaps the best parody ever on the subject put it, he never claimed to be the messiah: he really was a very naughty boy. Born into the Plymouth Brethren, a strict religious grouping, it was ironic that his family's wealth accrued from the brewing of Crowley's Ales at a brewery in Surrey. The young Crowley did not suffer materially, though mentally he was clearly conflicted.

His parents were zealots who believed that Christ's return was imminent. Such apocalyptic anticipation caused a frenzied reaction in their first-born son. The Bible was the only book he was allowed to read. There would be no deviation from its literal interpretation. Christmas was regarded as a pagan festival. Most other churches were viewed as 'synagogues of Satan'. Small wonder that this strict religious upbringing sparked his interest in false prophets and scarlet women – and that the very concept of The Beast ranged powerfully in his mind.

Sheltered, punished and austere, Aleister Crowley's was the enclosed childhood of the rich. At the age of 8, chubby and unworldly, he was bullied and tormented. Finding schools not to his liking, he was eventually allowed to study at home. While the young Aleister adored his father, he loathed his mother. Edward Crowley was, he claimed, his hero, who 'never allowed his religion to interfere with natural affection'. By comparison, he found his mother physically repugnant. With her oddly oriental features, the young Aleister considered the woman born Emily Bishop his father's social inferior. Some of his deeply ingrained misogyny stemmed from her prissy Victorian piousness.

At the age of 12, his father's death in 1887 devastated him and he soon rebelled. His mother became more devout (what he termed 'the hysteria of widowhood'). He revelled in sin and when he was 15, Aleister Crowley took great pleasure in losing his virginity to an actress – in one account – after which his mother termed him the Great Beast, wondering quite what she had spawned. Throughout his middle teens, he travelled, fornicated and, with what some might think divine justice, was handed into the care of a wilfully cruel uncle. Under this harsh regime, he became paranoid about people knowing what he was doing. This soon manifested itself, as his biographer Martin Booth notes, in making him 'regard everyone around him as a spy, a trait that allied to his occasional shyness, was to be an aspect of his character throughout his life'.

Yet there were more wholesome distractions for the teenage Crowley. When he was 16, on holiday in Skye, he became fascinated by the new sport of mountaineering, or what we would today call rock climbing (though these were, it should be noted, serious expeditions). It gave him a sense of freedom, a feeling of power and a curious inner harmony. Now he was ready to take on the world, for by now he considered himself a genius. Playing chess became an enduring enthusiasm, sometimes playing three games simultaneously, while blindfolded. In October 1895, he went up to Trinity College, Cambridge, supposedly studying moral sciences.

'I found myself my own master,' he later wrote, 'and settled down to lead a righteous, sober and godly life.'

It didn't last long. He was a loner and profligate, wasting his immense inheritance and time on such pursuits as esoterica and black magic. Yet by the same token, Crowley was well read, opinionated and witty. His arrival in Cambridge coincided with the Oscar Wilde Trial, which prompted his dandified appearance and sexual loucheness in the hope of being sent down. He devoted a great deal of time to reading and writing his own erotic literature – which would be difficult to get published – as sexual freedom was his greater interest of all.

Whether it was from having sex with prostitutes or women he met in taverns, Crowley caught the clap and syphilis. There were more dangerous liaisons, too, which led to his penning some lines of poetry, which, for once, are not opaque:

He who seduced me first, I could not forget
I hardly loved him, but desired to taste
A new strong sin

Several of his biographers believe that his first gay experience, while on holiday in Stockholm on New Year's Eve 1896, also helped awaken Crowley to magic possibilities.

'It was an experience of horror and pain,' he wrote, 'combined with a certain ghostly terror, yet at the same time it was the key to the purest and holiest spiritual ecstasy that exists.'

Far from being evil, The Beast was more a dilettante hedonist, the original Trustafarian who had nothing better to do – such as taking his finals. After leaving Cambridge without a degree, Crowley joined a local temple, the Hermetic Order of the Golden Dawn, and assumed the name of Perdurabo. He did indeed endure, impressing Samuel Liddell Mathers, one of its founders who had initiated him into the group. Yet the poet W.B. Yeats, who thought him an 'unspeakable degenerate' and considered him insane, did his best to get Crowley ejected. His repeated boasts of being higher up the order than he really was, his dubious sexuality and his lack of morals meant that many others turned against him.

Crowley lost interest in the group, determined to make his mark – and not just of 666 – and began on what one biographer has termed 'his magical way towards fame, infamy, vilification and a reputation he could hardly have foreseen'. Thanks to his inheritance, Crowley became an itinerant wanderer, first in Mexico, where he steeped himself in Mayan and Aztec Lore, then the Far East. In 1902, he took part in the first attempt to scale K2, the second highest and, by repute, the most savage mountain on the roof of the world. Its reputation as unassailable came true. Thanks to snowblindedness, malaria and hallucinations, Crowley went through sixty-eight days of horror, and the Himalayan mountain remained unconquered.

He next turned up in Paris, whose *belle époque* pretensions bored him. Sometime in 1903, though, a significant development took place at a spa near Edinburgh, where Aleister Crowley met what he termed his 'Scarlet Woman' – Rose Edith Skerret, the widowed sister of a Cambridge contemporary. 'Physically and morally,' he later exulted, 'Rose exercised on every man she met a fascination which I have never seen anywhere else, not a fraction of it.' And soon, after joining together in holy matrimony, his whole world was turned upside down with a series of visions and ecstasies that he alone was privileged to witness.

Mansfield Cumming's own interest in magic only ever extended so far as conjuring tricks for his family, and he was, in one contemporary estimation, 'an extrovert, bluff and charming man, a live wire of boisterous, outgoing nature and a great tease with the children'. He actively encouraged his youngest relatives to poke hatpins into his wooden leg. In later years, he did the same with a paper knife for potential recruits: those who winced were deemed unsuitable to join His Majesty's Secret Service.

Captain Cumming's need for a wooden leg came from a curious episode.[11] Just after the start of the First World War, in October 1914, he was driving in a car with his son in northern France when it crashed into a tree at full speed. Alastair Cumming was killed instantly. Finding his legs broken and trapped, Cumming somehow found a penknife and hacked at his left leg until he was free. Cumming crawled over to his son and put a coat over him ('That's the sort of chap old C is,' a later colleague marvelled). Cumming himself was found completely unconscious by soldiers a few hours later. His left foot was then surgically removed. Captain Cumming was fitted with a false leg and occasionally disconcerted people by tapping absent-mindedly at it with various unlikely (and often painful-sounding) objects.

C's curious physical appearance alone was a gift to future novelists and writers (who added to his mystique by never revealing his real name). Somerset Maugham, for example, who had worked for him, later recalled:

'The thing immediately noticeable about him was the closeness with which his blue eyes were set.'

So began the myth of the steely, secret servant.

'At first encounter he appeared very severe,' another of his more famous agents, Paul Dukes, later remarked.'His manner of speech was abrupt.Woe betide the unfortunate individual who ever incurred his ire!' And yet his sturdy reliability – like the clock he bequeathed to the service – means that even today, the latest chief of MI6 has termed Cumming 'our common ancestor', adding that the service 'feels like a surprisingly chief-centred organisation'.

It partly stemmed from his ability at infighting. The Secret Intelligence Service carried through the war in a strange bureaucratic limbo: created by the War Office, Cumming worked out of the Admiralty building, but was paid for by the Foreign Office. Cumming used this administrative blur-ring to his greatest advantage, for he was a shrewd Whitehall operator. 'C always used to boast that as he had three masters he had not got one at all,' a colleague recalled, 'as he could always set the two against any objections.'

The current chief notes that Cumming 'as steward of a fledgling organi-sation, faced a number of attempts by other departments to close him down and lacked the support he needed from some quarters in Whitehall'.[12] Though MI6 was limited by having no agents in Germany, it developed a highly efficient train-watching service in Belgium (with fifty-one sepa-rate posts at one time) which monitored German troop movements all along the Western Front. In the last eighteen months of the conflict, three-quarters of the intelligence gathered behind enemy lines came from a dedicated network codenamed the 'White Lady'. Cumming's officers also gained information from highly placed sources in other countries – notably Denmark, from a source known as TR-16, a German-born naval officer who had been court-martialled for insulting a relative of the kaiser – and now alerted the military to the shipping of men and materiel across the North Sea.

In other words, both Mansfield Cumming and MI6 had a good war.

When information came in to Whitehall Court, it was bound together in large books with red cloth bindings, a practice which continued until fairly recently. Today, MI6 reports are still distributed via the Foreign Office, more often than not electronically, and are still known as CX material. This is an abbreviation of Cumming Exclusively (as in, for C's eyes only), as they were known in those far distant times when Britain faced off the threat from Germany and His Majesty's Secret Service rose to the task splendidly.

There were certain revelations that were only ever meant for Aleister Crowley's eyes. As with all occultic visions, they were both horrible and fearful, yet ecstatic and enchanting, which proved, beyond all doubt that he was the prophet of a new age of humanity. In April 1904, he first became aware of Aiwass, a messenger of an ancient god, whom he saw during a séance as a tall, dark man in his 30s 'with the face of a savage kind and eyes veiled lest their gaze should destroy what they say'.

It was the culmination of three days of magickal activities in Cairo. They would set the seal for his own fate along with Rose, his wife and Scarlet Woman, who had undergone a trance induced by hashish. She told him that Horus, the falcon-headed god of antiquity in Egypt, was waiting for him. He should, she said, go to a temple in their apartment, wherein he heard a man's voice as they started their rituals. This deep voice, 'musical and expressive, its tones solemn, voluptuous, tender, fierce', provided him with the words for what he called The Book of the Law, which he faithfully transcribed.

Saying this was the religion of Thelema, derived from the Greek word for will – and that he had been appointed the prophet of this same religion – Aleister Crowley had found his worldly vocation. Its central doctrine was 'Do what thou will shall be the whole of the law', which was, in its prophet's interpretation, nothing less than a clarion call for the hedonistic excess that he made all his own. Whatever else he might have been, Crowley was a gloriously unpredictable character, making up rules and then subverting them. Opinion veers from his being a blatant devotee of debauchery to a much-maligned mystic and, indeed, holy figure.

After his vision, he personally instructed people in the ways of magick, forming his own cult and sometimes joining others. With his trust funds, he bought a house, Boleskine, on the shores of Loch Ness (later bought by the guitarist Jimmy Page), where he acted like a laird, intimidated the locals with his reputation and attended to his magic and writings. To the average reader they were obscure and, at times, unreadable. He had to publish his own luxuriously bound poetry – corny, trite and invariably incomprehensible – privately as they didn't sell.

At Boleskine, Rose gave birth to a daughter, but then Crowley travelled again to the Far East, setting out to climb another Nepalese mountain, Kangchenjunga, the home of the gods in folklore. When he first saw it, 'faint blue, clear white in the dawn', Crowley claimed he was only interested in establishing an altitude record. Arrogance and egotism would be his undoing on this expedition. There was near mutiny when a porter deserted and died. Another slipped, caused an avalanche and Crowley refused to help.

When he eventually returned to Britain, he found that his daughter had died from typhoid in Rangoon. Shocked, his health failed and he was clearly in agony. 'I want blasphemy, murder, rape, revolution,' he said, eventually abandoning Rose while he continued on his life of magical indulgence. He didn't resume his occult activities until 1909, and when he did, they were often ridiculously theatrical in public demonstrations of magic and symbolism. By now, the money was starting to run out, and his shouting of 'there is no god' had more to do with his own lack of faith than anything blasphemous.

During the Great War, Mansfield Cumming was not the biggest chief in the secret world. C was outranked, and, it has to be said, eclipsed by the much more bullish character who had been appointed to the post of Director of Naval Intelligence (DNI) in November 1914. Reggie 'Blinker' Hall was cut from a similar cloth and on one occasion would declare that Cumming's motto was very simple: 'Wisdom is better than weapons of war.' Hall would have an even better war for, in several estimations, he was one of the most impressive intelligence officers of his generation. Another went so far as to baldly state that the Great War was won by 'the uncanny ability of this great Sherlock Holmes'.

Like Cumming, Hall's was an unfortunate physiognomy: to some he was reminiscent of Mr Punch – and similar to Cumming – with a hook nose, which to Compton Mackenzie, was better suited to 'a nut about to be cracked by a toucan'. His screwing-up of his eyes and rapid blinking led to his unfortunate nickname. Appearances were deceptive, for 'Blinker' Hall was fearless, demanding, but highly imaginative. His piercing stare and conspicuous false teeth helped disconcert anyone he was interrogating. An energetic, fantastic organiser, his was, in the awed respect of the US ambassador, 'a clear case of genius'.

The organisation he took over in October 1914 prospered. Captain Hall had been a successful, innovative commander of the *Queen Mary*. With the outbreak of war, the Naval Intelligence Division's role was transformed into gathering as much information as possible about the kaiser's navy. The main problem facing the NID was simple: how to detect the German High Seas Fleet as they left the Kiel Canal. So NID developed a network of volunteer coastal observers all around the world to record shipping movements and, in Nigel West's apposite phrase, transformed them into a human radar chain.

Hall's men were helped when they received a signal book from the Russians, removed from the body of a drowned officer, 'a gift more precious than a dozen Fabergé eggs' in the First Sea Lord's eloquent estimation. Nevertheless, the voice of Winston Churchill, as well as his DNI, echoed in the wilderness. More than anything, Blinker Hall's appreciation of cryptography meant he gathered together a unique collection of what one later review termed 'an inner body of some half-a-dozen officers attempting the impossible'.

Despite decoding German intentions at the Battle of Jutland, higher officers did not use them to significant advantage and the codebreakers 'simmered with resentment' over what had happened. Ironically, in that exchange, Hall's old ship was blown up. Had the DNI remained at sea he would have almost certainly been killed. Within months, though, their work would change the fate of the world when they unbuttoned an enciphered message from the German foreign minister to his counterpart in Mexico City. America's entry into the First World War was assured. The Zimmermann message thus ensured Germany's defeat. Hall finished the war with his reputation riding high (supposedly, his greatest ever achievement was seeing through the most famous femme fatale in history, Mata Hari).[13]

Yet Reggie Hall was a maverick who had a greater feel for the great game. As one naval historian who knew him well has written, the DNI ensured 'the world of spies, agents, deception, bribery, disinformation, destabilisation, all that side of Intelligence now stigmatised as the "Dirty Tricks" department'. And as a result, Hall's organisation, too, would have another strange claim to fame, when in the spring of 1916, another curious character came into the view of British Intelligence: Aleister Crowley.

If there was another myth that took hold after the fighting was finished, it was that of the superiority of British propaganda. Yet as one historian has noted, it 'required five years of honest effort in order to devise a psychological warfare system sufficient to meet the needs of a great power at war.' In later years, German writers ascribed this supposed pre-eminence to an inherent fiendishness in the British character compared to the gullible purity of the Teutonic spirit. No greater partisan was the corporal who claimed to have been blinded by a gas attack in the final year of the fighting.

Adolf Hitler would note that 'propaganda was a weapon of the first class, while with us it was a sop to unemployed politicians.'

Or, for that matter, underemployed sages.

To understand Aleister Crowley's involvement in British propaganda, it has to be seen in the light of a starker reality: that after those first few years, the confusion and duplicity of the effort prompted one senior official to take the initiative, as he always seemed to do, and exceed his own authority. Admiral Reggie Hall would use guile and deception to get his own way and make his own mark. It would also lead to a reversal of fortune for Aleister Crowley, who had arrived in New York City on the equally doom-laden *Lusitania* in 1914. Nothing was as it seemed during the great Beast's subsequent American interlude.

'What followed were five years of frequent penury,' writes Professor Richard Spence of the University of Idaho, 'and scores of occult workings, mostly of the sexual variety.' In some accounts, Crowley had moved to America because he had taken the huff over not being employed as an agent of intelligence. He subsequently authored a handful of virulently anti-British articles, which led to his vilification in his homeland.

The reasons why are worthy of examination. Within two years of the fighting, a certain heavy-handedness had come to characterise the British response to dealing with the neutral United States. The British censors interfered with the transatlantic mails and would blacklist US firms suspected of dealings with the Central Powers. When one newspaper censor in London came across the story of a Briton proclaiming Irish independence from the Statue of Liberty he took notice.

The name was at least familiar. Aleister Crowley was up to his old tricks again. Or was he? Crowley himself later claimed that he was involved in the prosecution of propaganda, that, as he later explained it, was 'so blatantly extravagant only a German would have believed it'. As to how and why, greater mysteries than those of the occult now gather. When applying to visit the US thirty years later, Crowley claimed he was in Switzerland when the war broke out. He was, he claimed, hoping to be commissioned into the RNVR, but a few weeks later was 'attacked by phlebitis, which bars me permanently from active service'. In another interview with a New York paper, *The Evening World*, he claimed he was shot in the leg while 'in the confidential service of the British government'.

Many other rumours about Crowley's supposed connections with British Intelligence have proliferated. Certainly, it is true that he had dealings with the Naval Intelligence Division. His contact was the

Honourable Francis Everard Joseph Feilding, who, like Ian Fleming in the next war, was commissioned into the RNVR as a lieutenant. Like Fleming, Feilding had many connections in the city, but, unlike him, also had many interests in exotica. A charter member of the Masonic Order of Christ and a former secretary of the Society for Psychical Research, Crowley based a character on him in *Moonchild* who says, 'investigation of spiritualism makes a capital training ground for secret service work, one soon gets up to all the tricks'.

Feilding's own, more reliable recollections sometimes muddy the picture further. Aleister Crowley wrote to him, was anxious to work as a spy and, 'by various preposterous performances', made out that he was disaffected. But it was most likely the other way around. In a note to the historian Gerald Yorke, Feilding claimed that the Beast's 'taste for farcical situations' was a reason for the reluctance in employing him. And yet Crowley, as would be expected, crowed that even that was all part of a greater plan.

'I knew that the only way I could combat the influence of German propaganda in the States was to identify myself with it in every way and by making it abhorrent to any sane being,' he claimed, 'gradually get the minds of the American public to react against its insidious appeal.'

Feilding noted that Crowley also asked him to start a defamation campaign against him in the English press, 'with the idea that this would confirm his evil reputation in America so far as British Intelligence was concerned'. And when that did eventually take place, because Crowley was well known and lapped up the attention, Feilding noted that 'treachery to his country was not one of them'. Certainly, he was useful to the NID for he could inveigle himself (as he seems to have done) into pro-German circles. Behind that was the hidden hand of another master at work.

'Admiral Hall's policy appears to have been to follow the perpetrators, let the outrage happen, expose the culprits and turn American opinion against Germany,' writes Tobias Churton, an academic who has done much to illuminate these developments.

American national opinion had also been inflamed by the fallout from the Easter Rising of 1916. Even Crowley remained coy about the Irish aspects of his work, some of it carried out with John Quinn, an Irish-American bibliophile who had earlier hosted Sir Roger Casement,[14] an Irish-born consular official for the British Government who appointed himself ambassador to the Irish state. As part of a greater propaganda effort, all that the British could do to fight back was to destroy Casement's reputation. Professor

Spence speculates that Quinn could well have been Crowley's contact, and a report for the US Army's military intelligence division states specifically that it had been 'determined that Aleister Crowley was an employee of the British government'.

As to his real feelings, Crowley later claimed he was patriotic. 'I still think the English pot as black as the kettle,' he later confessed, 'and I am still willing to die in defence of the pot.' Even today, nobody is completely certain if that was true or just how far he was willing to bend his own beliefs in the employ of a country that soon turned against him.

With the cessation of hostilities in November 1918 came the most potent myth of all: that there had been a 'stab in the back' of the kaiser's forces by the *Deutsches Volk*. And, for good measure, claimed Field Marshal Ludendorff himself, it was even more insidious than that. German troops had also been hypnotised by propaganda, 'the traditional British weapon', as he described it to anyone who would listen.

And so, as Professor Nicholas Goodrick-Clarke aptly explained, Adolf Hitler was 'born' in Versailles. By blaming Germany's defeat on such a spiritual malaise, the stage was set for the rise of Nazism and rearmament. The roots of the subsequent global conflagration came with the unrelenting harshness of the Versailles Treaty, a travesty which directly inspired the excesses of the Nazi regime. Adolf Hitler's motivation was always in 'tearing the treaty to shreds'.

Yet this myth of the stab in the back was nothing compared to one which was, if possible, even more pervasive. It would soon come to occupy the mindset of the 'golden pheasants', the leaders of the Nazi regime: that of the insidious influence of the British Secret Service, which continues today with its supposed involvement in the death of Princess Diana or its Machiavellian posturing which led to the recent invasion of Iraq.

The Nazi leaders held an unshakeable belief in the malign, mysterious powers of the British Secret Service on a level that matched the occult. Associated with both came vast skeins of intrigue and mystery which would see the creation of a whole new set of inter-related myths. In the early twenties, a prominent astrologer was sent details of Adolf Hitler's birth, after which the otherwise obscure political leader was revealed to be 'a fearless man of action' who was 'fated to sacrifice himself for the German nation'.

And that was when all the trouble started.

2

Higher Authorities

The supposition that Hitler believed in astrology and employed astrologers was current from 1933 onwards. It is clear that many thought that the only possible explanation for his uninterrupted and increasingly threatening run of political successes and territorial gains was his access to advance information obtained by paranormal means, of which astrology was the most likely.

Astrology and the Third Reich, Ellic Howe

That the Nazis did not use magic – either white or black – in the prosecution of war is, in some estimations, one of modern history's more enduring puzzles. The 'golden pheasants', as the Nazi leaders were known by the man in the street, had many strange, often contradictory obsessions with both mysticism and the occult. This supposed predisposition to all manner of mysticism forms a strange backdrop to the rise of Nazism. Various mystical pronouncements supposedly provide a particular (not to say peculiar) explanation for its successes.

There was, however, no black magic to guide the men in black shirts.

To paraphrase Mark Twain, rumours of an astrologer were greatly exaggerated and so, too, were the supposed occultic roots of Nazism. Though a number of historians have argued that the whole basis of National Socialism stemmed from the almost occult-like Thule Society, which in both its anti-Semitic and anti-Communist roots appealed to the Nazi leadership, the reality was less clear cut.[1] As Michael Burleigh has elegantly diagnosed, the German people took to a politics based on 'faith, hope, hatred and sentimental collective self-regard for their own race and nation'.

The supernatural provided an immeasurably better explanation for the Fatherland's loss of face and the post-Versailles malaise in which a once-proud nation found itself. The occult helped alleviate much of the pain of the *Zeitgeist*. It was so much easier to blame the social and economic woes of the Weimar Republic on malign forces beyond their control. At the same time as Adolf Hitler's rise, Germany's best-known mediums and card readers were able to fill large concert halls for their demonstrations. Immediately after the Armistice, many educated Germans seriously started to believe in the supernatural. Astrology, hypnosis, clairvoyancy, tarot readings, palmistry and fortune telling would all reach their apotheosis in the Weimar Republic. So, too, would 'criminal telepaths', clairvoyants consulted by the police to shed light on unsolved crimes.

Healers, seers and prophets proliferated. A champagne-maker became famous for prophesying the apocalypse and that the only way to stop it was by penance. 'They were all around, these people promising the messiah, all of them together created a mood from which Hitler could arise,' noted one journalist. And, as a result, a rabble-rouser from Bavaria was hardly out of place. 'I believe that it was also God's will that from here a boy was to be sent into the Reich, allowed to mature, and elevated to become the nation's Führer, thus enabling him to reintegrate his homeland into the Reich,' Adolf Hitler would famously declare just after the *Anschluss*. 'There is a divine will, and we are its instruments.'

Worse, Hitler saw himself – as did his many followers – as a magical figure of supposed wisdom and oracular power. He would, he claimed, deliver the German people from the humiliations of Versailles, leading them into a glorious future. Indeed, his self-belief became maniacal and his messianic fervour the source of his personal power. Adolf Hitler found a willing audience amongst the rancour, defeat and desperation of the Weimar Republic. And yet for all his railing against religion, especially ones based in Jewish traditions, on one occasion, at a Nazi Christmas celebration in 1927,[2] he would roar: 'The work that Christ started but could not finish, I – Adolf Hitler – will conclude.' A true warning from history that stands as one of the more astonishing.

In the years immediately following the Great War, when young boys eagerly devoured the fictional exploits of Bulldog Drummond and Allan Quartermain, the growing reputation of the British Secret Service was never higher. Its aura of invincibility and invulnerability was unmatched.

The ironic truth was that Mansfield Cumming's secret service was actually fraying at the seams, generally disbelieved and underfunded. In short, MI6 soon developed a terrible reputation and – worst of all – was irrelevant to the business of government it was charged to serve.

In some ways, MI6 had become a victim of its own success during the First World War. With the arrival of peace, the scope of officially sanctioned espionage quickly became superfluous to requirements. It was suggested that Cumming's department should be absorbed into one or more of the existing intelligence departments. MI6 was little more than organised chaos on which C seemed to thrive. Tales from this time are enlivened with reports of Cumming descending stairs on his behind or else negotiating corners on a children's wheeled toy. Today's service acknowledges that with a staff group called Scooter for handicapped officers, which refers to 'the mode of transport Cumming used to get around the building after he had lost his foot', in the words of the current C.

With the end of the fighting, there was another mysterious organisation which genuinely seemed every bit as dangerous as the occult and equally malign as the forces of the devil. The Secret Intelligence Service would now become preoccupied with combatting the menace of Soviet communism. It was Lenin's avowed intention, via the Comintern, to bring change and wage revolution throughout the rest of world. So the inter-war years for MI6 involved its preoccupation with undermining Lenin's revolutionaries, which involved many of the swashbucklers who established the secret service's reputation for derring-do and buccaneering. Various 'aces' such as Reilly,[3] Dukes and Hill were sent to the Soviet Union. There they established networks to encourage subversion, fund sabotage and stop the Red Menace in all its ugly manifestations by attempting to assassinate the Soviet leaders.

The most potent example was the remarkable Sidney Reilly, who had once plotted to kill Lenin and termed the phrase 'occult octopus' as a figure of speech, referring to the worldwide spread of capitalism. Many myths have emerged from this time which, as the former intelligence chief Alan Judd has written, 'undoubtedly contributed to the Great Game element of MI6 mythology in which the spy is not only a discreet seller of information but also a man of adventurous action'.

For one man, though, those adventures were virtually over. The greater truth was that Mansfield Cumming was worn out ('C later became a martyr to angina,' one contemporary recorded). Now in his 60s, he had fought hard to ensure the agency he had founded was autonomous and independent.

At a farewell dinner where various people eulogised him, as one attendee recorded, Cumming's reply was bittersweet: 'You have come to bury C, sir, not to praise him.' According to the legend which persists today within the Secret Intelligence Service, his heart gave out on the evening of 23 June 1923 after he had shared a drink with an agent who was about to head off on a mission abroad. Years later, when the sixteenth chief came to venerate and eulogise what he termed a Victorian predecessor, he got it about right when he said that Cumming was simply a hard act to follow.

The curious irony was that astrology had got off to a rip-roaring start in promoting the Nazi cause. In 1923 there was an astrologers' congress in Leipzig, where it was suggested that if their subject was to be taken seriously, a Central Astrological Office should be formed, and, in time, a new monthly astrological magazine was published as an official organ. At its helm was the first professional astrologer in Germany, Frau Elsbeth Ebertin, who, after being sent details of Adolf Hitler's birth, published a chart which showed the future Führer to be not only a fearless leader but a man of action who was 'fated to sacrifice himself for the German nation'.

Frau Ebertin, whose main claim to fame was her editing of an astrological annual called *A Glimpse Into The Future*, went even further, suggesting in that July's issue that the 'man of action' born on 20 April 1889 should not undertake anything of importance in November. 'What on Earth have women and the stars to do with me?' was, however, Adolf Hitler's perplexed response when Frau Ebertin's prediction was brought to his attention.

On 8 November 1923 he was arrested after the Munich Putsch, an event which would have much significance, 'the last desperate gamble of a man', in one historian's estimation, 'who feared he was being deserted by his fellow conspirators'. It failed and so Adolf Hitler was thrown into prison for nine months for treason, where he wrote his own wrong-headed 'masterwork', *Mein Kampf*.

Almost overnight, Elsbeth Ebertin and her horoscope became a sensation. Like all politicians, Hitler was astute enough to see through such bread and circuses for the masses – for now, at any rate, encouraged – not least in predictions made in his favour. Fortune telling had become so much part of the *Zeitgeist* that by the end of the 1920s, Weimar Germany was overwhelmed with spiritual activity. Berlin had become the capital of the occult world. There were seven astrological weeklies, along with more than 20,000 fortune tellers, astrologers, tarot readers and seers, ranging from quacks to 'bizarrely costumed leaders of secret brotherhoods and doomsday religious cults'. Small wonder that leaders, who were seen as cranks, became so ubiquitous and gained credibility in those worrisome times when the end of the world did not seem so very far away.

Irrational, sinister forces were sensed everywhere and, in these troubled times, no more acutely than in the unnerving stare of the former Director of Naval Intelligence. After the war, Reggie 'Blinker' Hall became convinced about the dangers of Bolshevism, and like so many others of his class and standing, became involved in various intrigues using his old intelligence connections. Hall had wanted to continue as DNI, but in pursuing a political career, for obvious reasons, had been forced to resign. Being Reggie, he threw himself bodily into subversion, particularly after losing his seat in the House of Commons to the growing Labour Party. The government needed to strengthen its domestic surveillance and ability to look at troublemakers who were part of the socialist menace.

So far as he and many others were concerned, MI5 was hardly up to the task. The gloriously anachronistic figure of the General – as Vernon Kell was usually known – was in one estimation 'short-sighted and timorous'. As with MI6, the peace dividend saw MI5's budgets cut back and, as its official history notes, over the next six years Kell had to fight to keep his organisation alive.[4] The Security Service, as it was later formally christened, was decimated, its staff numbers reduced from 800 to 30 and its budget slashed by nearly two-thirds.

It was hardly a crackerjack operation, and for Kell personally the greater fear was of amalgamation. It hardly helped that the General's gaze never seemed to reach beyond military or well-bred personnel – truly pukka chaps, given that many were retired from the Indian Police – supported by either private incomes or drawing upon pensions drawn from the flickering embers of the Raj.

Yet Bolshevik subversion was a potent clear and present danger. The fear of red communism would inform its greatest pre-war success in the ARCOS raid in May 1927, which involved 150 police officers breaking up a Soviet spy ring,[5] after which diplomatic relations were broken with the USSR. As his organisation had been wound down, Kell had little choice but to rely on operators from various private organisations. And that included some of the stranger coves who also existed in the murky, strange overlap of state and far right intelligence groups. Any number of curious, private intelligence organisations had come into being, with none as shadowy as the Makgill Organisation.

Sir George Makgill was a writer, businessman and fervent right-winger who stood as a candidate in the early 1920s for the Anti-Waste League. During the First World War he had been involved in a court case where a servant felt he had been slandered, and later still, head of the Anti-German Union, which famously had led to the expulsion from the Privy Council of two lawyers who did not have British parents. By 1917, he was listed in the London telephone book as being Honorary Secretary of the British Empire Union.

The organisation he set up in the early twenties, with backing from various captains of the coal, mining and ship-owning industries, was described by Kell as secret: 'somewhat on Masonic lines'. The Makgill Organisation had the distinct advantage of being disavowed by official sources. Its aim was to root out subversive influences such as anarchists, communists, Fenians and, from some of the surviving notes, people they didn't like the look of.

Small wonder that secret societies and extreme politics seemed to go in hand in hand: the question is simply one of how far their tendrils extended? From this remove, it does seem curious that many who were interested in the occult somehow converged in cabals of right-wing intrigue. Conspiracies do not thrive in a vacuum and communism became a potent bogeyman. But of especial note to this story, in one account, Makgill 'also devoted a considerable amount of time unmasking the cult of evil of which Aleister Crowley, alias "The Beast" was the centre'. This apparently, concerned an international traffic in drugs, women, children and blackmail, the result of the most notorious phase of the Beast's life upon which much of his subsequent reputation falls.

When Aleister Crowley returned home from New York in 1919, he arrived with a new mistress, failing health but a renewed dedication to the cult of Thelema. And for that he travelled all over Europe, trying to drum up support, having used up most of his inheritance. To make ends meet, he wrote *The Diaries of a Drug Fiend* in twenty-seven days, a kind of *Trainspotting du jour*, for he had been prescribed heroin by a doctor for his various ailments, asthma the most prominent. To say his writing was obscure would be an understatement, for in one review it was dismissed as 'a phantasmagoria of ecstasies, despairs and above all, verbiage'.

The diaries provided more unwelcome publicity and a campaign began against him by some of the more censorious journalists of the day in the rabid tabloid *John Bull*. His wartime pronouncements against Britain, however well intentioned, were not forgotten. So began a new chapter of wanderings. Crowley was determined to establish a monastic, liberated community for all his followers. By April 1920 they had congregated at a hilltop in Cefalù on Sicily where, in an oblong farmhouse, he established the Abbey of Thelema. Better known as Villa Santa Barbara, it became notorious as a kind of glorified crack den for his initiates.

Everywhere you looked was a mess. The paraphernalia of drug use and magick coexisted with a staggering lack of sanitary facilities. Crowley and his followers regularly imbibed cocaine, opium and heroin, and lived in a junkie's paradise. Even one of the dogs that was adopted as a pet was called Satan. So many rumours evolved from this time that they took on a life of their own. Drug-induced orgies and debauchery were so prevalent that one reviewer of Crowley's life later noted in mockery: 'He had sacrificed a goat to a youth – or was it only a youth to a goat?'

And there grew another rumour that during another ceremony a baby disappeared. 'Children under ten, whom the Beast keeps at his "abbey",' records another contemporary chronicle of the gothic horror to be found there, 'are made to witness sexually debauches unbelievably revolting. Filthy incense is burned and cakes made of goats' blood and honey are consumed in the window-less rim where the Beast conducts his rites.'

For the rest of his time in Sicily, Crowley went rock and hill climbing, trying to portray himself as at peace – thanks to his sex magick – with himself. 'I care nothing for public opinion,' he wearily declared. 'I care nothing for fame or success. I am perfectly happy in my retirement.' And that peace might have continued had it not been for a twice-divorced artist's model called Betty May. She wouldn't be the first spouse of someone else to come under the Beast's spell. Yet all along, from when he first answered a door in a kilt with make-up and black wig, she felt uneasy in Aleister Crowley's company.

It was reciprocated in full by the Great Beast.

In the events which followed, Betty May was hardly an innocent. She had been part of a criminal gang and was called Tiger Woman because of her fierce, feline nature (and looks). Yet all that was behind her when she and her husband, a beautiful spirit ten years her junior, turned up in Cefalù in the autumn of 1922. Frederick Loveday was enchanted by Crowley's spell. A bohemian who called himself Raoul, he too existed on a surfeit of hedonism, self-indulgence and thrill seeking. Aleister Crowley was besotted, terming him 'extraordinary', a fascination that was reciprocated in full.

Over the winter, the atmosphere at the Abbey of Thelema turned ugly. As well as the drugs, Crowley lay down the law. Any infraction of his word was treated with enforced self-mutilation. Many of his magick rituals seemed to involve feasting on various offals, like black pudding made from goat's blood. Worse was to come early the next year when a cat was ritually sacrificed when Crowley announced it was an evil spirit. When the poor animal was brought into the ceremony, it spat and hissed. In the most popular story of what happened next, Raoul Loveday slit its throat, which sprayed blood everywhere. Shortly afterwards he became ill (though others suggest it was because of unhygienic drinking of water).

Either way, Loveday died shortly thereafter from gastroenteritis. His wife had her revenge. All hell broke loose.

There was nothing like a bit of devil fighting for a newspaper on the Sabbath. So it came in February 1923 with an exclusive in the *Sunday Express*. 'More Sinister Revelations of Aleister Crowley. Varsity Lad's Death. Dreadful Ordeal of Young Wife.' It told the harrowing story of 'the girl-wife' who was left alone to fight the Beast: 'Since she defied him in every way and managed to keep herself clear of the bestialities of the house, he turned her out into the night.'

All this turned Crowley from a mild curiosity into public enemy number one – the man everyone loved to hate – and the infamy he had always craved was suddenly upon him. The Great Beast was stunned. In his own mind he was a great leader and great man, not a sinister pantomime villain. Soon he came to the attention of another with political pretensions. Benito Mussolini, like most Italians, had good reason to fear secret societies, not least the Freemasons, who were decidedly anti-fascistic.

The fascist leader had Crowley booted out of the country, whereafter he commenced his wanderings. Yet for all the tabloid vilification, Crowley had become more of a pathetic figure. One Englishman who caught up with him a few months later found him a large man of 47, inclined to corpulence and a sallow complexion. 'His manner was peculiar and he had a slight cockney accent.' He was 'disappointingly unsinister', and in time many also changed their opinion.

Aleister Crowley was, in this fellow Englishman's estimation, 'a very silly man'. And, for all the vilification that was meted out, a later review of this time of the Great Beast's life – even allowing for some latent misogyny –

gets it about right when it asks, 'in a period defined by the authentic evil of
the SS and Ogpu, can we be expected to shudder at Crowley's unhygienic
carryings-on with loose and hysterical women?'

After Mansfield Cumming's demise that same year of 1923, MI6 remained
underfunded and understaffed, its expertise stretched too thinly. It was
unloved too, for useful information was hardly forthcoming. Whitehall
awarded it such a slender budget that most of its agents couldn't afford to
use wireless sets. Lack of money also meant downsizing its staff, generally
perceived as amateurs who were highly dependent on voluntary assistance,
which could be fitted into a single house off Kensington High Street, on
Melbury Road.

But not all at the same time. When officers unexpectedly returned from
overseas, C's own secretary had to be temporarily accommodated in the
greenhouse outside. Perhaps this explained why the location of the house
wasn't exactly a state secret. When the new chief arrived at the Kensington
house in 1923, he asked a passing milkman who lived at this apparently quiet
residential mansion.

'The secret service,' was his reply.

With this temporary move to Melbury Road, MI6 hoped for greater
prosperity. A new broom was needed and after Cumming's demise it
arrived in the resplendent form of another naval officer who, despite superficial similarities, was cut from a very different kind of cloth. After replacing
Reggie Hall as Director of Naval Intelligence, Admiral Hugh Sinclair was
well regarded, loyal and fair to his staff – 'a good team captain' in a recent
assessment – whose charisma and dynamism often worked against him.

A nice, eminently clubbable fellow who revelled in a nickname from a
play about 'the wickedest man in London', Sinclair called himself 'Quex'
because of the raffish associations with Sir Arthur Pinero's *The Gay Lord
Quex*. Though later dismissed as 'a thoroughly unorthodox and somewhat
arbitrary commander' by one, to most of his staff, the new C was always a
pleasant, paternal figure. For the caricaturist, Sinclair was yet another gift:
'the little man with the face of a faintly surprised frog' in one estimation.

In many ways, Quex Sinclair would not have been out of place in a
drawing room comedy. One visitor recalled having to enter via the trades-
man's entrance through a bathroom with lavatory pans, and entered an
inner sanctum that was 'out of this world'. He recalled a table on which
was a mother-of-pearl handled pistol, a cigar box and a deep Turkish carpet

('that you nearly got lost in'), and a desk behind which sat the squat figure of the chief himself.

Another officer would recall being asked to see him as very much in the style of 007 being called in by M:

> As the Admiral got up from behind his large carved mahogany desk to greet me, I saw a rather short stocky figure with the welcoming smile of a benign uncle. His handshake was as gentle as his voice, and only the very alert dark eyes gave a hint of the tough personality that lay beneath the mild exterior.

At this remove, the second chief of Her Majesty's Secret Service seems yet another incongruous choice, for Quex Sinclair also seemed to delight in taking every opportunity to draw attention to himself. The new C sped around the capital in an ancient Lancia touring car, sometimes wearing a hat too small for his head, often with shoes that didn't match his suits. A *bon vivant* (with a large crocodile-skin case containing a hundred cigars somewhere to hand) paradoxically, Sinclair wanted to reform and modernise the service. Today, his time in office is overshadowed by a murky episode involving a forged document which led to the collapse of the first Labour government in 1924.

The Zinoviev letter,[6] supporting a call to agitprop by the president of the Comintern, was most likely forged by serving intelligence officials. Blinker Hall, by now the Union MP for Eastbourne, as well as the serving heads of MI5 and MI6, Kell and Sinclair, were involved in handing the letter to the *Daily Mail*. Widely seen as a triumph of the Occult Octopus and the shady right-wing elements who passed the letter on, it would lead to suspicions of conspiracies by those on the left for years to come. In this case, as the former Foreign Office archivist who looked into the matter termed it, the result of a 'very, very incestuous circle' of a conservative elite network which populated the intelligence world.

Early the next year, the Secret Intelligence Service moved to Broadway Buildings close to St James and hard by Parliament Square, thereby relieving some of the pressure in having to house staff in the greenhouse. More than that, it was agreeably symbolic, for the new C would now be nearer to the seat of power. Though he was rather more visible in Whitehall than his predecessor, it was said Quex Sinclair 'spent most afternoons at tea time quaffing brandy and soda under the great portrait of Nell Gwynne' at his club.

The problem was that the service was facing the wrong way and spent too much time staring off the Soviet bogeyman. Quex Sinclair was a dedicated anti-Bolshevist. He would dismiss the Nazi threat almost until it was almost too late, viewing it through an unappealing prism of anti-Semitism. C thought that reports of Germany's aggressiveness was a specious claim 'put forward by Jews and Bolshevists for their own ends'. Only too late did MI6 realise the extent of the menace of Adolf Hitler, for, as a recruit to its Air Section in 1929 would later write, attention to the Nazi Party was small and 'official minds seemed to shrug the matter off as just another political party of little consequence'.

It is perhaps significant that in April 1930, Aleister Crowley had settled, for the moment, in Weimar Berlin. He fetched up with a new 'scarlet woman' and exhibited his paintings, but for someone who was supposedly skint, he generally behaved with his usual breezy self-indulgence. A singular question remains about this period of his life: was he in the employ of intelligence? In the early thirties, he was possibly an informant for Britain in Weimar Germany, but his time there, on the available evidence, was more to allow him to spend time with Stephen Spender and Christopher Isherwood searching out male prostitutes.

But as Richard Spence has pointed out, occult assemblies provided the perfect cover for recruitment, and by now he had become a leading light in the Order of the Oriental Templars (*Ordo Templi Orientis*, or OTO). In this regard, it always seemed odd that Crowley had met one of the order's founders, Theodor Reuss, in pre-war London. The circumstances prompted Peter Quennell to note that Crowley happened to meet a mysterious stranger 'with prim pince-nez and handle-bar moustache, who one night appeared in Victoria Street, bearing the salutations of a powerful society of German seekers after the occult, and who turned out to be in his spare time, an agent of the German secret service'.

Subsequently, Crowley and Reuss had corresponded, and when the German leader of the OTO subsequently suffered a stroke, Crowley sensed an opportunity. When Reuss died in October 1923, Crowley claimed he was the natural heir to lead the Templars.

The fact an Englishman would now aim to be in charge hardly went down well in Weimar Berlin. It led to a chaotic Leadership Conference of Grand Masters in the summer of 1925 during his first visit to Germany. The result was that, as with all sects, it split and Crowley had to settle for running a diminished offshoot. In his later writings, Crowley confessed that he also met Hitler's fellow conspirator, General Ludendorff, with whom they had a discussion on 'Nordic theology'. Crowley later claimed it was his suggestion to adapt the swastika for the growing political movement.

And then came what was known as *l'affaire Crowley*, for in one French newspaper account, the Beast had 'been proven to be a secret agent in the service of Germany'. By the spring of 1929, he was living in some comfort in Paris, had resumed his writing (his masterwork *Magick In Theory And Practice* was the result) and had a new wife in the form of a voodoo princess from Nicaragua. Suddenly that April, without warning, the French authorities kicked him out on 'moral grounds'.

Nobody ever got to the bottom of what really went on. But why, as Richard Spence asks, would the Germans have ever employed someone who had worked against them in the Great War? As one of the leading Weimar spymasters noted, 'the full value of a secret service depends on the number and standard of double agents'. Some suggest Crowley may well have been spying on the communists. A couple of years later he had a lodger called Gerald Hamilton, who had been a friend of Sir Roger Casement, and was also a German spy and communist.

Around this time, in several accounts, Crowley became a part-time informant for the British, for he met a man with intelligence connections whom some believe was his handler. And, as prophesised in *The Book of The Law*, he was the rich man from the west, a charming old Etonian called Gerald Yorke, who soon became Crowley's business manager, helping promote the cause of his beliefs. Yorke had an intriguing background as a journalist in the Far East and had suspected connections with MI6.

As the Nazi party rose to power, it is easy to see why Crowley would be a person of interest to British Intelligence. In the early thirties, one of the Beast's German devotees, Martha Küntzel, had sent Adolf Hitler a copy of *The Book of The Law*, suspecting the German leader's supposed interest in the occult. Some have claimed that the Führer was a devotee of the beast, but within a year of coming to power he had banned most of the organisations of which Crowley was a member.

Yet as Gerald Yorke noted, there are similarities between *The Book Of The Law* and *Mein Kampf*. Both are, at some level, Nietzschean rants, and in his various drugged states, Crowley had some very odd dreams: in one, the Führer made all his books compulsory reading in Germany, while in another, Crowley was running Germany on Hitler's behalf. Magickal philosophy was the ultimate in the triumph of the will.

Rather than welcome him, as some have suggested, the Nazis did the worst possible thing so far as he was concerned; they simply ignored him. And by the time he fetched up back in London in 1932, he was penniless and still trying to attract attention. Crowley would joke in later years that 'legend says that my dossier at Scotland Yard fills a whole room', but there is little evidence to support this.

Yet one thing remained unchanged. When a *Daily Sketch* reporter happened upon the Great Beast around this time, he left no doubt for his readers how scary he was. It was the unwavering, hypnotic aspect of the eyes that continued to draw attention. 'Crowley has an amazing appearance,' the reporter noted, 'when you first look into them [they] are literally terrifying. I hate to imagine what they must be like when he is not in a benevolent mood.'

It was another pair of eyes that were equally terrifying.

They were of such an unwavering, cold blue intensity that when a former Great War pilot looked straight into them in pre-war Berlin, they struck him as being akin to those of a dead cod. The words that accompanied his staring were startling in their other worldliness. 'There should be only three major powers in the world,' the Führer flatly declared. 'The British Empire, the Americas and the Germanic Empire of the future.'

The ice was broken when the Englishman acknowledged that he was not bitter for having endured eighteen months as a prisoner of war. They were soon chatting away like old pals, not least when the Nazi leader became het up about the dangers of communism. And given that his visitor was head of the MI6 Air Section, there was at least some common ground in their discussion.

Squadron Leader Freddie Winterbotham had been restless when asked by the Deputy Chief of Air Staff to join the secret service. An old Carthusian, he had been shot down after a dogfight in the First World War and was finding the work of being a pedigree stockbreeder uninteresting. His arrival in MI6 was propitious. Winterbotham was posted to Berlin from 1933 to 1938, where he would witness German rearmament first-hand. Though listed as a member of the Embassy Air Staff, his secret connections soon became well known to the Nazis.

Winterbotham's greatest source of information was a one-time Baltic baron called William de Ropp, who had worked as a journalist and by the start of the thirties was just about the only MI6 source within Germany. Ropp (or Code 821 as he was known) provided Winterbotham with details of the emerging Luftwaffe. The Nazis, though, were equally ignorant about the Royal Air Force. So Winterbotham would trade information back and forth. As with much of the espionage world, it was never quite clear who was using the other to better advantage.

The Nazis would soon refer to Winterbotham as 'our English agent', whose role, in one account, was 'persuading people in Britain to see things the Nazi way'. Winterbotham had arrived in time for the Reichstag fire where, he would memorably recall, the 'writing was on all the walls, illuminated by the swastika'. One day he was met by Alfred Rosenberg, one of the principal architects of Nazi ideology, in full uniform, who astonished him by giving the Nazi salute.

While staying with de Ropp, Winterbotham was later taken to the Chancellery to meet the Führer, an experience he vividly likened to entering 'straight into Alice's Looking Glass land'. Within months, Winterbotham met virtually all the other leading Nazis and became aware of the full extent of German rearmament. In the face of official scepticism, he repeatedly briefed London on the self-evident expansion of the Luftwaffe. He was able to obtain photostats of its training 'bible' and went to visit some of the flying training schools.

Yet nobody in Broadway Buildings wanted to know.

'I found a rather smug complacency within MI6,' Freddie Winterbotham would later recall, 'an attitude that was also common around Whitehall.'

By now, the Secret Intelligence Service had made itself very unpopular over its very same estimates for the growing emergence of German air power. In May 1935, C himself threatened to resign when the prime minister made a misleading statement to the House about the extent of Nazi aerial rearmament. A secret cabinet enquiry vindicated Quex Sinclair's estimates, though Stanley Baldwin saved face by claiming that he, too, had been misled. The point was, dodgy dossiers or not, C's figures were accepted. Freddie Winterbotham would write that this would be the turning point of his career as a secret servant and a highlight for an increasingly embittered service. 'We all had a drink in the Admiral's flat,' he would recall.

Though some subsequently claimed the Führer had the devil at his side, it was clear that Adolf Hitler had little need for supernatural forces in his extraordinary rise to power. Resentment and the various prejudices of the day were sufficient. Bolstered by what one historian called 'the intellectual detritus of centuries', Hitler was a canny enough politician to invoke ancient symbolism. Historically, the swastika had symbolised everything from good luck to fertility. The red, white and black of the SS uniforms were taken from the priestly robes of the Manichean order, an occult-based religion. The skull and crossbones symbolised the work of the devil and the SS lettering was based on the Runic alphabet. In other words, death-fixated kitsch and sinister sentiments, though largely peripheral to the actual cause, represented its best foot forward.

Other senior Nazis were equally shrewd enough to invoke ancient symbolism to pitch politics to a largely superstitious *Deutsches Volk*. Hess and Himmler often conjured up the occult to support their more hare-brained schemes. 'Göring is worried about the stars on his chest,' Reinhard Heydrich once famously remarked, 'Himmler about those in his horoscopes.' In 1935, Heinrich Himmler founded the Ahnenerbe (Ancestral Research) branch of the SS, an academy where he could indulge some of his nuttier fantasies. Indeed, the Reichsführer-SS was hooked. At various points in his life, Heinrich Himmler believed that he was a reincarnated monarch, which no doubt prompted the Ahnenerbe to investigate the occult origins of the Aryan race.

Most famously, this involved the dispatch of an expedition to Tibet to look for the fossils of giants. 'The usual view of Himmler is that he was an ice-cold, cynical politician,' one SS officer in his immediate circle crisply recalled. 'This view is almost certainly wrong. Himmler was a mystic.'

Even Hitler viewed him as a crank, but a loyal one.

In Wewelsburg, Heinrich Himmler established an SS School in an area of Westphalia long associated with Saxon paganism. A training camp close by a seventeenth-century castle was built and was soon decorated with all sorts of signs and symbols, including one in an entrance hall akin to the shape of the Spear of Destiny, perhaps the starting point for some of the more curious myths. Every year at midnight on 2 July, some accounts suggest, Himmler held a ritual in the crypt at Quedlinburg Cathedral after a formal procession.

It was there, in 1937, that he had had the bones of his namesake, King Heinrich I, reinterred. The *Reichsführer-SS* seriously believed he was the reincarnation of the king sometimes known as Henry the Fowler. Himmler, others have suggested, communicated with him in his sleep. Although this suggests Himmler was a true crackpot, if anything, the deputy leader of the Third Reich was even nuttier. Rudolf Hess was susceptible to various 'mad' theories and surrounded himself with mystical mountebanks of varying degrees. 'His was a Manichean universe in which the forces of good, the

Aryan and particularly the German race, were constantly at war with those of evil, the Jews,' writes the late historian Hugh Trevor-Roper, 'and Hitler, to whom his loyalty was no less absolute, was not merely a political leader but a Redeemer sent by Providence.'

The Deputy Führer often slept under magnets to draw out any harmful substances in close proximity, and routinely tested bedrooms with divining rods to ensure no underground waters could cast any lingering malevolence while he slept.

Given all these flirtations with the mystical, it is hardly surprising that the notion of Hitler having his own astrologer gained credence in the years before the outbreak of the Second World War. Increasingly thereafter, innumerable spurious accounts talk of an unknown *éminence grise* behind the scenes who advised and counselled him on the ways of the stars. Stranger still, British Intelligence had also come to realise that the Führer had appointed a new chief of military intelligence who was a surprisingly sentimental fellow and, in London at least, some considered him a kind of Catholic mystic.

It was a salutary lesson for anyone interested in the occult in Nazi Germany to learn what had happened to one of the few practitioners who had been allowed free roam within the Führer's inner circle. That Erik Jan Hanussen was Jewish adds a curious piquancy to his story, though, almost inevitably, within months of Hitler's coming to power, he disappeared from view in mysterious circumstances. Hanussen had long since styled himself as the 'Magician of Berlin', where he would routinely stage elaborate séances which – through astute toadying and promotion – he made into a kind of must-see for any self-respecting Nazi. Quite how he came into the orbit of the Nazi leadership, and even when, have been the subject for much debate.

Before the election of 1933, Adolf Hitler called in the Viennese-born Hanussen, who had already predicted that he would become Führer. In one, admittedly febrile account, the politician came to visit him and fell into a trance. 'I see victory for you,' the seer said. 'It cannot be stopped.' So the man born Hermann Steinschneider was allowed to help the man sometimes wrongly identified as Adolf Schicklgruber.

In his youth, he had become a hypnotist, seer and self-styled psychic detective who had started out in the carnivals and music halls of his native

Austria. By the time of the Weimar Republic, Hanussen was one of the more famous magicians in the capital. Weimar Berlin was full of seers and mystics who all competed with each other. Petty jealousies and battles for primacy characterised both them and their work. All vied for supremacy but Erik Jan Hanussen, through a canny but clever series of self-promotions, became pre-eminent. He bought his own luxurious cabin cruiser nicknamed 'The Yacht of Seven Sins', on which he experimented with mescaline and peyote, as well as hypnotising women into sustained frenzies of sexual ecstasy.

As a result, Hanussen was alternately condemned and supported by the press, depending on whether they supported Hitler or not. It was almost inevitable that Hanussen would bring out his own weekly, in which he could draw attention to the startling accuracy of his own predictions. When his own newspaper, *Berliner Wochenschau*, carried a story under the headline 'Hanussen In Trance Predicts Hitler's Future' in March 1932, people sat up and noticed.

Adolf Hitler would, he calmly predicted, become Reichschancellor in a year's time. Later that same summer of 1932, Hanussen was ushered into the company of the future Führer, an event which has become totemic and around which much mystery exists. Some accounts suggest this occurred in 1926, but more recent biographers point out it was actually later in the Führer's rise. Certainly, the magician suggested ways of making his ascendancy more assured.

'If you are serious about entering politics, Herr Hitler, why don't you learn how to speak?' Hanussen asked.

After teaching him about elocution and body language, Hanussen would become part of the leader's reinvention and eventually cast the Führer's horoscope – by which his fate was sealed. Now in the frenzied atmosphere of divisive politics which consumed Weimar Germany, where Hanussen was seen increasingly as a Nazi stooge, it emerged that he was Jewish. In September 1932, a Viennese chorus girl was gossiping that the 'Aryan prophet' was circumcised. In communist newspapers, Hanussen was described as 'Hitler's Jewish disciple', 'a religious quack' and 'an outrageous swindler'.

And when another enemy revealed that not only was he fully Jewish – by the Nazi definition of bloodlines – but the nephew of a rabbi from the Austrian ghetto, it was reported as a fact in one of Josef Goebbels' propaganda sheets. Erik Jan Hanussen denied the charges and soon turned his greater attentions to a shining beacon of his own self-aggrandisement.

In early 1933, he was ready to open his own 'Palace of Occultism' in Berlin. By now very rich, as his biographer Mel Gordon notes, the whole enterprise was glorious, 'like a spiritual appendage to Versailles'. In some ways, it sounds more akin to a tart's boudoir crossed with a gold-bedecked Taj Mahal and an Egyptian temple. Decorated with astrological signs and pure-white marbled religious statues, it also contained a vast bronze statue of the man himself, dressed in a Roman toga, his left arm rising in a Nazi salute.

The innermost sanctuary, The Room of Glass, was Hanussen's throne. There he sat by a large glass table under which a wheel, covered with various occult symbols, would be spun. Hanussen would divine meaning like a croupier attuned to the occult. On the opening night, he enthralled the crowds of visitors. 'He predicted the blood purge that was to come later and the war with England, Russia and America,' recalled one.

The next night, something terrible happened. The Reichstag was burned to the ground. Hanussen's prediction of the Reichstag fire – or rather of a great house in flames – has led some to speculate that he had even hypnotised Marius van der Lubbe, the anarchist supposedly behind the outrage.

But then within a month, Hanussen himself disappeared. Ten days later, his body was found. The perpetrators were never found but everyone knew who they would be. The savage irony was that the great seer couldn't see what was right in front of him. 'I always thought that business about the Jews was just an election trick of theirs,' he had said a few weeks before. 'It wasn't.'

Unlike Winston Churchill, who had a natural predisposition to intrigue of any kind, Adolf Hitler said he would never shake hands with a spy, generally dismissing intelligence warnings as fanciful or fantasist. So when, in the early autumn of 1935, the Führer himself summoned his new espionage chief to his mountaintop lair, very little was expected. Against the suitably Wagnerian backdrop of the Berghof, something entirely unexpected happened that September morning.

Both Führer and spymaster bonded.

In fact, Captain Wilhelm Canaris was just the kind of person Hitler would have hated and normally blamed for the country's failures. His newly appointed spy chief was a fairly typical Wilhelmian brahmin of wealth and bourgeois sensibilities who ran the Abwehr, as German Military Intelligence was known. After a family cruise around the Aegean, the young Canaris – whose childhood inquisitiveness led to his nickname of 'Kika' (snooper)

– joined the Imperial Germany Navy in 1905. In time, he became one of the finest officers of his generation, despite his shortness, his inscrutability and what seemed to be a frail appearance.

During the Great War, Canaris 'showed a penchant for clandestine operations and secret negotiations which earned him a reputation as being something of a super-spy', as one biographical entry has it. Something of his reputation preceded his meeting with Adolf Hitler, which was by all accounts highly convivial. 'You can talk to the man,' Canaris later told his associates about the Führer. 'He is reasonable and sees your point of view, if you point it out properly.'

Within a four-month period, Canaris had seventeen private meetings with the Führer. With his baroque and old-world politeness, the canny spymaster would listen and flatter. Canaris was determined to make his service pre-eminent – there were at least another half dozen agencies competing with his – and by a canny mixture of mending fences, playing off rivals and, in the first few years at least, scoring some notable successes, he did so. Small wonder that in time, the Abwehr's rambling headquarters on the Tirpitzufer came to be known as the 'Fuchsbau', or fox's lair.

As befits someone named for such a wily creature, nobody could ever quite pin down the exact loyalties of Wilhem Canaris. The head of the Abwehr remains a remarkably opaque figure because of the enigma of his personality, living up to his billing – by Russian military intelligence, who knew a thing or two about such matters – as the most dangerous intelligence man in the world.

In some accounts, including official government ones, it is said that before the war British Intelligence had no idea what its German equivalent was called, who ran it, where it was based and what it was up to. Thanks to the recent release of MI5 papers from 1938, which cross-reference some CX material from MI6, it is clear that Canaris's opposite numbers were perfectly well aware who he was and what he was doing. An MI6 report from Prague dated 25 July 1938 reveals that C's staff knew the Abwehr was a function of counter-espionage in the German Armed Services. The admiral was recorded as having been Chief of the Defence Section (*Abwehrabteilung*) in the two previous years. And in another CX report it says: 'CANARIS was described as essentially a southerner, and in tastes as well as appearance, more Greek than German.'

There, though, the certainties end.

In the years to come, Wilhelm Canaris – who was promoted to vice-admiral in 1938 and admiral two years later – would become known to MI6 as Theodor. As the official MI6 history notes, there has been a great deal of speculation about such breathtaking links.[7] Though he never reported to anyone in the direct employ of British Intelligence, it is clear that Canaris used various cut-outs and intermediaries to let London know exactly what he was thinking. These odd, shifting sands of contacts were amongst the closest-guarded secrets of the war to come.

In the same way that Mansfield Cumming had dominated the early years of the Secret Intelligence Service, Wilhelm Canaris would set the tone for the organisation which he came to command. The Abwehr had actually been in existence since 1921, though such an agency had been forbidden by the strictest terms of the Versailles Treaty. Its title meant 'defence', as in the sense of warding off, for 'defensive' counter-espionage was allowed. Originally, the Abwehr was a small, yet surprisingly effective adjunct to the Supreme Command. Rather like its equivalents in MI6, throughout the twenties the Abwehr's officers and reservists were recruited from the old school, all keen to maintain the glorious certainties of the older imperial order.[8]

In these early years of Wilhelm Canaris's ascendancy, he built his staff up from 150 to just under 1,000 in three years. It steadily grew, until it took over several buildings to the west of Berlin. The small 'defensive' organisation was reorganised into five separate sections, including a large department which would be responsible for sabotage in enemy countries. Much of what happened to the Abwehr in the subsequent intelligence war can be explained by Admiral Canaris's curious, invariably inscrutable character. The admiral's white-haired countenance led some to call him Father Christmas, for he was generally seen as an avuncular figure who spoke hesitantly and walked with a stoop, his hands firmly clasped behind his back.

From his Spartan office, Canaris would look out on to the limes and chestnuts of the Tiergarten. Most mornings, he would go riding in this park which bisects the centre of Berlin. 'The room where Canaris worked symbolised the man and his character,' his executive officer, Erwin Lahousen, would later recall. 'You could not but notice the simplicity of his surroundings.' The floor was covered by a threadbare Persian carpet, along with a small safe and a handful of portraits. The admiral spent much of his time looking at his faithful pair of dachshunds asleep on a cot in the corner. It would later be said that Canaris preferred animals to people[9] – like the Führer himself – and with good reason. If a man didn't like dogs, Canaris would say, he couldn't be trusted.

Outside the office, there were equally unlikely pursuits.

He enjoyed cooking, often preparing meals for a near neighbour whom he had known on active service at sea. Their gardens directly backed on to each other's in a pleasant suburb of the capital. This younger man, highly regarded for his mellow and delicate violin playing, was often invited over by Frau Erika Canaris[10] to join her in musical recitals at their home on Sunday evenings. And in time, perhaps, both she and her husband would rue the day that they had let Reinhard Heydrich enter their lives; his ruthlessness was only ever matched by an overreaching certainty in the malign influence of the British Secret Service and whose many pretensions involved signing himself as 'C'.

By now, the tide had turned against the occult in Nazi Germany.

Within a couple of years of reaching power, the Nazis had banned all public displays of occultism and astrology. Just two years before the outbreak of the Second World War, it had become a punishable offence to publish or even cast a horoscope about Der Führer. The head of the Central Astrological Office – a kind of puffed-up, self-congratulatory body to which most astrologers belonged – was arrested. He was released and became, perhaps understandably, more circumspect in his predictions. Newspapers were banned from carrying astrological advertising. Fortune telling and astrology was also banned in Berlin. Police raids on occult bookshops and publishers became a regular occurrence. All occult societies were outlawed and their members found themselves under investigation by the Gestapo.

The reasons were simple enough.

Despite some of the more specious claims, the Nazis only ever used astrology and occult practices to suit their own needs. 'We cannot allow astrologers to follow their calling unless they are working for us,' Heinrich Himmler said at the time. 'In the National Socialist state, astrology must remain a *privilegium singularum*. It is not for the masses.'

For partisans of the occult, this became an all too inevitable axiom. Such secret knowledge was simply too dangerous to be allowed in the hands of the *Deutsches Volk*. The greater truth is that the Nazi hierarchy didn't want to allow its influence to be allowed unchecked, nor to have any control. The Führer agreed. In private, Adolf Hitler referred to horoscopes as 'a swindle whose significance should not be underestimated'.

The German leader's interest in the occult was only ever fleeting and dictated by political expedience. An autodidact with various quotidian chips on his shoulders, his ostracism was a *sine qua non* of higher insight which the Führer felt. Most of it centred, unsurprisingly, on the Jews. Yet despite Hitler's ambivalence, that did not stop his immediate circle from promoting any number of bizarre ideas.

A Munich physician in the Führer's employ regularly used an astrological contraption he called 'the sidereal pendulum', which supposedly gave him the power to sense the presence of Jews or those of Jewish ancestry. Adolf Hitler would supposedly call upon its peculiar 'mystic' powers and discuss questions of racial purity with its creator. Various surreal 'cosmic theories' would also come to be taken up in much of the Nazis' cack-handed interest in history: of universal ice, of ancient history and human origins from giants, all fuelled and matched in the operatic range of Wagnerian grandeur (the composer whom, it should be noted, Adolf Hitler idolised as the greatest interpreter of German folk spirits, yet another wrong-headed interpretation of history that propelled the Nazis on their way).

The key to understanding Wilhelm Canaris's disquieting protégé was, it was always said, the almost operatic side of his nature. When he had first met Captain Wilhelm Canaris in 1923, Reinhard Tristan Eugen Heydrich had been a lanky, blonde cadet most notable for his high-pitched voice, arrogant disposition and occasional histrionics. His was a complex character and a personality which one historian aptly calls 'a cold, calculating, evil genius and a very real man of many weaknesses'. So successfully did he hide the latter that even Adolf Hitler referred to him as iron-hearted.

With a cruel, thin face which would not have looked out of place in a Van Dyck portrait, Reinhard Heydrich's arrogance was a mask for crippling insecurities. Being the son of an equally arrogant, often harsh actress and an opera singer perhaps explains his highly strung nature. Heydrich came to be the most feared spy chief in pre-war Germany when a former pig farmer asked him to write the synopsis for an intelligence apparatus for the Nazi Party. After twenty minutes, he returned, paper in hand. In this, he gained Heinrich Himmler's eternal gratitude.

Reinhard Heydrich thus bluffed his way into the intelligence world, soon establishing himself 'the master of the necessary mysteries' of counter-espionage and threats to the Nazi movement. Soon, his grander pretensions rubbed up against the harsher realities of the time, in that he could only afford to buy garden furniture for his office. Often rash and impetuous, he had an impressive memory for detail and a love of the theatrical.

In short, Heydrich loved playing the role of a secret service chief, filling the SS library with all the trashiest spy novels – Le Queux, inevitably, amongst them – and even signing correspondence with an ornate letter C, as the head of the British Secret Service was known to do. Such pretensions informed a peculiar vision of MI6. He was told, for example, that the Secret Intelligence Service was self-financing (by selling its secrets to the government of the day). Reuters, the *Daily Express* and the YMCA were also viewed as supposed pawns of British Intelligence.

Soon he was the de facto intelligence chief for the Nazi Party. Established as part of the SS, Heydrich came to command the *Sicherheitsdienst* (SD), which would be staffed by other sons of the middle classes who had been alienated and repelled by the rootlessness of Weimar society. The SD was created by Heydrich specifically to alert the Nazis against threats to the party. Though the Abwehr was supposed to provide intelligence for the German General Staff, it was inevitable that it would brush up against Heydrich's upstart agency. The result was much how Nazi Germany liked to carry out its official business: a vast, competing, uncoordinated mess, with often contradictory information reaching the top via whichever minister or bureaucrat could vie for the attention of the leader.

Ostensibly, the Abwehr was responsible for military espionage and counter-espionage, while the SD looked after 'political' crime and espionage. 'Usually the two agencies worked together well, despite extensive duplication of effort,' one historian has written. Though outwardly maintaining a friendship, Admiral Canaris and his former cadet would become the deadliest of rivals by the end of the thirties. As well as post-war myths, there is much mythology surrounding the relationship of Heydrich and Canaris, almost a Manichean struggle, a delicate dance like that of two tarantulas.

Sicherheitsdienst agents spied on their Abwehr counterparts. Officials placed microphones in opponents' offices. Heydrich and Canaris recorded intimate details about each other's supposed indiscretions in secret files. All telephone calls from the Fuchsbau were monitored by Heydrich's wiretappers. Each jealously guarded his own sphere of influence in the hope of gaining pre-eminence with the leadership or, at the very least, that the other would make some sort of terrible mistake that could be used against them.

When Wilhelm Canaris started to become aware of the excesses of the Nazi police state – particularly investigations of the links between the Wehrmacht and the Red Army – he was dismayed that they had been orchestrated by his former cadet.

'Heydrich is a barbarous fanatic with whom it will be very difficult to collaborate in a frank and loyal manner,' Canaris said on one occasion. But an even more illuminating tale comes from the admiral's nephew," an SS officer who was interrogated after the war. Constantin Canaris said that his uncle was a religious man who had, in 1937, approached Heydrich on the party and SS attitudes to religion. The admiral told his nephew he had lent Heydrich a book on the great religions of the world, 'telling him that he ought to learn something of the meaning [of] faith which he was attacking. After a few days, Heydrich returned the book, saying that it was beyond him and that he was not interested in such matters.'

In the battles to come, Reinhard Heydrich – and others in the Führer's immediate circle – never lost their faith in the ubiquity and infallibility of the British secret service. Yet, ironically, the advice given by MI6 to the British government was, by the latter part of the thirties, largely being completely ignored. Having failed to warn of Italy's invasion of Abyssinia, funding for the Secret Intelligence Service was reduced by disgruntled Whitehall mandarins. C protested in vain that lack of money meant it had no presence in those countries which could have ever spotted the Abyssinian attack.

To be fair, the Secret Intelligence Service was now preparing for the fighting to come by establishing a new espionage network across Europe. Purely as a form of insurance, one of Sinclair's deputies, Claude Dansey, a larger-than-life character known, not entirely fondly, as 'Uncle Claude', wanted to create a parallel structure in case the 'official' networks based around British Embassies became compromised. Colonel Claude Edward Marjoribanks Dansey was an *éminence grise* within MI6, an acerbic, querulous figure who, as one who knew him well said, seemed to be consumed by hatreds. Yet another Indian policeman who surrounded himself with placemen from the same inefficient old boy network, his arrogance and incompetence ('a snob, a bully and a shit') ensured that he vetoed the recruitment of graduates. As a result, the overall calibre of MI6 officers still left a lot to be desired, with one later remarking that they were 'by and large pretty stupid – and some of them very stupid'.

Existing only in continental Europe and Greece, Dansey's Z Network employed a curious mixture of businessmen and journalists who would obtain political and economic intelligence. They used, as cover, London Films, run by Sir Alexander Korda, the Hungarian-born film director who got a knighthood for his trouble. 'It was a very well kept secret,' Dansey's widow said many years later. Her husband sat on the board, which allowed MI6 to keep in contact with its agents all over Europe. The Z Network also used a tour company (to inveigle agents abroad) and some kind of chemical one. The problem was that refugees would come up with any old nonsense ('prepared to sell anything to anybody') and, as they were untrained, were often comically inept.

The more formal MI6 network hardly fared any better.

The Foreign Office remained unhappy at C's men using diplomatic cover as passport control officers (PCOs) and there was a long and bickering correspondence about its general unhappiness. Worse, because MI6 officers mainly existed on private incomes, financial temptation proved too great, particularly with the exodus of the disaffected from Germany.

To be fair, the passport control officers were overwhelmed. Some behaved despicably. Exit visas for Palestine were preferentially issued to richer Jewish émigrés who would hand over vast sums for the privilege. When it became clear in 1936, for example, that the PCO stationed in The Hague had been accepting bribes, he shot himself. In Germany, the demand for exit visas was so great that Frank Foley – a true-life Schindler if ever there was one – would lament that his workload grew to such an extent that he had to restrict the time he had available to devote to genuine intelligence gathering.

With its officers overwhelmed, whenever genuinely useful information came in from Broadway Buildings – the CX reports still elaborately bound in red books – very few civil servants tended to believe it. 'Such a service as the Secret Intelligence Service ought properly to regard itself as always at war,' the MI6 War Book had noted at the end of 1937. 'An actual state of war does not radically alter its functions, it only intensifies them'. In fact, the greater truth, as the former Foreign Office archivist Gill Bennett has wryly noted, was that MI6 was always at war with Whitehall.

Its coverage of Germany was dismissed as spasmodic and fragmented, for in such a harsh, totalitarian police state the usual diplomatic rumours did not filter through. Worse, as the official history of wartime intelligence notes, 'clandestine sources were in no position to fill the gap'.

Around the corridors of power, an even more pervasive belief was that the agency was a kind of gentleman's drinking club for middle-aged nobs – with officers named Cuthbert Bowlby and others like 'Biffy' Dunderdale and 'Lousy' Payne[12] – who had also been at Eton, served in the Guards or married well. Suitable candidates for the secret world were either metropolitan young men drawn from the London clubs or else ex-Indian policemen.

And when, a few weeks after war was declared, Quex Sinclair passed away from cancer, the appointment of his successor produced puzzlement at the apex of the establishment. In one especially damning estimation, it was a complete mystery why someone so stupid had been shooed in as the new C. That such a complaint came from the Duke of Buccleuch, whom he had fagged at Eton, shows just how seamless the robes of entitlement fitted the appointment of His Majesty's new spy chief.

With his inheritance of vast estates across the Scottish Highlands and a name whose pronunciation invariably confused foreigners, Colonel Stewart Menzies sounds suspiciously like a character from a John Buchan novel. The scion of Scottish mercantile aristocracy, the chief who would direct MI6 in the Second World War was, in his biographer's telling phrase, 'exceedingly good-looking in the Hannay fashions of the Edwardians'. Born to the powerful elite who ruled half the globe, Menzies (pronounced Mingiss) was memorably described as 'sandy-haired, with a soft handshake and an air of indolence, belied by a glint of cunning in his brown eyes' by one of his later underlings.

The Duke of Wellington famously said that the Battle of Waterloo was won on the playing fields of Eton. Now, in the glorious age of Edwardian England, it helped that Stewart Menzies had been a contemporary there with most of the Cabinet. Many of the intelligence battles in the Second World War evolved from those same fields, where sportsmanship had been set at a premium. A contemporary noted that 'Stewart was a beautiful athlete', often winning the steeplechases, 'probably the most coveted race to win at Eton'. During what his friend termed 'four blissful years', Menzies had been a Master of the Eton Beagles, became Captain of the First XI and was elevated to yet another élite within an élite – the President of Pop.

But more significantly for this narrative, Menzies and his cronies were introduced to the works of Kipling by a kindly housemaster. As a result, life imitated art as the teacher 'had a profound love and admiration' for his seminal *Kim* which his pupils came to share. Menzies was hardly the intellectual duffer others had made out, for in Rex Benson's estimation he 'had a habit of plying you with questions and like "Kim" of acquiring knowledge which he put to good use in his later professional life'.

When war broke out, Menzies joined the Life Guards and in November 1914, during battles in the Ypres Salient, was awarded the Distinguished Service Order. His regiment was virtually decimated – nearly a million men were either killed or maimed – and, on that occasion, he had a remarkable escape when he jumped into a trench full of Prussians. In later years, when opinion was sharply divided over his effectiveness, Stewart Menzies' bravery was never brought into question. A year later, he joined Field Marshal Haig's staff, where he became attached to the British Expeditionary Force Headquarters as part of military intelligence (and, at that stage, it was a collateral branch that was entirely separate from Cumming's service).[13]

His attachment was to the Counter-Intelligence Division based in Montreuil, where he was engaged in 'secret service and security work' (the lapidary words on his military record). There he took charge of a large staff that was alert for potential spies and saboteurs. In later life, Stewart Menzies remarked that those three years of secret service in the Great War gave him thirty years' experience of the ways of humanity.

Opinion has been divided over how useful the chief of MI6 in the next war really was. Some of his more vociferous critics suggest he was rather hasty and superficial, yet Menzies himself was generally liked as a person. One assistant later noted that 'no-one could work closely without feeling for him real respect and great affection'. Some said he was not a particularly good judge of character,[14] and in another assessment he 'had more common sense than learning'. Yet Menzies hardly needed to be a towering intellect, a point lost on (inevitably) towering intellects, for in the fighting to come academic abstraction was hardly necessary.

The role Stewart Menzies would play was that of the good and faithful servant. 'C rarely left his desk during the war,' his assistant Robert Cecil wrote. 'One reason was his feeling that he should be on hand if a summons came from the PM, which might come on any day of the week and at any hour of the day.' The new C's greater problem was that he could not escape the shadow of the larger than life Sinclair. Unlike the rascally Quex, Menzies was reserved – and diffident, so much so that his ability to remain in the shadows and achieve things covertly was almost psychological.

As deputy chief, Stewart Menzies had capitalised on rumours from Germany about an inexpensive new 'secret writing' machine which were emanating from the mists of Eastern Europe. Though adopted by the German military under the impression it was unbreakable, the Enigma machine was vulnerable. As is now well known, the work of two Polish mathematicians prompted a systematic unbuttoning of its fearsomely complex internal encoding, with help from MI6.

In this determination to unravel the secrets of Enigma, the fortunes of the new chief, Sir Stewart Menzies, became inextricably linked. 'He would not have held the job for more than a year if it had not been for Bletchley,' said another observer at the time. The new C was hampered by the fact the Secret Intelligence Service had remained chronically underfunded. Starting from a low base, things could only have got better for, in the assessment of another intelligence professional, 'if they had had the money, [they] would have provided us with a splendid organisation when the war broke out and [would be] capable of rapid expansion'.

As befitting a future Chief of the Secret Service, the life of Sir Stewart Menzies threaded the various seamless robes of the establishment, for he was well born, well connected and, even more significantly, had friends at Court.[15] Early in the 1920s, the then Colonel Stewart Menzies happened to be having dinner with King George V, whom he knew well from his family's connections to the throne. Despite his reputation for lack of mental acuity, a certain dry wit – along with an unquestioning devotion to the monarchy – was very much in evidence. Despite his closeness to the royals, he was commendably discreet when the king asked him for the name of the Secret Service's man in Berlin.

'Sire,' Menzies replied smoothly, 'if my service has a man in Berlin, I may not divulge his identity.'

The king decided to offer some royal prerogative.

'What would you say if I said "Menzies, give me the name of our man in Berlin or off with your head"?'

'Sire, if you were to give such an order, and when your order was carried out, my head would roll with lips still sealed.'

With his subsequent elevation to the coveted role as C, Stewart Menzies would become an important player in the most furtive and influential cabal of all: 'the spider in the centre of such a network', in the estimation of his obituary. He was protected by a real-life Miss Moneypenny, Kathleen Pettigrew – 'a formidable gray-haired lady with a square jaw of the battleship type' and – to the endless procession of visitors who came to gaze upon her beauty – her younger assistant, Evelyn Jones.

And then there were the curious traditions that the chief would now inherit, every bit as preposterous (in some estimations) as the accoutrements and artefacts associated with occult gatherings. The green light above his door, his habit of using special green ink and signing documents with the letter C, as well as his frequent disappearances down a secret passageway out of the building, seemed like amateur theatrics better suited to a more innocent, if not heroic, age. Sir Stewart Menzies would thus become the highest secret servant in the land, living in a twilight world of shadows, where, as one historian has remarked, 'it is hard to distinguish with certainty between the menacing and the merely ludicrous'.

Queues usually formed, as he could never quite delegate to Claude Dansey (whom Menzies had appointed assistant chief of the service) at the other end of the corridor. The difficult architect of the Z Network spent most of his time fighting the deputy chief, Colonel Valentine Vivian, usually called Vee Vee, who was equally serpentine: 'a nice wet man with no guts', in one assessment and, to many, the ultimate 'yes' man in his cloying humility and insincerity. To the lower ranks, they were all mysterious, unfathomable figures. Many of the new wartime recruits to the service never quite knew what to expect. And for all the rumours of its infallibility, there seemed very little by way of practical information available to recruits. 'You'll have to work it out for yourself,' said one station chief.

Most were equal to the task. There was something unique about the British character which lent itself to the swift management of deceit, treachery and double-crosses. Espionage operations carried out in the name of statecraft required great imagination, extreme subtlety and, often, sheer improbability, none more so than one of the more remarkable in the story that follows, a self-promoting astrologer who, if his own memoirs are believed, helped win the war single-handedly.

3

THE DEVIL IN THE DETAILS

My aim is to bring light. But then Lucifer was also a bringer of light ... A doctor's poison cupboard contains wonderful means of healing. But what would they become in the hands of a layman who did not know how much he should take of them? Astrology can be poisonous in the wrong hands ... Anyone should not be allowed to study astrology, only those who take a solemn oath to us it only for good.

Louis de Wohl, *Secret Service of the Sky* (1938)

For someone supposedly so mindful of the heavenly runes, the late Ludwig van der Wohl admitted that he got the timing of his birth wrong. What seems like a curious admission for an astrologer is, in fact, telling. In his autobiography, *I Follow The Stars*, van der Wohl claimed he was born at 7.45 p.m. on 24 January 1903. Later, he admitted it was nearer to 3.30 p.m. This was a deliberate obfuscation, he maintained, as he didn't want anyone to meddle with his own charts for their own advantage.

This discrepancy speaks volumes about the man whom one secret servant would later dismiss as 'that German astrologer and exhibitionist'. With an ego the size of Jupiter (and a stomach to match), van der Wohl would eventually claim to have played a starring role in the secret war and more or less defeated the Nazis single-handed. He would famously declare in another volume of entertainingly immodest memoirs: 'In the Second World War astrological warfare was waged for the first time since the Thirty Years' War, 1618–48. It was waged by no more than a handful of men. There were six, as far as I know, on the Axis side: on the Allied side, I believe, I had the honour alone.'

The truth was very different, and thanks to the release of his hitherto restricted Security Service files, the story of the Hungarian astrologer can now be told. The man who anglicised his name to the less Mitteleuropean and therefore unthreatening Louis de Wohl would come to alternately bemuse, amaze, amuse, annoy and enrage British Intelligence – often, all at the same time.

Louis de Wohl would also have a strange impact on the secret world with a series of subsequent events about which so many half-truths have been claimed. So far as Louis de Wohl is concerned, nothing was ever quite what it seemed. It is a story that links high policy and low farce, accompanied by a chorus of naysayers such as the MI5 informant who noted that he was 'a charlatan and a fake', a view that many in British Intelligence later came to quite quickly.

Yet the curious character who had actually been born Mucsinyi Wohl Lajos had, as his later handlers noted, 'crowded a most adventurous career' into his short life to date. 'He has lived a large part of his life in Germany and came to the United Kingdom in 1935,' MI5 later noted when it came to summarise his background, 'where [he] had made quite a name for himself as an astrologer.'

Although claiming to be Hungarian, de Wohl spoke with a distinct German accent. After settling in London, he never had his passport renewed and the Security Service recorded that he was Hungarian in 'little more than name'. 'De Wohl does not speak a word of Hungarian and has never at any time lived in Hungary although claiming to be the son of a Hungarian nobleman,' its officers noted. As Hungarians often say of themselves, de Wohl was the kind who would follow you into a revolving door and end up coming out of it first. The astrologer also claimed to be related to a former Lord Mayor of London, notable musicians, poets and bankers – and nobody could ever quite determine if any of them were even ever so slightly based in reality.

Mucsinyi Wohl Lajos had been born of Hungarian parents and was partly Jewish, but became a devout Catholic. His mother was a baroness – more formally known as V. V. Decifur – while his father came from a lower-middle-class background and had served in the cavalry. De Wohl senior then worked as a journalist and a politician, 'but what his brand of politics was, de Wohl professes not to know', the Security Service noted. Within a few years, the family had moved to Berlin, where his father had mining interests and became wealthy. Most of this money was lost and the family faced an unfortunate future, not least with the father's passing five months before the outbreak of war in 1914.

Louis de Wohl had been too young to enlist, and then the certainties end. By the start of the twenties, he was working in a bank in Berlin, where he started to write. Within four years, he had been sacked. 'He struggled to become an author,' a good friend of his later wrote, 'though the actual dates given by him in passages in his books are contradictory.'

And that was always the problem with Louis de Wohl's stories about himself. Nothing ever quite added up, such as his claim that he got by with designing dresses and doing film publicity work. 'He wrote in Germany some twenty to thirty novels of extremely dubious value,' the Security Service later noted. 'He has been a bank clerk, film scenario writer, a traveller – commercial and otherwise. He claims in his books to have travelled widely in the East in Arab disguise.'

The mention of such masquerades is significant, as there is an exotic tinge of the tales of Baron Munchausen suffusing his exploits. In his autobiography, he tells of visits to exotic places, tracking down drug traffickers, helping police and so forth. If nothing else, Louis de Wohl had a vivid imagination. But what was self-evidently true was that he had a capacity for survival, reinvention and was, as the authorities noted, 'an extremely clever man with multifarious connections'.

Somehow – and not for the last time – Louis de Wohl broke into high society in Weimar Berlin. The instrument for this was most likely a female companion who styled herself as 'a Rumanian princess' by the name of Alexandra, whom the astrologer married in the mid-1920s. The daughter of a German Jewish businessman, the British security authorities noted again with some relish that 'his wife is really illegitimate, being the fruit of sin of a liaison between "the princess" and an Aryan German'. The relationship between Alexandra and Louis de Wohl would come to bemuse and baffle British Intelligence, not least because he seemed 'to have often frequented cafés in Berlin in feminine attire' (though disguise was crossed out and replaced by attire).

His later time in London, as several other people who knew him have attested, also involved curious episodes of blatant transvestism of the exhibitionist variety. Louis de Wohl's sexuality became the subject of much speculation. Despite his marriage, the astrologer seems to have been mothered by various older women into whose company he regularly seemed to fall.

Many people who met him assumed he was gay. Even allowing for the engrained attitudes of the time, another astrologer who later knew (and

liked) de Wohl noted this marked streak of femininity. At the start of the
fighting, this fellow devotee of astrology, Dr Felix Jay, visited his friend at
a party, where he was asked to accompany him on the accordion. 'Louis
indulged in one of his favourite pleasures,' Dr Jay later recalled for an astrological magazine, 'that of dressing up as a woman. And, indeed, he looked
the part, that is if you like Peter Paul Reubens' "compleat ladies".'[1]

Whatever the true nature of his sexuality, Louis de Wohl's life in the
twenties had been that of a social whirl, which often included the glitzy
gatherings such as the one he attended at the Hotel Esplanade in Berlin
at the end of 1930. Here, it seems, the son of Prince Heinrich of the
Netherlands was introduced to him. After a discussion, Ludwig agreed
to cast his horoscope. At first, the Hungarian was ambivalent about these
kind of fripperies, until it became clear there was good money in making
such predictions.

And then, as if by magic, he was hooked. Astrological forecasts became
part of his money-making activities. According to his memoirs, the man
then still known as Ludwig van der Wohl was approached in 1935 to do
'very important' work for Adolf Hitler. A party member who 'wore a smart
uniform and had lots of minions working for him' came to see him. In der
Wohl's recollection, this sinister figure was part of a dedicated office which
considered astrology for Adolf Hitler (the German Geo-Political Institute
in Munich) 'which employs 1000 experts to plot Hitler's stars', he later
claimed. This was a complete exaggeration but one which der Wohl would
later elaborate to great advantage. The only Party member engaged on any
such work at that time was Karl-Friedrich Schulze, whose role was much
less prosaic. He acted as a censor to stop the more lurid forms of fortune-
telling from appearing in the public prints.

In his own estimation, der Wohl hated the Führer and his politics, not
least because of his own Jewish origins. As he didn't want to end up in hock
to 'a tyrant with one of the most dangerous horoscopes I had ever seen',
he made his way to London that summer of 1935. Though, as MI5 noted,
not technically a refugee from Nazi oppression – he had left 'somewhat in
a hurry' and, more to the point, did not 'know how much Jewish blood he
has'. He later claimed in a press interview that he had endured three years
of Hitler and knew how evil his regime was.

'Neither I nor members of my family were ever molested,' he later
claimed to an American reporter, 'but I saw and heard stories that sickened
me.' The sense of suspicion, distrust and disbelief about all these claims
suffuse all the various later British Intelligence reports, with one, oddly,

picking up the rumour that he was 'well known in post-war Germany as a Nazi' rather than being a victim. Yet despite his Walter Mitty-like tendencies, Louis de Wohl soon made his mark in pre-war Britain. In the same way that the devil's greatest trick was to show he didn't exist, then Louis de Wohl's was to summon a plausible enemy out of nowhere, the so-called *Führerastrologe*.

If there was one thing which Karl Ernst Krafft would never do, that was to leave things well and truly alone. Most people who ever encountered him thought he was downright peculiar. The word many used in their descriptions was 'difficult', for most were always negative in their initial reactions and subsequent memories. Partly it was because Krafft had no sense of humour, but also because he contrived a deliberately bizarre appearance.

'[He] was short – dark-haired, dark-eyed and with sharp, peering, pale features,' recalled one contemporary. 'For a long time he looked more like a gnome than a human being.' Another who came to know him well later said of Krafft – independently echoing MI5's assessment of Louis de Wohl – that 'he had glimpses of genius, but sometimes behaved like a charlatan'.

In other words, like most of the astrologers encountered in this story, he fitted right in. By all accounts, Karl Ernst Krafft was a brilliant mathematician who developed, over the best part of a decade, an elaborate theory of predicting the future based on an individual's personality. Born in Switzerland to German parents in 1900, he was a well-known contributor to Swiss newspapers. While an undergraduate, he became convinced by his own elaborate explanation for human behaviour based on statistics and character. But when he presented a paper in his last term in Geneva, 'Cosmic Influences On the Human Individual', one of his professors said: 'You can prove as much as you like, but your theory is complete nonsense.'

Not only would Krafft now be barred from submitting a PhD on the subject, he would spend many years trying to find a suitable berth, including, bizarrely, his appointment to a department store in Zürich where he cast horoscopes for customers. A certain bitterness set in, which would be fanned by the rise of Nazism. Always highly strung, Krafft would spend time in an asylum before earning a living as a 'psychological adviser' in the thirties, helped by a financial legacy from his estranged family. Steadfastly, he was scribbling away on what he hoped would become his magnum opus that tied everything together. Eventually, it was published in Brussels as *De L'Astrologie par la Cosmobiologie à la Typocosmie*.

To support these ideas, Karl Krafft lectured in Germany, France and England. The book – a 'wonderful mismash' in one estimation – appeared in August 1939. It is significant for his supposed abilities that Germany's signing of the non-aggression pact that month with the Soviet Union was not foreseen in his *Meisterwerk*.

Yet his entry into the orbit of Nazi ideologues was almost preordained.

Krafft also felt that he was unappreciated in his native land. That he was anti-Semitic, pro-German and hated the Swiss had much to do with what happened over the next few months. That same autumn, when war broke out, Krafft was back in contact with a former schoolteacher and classical scholar who knew some Sanskrit. Dr Heinrich Fesel was employed at SS Headquarters (later known as the RSHA, Reich Main Security Office) on Prinz Albechtsrasse on various strands of ideological research that encompassed freemasonry, cults and occultism.

As noted earlier, Himmler's various bizarre obsessions informed much of this work and, in Charles Wighton's elegant phrase, the section Fesel worked for could best be described as the wastepaper basket for half-formed ideas and prejudices.[2] 'There the SS cranks whom even Himmler found too much found shelter,' one biographer of Heydrich's has added.

There is little doubt that Karl Krafft's various musings found a mildly appreciative audience. Paid just 500 Reichsmarks per month, the Swiss-German would submit memoranda on economics, politics and various speculations for Herr Fesel from his various astrological perspectives. Given that he also had a Swiss passport, Krafft could also travel freely and spread the word. Why anyone would want to listen to him is hard to explain, but in his own mind, he now had a starring role.

Karl Krafft would have dearly loved to have been Adolf Hitler's astrologer, for he often gave readings and public sessions. In pre-war Germany, he more or less claimed that he was indeed the *Führerastrologe* to the more credulous of his followers, a fiction that many within the RSHA were happy to endorse so long as he didn't go public. And when it became clear that even as innocuous a subject as astrology could be used and controlled, it was obvious that Reinhard Heydrich, and more to the point, Heinrich Himmler, envisaged it as some sort of long shot in the war to come. Karl Ernst Krafft provided Louis de Wohl with his greatest raison d'être, who could be cultivated and used as a weapon against the Nazi regime.

That Louis de Wohl and Aleister Crowley would come to the attention of the British security authorities was hardly a surprise. Despite the cutbacks, MI5 was still alert for saboteurs, anarchists and troublemakers. By the time he showed up in the mid-thirties, Louis de Wohl was part of the great tide of refugees – mainly Jewish – which had started to arrive from Nazi Germany. The problem was that it was hard to determine just how honest and truthful some of those refugees were.

Aleister Crowley had returned home very much with his tail between the legs, and though the security service has admitted keeping an eye on him – after all, he was a rabble-rouser of some note – it says that his files were destroyed long ago. Some see a great cosmic significance in this. Yet by this time, he was more a figure of fun than anything else.

By now, Aleister Crowley had passed the pinnacle of his infamy. With his shaven skull, piercing eyes and general air of louche bohemianism, he picked fights, promoted myths and laid claims to various titles to which he was not entitled. Like so many ne'er-do-wells, he had gone to the last resort of the law in attempting to earn easy money. He sued a bookseller which claimed it had suppressed Crowley's *Diary of A Drug Fiend* (it had only gone out of print) and, more importantly, the publisher of Nina Hamnett's *Laughing Torso* for libel, which came from a mere three sentences referring to his time in Cefalù a decade before.

When the case came to trial in April 1934, he seemed to relish in the attention. So did everyone else, for some of the exchanges were priceless, such as the one where prosecuting counsel claimed the defendant was hardly in a position to assume a higher sense of purpose.

'For many years you have been publicly denounced as the worst man in the world.'

'Only by the lowest kind of newspaper.'

'Did any paper call you the monster of wickedness?'

'I don't remember which papers.'

'Have you from the time of your adolescence openly defied all moral conventions?'

'No.'

It was obvious how it would play out.

In his summing up, the judge said: 'I have never heard such dreadful, horrible, blasphemous and abominable stuff as that which has been produced by the man,' indicating Crowley, 'who describes himself to you as the greatest living poet.'

He lost and had to pay court costs. He was left penniless and was eventually declared bankrupt. Even more so than before, he became a shambolic figure whose *joie de vivre* had also evaporated. 'People meeting him for the first time often feared that he would make indecent advances,' notes one chronicler, 'but in practice, he was more likely to borrow a fiver.'

And yet he was still consulted as the titular head of the OTO.

It had grown thanks to a disciple – whose first wife had characterised Crowley as the 'international crook' – who had actually worked in Military Intelligence. Now, in the run up to the Second World War Crowley's protégé would become possibly the only person ever to have ever been kept in custody by the German, Belgian and French police and then investigated by the Federal Bureau of Investigation.

When Charles Henry Maxwell Knight passed away in the late sixties, he was better known to a generation of children as Uncle Max, a kindly and avuncular naturalist who taught them how to explore the natural world via many engaging books and, more famously, his weekly radio broadcasts. Few of his many listeners would have ever suspected his earlier role as an indefatigable hunter of spies and subversives. In some ways it is not surprising, for the same skills needed to track, observe and tame wildlife had been put to better use in Max Knight's own youth.

From the twenties onwards, Knight had been one of the most formidable agent runners of his generation. As several writers have suggested, he was indeed one of the most enigmatic and, with a marked interest in the occult, certainly one of the most unusual. As a gadabout in the twenties, socialising with debutantes and jazz musicians, Knight had the perfect cover. 'In a world where we are all tending to get more and more alike,' he had noted in a minute for the files, 'a few unusual people give a little colour to life!'

Max Knight had met Vernon Kell, the Director General of MI5, at a dinner party in 1925. The general had thought him a splendid chap and recruited him to root out communist spies. He seemed a perfectly good fellow.

That, in Kell's eyes, was usually enough.

Tall, thin with delicate features, he had subverted the miseries of his own childhood into a charming, yet inscrutable exterior. Mixing with a fast set of bright young things with private incomes, Knight was in his element and, after having visited Manhattan, was very much into the new jazz music.

Born into genteel poverty, his solicitor father wasted time and money on mistresses, which ended up bankrupting the practise. The young Max was partially brought up in the Glamorgan home of a miserly uncle, a tyrant, from whom he could escape into the countryside. After his older brother was killed in the trenches, he volunteered for the navy and served in armed merchantmen. After the war, Knight taught Latin at a prep school and lived with his mother and sister in a small flat in London that he soon filled with animals.

As a result, he sometimes struck an incongruous figure.

According to one who knew him, 'he used to come round to our house on Sunday afternoons after riding in Hyde Park. He had a pet bear that used to go round with him on a chain.' Max Knight and his amazing dancing bear, Bessie, was probably the most arresting of the beasts in his menagerie. Sometimes, a bulldog or a baboon would follow them both.

At his home in Sloane Street, there were white mice in the living room, grass snakes in the bath, a parrot in the kitchen and ferrets in the garden. He played his adored jazz to all of his animals. He once incubated a nest of adder eggs in his pocket and later in life, so his obituary remarks, visitors might find him nursing a bush baby, feeding a giant toad or 'engaging in masculine repartee with a vastly experienced grey parrot'.

Max Knight always liked to maintain that this interest in animals informed his career as an agent runner. And that meant he would come across some very unusual animals indeed, where, in the words of another agent runner, John Buchan, he would meet 'with odd people, in odd places, of fantastic duties which a romancer would have rejected as beyond probability'.

Karl Johannes Germer had been Aleister Crowley's leading disciple in pre-war Germany, where he ran the OTO, Ordo Templi Orientis. He had originally met Crowley in 1925 on a visit to Germany, where he became transfixed by the self-styled Beast. Before the Great War, Germer had been the Berlin representative for a British machine-tool company based in Coventry. Travelling all over Europe, he had been in Tsarist Russia when war broke out and narrowly avoided internment. In one account, Germer served in military intelligence on the Eastern Front, where he received an Iron Cross First Class.

An obvious question is: did he stay in contact with his masters?

He certainly became an important acolyte of Crowley's and became such a baleful influence that the master's presence – and her husband's devotion – led to a divorce from his first wife. Like Crowley, Germer was peripatetic and when the Nazis came to power, wanted to leave for America with his new wife, Cora Eaton. As he later explained, 'I failed to get my visa in time' and remained in London until the Home Office refused to renew his British visa. It was thus Germer's misfortune to return to Germany when the Nazi crackdown on occultism came into play. Along with all other occultic organisations, the Ordo Templi Orientis had been declared illegal and suspected members were arrested by the Gestapo. On 2 February 1935, this happened to him in Leipzig, where he was charged with recruiting people to 'follow the Highgrade Freemason Aleister Crowley'. Perhaps when the Nazi state police found out Germer had sold Elixir of Life pills – manufactured from a neutral base and Crowley's semen – it had swiftly prompted his dispatch to Esterwegen concentration camp.

Nevertheless, he was released a few months later as more of a nuisance than anything else. Herr Germer then moved to Brussels, where he was arrested, deported to France in 1937 and then interned once more. He eventually emigrated to the United States in June 1941, where he supplied money and material to support the perennially skint Aleister Crowley with the proceeds of his various writings which were being sold through occultic bookshops in the US.

Most of Karl Germer's own income came from his fortunate predilection for marrying heiresses: after being widowed in the thirties, he subsequently married a Viennese piano teacher, Sascha Ernestine André, who continued to support him. When the FBI started to target the Germers, they became so paranoid that they stopped talking in their own house. 'His conversation is violent Nazi propaganda,' is one comment from one particular FBI informant, while another had overheard him say: 'Hitler is right in believing Germans are the Master Race.'

The G-Men thought Aleister Crowley was Karl Germer's controller because of the Beast's previous pro-German sympathies which had been expressed over the years, not least in the First World War. 'I do feel something is very wrong with these two men [Crowley and Germer] being in constant contact with each other,' is one typical assessment. 'Mr Crowley seemed the brains behind Germer. The latter seems to be a tool in his hands.' Tool is an unintentionally hilarious choice of word, as there is also an unsubstantiated rumour that the German had acquired syphilis from his master.

In this sense, Aleister Crowley was an ideal candidate for espionage operations as his often eccentric outlandishness blinded many to his rather more complex nature. As several people have also noted, Crowley was also adept at projecting disguises, deceiving people and, in that sense, never quite revealing his hand in all the years to come. In other words, he made a perfect paradox on the fringes of intelligence; well known, yet secretive when he needed to be.

Even without his obvious eccentricities, Maxwell Knight provides some sort of link from the occult octopus to the occult in which he was interested. It was hard to determine his true politics, for one colleague who knew him recalled that he 'had no time for democracy and believed the country should be ruled by the social elite'. Perhaps it is no surprise that he was originally recruited by Sir George Makgill, and in Knight's later recollection, at his command had joined the first Fascist movement in Britain at the end of 1923.

For the Fascisti, as they were known, Knight worked in various capacities – publicity officer, deputy chief of staff and, most importantly, its director of intelligence. In this latter role, he carved out some practices which served him well in later years. Getting to know people, compiling dossiers on them, as well as establishing and maintaining cells within other organisations were all part of his approach.

This remains the most controversial part of his career, the wellspring for any number of conspiracy theories. As a review of this part of his life notes of his work for the Fascisti: 'Maxwell Knight quite clearly stood at the nucleus of the movement, its locus of power, and whatever competence and sophistication it displayed, were very largely his handiwork.' To some, he was nothing less than a fascistic agent provocateur who inveigled himself into left-wing organisations.

For others, it was almost inevitable that someone so right wing would become interested in the supernatural. For those who hated change, the occult appealed to conservative – with a small c – beliefs as it held everything in stasis. The occult world never changes, its myths are eternal verities and, as the writer Phil Baker notes, it is 'as if nothing essential had changed since the days of ancient Egypt'.

The occult was an attractive alternative to the lingering effects of the global slump and the rise of unemployment by the end of the twenties. By the early thirties, a sense of doom pervaded the whole of the country. It was, as several people noted, an ominous time, 'a low dishonest decade' in W.H. Auden's famous estimation.

In another, it was even simpler – 'the devil's decade'.

Yet so far as Max Knight is concerned, it might not be quite so clear-cut.

As he later noted in his own history of his own work – especially the recruitment of agents – anyone could 'find amongst his own circle of friends at least one person who would be suitable for employment as an agent'. An agent runner should go with the flow: if you were interested in right wing politics, you should mix in right wing circles. The same would be the case for those interested in the left.

One thing he always would ensure was plausible deniability.

In the early twenties, MI6 had all the experience of running agents, while MI5 did not. So Max Knight was employed on a freelance basis by MI6. As its official historian said when his book came out, Knight 'had a small amateur detective or secret service in London, consisting of about a hundred individuals in all walks of life, many of whom spoke foreign languages'.

They formed a group of what were called 'casuals' until there was a major row and were eventually transferred to MI5. And as Knight later wrote in a semi-confessional note: 'My association with this body was at all times for the purposes of obtaining information for HM Government and also for the purposes of finding likely people who might be used by this department for the same purposes.'

Knight claimed he worked for this organisation until 1930, after which, as he later said, 'it more or less became ineffectual'. After that, he was allowed some latitude in running his own small department – sometimes known as M Section – because of the rise of the extreme right, not least the brief and self-destructive flowering of the British Union of Fascists.

By then, he had shown his mettle and had made, in one official appreciation, 'an excellent impression, is perfectly honest, and at need, prepared to do anything but is at the same time not wild'. The same, alas, could not be said for the unfortunate woman who was his first wife, whose death is axiomatic for some in that it had to do with their dabbling in the occult.

It was almost inevitable where Louis de Wohl would end up when he landed in London. The Esplanade Hotel in Maida Vale was home to many émigrés and, famously, hosted Sigmund Freud while he and his family were having their house decorated (but only after being reassured about the quality of the hotel's cooking). It is a delicious irony in his often quoting Freud – and Jung and Adler – that Louis de Wohl had never studied them in detail and, more to the point, didn't understand what he was talking about.

At one point, the whole of the Polish government-in-exile later stayed at the same hotel, and it was clear that the Esplanade appealed to the Mitteleuropean astrologer's own ornate tastes. The ostentaciousness – a heavy continental style called *Klubsessel* – oozed rococo opulence and was presided over by a bespectacled White Russian who was the owner.

Louis de Wohl's was a large room where he received his many visitors, lined with books, piles of paper, mementoes and bric-a-brac. 'Most objects of daily use were engraved with a baronial coat of arms,' one later remembered, the host himself often dressed like an archduke in his chair. There were large cigar cases, for Louis de Wohl was often wreathed in cigar smoke. Here he deliberately cultivated a Sydney Greenstreet air of mystery and grandeur, and what one visitor found an 'aura of questionable taste'. The same could have been said about the astrologer who always seemed to wear 'a flowing robe or a silken dressing gown'.

After anglicising his name to the more acceptable Louis de Wohl, he became reasonably well known in a short space of time. In Germany he had already been a successful novelist, journalist and scriptwriter. Within three years of his arrival in Britain, he had written a few more novels, had some earlier ones translated from German and created a few potboilers of the reading-on-the-beach variety. Consider *Satan In Disguise*, in which, *The Observer* noted in its review at the end of May 1937, 'Both dialogue and characterisation are very much above average'.

A year later, Louis de Wohl had written his own autobiography and a reference book on astrology. Industriousness, then, was one of his greater virtues. In a later interview, his very accuracy, he claimed, 'gained him respect in the super exclusive international astrological circle'. Yet his good friend Dr Felix Jay begged to disagree. Having made his own study of astrology, Jay never fell for what he terms 'the scintillating astrological canvasses [de Wohl] painted'. The Hungarian's astrological wisdom 'was entirely second hand'. Thanks in part to his film background, Louis 'served up the evergreen ingredients garnered from others in an attractive, amusing and often sensational manner'.

Yet in de Wohl's own estimation, his 1938 book on astrology, so he liked to claim, was one of staggering exactitude. 'There's nothing supernatural or uncanny about it,' he said in a later interview in the United States. 'It's just cold logic. Stars can affect our doings only 40 per cent and human wills affect the remaining 60 per cent. But you can't ignore that 40 per cent.'

According to the Hungarian, he would never make impulsive predictions.

Weeks of studies of charts, dates and what he liked to call 'other technical considerations' would then prompt his drawing up a prediction. And, unsurprisingly, what that really meant was that he was soon developing his own private clientele for readings who also believed his own unshakeable self-belief. Several future colleagues remarked that he had an obvious capacity for falling on his feet. In the estimation of one, Louis de Wohl was imaginative, gifted and had the quickest working brain she had ever encountered.

In Dr Jay's more honest – yet affectionate – account, the Hungarian simply made dull lives seem more interesting. His clients accepted him as more than an astrologer: 'philosopher, saint, prophet and father-confessor' whose own 'quasi-theological pronouncements often bordered on the ludicrous'. And yet, by an intriguing, entirely characteristic mixture of social climbing, blatant grovelling and almost feral sense of self-preservation, Louis de Wohl was able – as he later claimed – 'to convince the highest in the land that astrological warfare against Hitler was a necessity'.

It had all the hallmarks of the plot of the potboilers so beloved of the time. A beautiful, rich and somehow tragic redhead passes into a coma, her body is discovered and cannot be revived by her secretive, repressed husband, who – when it came to a spectacular hearing into the circumstances of her death – was more or less accused of bumping her off for her money. When he appeared at a hearing into his wife's death, Maxwell Knight had to endure such an accusation in public. His defence lawyer deemed it not a proper question. 'What I was asking were questions in order to elucidate if this man was in any way responsible,' the prosecutor then said, 'not criminally, for his wife's death.'

There were, as with all unexplained deaths, even more lurid rumours: that his wife had died because of an occult ceremony which had gone horribly wrong, and that somehow, Aleister Crowley was involved. The fact that Max Knight's good name was effectively traduced in court meant a public scandal that could so easily have derailed his career in intelligence.

In the the same year that he met General Vernon Kell, Maxwell Knight had met a ravishing, wealthy redhead by the name of Gwladys Poole. With her money they bought a flat on London's smart Sloane Street, into which Knight moved his menagerie. Gwladys was hardly a fan, for as his biographer notes, aged just 25, she 'had not expected to become a zookeeper in addition to her other troubles'.

Not only did Max flirt with other women and was largely affectionate, but their marriage was never consummated. Nevertheless, Gwladys's devotion meant she worked with him in the British Fascisti, where she acted as a secretary. Seeking to invest some of her family money, the Knights bought a pub in Somerset that Gwladys ran during the week while Knight worked in London. She was, at heart, a countrywoman. In Somerset, Gwladys had her own set and friends. At weekends, her husband did travel down to meet her – only to then disappear, fishing for hours.

It was thanks to such gathering abandonment that in November 1935, Gwladys Knight took an overdose of barbiturates. Her family accused Max Knight of driving her to suicide. There were more lurid rumours. According to his later assistant, Joan Miller, Gwladys 'died in the Overseas Club after some sort of occult misadventure in which the notorious Alesteir Crowley was involved'.

At the time, though, the newspapers reported that it was an open verdict. 'Mrs. Knight died from poisoning by a barbitric hypnotic preparation,' the coroner concluded, 'there being insufficient evidence to show in what circumstances her death occurred.'

Such lurid publicity was anathema to MI5. Yet within months, Max Knight's reputation was rescued by his first great coup – that of the Woolwich Arsenal conspiracy, where the case was saved by one of the braver women Max Knight ever recruited, whose work set the standard for much of his later penetration of extreme political groups – of both the left and right.

Though his wife's suicide had been reported in her real name, the woman Max Knight used for his first – and possibly greatest ever – coup was only ever referred to, even in his own reports, as Miss X. By the early 1930s, the clear and present danger represented by communism had grown and, as part of his almost routine activities, Max Knight recruited the first of his long-term agents. It is instructive to see how. Olga Gray was, as he describes her in his own official report, 'a girl of 25 from a provincial town' who was trained as a commercial secretary with six years' experience (with the Automobile Association).

By all accounts, she was spirited, quick and had a photographic memory. Over cucumber sandwiches, she had been asked by another secretary if she would like to join the secret service. Eventually, she was met by Max Knight at Euston. She was the perfect mole: she didn't know anyone in London.

Olga was just 19 when she began attending meetings of the Friends of the Soviet Union, a front for the Communist Party. Working as a typist, Olga soon won the confidence of Harry Pollitt, the Communist Party of Great Britain leader, who sent her on a 'secret' mission to India to pay a recruit. Despite her carefree exterior, as Knight himself noted, 'some years of literally leading a double life, cut off from most of her friends, and under conditions of considerable strain, still further affected' Miss X's health. In the account she related to Anthony Masters, Olga and Max Knight went to a cinema and a black cat crossed the road. 'The next evening Pollitt asked me to go to India on a mission,' she recalled. The bank notes were scored with invisible ink and she hid them within some sanitary towels. When she met her contact – a jazz band conductor at the Taj Mahal hotel – she was scared. 'This was the first time I had been really afraid,' she said, 'and suddenly I realised I wasn't playing spy games any longer.'

Yet as Max Knight realised, working as a secretary gave someone very good access to what was going on. As he later remarked, any woman who had some basic secretarial skills offered a unique chance for exploitation. 'I would state categorically that it were possible for any business magnate or government official to be able to see into the mind of his secretary,' Knight later concluded, 'we would be astounded at the amount of knowledge concerning the general affairs of the business or department in question which lay in the secretary's brain.'

Ultimately, it was a slow burn of an approach.

As Knight himself described it, the aim was always to 'eventually [get] into a position of responsibility [to] obtain reliable information about the more sinister plans of the organisation concerned'. The approach, as he noted, should 'always be made by the body to the agent, not the agent to the body', so Olga Gray waited, as he describes it, to be invited to join the party, 'the first major step, without laying herself open to any accusation of "pushing"'.

It would be another seven years before she came to uncover the Woolwich Spy Ring, where it became clear that the most secret details of anti-submarine bombs and detonators had been handed to the Soviets. The conspirators – led by Percy Glading – were jailed thanks to her evidence. The proceedings were held in camera, where Olga Gray was known as Miss X: she was terrified there might be revenge, so her name was kept out of the newspapers. 'She must be possessed of extraordinary courage,' the judge said. 'She has done a great service to her country.'

The Woolwich Arsenal spy case was a personal triumph for Max Knight, who began to rise through the ranks of MI5, being appointed head of B5b, a newly created section that dealt with subversive organisations. As such, he became more involved in monitoring right-wing organisations, an irony not lost on several reviewers of his life. Keeping his eye out for troublemakers was, as one colleague noted, 'all of a piece with his feeling for the occult and his clandestine sexual leanings'.

But Max Knight had another surprising sideline. As noted earlier, many of the figures who became involved in espionage were often writers, an occupation which invariably allowed their imagination free rein. So it was with Knight, who had found writing another way to supplement his income when married to the unfortunate Gwladys.[3] Most were – by common consent – dreadful, though did contain the occasional nugget of autobiographical note. In one, *Crime Cargo*, our hero had served on HMS *Worcester* – a training ship that both Knight and, a couple of years earlier, another writer who would come to resemble one of the characters in his own books and would become a very good friend of Maxwell Knight.

Dennis Wheatley, by the mid-thirties, was one of the most popular authors in the western world, the Stephen King of his day, earning the equivalent of half a million dollars in today's money in the years immediately before the war. Looking every inch the former wine importer he had once been, Wheatley was short and bibulous (with the build and red nose of a true *bon vivant*), whose interest in the occult came only as a result of its entertaining possibilities. Today, his clubland snobbery, unapologetic racism and borderline anti-Semitism are a little difficult to digest, yet he was hardly alone in his attitudes at the time. Always acutely aware of status in society, Wheatley's own background was trade, and when, many years later, he joined White's Club, he remarked it wasn't 'bad for the Streatham-based son of a shopkeeper'.

Growing up in the Edwardian era, Dennis Wheatley yearned to be a gentleman in the Victorian mould, devoted to, in various degrees, decadence, esoterica and the pursuit of hedonism on a truly magnificent scale. All would be important in his later life and, as a result, Dennis Yeats Wheatley casts an important shadow in the shadowy world where the occult and espionage were joined together. Though considered an expert on such arcane matters as the supernatural, satanism, the practice of exorcism and black magic, Wheatley genuinely disdained them. He was only ever interested in them as a plot device and, as part of his characteristic assiduity, made sure he consulted what he termed the 'top chaps' in the field.

As a result, many rumours have asserted themselves about his involvement in both the occult and, later, how that informed his employment
by the secret services. It is a measure of his interests that his first volume
of memoirs was called *Drink and Ink*. Dennis Wheatley only ever got into
writing after a decline in the family business during the Depression. The
author of *The Devil Rides Out* and *The Haunting of Toby Jugg* was gassed
in a chlorine attack at Passchendaele. As a result, he had been invalided
out of the Army as a second lieutenant in the Royal Field Artillery
after seeing service in Flanders, on the Ypres Salient. That unfortunate
circumstance meant that he would have something in common with a
rascal whose body would later be found riddled with bullets and encased
in concrete.

Eric Gordon Tombe was, in one journalistic assessment, 'impaired in
health and possibly in moral character', and met fellow invalid Dennis
Wheatley in a hospital in a camp in Marylebone. After demobilisation and
peace, Tombe took good times into the stratosphere, chasing women and
gadding about town, with Dennis often in tow. He took great delight in
turning his army buddy into what Tombe called 'a conscious hedonist'.

The pursuit of such sybaritic pleasure would come to a sorry and sudden
end with a disappearance which never made sense. It was the newspaper
sensation of 1923. Tombe had been shot in the back of the head and forced
via a manhole into a well, which was then covered in rubble. It transpired
that Tombe's friend, Ernest Dyer, had shot him and then attempted to empty
his bank account. Rather like an Agatha Christie story, Dennis put a private
detective on him and the circumstances of what happened affected him
deeply. Distressed, Wheatley never talked about it.

After his first marriage failed, Dennis developed other, suitably eclectic
aquaintances whose odd stories and experiences would inform his writing.
There was, for example, Montague Summers, 'a mysterious figure with his
large moon-like face, wearing a black shovel hat and flowing cape', who
some wondered whether he had actually been ordained or not. It was
Summers' 1936 tome on witchcraft that, as Wheatley's biographer notes,
'with its list of black mass and infant sacrifices set the subject back four
hundred years'. Others say he was a satanist who liked to dress as a priest
and was sexually aroused by devout young Catholics boys.

There was also an Egyptian black magician called Rollo Ahmed who
had done time for forgery, was a friend of Aleister Crowley's and could, it
was said, consume a whole bottle of whisky and remain sober. It was also
said that he had lost his teeth when he had messed up a ritual and failed

to master a demon. In time, all these friendships would wane, but another would provide Dennis Wheatley with great pleasure and a sense of unabashed fun in the company of his new wife, who liked him too.

His name was Max Knight.

One evening, Dennis and Joan Wheatley had gone to a party in Hallam Street where, amongst the debutantes and socialites, they met a tall, charming man in his mid-30s with a striking Wellingtonian profile. 'The three of us settled down in a corner to talk and it transpired that, like myself, he had been a cadet on HMS *Worcester*,' Wheatley later said. They had other interests, too, and in time Dennis Wheatley encouraged Max's writing. By now, Max had published a handful of stories and, indeed, the following year he would dedicate his next book to both his new friends.

Charles Henry Maxwell Knight enjoyed the Wheatleys' company greatly, and his influence grew. One thing he then did was to keep it in the family, for he wanted to know about suspected communist subversion at Oxford. For this, Knight wanted to enlist the help of Wheatley's stepson – Joan's son from her previous marriage with Jack Younger – at Christ Church, where his history tutor, J.C. Masterman, had Establishment connections.

The Honourable William Younger, to give him his full name, had just come down from Oxford, and, as Knight later minuted, 'we had a young man completely inexperienced but whose flair for political investigation had attracted my attention during the previous year'. He would be an unlikely spy – he had a withered arm from childhood polio – yet he was secretive and found, like many others drawn into espionage, an outlet with his poetry. That he used the name William Mole was another curiosity, going so far as to dedicate one book to CHMK.

'It's easy to see what made Max's department such a literary one,' said a later colleague from the war years, 'with so much dramatic material to hand, the impulse to make a high class story out of it must have been pretty well irresistible to anyone with the least degree of narrative ability.'

As Nigel West has noted, there was an 'almost incestuous' overlap between MI5 and various literary types. Knight often recruited his staff at the Authors' Club in Whitehall. His protégé, John Bingham, was also the model for George Smiley, and Bingham's wife and daughters, who worked for MI5 and were novelists too. Bill Younger, late Bingham's MI5 assistant, wrote *Skin Trap*, using the odd nom de plume of William Mole. His mother Joan was married to Dennis Wheatley and used the name Eve Chaucer to write *No Ordinary Virgin*. Younger's sister also worked for MI5, as did their cousin Kenneth, a later Labour MP, whose 1964 book *Changing Perspectives in British Foreign Policy* was hardly a page-turner.

It is striking that in this milieu, authors who were interested in the occult were all used to weaving lies and deceptions. But in his later remembrance of his wartime work, Knight said he would use 'as far as possible the service of persons whose personal honesty and motives are beyond reproach'. That way, he reasoned, it saved time and effort in checking on the information, though that was hardly ever reciprocated.

'If you are going to tell a lie,' Max Knight would say to his agents, 'tell a good one and stick to it.'

If Max Knight was a repressed homosexual who liked animals and was interested in the occult, then so too was Evan Morgan – but there the resemblance ends, for Morgan, better known in the thirties as Viscount Tredegar, was even more curious. At times, it seemed that members of his family also considered themselves to be birds and, around the family pile in Monmouthshire, were gathered even larger – and scarier – animals than those the MI5 agent runner used to take for walks. Small wonder that a fellow aristocrat, the Duke of Bedford, called the Morgans 'the oddest family I have ever met'.

Though a complete gentleman, Evan Morgan – exactly as the fictional James Bond had done – left Eton under a cloud. A gathering storm seemed to follow in his wake for the rest of his life, whipping up myth, scandal, rumour and, in one biographer's recent estimation, a cursed life. 'Why even both trying to make up characters for one's books when real people like Evan Morgan exist,' asked one of his good friends, Aldous Huxley.

Viscount Tredegar soon became well known for a collection of animals which formed a surreal menagerie at his family home in the Welsh hills. At Tredegar House, a restoration mansion in Newport, the young Evan Morgan kept a curious collection of beasts within the stables. He kept a fierce white arctic owl in his bedroom and boasted that he was the only person who could handle it. There was also a small alligator which wandered around freely, as well as kangaroos and monkeys outside. A baboon called Bimbo had the run of the house and there was also a macaw called Blue Boy, whom he trained to climb up his trouser leg. The bird would emerge from Tredegar's flies and would fly around, often shocking dowagers with the ripeness of his language (the macaw, not the viscount).

On one occasion a black widow spider that was kept in a glass case in the most formal of the State rooms, the Gilt Room, escaped during a party and was eventually found climbing up a curtain. Evan's guests were both entertained and terrified in equal measure.

Some explained his interest in birds as coming from his mother, Lady Tredegar, who made ever greater birds' nests and dotted them around her estate. Some were so large that people could actually sit in them. So eccentric was she that towards the end of her life, she was convinced she was actually a bird.

Young Evan always liked to think he was related to the pirate Henry Morgan, and was, in every sense, a gay young thing of the twenties. On the occasion of his death, even *The Times* obituary called him 'a man of many parts to whom the word dilettante may appropriately be applied'. After the First World War, he was accepted as a Privy Chamberlain of the Sword and Cape by Pope Benedict XV. Quite why he turned to Rome was never really explained. 'Lord Tredegar was gifted and versatile,' notes another contemporary profile. 'He painted cleverly and when quite young exhibited at the Paris Salon.' Also a talented musician and poet, he was, by all accounts, completely crackers.

Yet Lord Tredegar's social conquests were vast. He married a Russian princess, though it was, as was said at the time, a marriage of convenience. The Royal Family enjoyed his antics and the Queen Mother termed him her favourite bohemian. His friends included the writer Somerset Maughan, the heiress Nancy Cunard, Noel Coward, H.G. Wells, Aldous Huxley, Augustus John and many more. When he became a viscount, he continued to live in London but often spent the weekend at Tredegar House, holding lavish parties, invariably enlivened by his mother. 'She makes the most wonderful nests,' he would say.

And it is here that, once more, a bird of a different feather appears: Aleister Crowley. It is a matter of record that Evan Morgan met Aleister Crowley in the Paris of the 1920s. That much can be stated with certainty; the rest is difficult to know, because neither were exactly rational or reliable and both enjoyed making outrageous and often ridiculous claims. In the case of Viscount Tredegar, upon his death, most of his papers and letters were destroyed.

Conspiracy theories swirl around him – and, as a result, many of the stranger episodes of his life are invariably explained by the occult. The very odd thing was that Evan was allowed to stay in the Vatican even though it was rumoured he would head to Shelley's grave to make incantations. Though his beaky nose stuck out from under a cowl, it was always rumoured that he wore robes so as to take part in magic ceremonies, and at the family home in Wales was a black magic room, so great that Aleister Crowley is said to have expressed his amazement. It was only a matter of time before Evan Morgan, too, would be recruited into one of the more rarefied branches – literally – of the secret world.

At this point, the names of Max Knight, Evan Morgan and Dennis Wheatley form an unholy trinity surrounding the Beast, all the more piquant for their subsequent involvement in secret warfare in the Second World War. As a result, the more preposterous claims can be – and indeed have been – made about their influence. Max Knight's nephew told the late Anthony Masters that towards the end of 1936 or the start of 1937, Knight and Wheatley applied to Crowley as novices and were accepted.

'But my uncle stressed that his interest – and also Wheatley's – was purely academic,' Harry Smith added. The only problem with this statement is that by this time, in the later thirties, Crowley no longer conducted any such ceremonies. He was only interested in cadging food, which is rather more germane to how Dennis Wheatley met Crowley at a Hungarian restaurant on Regent Street sometime in 1934.

As Wheatley's most recent biographer, Phil Baker, has noted, they had a lot in common – a devotion to hedonism, Edwardian in their complete rejection of Victorian rectitude – and, by rights, they should have got on like a house on fire. 'So it is remarkable that Wheatley never says anything whatsoever about this lunch,' Baker writes. 'It provided him with not a single anecdote.'

Later on, Wheatley had variants. 'We had Crowley to dinner several times,' Dennis says in his memoirs. 'His conversation was fascinating. He gave me much useful information and several of his books.' Crowley gave him a copy of his book *Magick In Theory and Practice*, inscribing it to the more successful author (Wheatley), 'in memory of that sublime Hungarian banquet'. The Beast would also provide the inspiration for Wheatley to base one of his own villains, Mocata, on Aleister Crowley in his novel *The Devil Rides Out*.

Any death, however unfortunate, within such gilded company always seems to have involved occult practices. The supposed involvement of the intelligence agencies adds even more smoke. The rumours about Gwladys

Knight's demise and Aleister Crowley's supposed involvement are often reported as fact. Though MI5 says it had indeed kept an eye on Crowley – quite possibly via all the Wheatley relatives – he was now approaching his 60s. By now, his life was quiet, on an even keel and, as Martin Booth notes, he spent most of his time reading, carrying out magical rites, studying the tarot, entertaining visitors and playing chess.

And just weeks before his death in 1977, Dennis Wheatley was most insistent what he really learned from them. He told the *Guardian* that he had met a lot of the most prominent occultists of the twenties and thirties. Crowley and that lot, he called them:

> They came to dinner but knew better than to try to inveigle me into any funny business. I've never even attended a séance. I've only seen one ghost and at that the time I thought it was a burglar. It cannot do you anything but harm. You can become so interested that you neglect your work and family and if you are at all weak-minded you can pop off to the loony bin. There is no question about it that quite a lot of people who are in the loony bin today are what in the Middle Ages would have been described as victims of possession.

For the rest of the thirties, Max Knight had his work cut out for him.

It is a matter of public record that in the six years after the Führer came to power, thirty agents suspected of working for Germany – twenty-one of whom were native Britons – came to the attention of the British Security Service. 'Quantity, not quality in agents, seemed to be the aim,' wrote the service's deputy director, Jack Curry, in a first official history of its pre-war activities, 'but it was and is impossible to say whether a cloud of agents of low quality served to hide a few good ones.'

Even though hostilities with Germany were seen as increasingly likely, the Soviet threat continued to overshadow everything else (as was the case with its sister service, MI6) until it was almost too late. Writing a few years later, Curry added that 'it was obvious that in official but wider circles there was a general failure to appreciate the character of the Nazi Party'. Based in his new offices in Dolphin Square, Max Knight's M Section confined itself to communist and fascist organisations:

> But in 1938 it was obviously necessary to pay some attention to the desirability of having agents who could be used in connection with

that branch of German espionage which had an affinity with either the NSDAP organisation – in Great Britain, or pro-German societies and groups which did not properly fall under the heading of the fascist bodies.

On the eve of the fighting, the Security Service began to expand. In 1938, it still numbered thirty officers and just over 100 secretaries. A year later, MI5 recruited another 750 new staff. In a summary of his own work, Max Knight pointed out that he had only employed fourteen agents, one officer and one secretary.

He noted: 'It will probably come as a surprise – even for personnel of the Security Service – to learn that during the vital years between 1935 and 1939, such a small number of agents was available to cover such a vast field of work of the first importance.' The reason was lack of money, and the fact that good information came out was as much due to good luck as anything. Improbably, his happening upon one of the most beautiful women in London who was nothing more than a glorified striptease artist would soon come to have an important impact on the secret war.

In the run-up to the fighting, then, any number of curious undercurrents and even stranger characters were flowing around the periphery of the secret world. When the Nazis came to power, they regarded some sort of agreement with the British as highly attractive. Indeed, despite their later propaganda claims denigrating its excesses, the Nazis saw the British Empire as an exemplar they should follow. But they had no direct understanding of Britain, and the academic Gerwin Strobl has written of 'the extraordinary limited factual knowledge upon which the regime attempted to base its policies'.

Yet the Führer was envious of the prestige of the British Secret Intelligence Service, MI6. Indeed, most of the German leaders had an unshakeable belief in the power of the British secret service, so much so that when anything went wrong, they would invoke its mysterious powers. At the time of its supposed greatest influence, the secret service's powers were limited. MI6 was hardly the most efficient and powerful organisation which the Nazis feared. As it was, a remarkable cast of characters was ready and waiting for the fighting which would soon consume the whole of the globe, none more extravagantly than a couple of writers – and professional rivals – who found themselves squabbling on a train in the halcyon spring before war broke out.

4

FROM RUSSIA, WITH CONDOMS

At the outbreak of the Second World War, the bodies which carried out [intelligence] functions for the British government were not so well organised, either individually or in terms of the co-ordination of their work, that they constituted an efficient system. They had been handicapped by financial stringency and by the lack of priority given to intelligence in the inter-war years, disadvantages which were reflected less in the small size than in the indifferent quality of their staff.

From the *Official History of British Intelligence in the Second World War*

The cold and colicky fear of a customs inspection at eight in the evening was bad enough without mistrustful, white-gloved security officers in attendance. Yet as the Warsaw Express thundered on through the night, the searching was inevitable. The two English journalists who were sharing a luxurious compartment in a Pullman carriage were as impassive as only men of their class and calling could ever be.

Both found the inspection amusing, though probably for very different reasons. In some ways, they were as different as chalk and cheese. Physically, they were a study in contrasts: one was tall, languorous and, in the recollection of the other (who was larger and louder), had 'the profile of a Tarquinian piper'. Together, they enjoyed a friendly rivalry, the mildest form of one-upmanship which, at times such as this, saw them winding each other up.

The two Englishmen watched, aloof and impassive.

The mood changed suddenly when one of the guards found a packet of latex prophylactics and held each one of them up to the light. Their owner, for whom espionage and protected sexual intercourse became something of a métier, shrugged it all off. His companion, older and much more amused, was succinct after the guards had departed.

'You should have swallowed them,' Sefton Delmer said to Ian Fleming.

The train continued on into the night with no further interruptions. It was March 1939 and war, as a mutual friend of theirs would write, was 'striding inexorably across those months'. The younger, rather more suave of the pair, who had actually been on a freelance spying mission in Moscow, would be provided with the germ of an idea.

The train journey in Eastern Europe – with all its inherent dangers and permutations of menace – was stored in the ever fertile imagination to become a set-piece action sequence in a book which became the favourite reading of a later American president, whose father would shortly declare that the outbreak of hostilities meant the end of the world. But as John F. Kennedy – who claimed that *From Russia With Love* was one of his favourite novels – would later acknowledge, that halcyon spring, it wasn't too late for the country to awaken from the slumbers of appeasement. 'The result was that Britain felt secure in her defences,' JFK himself would write, 'and believed that if they would get through the winter without a knock-out blow England would have so built up her defences that she would easily be able to outlast Germany.'

Today, the younger man on the Warsaw Express is known throughout the world, not least for his remarkable literacy legacy which continues to promote the myth of British pre-eminence in the secret world. Ian Fleming's wartime experiences would inform many of the later adventures of James Bond, though, sadly, the fame and vast fortunes he craved would prove elusive until the end of his life. Yet a former MI6 chief has called 007 the best recruiting sergeant the service ever had and, as real-life officers have found, in Alan Judd's apposite phrase, 'you can go to the most remote and enclosed communities in the world and say "I am from British Intelligence and I'd like you to help me" and get a response.'

At the time of this trans-European train journey, though, Fleming was eclipsed by the career, accomplishments and sheer circumference of his companion. Denis Sefton Delmer was a larger-than-life character, blimp-like but not at all Colonel Blimp-like, with 'a genial and Rabelaisian nature' in the estimation of one colleague. Delmer was a well-known journalist and *bon vivant* celebrated for his various visits to the capitals of Europe. To most of its readers, he represented everything that was admirable about the pre-war *Daily Express*, for whom he was chief foreign correspondent.

That he would eventually be overshadowed by his younger companion, there was little doubt in his own mind. Even then, Sefton Delmer formed the impression that the indolent old Etonian who had been representing *The Times* on their journey to the Soviet Union was something more than a reporter. 'As soon as I saw him,' he recalled, 'I knew he was on some intelligence job or other.'

As to what exactly, the files are somewhat opaque.

'Mysteriously seconded' seems to be the best way to describe what he had been up to. Ian Fleming, Delmer later added, tongue in cheek, 'seemed to be acting the part of one of the Secret Service men he had read about in E. Phillips Oppenheim' – a famous interwar spy novelist. *Pravda* would come to hold the same view and, at the height of Bondmania in the mid-sixties, railed about the twin evils of Western decadence and such bourgeois symbols as 007 himself. 'His creator is Ian Fleming, who posed as *The Times* correspondent in Russia in 1939 but was in truth a spy for the capitalist nations'.

Sure enough, on their return to London, Fleming submitted a lengthy report to the Foreign Office on the state of the Soviet armed forces. The condoms, he thought with characteristic ingenuity, could also be analysed for their rubber content, a telltale indicator of the state of Soviet industry. Very little had changed in the six years he had been away from the country since his first visit. Stalin's Russia was still as grim and menacing as it had been in 1933, when Fleming had reported the trial of Metro-Vickers engineers accused of espionage (at which the chief prosecutor had declared that C was the 'power behind the throne', so convinced was he – like the Nazis – of the omniscience of the British Secret Service).

If anything, the USSR was now even more depressing, for the dead hand of Stalin's paranoia seemed more pervasive. Their trip to Moscow was ostensibly part of a trade mission, where Fleming, again in his friend's knowing estimation, 'introduced me to some very enjoyable characters'. Many, Sefton Delmer later realised, would have fitted nicely into a James Bond story. The two British journalists spent a fruitless evening searching out the private flat of the Commissar for Foreign Affairs – and instead booked into a suite in the National Hotel. A junior member of the British Embassy, Fitzroy Maclean, came looking for Ian Fleming later that night.

He found *The Times* writer in bed with a girl. With typical aplomb, Ian Fleming apologised to Maclean that he wouldn't be able to join them for dinner. He was, as Maclean later explained to his wife, 'very, very busy'. Fleming's female companion was one of a pair from Odessa whom he and Delmer had picked up in the bar of their hotel. Whether joking or not, Fleming left the lower half of his silk pyjamas as a present for his own particular girl.[1]

Small wonder, Fleming always claimed he enjoyed the visit. Ever tongue in cheek, he claimed that the Soviet capital was akin to the Gorbals – a well-known slum of the period – in Glasgow. The paranoia engendered by the unknown hand of Soviet Security remained palpable. Throughout their time in Moscow, Ian Fleming and Sefton Delmer were constantly tailed. On one occasion, the car following them burst one of its tyres. Obligingly, their own official driver waited while it was fixed before driving off again, a scene reminiscent of the cat and mouse antics of the Russians in the film version of *From Russia With Love*.

That Ian Fleming and Sefton Delmer had first met in appropriately authentic circumstances of mystery and intrigue in pre-war Moscow is significant for the secret war to come. They were drawn to each other not least because they were journalists. Both Fleming (the scion of an illustrious banking family) and Delmer (because of his Australian parentage) were outsiders. More exotically, Delmer had actually been born in Berlin and had even been repatriated during the Great War when he was 13. After a scholarship to Lincoln College, he joined Beaverbrook's *Daily Express* in its pre-war heyday. When hostilities broke out, the fact Delmer was born in Berlin and knew all the Nazi leaders personally was actually held against him.

Fleming, the youngest son of a banking dynasty, was the nearest to an outsider within the gilded cage of the Establishment. To some, his aloofness was typical of the withdrawn superiority of the old Etonian; to others, part and parcel of the introspection of his family.

Yet – no pun intended – they bonded.

Tongue in cheek, Fleming's one-upmanship extended to the literary milieu. He included a sly reference to his friend in the novel *Diamonds Are Forever* – 'Isn't that chap Sefton Delmer a boyfriend of yours, Lil?' 007 asks his glacial secretary, Loelia Ponsonby, one of the few characters who was never transferred to the big screen versions of the books.

Within months, they would both make their mark on the secret world, particularly when Fleming took his friend to lunch and disingenuously announced: 'I have been given a special desk job at the Admiralty.' In this way Ian Fleming would let his closest friend know that he had been drawn into the secret world as a special assistant to the head of the venerable

Naval Intelligence Division, who had merely specified that he wanted 'the outlandish, the unorthodox and the inspired' to be available to him. In Lieutenant Fleming RNVR he got all three, and within weeks, his success and charm inspired the First Sea Lord no less to remark that he was one of those people who could see in the dark.

That acuity would be needed to work through the mire of operations concerning propaganda and psychological warfare. Aiming to drive a wedge between the Führer and his people, inducing 'war-weariness and defeatism by every means, open and clandestine', the greater plans in Whitehall were farcical and futile to the point of absurdity. For the next couple of years, infighting, lack of co-ordination and personal enmities would come to characterise the greater story of British wartime propaganda.

Equally pervasive myths and shadows would consume his travelling companion on that pre-war journey, for at the start of his life, Denis Sefton Delmer had been interned as an enemy alien in Berlin during the Great War. Universally known as Tom, it was Delmer's curious fate to have been in Berlin, where his father was a well-known lecturer in English literature. As a later stringer for newspapers, Delmer was determined to enjoy the many social excesses of the Weimar Republic, reporting with relish and enjoyment stories of scandal and corruption. He was fascinated by the variety of charlatans of one form or another who were flourishing in the country. When he first attended a meeting of the National Socialist Party in 1929, Delmer soon considered Adolf Hitler a lunatic for exhorting his audience not to eat foreign fruit such as oranges.

His own appetites were vast. With the outbreak of the next war, as his son Felix Delmer ruefully remarks, weighing seventeen stone (240lb) meant Tom Delmer could hardly take part in the fighting. Ironically, the security authorities were wary of him and his German background appeared more sinister than it was, so was held against him rather than seen as an asset.

With his near-fluent German, Delmer thought he was ideally qualified to become a spy or at least help in the evaluation and interpretation of intelligence. 'I knew something of the mentality of Germans at war from having been at school as a lone English boy in starving Berlin during the first war,' he reminisced.

After his strange visit to Moscow in the company of Ian Fleming, Delmer managed – just – to stay ahead of trouble. He was still working for the *Daily Express* in Warsaw when the first bombs landed, and escaped through Romania before making it back to London. He became an official war correspondent, attached to the French Army. Delmer managed to escape from Paris just hours before the Germans arrived and thence undertook a nerve-wracking journey to Bordeaux and back home. Ultimately, Tom Delmer was one of those innumerable square pegs who would not fit into any predetermined circular holes. It would not be long before feelers were extended towards him from the secret world, and when they did, he would seize it as hungrily as he could.

That spring of 1939, it was clear that war would not be long in coming.

The Naval Intelligence Division had, like most arms of British Intelligence, been neglected since the end of the Great War. At the start of the year, a new Director of Naval Intelligence was appointed; when he took over, Admiral John Godfrey would admit that he did not know much about intelligence. But, in the time-honoured way of all clever operators, he took care to find enough people who did.

As raging torrents of information swept into the Admiralty, Godfrey would ensure the right people got exactly the right information they needed. If nothing else, he was a superb organiser, so his biographer attests, 'of the devices and unscrupulous art of Intelligence'. Thanks to his energy, determination and enquiring mind, the eyes and ears of the King's Navy were finally gearing up for the inevitable.

Under Godfrey's stewardship, Naval Intelligence was soon ahead of the game with a shipshape sense of its purpose. 'Both MI5 and MI6 tended to be amateurish and old-fashioned in their outlook and methods,' writes Patrick Beesley in his biography of Godfrey, *Very Special Admiral*, 'a weakness that was to become painfully apparent before the war was three months old.'

Ironically, the German naval attaché in London was in agreement. 'The Admiralty appears to have exerted to place one of their best officers in this important position,' Godfrey's biographer records. With a stern, weather-beaten face, the Director of Naval Intelligence had, in the later estimation of one who worked with him, the manner of a relentless advocate. He would never suffer fools and, as yet another recalled, 'with his own quick and penetrating mind he expected others to keep up'. Another who knew him well got to the heart of the matter by observing that he was nothing less than 'exacting, inquisitive, energetic and, at times, a ruthless and impatient master'. Arousing admiration, loyalty and downright antagonism in other departments, Godfrey was, in short, the hardest of taskmasters.

The admiral was a seasoned naval officer who was regarded as one of the best navigators in the service. Godfrey had patrolled the Yangtse in a gunboat, sabotaged munition dumps in Sebastopol and most recently commanded HMS *Repulse* in the Mediterranean at the time of the Spanish Civil War. When he was appointed as DNI in early January 1939, his most immediate task echoed that of his most illustrious predecessor. In the Great War, 'Blinker' Hall had found a stockbroker to act as his assistant.[2]

Godfrey, through contacts that included the Governor of the Bank of England, sent out feelers to search out the same. One name kept cropping up. Ironically, very little had ever been expected of this dilettante old Etonian, for up until now, he had been something of a dabbling failure at everything he had turned his hand to. Word soon spread that 'someone rather dim in the city who happens to be Peter Fleming's brother' had been appointed at the very heart of British Intelligence. To many it was a great surprise, for they were inclined to dismiss him as nothing less than a mountebank, often supercilious and aloof.

In so many ways, though, the appointment of Ian Lancaster Fleming was an inspired choice, particularly when later working in harness with his old friend Sefton Delmer. Fleming was, as Admiral Godfrey would later write, 'the man for the job' and, in this way, more by oversight than anything, James Bond's future creator was able to make his mark in areas like propaganda, subversion and press manipulation, along with prompting the creation of both psychological and political warfare. Along with his pre-war friend and rival, they would eventually take it to literally new heights and, in the admiral, Fleming would encounter the prototype for the steely, imperturbable M of the later Bond novels.

The most obvious ingredient for those later stories – 'sex, sadism and snobbery' in one famously shrill review of *Dr. No* – contrasted the fact that the former was seen as more of a hindrance in real-world espionage. That was certainly the view of yet another supposed candidate for the role of M,[3] Maxwell Knight, whose own aversion to physical satisfaction with women has been well chronicled. This was reflected in his views on running female agents which, in some ways, were curiously liberated for the time. Knight supported the use of female agents and took care to dismiss a 'very long-standing and ill-founded prejudice' against them.

'A clever woman who can use her personal attractions wisely has in her armoury a very formidable weapon,' Knight recorded. If a woman was a casual interest – as in just a short-term fling based on physical attractiveness – then a male source of potential information 'will very speedily lose interest in her once his immediate object is attained'. If the reasons for the contact had more to do with companionship and sympathy ('than merely those of physical satisfaction'), a woman would make a much better and longer-term agent. The best way to ensure that female agents did not fall in love with the men upon whom they were spying was simple: steer clear of femme fatales.

After the Great War, such temptresses were considered to be the worst sort of recruits. Maxwell Knight namechecks Mata Hari as a figure whose greater fame came thanks to her lovers rather than any accumulated wisdom or activity in espionage. 'I am no believer in what might be described as Mata Hari methods,' he wrote in a post-war review of his activities. 'I am convinced that more information has been obtained by women agents by keeping out of the arms of the man, than was ever obtained by sinking too willingly into them.'[4]

Though in the modern era many of these musings sound rather like the unabashed comments of a fully paid-up, card-carrying misogynist, at the time – not least after the trauma of his first wife's death – Max Knight was a new man by the standards of the day. He took care to note that his own experience showed women were not the neurotic creatures many dismissed them as ('ruled by their emotions and not their brains', 'intuition rather than reason' and 'that sex will play an unsettling and dangerous role in their work') and were valuable recruits.

A further insight into his attitudes came from his peremptory dismissal of agents of his own gender. 'Taking him generally, Man is a conceited creature, while woman is a vain creature,' Knight wrote. 'Conceit and vanity are not the same.' The former, Knight added, made men indiscreet, especially when trying to impress women, for which 'their outlet for this form of self-expression is their personal appearance, dress etc.' Knight also noted that as well as her sexual allure, closely allied – and ultimately more important – was 'the quality of sympathy'. '[N]othing is easier for a woman to gain a man's confidence [than] by the showing and expression of a little sympathy; this cannot be done by an undersexed woman.'

He had chosen well. None of his agents seemed to have fallen in love with the people they were spying on. In his own life, though, matters were more complicated. By the time he had written these words, Knight had married again, to a pretty young woman ten years his junior by the name of Lois Coplestone. Though clearly distraught about the death of Gwladys, his new bride was charmed by him and consoled him through his grief. 'We didn't lead much of a social life,' Lois later told Anthony Masters, 'and often we used to sit in the dark in Sloane Street because it was the animals' bedtime.'

Fairly swiftly, Max had installed her in his flat, which by now housed a white bull-terrier, a bullfinch, snakes, salamanders, an incontinent bush-baby, a bear cub, a baboon, monkeys, rats and several birds – including a blue-fronted Amazon parrot who took a virulent dislike to her. Ominously, Lois Knight became aware of something disturbing: how her husband liked to control people. And according to another woman who later worked closely with Max Knight, behind that carefree façade of a happily married man was, in reality, a repressed homosexual who had an interest in rough trade. Or at least that was the claim of Joan Miller, who later wrote a book which, ridiculously, the British government tried to ban in 1986.

One Girl's War was fairly harmless, containing, as one review put it, 'all the ingredients of a class yarn – deceit, double bluff, clandestine meetings and finding betrayal'. Later, using her real name of Joanna Phipps, this particular Miller's tale reads more like a cross between an Enid Blyton story and a Mills and Boon romance than a systematic attempt to subvert state secrets from four decades earlier. Joan Miller herself could have walked straight in from a drawing room comedy, a spirited, upper class 'gel' so typical of the time. Yet beneath the surface, Joan Miller was clearly lonely, restless and rootless. Her story is tinged with the sadness that her father had gambled away the family's money, as a result of which her mother had turned to drink.

Working as a mail clerk at Elizabeth Arden, one of her school friends was working for MI5 and politely enquired if she would like to join. 'I want all my girls to be well bred,' the director of the service, Vernon Kell, had decreed, 'and have good legs.' In this regard, she seemed to fit in. She quickly came into the orbit of the general's most illustrious agent runner. In some accounts, Joan Miller was like a lovelorn puppy in Max Knight's presence and would, another recruit said, follow him to the ends of the earth. Joan quickly became enthralled by Maxwell's magnetic personality, which bordered on hero worship.

Yet, as she freely admitted, she found him a paradox.

Fairly close to the surface he exhibited any number of unappealing prejudices, such as a marked aversion to Jews, gays and communists. Intriguingly, Joan seemed to think 'his intolerant attitude wasn't altogether consistent'. Sometimes, he seemed to parody himself and, in time, his lustre palled as she became increasingly embittered by his never seeming to notice how smitten she was. In other words, she may not be the most reliable of witnesses.

Many of her claims are all the more puzzling for others had noted Max Knight's own intuition when hiring people. He had an uncanny ability to get under the skin of people – something he approved of in others when they tried to recruit agents, especially females. 'That a woman's intuition is sometimes amazingly helpful and amazingly correct has been well established,' Knight noted, 'and given the right guiding hand, this ability can at times save an Intelligence Officer an enormous amount of trouble.'

When, in the early stages of the war, Tom Delmer went to visit Ian Fleming at the Admiralty, he could – like several others – sense that his friend was in his element. Room 39, Delmer thought, was vaguely reminiscent of a busy bank in Tangier. Later termed 'that legendary room through which all the Navy's secrets passed', it was the bustling antechamber to Admiral Godfrey's inner sanctum next door. It was, as Andrew Lycett has aptly termed it, nothing less than the bridge of Godfrey's ship.

To call in his staff, the admiral employed a deliciously camp nautical touch which Ian Fleming doubtless enjoyed: the DNI simply rang a bell with the Morse letter which indicated the surname of the officer he wanted to speak to. To Tom Delmer's amusement, Fleming was wreathed in cigarette smoke, sitting in his chair by a large corner window. The DNI's assistant always liked to claim that he was prone to suffering corns on the backside. When he took his friend in to see 'Uncle John' (as the admiral was called, and not always affectionately), the encounter was startling. Delmer later recalled him as having silver hair and the kindest, shrewdest eyes he had even seen.

Room 39 had twenty or so hand-picked officers who collated information from amongst the chaos and echoing cacophony of noise. Fleming's colleagues sat amongst tightly packed desks, surrounded by ever-increasing mountains of paper. All this frantic activity was accompanied by the constant clack of typewriters and the ceaseless ringing of telephones. Fleming appeared to be chief clerk in the mêlée of seven commanders, one captain, two lieutenants, two civilian assistants and four female secretaries, along with female admirers or anyone else who happened to be walking by.

Each day the tall, languorous old Etonian would enter Room 39 to enquire archly of a stiff colleague just to annoy him: 'I say Quacker, what's happening?' Most in Naval Intelligence – including the intended recipient called Charles Drake – ignored his barbs. The most fertile imagination in Room 39 of the Admiralty invariably indulged his whims.

Yet typically, 'Quacker' Drake became one of Fleming's greatest fans.

Because most of those people surrounding and outranking him were peacetime naval officers, they suffered from what Fleming called 'Senior officer veneration'. As Drake later explained, that meant 'you were always a bit nervous of somebody firing questions at you [who] was wearing twice as many stripes as you were wearing'.

Fleming didn't have that. He would speak to people as equals and get his own way. He knew most people – either socially or from school – and was on first name terms with them. Fleming's list of social contacts was astounding, often meeting them in the Dorchester Hotel, which his future wife Anne called the 'gilded bird-cage of the rich'. In his naval reserve uniform, he was invariably dismissed by some of his social clique as a 'chocolate sailor' – someone who had never been to sea or taken part in any action.

Yet despite the sneers, Lieutenant Fleming, RNVR, had taken to the navy with characteristic self-possession and, against all expectations, revelled in the paperwork. The nature of his work was perplexing and restless. Despite the fact, as another colleague famously joked, that Fleming 'hated anything in triplicate – except a large martini', his reporting background helped. The DNI's fixer was, in Drake's estimation, brilliant at 'drafting papers without being verbose' which, in the Royal Navy, guaranteed action would be taken.

Fairly soon, Room 39 would reach far beyond its remit of co-ordinating information that streamed into the Admiralty, which was 'regularly coming from here, there and everywhere'. Ian Fleming soon became Godfrey's emollient and, in his own words, 'a convenient channel for confidential matters connected with subversive organisations'. In another colleague's estimation, nobody was able to jolly along the obstinate admiral more effectively than his special assistant. Fleming was simply brilliant, the best kind of ideas man who, working in harness with his boss, would come to make their own unique contributions to the prosecution of the secret war.

For all his railing against the use of femme fatales, Maxwell Knight did make good use of one particularly beautiful and beguiling woman who lured the unsuspected to reveal information – or more besides. In pre-war café society, the stunning female with the Viennese accent would be able to make her way in the higher echelons of society, listening in to tittle-tattle and titbits of gossip. After all, her sister was often to be found sitting in a seashell like a siren of old[5] and somehow had married the brother of a rising star in British Intelligence.

Friedle Gärtner was well connected. Working as a part-time informant for Max Knight, he later noted, she 'did very excellent work for us between 1938 and the outbreak of war'. By posing as a Nazi sympathiser to flush out potential fifth columnists, Friedle had used her looks to gain confidences. Today, she would be called a knockout. Then, the pukka chaps merely noted, 'there is no doubt whatever about her very considerable personal attractiveness'.

That new year of 1939 had seen Maxwell Knight write a letter to his old friend Dennis Wheatley to introduce her as a potential 'research assistant'. They had already discussed her and, as Max noted, 'it is absolutely essential for the scheme and her own peace of mind that she should not suspect that the job is not an entirely genuine one'. This particular *ménage à trois* adhered to another of Max Knight's approaches in recruiting people. '[It] is nearly always necessary for our official contact to call in some colleague,' he noted, who would then tell someone else, 'and though it is perhaps a little sweeping to say that a secret between three persons is no secret', at least there would be a sense of trust between them all.

But then a typical complication arose.

In Joan Miller's account, Friedle had also fallen in love with Max Knight, but realised that Joan herself was already – at least in her own mind – *maitresse en titre*. A good time girl, Friedle Gärtner was always forgetting the curfew or being picked up by the police, thrown into a black Mariah and finding herself in lock-ups with ladies of the night. 'The clothes we wore in those days were very tarty,' Joan Miller said about the both of them. According to Joan, Friedle used to call Tommy Thompson of Special Branch to get her out.

Even though there was a war on, she didn't seem to have a care in the world. She would fall in and out of love – and dresses, too. One of her devoted swains was Bill Younger, Knight's protégé and Dennis Wheatley's step-son, who consulted his mother on what sort of ring to propose to her with. Joan Wheatley was, to say the least, horrified.

Thankfully the engagement never happened and Friedle carried on much as before, a cross between flibbertigibbet and smouldering siren. For Friedle, at least, one marriage had been enough. A gentile by birth, she had worked in her native Vienna as a stenographer and, in 1934, married into a very Orthodox Jewish family. Though she emigrated with her husband for Palestine, the marriage was not successful. 'I can't tell you how frightful it was,' she later told a friend. In the meantime, her sister, Lisle, had married Major Ian Menzies of the Scots Guards, who just happened to be the brother of the Chief of the Secret Intelligence Service.

This would prove to be her most useful connection in the secret world.

Sir Stewart Menzies saw that Friedle could become a useful agent overseas, even though she wanted to remain in the United Kingdom with her sister. 'Her reason for coming to me is that her sister married a brother of mine,' C noted in a letter to MI5 in May 1938, 'and it is with these relations that she is temporarily staying.'

Both Knight and Miller used to stay at Ian Menzies' house or party amongst his well-to-do set. 'The family was rich and Ian's house was pretty opulent, as I remember it, without containing a single tasteless item,' recalled Joan (who became a good friend of Friedle's). The parties, she recalls, involved gambling and the most memorable attendees were 'Greek shipping magnates, middle-aged, lecherous and wearing pure silk shirts'.

In time, Friedle would be introduced to even more exotic specimens from the secret world. For now, as a native German speaker, she was soon attending events at the Anglo-German Fellowship, which included dinners and cocktail parties. After the *Anschluss* in her native land, she had called at the German Embassy to offer her congratulations. She even tried to join the *Arbeitsfront* – the German Labour Front, to which waiters and barmen were often accredited – though it had proved rather more difficult than she expected. A typical 'Nazi Prussian', as she described him, had barked, unconvinced: 'Why are you here anyway? You had better go home.'

A strange sense of uneasiness accompanied Prime Minister Neville Chamberlain's announcement over the BBC at 11.15 a.m. on the first Sunday in September 1939 that 'this country is at war with Germany'. Within minutes, an unidentified aircraft – later revealed to be a French courier plane – triggered an air-raid warning. At the same time, the congregation in St Paul's Cathedral were singing a hymn with the lines:

'O God of love, O king of peace –
Make wars throughout the world to cease'

when the sirens sounded. The service was temporarily abandoned and continued a little while later in the crypt.

All the terrifying predictions about aerial bombardment which had preoccupied the population before the war now crystallised into public panic. 'In London there was an air of 1918 and even a touch of 1665,' one author would write. 'Not since the Great Plague had there been such a flight to the country.'

Schools and swimming baths were prepared to receive corpses; a million women and children were taken outside the capital to live with strangers; and 8,000 TB patients were sent home from hospital and – in a marvel of epidemiological control – told not to cough over young people. Their beds, they were told in all seriousness, would be needed to accommodate the victims of bombing. Within days, newspapers were no longer carrying weather forecasts in case they gave aid to the enemy. Soon, they were reporting another very curious phenomenon. 'Englishmen were speaking to each other.'

Yet for all these apocalyptic pronouncements, there were no massed raids by German bombers nor tidal waves of casualties. More civilians were killed over the next two months from road accidents than any indiscriminate bombing. Reluctance was also apparent at the highest levels. While the army dug trenches in Hyde Park, the Cabinet argued over its strategy for bombing Germany. When it was later proposed that German forests should be set alight, the air minister – a former insurance consultant – was horrified.

'Are you aware that it is private property?' Sir Kingsley Wood exclaimed. 'Why, you will be asking me to bomb Essen next.'

A more refined approach was attempted with what was termed 'bomph', leaflets that were printed up to try to alter the population's view of the fighting. Greater numbers of leaflets than bombs were dropped by the Royal Air Force in those first few weeks of war. There was a feeling that if done properly, propaganda would turn the *Deutsches Volk* against their leaders.

But how? It was a simple question with a ridiculously bureaucratic answer.

As with much of the subversive activities undertaken by the British government at the start of the war, there was no coherence nor clarity of purpose between the trio of separate agencies whose 'objectives were obscure and overlapping, their relations to older departments ill-defined and often bad-tempered'. As a reaction to the Munich crisis, a senior Air Ministry officer realised that propaganda could fill the gap to show British grit and determination. 'A sort of department,' he loftily proclaimed, 'should be set up which would let all the world know that the lion had teeth and would use them.' Kingsley Wood, the minister who didn't want to bomb private property, caught the ear of the prime minister. Sir Campbell Stuart, a Canadian who had worked under Lord Northcliffe during the Great War, was given four rooms, three staff, one typewriter and the wherewithal to keep quiet.

'There is only one answer to a lie,' he would declare, 'the truth even if you have to bend it a little.' It was kept off the books as CS or Electra House, EH, close by the Embankment on the Temple. As M.R.D. Foot termed it, Stuart 'was no Goebbels, but he collected a few sensible journalists and broadcasters

around him'. But no sense of common purpose was forthcoming and something as simple as dropping leaflets became a very different battleground.

The night war broke out, the Cabinet discussed dropping propaganda
leaflets in the hope of having 'an important effect on German opinion'.
From the outset, it was only ever envisaged as the military equivalent to
ringing a doorbell and then running off. 'Bomber units of the Royal Air
Force carried out a leaflet raid on Western Germany during the night,' Alvar
Liddell would later broadcast on the BBC. 'None of our aircraft is missing.'
Chamberlain, delighted to be able to 'speak' to the German nation, never
really appreciated what was being done in his name.

The dropping of propaganda leaflets and leafleting was half-hearted. An
Air Ministry official had the right to veto – in case it brought about retaliation – any material that was prepared. The leaflets themselves were translated
into German by a mining engineer called Schmidt, who seemed to have
walked in from central casting so far as pedantic Teutons was concerned.

'The results were not good,' recalled the person in charge.

There was incessant wangling over costs and bailiwick disputes between
the Treasury and the Foreign Office. Much more time and effort was wasted
on arguing for its own sake and what one historian aptly termed 'an interdepartmental game of beggar-my-neighbour' resulted which would need a
firecracker to sort it all out into something coherent and useful.

It was hardly an act of hagiographical toadying that the title of a splendid
biography of Admiral John Godfrey was called *A Very Special Admiral*. Like
his assistant, Godfrey was used to thinking outside the box when it came to
deceiving the enemy and, as he later noted, 'to be successful, false scents must
be laid and something done to tempt the enemy to the spot'. The interests
of the Director of Naval Intelligence were suitably eclectic, especially with
what he termed 'deception, *ruses de guerre*, passing on false information, and
so on'. As he would write a few weeks later after the outbreak of war, all
came under the 'general heading of deception and "dirty work" – which,
for some reason is regarded as the DNI's prerogative'.

Perhaps that was the legacy of the Machiavellian Blinker Hall. Yet a
new war and technology which accompanied it ushered in great changes.
As his biographer notes, Godfrey would 'almost certainly be confronted
with a whole range of problems which had not existed in Hall's day'. The
admiral's own attitudes to what were generally termed 'the funnies' had
been informed by a curious pre-war experience at sea. While on duty in

the Mediterranean, as he noted for the records, Godfrey 'once saw a large red turtle, east of Gibraltar, 4–5 miles away, floating idly on the surface. It looked very like the red head of a torpedo for which we were searching.'

So a few weeks after war broke out, Admiral Godfrey made the first ever notes on the subject of dirty tricks, deceptions and decoys. They are worth examining given some of the operations which later came to have the admiral's imprimatur upon them. In his lapidary way, Godfrey noted that the difficulty behind any such operations was how to get the information across and the quality of that information itself. And nobody would do it better, 'probably', the admiral noted, than the British.

He went through a number of ideas and warned that they might be somewhat fantastic, 'but nevertheless contain germs of what I feel to be some good ideas'. The more you examine them, he reasoned, the less fantastic they seem to appear. All would culminate in perhaps the most fantastical of all, the infamous 'Man Who Never Was' operation. Despite a recent hyped book on the subject, Admiral Godfrey was behind the idea – though it was 'not a very nice one', as he termed it. This would involve a corpse dressed as an airman, as though his parachute had failed ('I understand there is no difficulty in obtaining corpses at the Naval Hospital, but, of course, it would have to be a fresh one').

Other ideas proposed by the admiral could equally have been employed by Q branch in the later Bond films. Removing food from enemy ships and making them more palatable by use of plausible instructions to be printed on the outside was one. 'Explosives and means of detonation might thus be introduced into enemy submarines,' he minuted, an idea that, sadly, never seemed to see the light of day.

Nothing – no matter how outrageous – would be rejected as possible weapons in the fight for survival which would come. It helped that the admiral could call upon an imagination as fertile as that of Ian Lancaster Fleming. For the writer who effortlessly created a memorable hero and macabre villains became the initiator for other irregular projects at the start of the war. Lieutenant Fleming was interested in the use of rumour, disinformation and propaganda. He suggested metal discs with a five mark note on one side and a propaganda image on the other, forging German currency and a radio propaganda ship, a kind of Radio Caroline that would draw German fire and ire ('the tone of the broadcasts should be peremptory and occasionally scornful').

For all those who knew him, Ian Fleming was, for all his indolent dilettantism, in his element at the Admiralty. Robert Harling, who knew him well during these war years, later wrote that he became his own brand image for James Bond around this time. 'He had a sad, bony, fateful face, strong featured and with very clear eyes,' Harling wrote in an appreciation a few days after his friend died in August 1964. It was illuminating, he said, when the two old friends had discussed the war years, Harling had suggested that most middle-aged men see themselves as between the ages of 28 and 32. It was significant that when war broke out, Fleming was 31. James Bond's creator grinned by saying 'touché'.

The literary father of James Bond would represent the admiral at meetings he didn't have the time – nor inclination – to attend. In this way, more by oversight than anything, Fleming was able to make his mark in new, often bizarre, forms of warfare. These included subjects like propaganda, subversion and press manipulation, along with developing psychological and political warfare as the fighting progressed.

As Admiral Godfrey was to remark, war changed intelligence officers from Cinderella into princesses.[6] Ian Fleming not only went to the ball like that mythical figure, but had one, too. It would be too easy – as some more questionable accounts have done – to read too much into Fleming's own wartime secret service. Yet it should be noted that, like so many others, Fleming was never inculcated into the greatest intelligence secret of the war. Ultra, the fruit of the labours of the codebreakers at Bletchley Park, was known only to a handful of people at the apex of the secret world.

James Bond's creator was pointedly excluded from knowing about the unlocking of the Enigma machine. That probably explains one of his more hare-brained schemes, which he proposed the following autumn of 1940.[7] Operation Ruthless would, according to a note he minuted Admiral Godfrey, have seen Royal Naval personnel pretending to be a shot down crew of a German bomber. By luring an air-sea rescue boat to retrieve them, they could, Fleming suggested, then hijack the aircraft and steal its Enigma codes. Ultimately, the Bletchley codebreakers were helped when sailors retrieved the settings from a sinking U-boat in October 1942, at a terrible human cost.[8]

For all these daydreams, Ian Fleming remained deskbound for most of the war and was never a man of action like the mythical hero he came to create. 'He wasn't James Bond,' one of his Naval Intelligence colleagues would caution, 'he was a pen pusher like all of us.'

Yet occasionally, Fleming would employ the kinds of rascals who seemed to think that they were. And for that, some genuinely wild and crazy plans that would snugly fit into the earlier James Bond films seem to have been sanctioned in the early part of the war. 'What nonsense they were,' Fleming would later write disparagingly, 'those romantic, Red Indian daydreams so many of us indulged in at the beginning of the war – to blow up the Iron Gates of the Danube.'

The latter, concerning the great arterial river of central Europe, were a case in point. The Iron Gates are a gorge which forced the flow of the Danube into 25 miles of dangerous narrows below Orsova. In strategic terms, they acted as a chokepoint between Romania and Yugoslavia, which commended them as a target because of German interest in Romanian oil. Even though difficult to transport and higher in cost than the market value – along with copper, chromium and manganese – Romanian supplies were important in feeding the Nazi war machine.

In some accounts, Fleming turned his mind to doing something about it.

So enters our story a remarkable buccaneer who – in his own mind, at least – was a prototypical 007. Others have termed Merlin Minshall a 'reach-me-down James Bond' who, in the tongue-in-cheek estimation of one official historian of intelligence, 'shared Bond's susceptibility to blondes'. In his obituary in *The Times* from 1987, Minshall was termed 'a rumbustious adventurer who was born three or four centuries too late'. Others have portrayed him more as a Munchausen-like fantasist whose claims, even today, are hard to establish as they have the barest basis in reality.

The son of a newspaper proprietor and nephew of a baronet, Minshall had sailed across Europe as an antidote to the tedium of studying architecture. He became a racing driver and somehow – like Ian Fleming – ended up a sub lieutenant in the Royal Navy Volunteer Reserve, though, as his obituarist noted, 'his was not in any sense a subordinate temperament'.

Inevitably, he got on with Fleming, through whom he claimed he found a suitably surreal sinecure with a junior consular post in Belgrade. It was here that, in 1939, Merlin Minshall became a very different sort of architect of what one newspaper later termed a plan 'as flamboyant as the RAF's Dambusters raid'. While there were a number of operations aimed at the Iron Gates, Minshall took part, in his own account, in a series of Bond-like adventures, all told in a racy autobiography that was ruined – in one reviewer's tart estimation – by inaccuracy and bombast. In this overheated account, *Gilt Edged*, Minshall claims that he travelled around Mitteleuropa with a cyanide capsule embedded inside a tooth, detonators stored inside a false-bottomed suitcase and had high explosives disguised as toffees sent via the diplomatic bag.

The Germans, in his account, were on to him and – with shades of *From Russia With Love* – he dropped poison into the drink of a German and then booted him out of a lavatory window on a train. All this was carried out against the backdrop of trying to block the oil supplies that passed through the Iron Gates by sinking barges. After failing to bribe local pilots, a couple of dozen Royal Naval ratings manned half a dozen ships which would then cause mayhem at the bottleneck. The denouement was equally improbable: unconvincingly acting as art students, the ratings were thwarted from planting bombs when the Germans stole Minshall's stock of fuel.

'No matter how preposterous it might be considered,' Len Deighton wrote, 'all of his references seem to check out.'

Others begged to differ. When Minshall first claimed these stories in 1975, a hornet's nest of criticism was stirred – leaving many others shaken – not least with public identification that the main animator of the plans was Mickey Mason,[9] another remarkable character who was an ex-naval boxer. According to newspaper accounts, Mason's plan was to have used 5 tons of explosive to blow up the banks of the Romanian side of the Danube, which would then block the Iron Gates.

But was Ian Fleming involved? When the noted military historian Ronald Lewin came to review Merlin Minshall's book for *The Listener*, he noted that all of Merlin Minshall's claims were called into doubt. 'Even the sophisticated Ian Fleming is made to talk like a character by Dornford Yates,' he wrote. There is a certain irony that Yates, too, is best known today for his clubland snobbery, xenophobia and silly-ass Englishness, along with another near contemporary who was finding his own berth in the secret world hard to find.

Despite the appearance of chaos and lingering claims from its more dismissive participants, Naval Intelligence – as Ian Fleming's most recent biographer has noted – was the most professional arm of British Intelligence in the opening weeks of the war. Its ascendancy was assured with a simple yet unequivocal communication that went out high priority via the short wave transmitters at Portishead. Routed from the Admiralty to every ship in the King's Navy, the 'snap' telegram read simply: WINSTON'S BACK!

It needed no further elaboration. Two days after war had been declared, Winston Churchill was re-appointed to the role he had last held at the start of the Great War. Within two weeks, his friend 'Chips' Channon recorded in his incomparable diaries[10] that 'Winston is already driving the Admiralty to distraction by his interference and energy'.

It was especially true for Admiral Godfrey's department.

For Fleming and his colleagues in Naval Intelligence, the outbreak of war meant a deluge of persistent, exacting queries from the office directly above theirs. The newly appointed First Sea Lord would almost drive them ragged with his unrelenting daily 'prayers', as they came to be known, on all manner of awkward subjects.

'Pray, what is being done about…' Winston Churchill would want to know.

Within minutes, some poor unfortunate in Room 39 of the Admiralty would have to find out. Lieutenant Fleming – with his incomparable ability at quickly writing the most lapidary of prose – usually ended up drafting the answer.

The First Sea Lord was hardly infallible and would, when it suited him, interfere with plans and operations. Winston Churchill had had a chequered career, including his years in the political wilderness, which had, in part, resulted from his chronic impetuousness. Indeed, the prevailing wisdom around the corridors of power was that Churchill was possessed of a wrong-headed kind of genius that had burned brightly but ended – as with all political careers – in complete and utter failure.

His brainwaves often teetered to the brink of disaster.

Appalled by the stalemate on the Western Front in the Great War, Churchill had articulated that an attack through the 'soft underbelly' of Europe would break the impasse. As First Lord of the Admiralty, Churchill had dispatched an expedition to the Dardanelles. When 250,000 troops had been killed as a result, his career as a wartime statesman was over.

Since then his political career had been resurrected despite his switching political sides with such disloyal careerism that it left some onlookers winded. Most recently, Winston Churchill had been a voice in the wastelands, a strident, increasingly monotonous portent of doom. But now, with a solicitous providence that he put down to fate, the First Sea Lord was where he wanted to be and, in a matter of weeks, the Royal Navy engaged the enemy in spectacular fashion. Churchill himself basked in the glory of victory with the Battle of the River Plate that December.

By comparison, the First Sea Lord's relationship with NID would be strained, not least with what the professional intelligence officers saw as his wishful interpretation – especially concerning U-boat statistics and the more vexed question of sightings and refuelling in Ireland and Spain. On this issue, the Director of Naval Intelligence later said that Churchill was at his most malignant. 'There will, of course, be occasions when ruthless criticism is a duty and irregular method a responsibility,' Admiral Godfrey would mildly record a few years later, 'but at no time should consideration of persons be allowed to impair intellectual integrity.'

As a result, the future prime minister would never bring John Godfrey into his inner circle. Their mutual distrust is reflected in the admiral later telling his biographer that the greater tragedy of Churchill's life was that although he loved strategy, the First Sea Lord was never particularly good at it.

Proof, certainly within the secret war, came with one of his Lordship's greater obsessions, an issue that would soon come to galvanize – in every sense of the word – his desire to prosecute subversion and guerrilla warfare. It was the vexed question concerning the often gloriously rainbow-hued mineral oxides from which metallic iron could be extracted which would have quite an unforeseen – and significant – impact on the secret war and its prosecution.

If Military intelligence was, as Groucho Marx famously quipped, a contradiction in terms, no better demonstration came with the War Office's own branch (known as Military Intelligence (Research)) which one recruit termed 'an organisation in which fact and fiction played so smoothly together'. At the start of the war, it was yet another department directed – though at times, that was overstating the case – towards sabotage and subversion, existing in a surreal, often topsy-turvy world of its own making. Though its staff did not officially exist, one would disconcert his colleagues by shouting 'Boo!' at them in the street. Another quickly went out of favour for not looking up and acknowledging the presence of Sir Stewart Menzies. 'I thought we were not supposed to know who he was,' said the unfortunate miscreant when C happened to pass through their office.

Whereas MI5 and MI6 were interested in gathering – or counteracting – intelligence, MI (R) was interested in developing weapons for use behind enemy lines. These would involve what one writer has termed the 'bizarre projects' expanding the role of deception in scarcely believable ways – not least to many of its own recruits.

Joan Bright, who became a secretary in the department, was told to report to St James's Underground Station at 11 a.m. on one particular day. She was told to make sure she wore a pink carnation. At the appointed time, she was led – after many changes of direction and what seemed obvious counter-surveillance – to an office where a colonel greeted her. Made to sign the Official Secrets Act, as she left the colonel pointed through the window to another man waiting at a street corner.

'When you leave here,' he warned, 'don't let him see you. Turn left and keep going.'

Although not explained at the time, this other fellow was most likely working for a rival department within MI6 with whom MI (R) shared a suite of offices at 2 Caxton Street, just round the corner from MI6 Headquarters at Broadway Buildings. Admiral Quex Sinclair had set up his own department within the Secret Intelligence Service, Section D – whose initial supposedly stood for Destruction – to look at attacking the enemy by unusual means. That meant sabotage, but as the intelligence historian M.R.D. Foot noted, Section D was also tasked to use 'propaganda to shift enemy opinion'.

For this, the agency employed a major and a typist. Though there was obvious overlap with Electra House, 'no one told Campbell Stuart about him', one official history notes, 'and no one told him about Campbell Stuart'. The duplicity hardly mattered because none was particularly effective in propaganda, nor, indeed, the greater needs of subversion. MI (R), Electra House and Section D ignored each other but somehow vied to be equally incompetent.

Though MI (R) eventually concentrated on work carried out by troops and Section D on undercover work, their two titular heads soon fell out. Even though they were both Royal Engineers, they bickered over approach and who should do what. It was a recipe for disaster which played out all over Europe with a series of farcical subversive activities that came to a head with a one-legged tea merchant who had been sent on a mission by someone who seemed to have read too many pre-war spy stories.

On that same first Monday in September 1939 – the day after war was declared, when Winston Churchill had been appointed First Sea Lord – another later entrant to the secret world began his own unique preparations for the fighting. Dennis Wheatley bought a stash of Hugo de Monterrey cigars and several bottles of champagne before stopping off at his publishers on his way home. He wanted to see if they might reprint his books while there was still enough paper left. Whatever else could be said about him, Dennis Wheatley certainly had style.

'During the first week of war, my failure to find any suitable war employment greatly depressed me,' Wheatley would later write. Indeed, his skill at writing, he felt, could become his entrée into the secret war and he offered his services to the Ministry of Information. His applications (three separate ones to different departments) were never formally acknowledged.

Through family connections – his wife, stepson and daughter were all working for MI5 – he was eventually asked to write some pamphlets and tips on how to resist the invasion (which were later published by Wheatley under the apt heading of *Stranger Than Fiction*). But he remained frustrated that he could not be put to more gainful employ, which even his good friend Max Knight could not assuage. Knight asked him to keep an eye on Rollo Ahmed, the curious Egyptian-born occultist, and asked if Dennis would 'sound him out very gently particularly with a view to finding out if he would be willing to do his sort of work abroad'. Knight does not say what that was and neither did Wheatley.

An obvious area for a wordsmith was in writing propaganda. But as Dennis himself noted, during the early stages of the war it 'was so bad that words fail to describe its rottenness'. It was, he felt, tantamount to treason to waste such an opportunity so, as the country prepared to fight the enemy, Dennis Wheatley turned his attention to a new novel in the hope that his own – and the country's – fortunes would change.

The MI6 officer who had been tasked to subvert and destroy the enemy by unconventional means as head of Section D was the most incongruous of figures who thought every operation he planned was a 'war stopper'. Major-General Laurence Grand was tall, slim and good-looking with a heavy moustache, exuding bonhomie with a curious air of mystery, usually to be found strolling around in a well-cut lounge suit with a scarlet carnation in his lapel. He was, as several people have pointed out, exactly the sort of figure whom Ian Fleming might have imagined to head up a department of the secret service. That he was, in effect, the head of sabotage and destruction within the real secret service meant that he tried to live up to his surname. On one occasion an instructor remarked in General Grand's hearing that he needed a real body to practice sticking a dagger in. 'I can let you have one, old boy,' Grand replied. 'Genuine German. It's in our freezer. I'll have it put in your car.'

After a lifetime in military service – India, Iraq and Kurdistan – Grand had been tasked to consider subversion without using anything akin to military action. 'Examining such an enormous task,' he later said, 'one felt as if one had been told to move the Pyramids with a pin.' Yet the recent MI6 official history describes him as 'a man of energy and ideas' whose fiefdom was his headquarters on the upper floors of the St Ermin's Hotel in Victoria.

Section D had been established on 1 April 1938 – which he thought appropriate. Everything was low key, informal and came under the purview of MI6 (to avoid prying Treasury eyes so that its budget was kept secret). This probably explains why C later handed him £100 in notes from a drawer and never mentioned the subject again. In the run-up to war, Grand had been in charge of military vehicle design but had also worked for MI6. One day, Grand was called in by Admiral Sinclair, whom he considered looked like a Mexican gangster with a wide-brimmed hat and a blue suit with brown shoes.

'I want you to do sabotage,' C told him.

'Is anything barred?' Grand asked.

'Not a thing!'

Despite the mutual loathing of their directors, the War Office's MI (R) would later be subsumed into MI6 within Section D in the guise of developing subversion throughout the world. A number of 'unusual' devices were developed including, improbably, a suggestion by J.B.S. Haldane FRS for mines to be attached by swimmers or in submarines. 'Prototypes were tested in The River Thames,' Joan Bright Astley,[11] recalled. '[Using] Boy scouts at strategic spots to catch them as they floated by.'

A number of other devices, including sticky bombs, almost inevitably drew the interest of the First Sea Lord. When during one demonstration, one bomb accidentally exploded behind some French generals, it disturbed them so much that they were never quite converted to the cause.

Vive la difference, then, for as the political situation in Europe had worsened, the vague notion of spreading revolt and guerrilla tactics had become, as one military planner noted, 'the only way'. Yet these were nothing compared to even more grandiose plans sanctioned by General Grand's Section D – into which MI (R) would be folded – which, as the authorised history of the service notes, was likened to 'arranging an attack on a Panzer Division by an actor mounted on a donkey'.

Iron Ore may not seem like the most crucial ingredient for prosecuting the secret war, but its availability to the Third Reich would act like a lightning rod for all the various glaring deficiencies of British attempts at covert operations. With the outbreak of war, no less a champion than the First Sea Lord had realised that one way to cripple the German war machine would be to strike at its Achilles' heel – Swedish ore exports.[12]

No longer having access to the extensive French ore fields, Germany's only source of iron ore was Sweden. The Third Reich's supplies had effectively halved. An attack against the Swedish ore fields, mainly in the north of the country, would effectively cut them off completely. Most was either transported via the Baltic port of Luleå in summer; or in winter, by train across the mountains to Narvik. There were plenty of places which could be attacked to stop the flow. The First Sea Lord wanted to seize supplies at sea, which horrified his colleagues, but over the next few months a variety of possible scenarios – many more improbable than the last – were suggested.

All showed the unreality of the British capability to sabotage the enemy.

At his first meeting with Sir Stewart Menzies in December 1939, Churchill discussed the matter and later authorised £300,000 to the NID to begin work. That new year of 1940, a Section D agent was sent to Stockholm. to spearhead this action. Alfred 'Freddie' Rickman had already written a book called *Swedish Iron Ore* as cover. Now, for reasons which were never clear, he employed a communist and a one-legged tea merchant to blow up some of the Swedish mines. By day, he was an importer of machinery, and by night, clearly, he may well have read too many trashy spy novels. Rickman communicated with London using invisible ink and smuggled in explosives disguised as rubber, chocolate or biscuits. It got even sillier: a military attaché who helped collect the explosives hidden within some books pretended to be a French chauffeur – with hat and accent – later terming the whole escapade 'real Edgar Wallace stuff, in a dark dirty wood at midnight'.

With several hundred pounds of explosive hidden in his cellar, Rickman was ready to go at any time in early 1940. There followed months of prevarication – during which Section D developed the notion of destroying the cranes at Oxelösund – the main port facing the Baltic that was ice-free all year round. Newly released files from 2013 show just how high the planning went. Both C and General Grand met with the Cabinet several times to discuss this pet project of the First Sea Lord's. All through the spring of 1940, Section D's efforts in depriving the Germans of Swedish iron ore –

and Romanian oil supplies – continued in a hopelessly amateurish vein. A high-ranking Foreign Office mandarin soon came to the conclusion that General Grand was 'almost always wrong, his knowledge wide but alarmingly superficial, his organisation in many respects a laughing stock, and he is a consistent and fluent liar'.

And still it went ahead with what another file terms 'a plan which we refer to under the Capital O'. This was aimed at Oxelösund – also known in some accounts as Operation Lumps – of which both the prime minister and Foreign Secretary were aware. Rickman said all that was needed was to press the button. His principal agent, a German refugee, panicked – and then the invasion of Norway intervened. At least now the fears of Norwegian complaints about interference in its rail system had been subverted.

A Royal Navy yachtsman called Gerald Holdsworth then flew to Stockholm. Working with Rickman, their first task was to move all the incriminating material in his cellar. Before they could, MI6 in London received a telegram stating that their man in Scandinavia 'was found in possession of five hundred weights of explosives'. Rickman didn't realise he had been under surveillance by the Swedish security authorities, who promptly arrested him in possession of explosives and maps detailing where they were going to be placed.

'In retrospect the Oxelösund Operation provides an excellent illustration of how not to conduct a covert operation and also of the price to be paid when things go wrong,' one academic review says with understated simplicity. Not only did Rickman anger his hosts, but also the minister – as the official British envoy was known – who noted 'they have achieved little in Sweden beyond putting me and themselves in an awkward position', as well as the local MI6 station chief (terming the potential saboteurs 'negligent or inefficient'). Rickman's handful of agents – supposed to be gathering shipping intelligence – were arrested and sentenced to short prison sentences.

During Alfred Rickman's subsequent trial – which brought unwelcome publicity – the prosecution suggested that the whole operation had been some sort of German provocation, engineered by undercover elements working for the Gestapo within the United Kingdom. 'Of course there were no "highly placed German agents in England",' notes the chief historian of the Foreign Office about this farcical denouement on the MI6 website, 'but with Britain's wartime fortunes at its lowest ebb, it was perhaps better that the Swedes should believe in imaginary German spies rather than the reality of British incompetence.'

Despite these ridiculous activities, the stage was now set for the greater battles of the secret war to come, with all the main players – certainly for the next few years – now in place. Despite some of the preceding nonsense, so far as the Nazis were concerned, there was a cunning, evil organisation whose tendrils got everywhere and seemed well-placed to stymie its plans and greater ambitions.

The British Secret Service.

As a result, on war's outbreak, the SS Intelligence Service attempted to understand the enemy forces they would be fighting. It gave especial attention to the field of foreign espionage. Intelligence, according to *Sicherheitsdienst*, was a peculiarly British métier, 'the virtue of their tradition, their experience, and certain facets of their national character – unscrupulousness, self-control, cool deliberateness and ruthless action – have achieved an unquestionable degree of mastery'.

The myth was widespread in pre-war Germany, so much so that when anything went wrong, the high-ups in Berlin would assume that His Majesty's secret servants – or their proxies – were somehow behind it all. But now, at the start of November 1939, came the confluence of two events which would link both the occult and the tendrils of the secret war. Both would be related to perhaps the most embarrassing incident in MI6's thirty-year history, which in the understated tones of the recent official history, noted simply that the Germans made tremendous propaganda capital out of it, as well as several heads on a plate and a sense that somehow, the occult had been involved.

5

Explosive Forces

The British Secret Service had a great tradition. Germany possessed nothing comparable to it. Therefore each success meant the building up of such a tradition and required even greater determination. The traitors who would stab Germany in the back during this most decisive struggle must be ruthlessly destroyed.

Adolf Hitler to Walter Schellenberg, immediately after the
Venlo Incident

The explosion, when it came, was unexpected and devastating.

There was an almighty flash, a deafening blast of noise and debris that killed and maimed several people. In the immediate confusion there was little sense of what had actually happened. But why was already obvious to the people who had congregated at the Bürgerbräukeller in Munich, sixteen years after the Führer had attempted to launch his ultimately abortive putsch. Now, it was aimed to kill both the leader and the most potent shrine to his remarkable rise.

Two months after the outbreak of war, Adolf Hitler's visit to the cavernous beer hall was an immutable fixture in the Nazi calendar. The Führer visited Munich on Wednesday, 8 November 1939, partly to see Unity Mitford recovering from a suicide attempt, but mainly to visit the spiritual home of his struggles which, in one estimation, eventually 'put the ertswhile denizens of the Munich beer cellar in the corridors of power in the Wilhelmstrasse'. That same Wednesday evening he would join 'the old fighters' where he had originally declared that he would save the German people, and, as ever, Adolf Hitler would not disappoint.

Even by his own standards, the Führer was in a belligerent mood.

Watched from the front row by most of the golden pheasants, he used the occasion to crow about the superiority of German culture. 'I believe that a single German, let us say Beethoven, achieved more in the realm of music than all Englishmen of the past and present together,' he began. For the next hour, his words rose to a screaming crescendo somewhere between ham and histrionics, concluding with a paean to the undying spirit of the fighters themselves. 'I cannot end this evening without, as always, thanking you for your loyal following through these long years!' he screamed.

And then, to riotous applause, he left the stage and departed from the hall early. Along with his entourage and local party faithful, he headed back to Berlin via train. Only bar staff and the musicians who had played the tunes that accompanied his entrance were left clearing up. Thirteen minutes later, there was an almighty flash, a fearful explosion of dust and debris which followed the collapse of the ceiling, and a gallery – under which Adolf Hitler had been standing – then crashed to the floor. Windows shattered, woodwork splintered and all exit doors were blown out.

Eight people – including a waitress – were killed instantly. Amongst the cries and screams, many more were injured. But, more significantly for this narrative, the intended target of the explosion came to believe – expertly stoked by Josef Goebbels and his propagandists – that his escape was thanks to divine providence. The story got stranger still when it became inextricably linked to two of the Nazi regime's other supposed obsessions: the occult and the supposedly supernatural powers of the British Secret Service, culminating a day later with a sting operation on MI6, which would also have many repercussions on both sides of the fighting and the secret war to come.

The stars, it seemed, had foretold events of great danger.

One strand of this already peculiar story had begun just six days earlier. Events had taken an extraordinary turn when the astrologer Karl Krafft had written to his friend Dr Heinrich Fesel at the Reich Main Security Office (RSHA) in Berlin. Since the outbreak of war, Herr Krafft had been regularly submitting his prognostications to SS headquarters on Prinz Albrechtsrasse. After deciding he didn't want to live in his native Switzerland – not least because of his anti-Semitism – Krafft was soon submitting papers on the blitzkrieg, the situation in Poland and the possibilities of invading the West. All were politely ignored but in this particular missive, however, he predicted something remarkable. *Der Führer*, Krafft predicted, would shortly be in danger from 'an attempt of assassination by the use of explosive material between 7–10 November'.

By the time the letter – dated the previous Thursday, 2 November 1939 – arrived in Berlin, plans were well afoot for Adolf Hitler's visit to Munich. There, at the Bürgerbraükeller, the Führer would address the local party on the anniversary of the putsch, about which a previous astrologer had made so much capital in the early days. As such, his visit was one of the few occasions when the Führer's movements could be predicted. What nobody could foresee were the actions – less still, the motivations – of a kind of über-Führer, someone who was adrift and bore massive grudges, who in one assessment had 'an abnormal need for recognition and acknowledgement which was reinforced by a thirst for vengeance for the alleged injustice which had been done to his brother'.

There is a certain irony that the person who planted the explosives – in a sense, a radicalised but hardly suicide bomber – had succumbed to an almost Freudian desire to destroy the Führer (Sigmund Freud himself had been forced to leave his native Germany thanks to Nazi persecution). According to reports at the time, Georg Elser would have made an ideal patient in a psychiatric ward. Or so Dr Goebbels' propagandists declared. Small, pale-faced with long hair, even Adolf Hitler later commented kindly on his 'intelligent eyes, high forehead and determined expression'. Significantly, Elser was a skilled artisan, a worker who many assumed would normally have been attracted to the Nazi Party. It was always thought that alienation had pushed him over the edge thanks to the repeated harangues from his overbearing father. As the historian Roger Moorhouse has written, in the unfortunate Georg Elser's mind the kind of people who were attracted to Nazism 'perhaps reminded him of the loud-mouthed bombast of his drunken father'.

Yet for all the portrayal of a misfit, Elser had a girlfriend who knew nothing of his plans. Born in 1903, Elser was never politically involved, rarely read newspapers and was the kind of introspective loner who few could imagine showing astonishing courage. He only ever joined the Red Front Fighters' League – streetfighters who enjoyed a good brawl with the brownshirts – to play in their brass band.

Yet in so many ways, Georg Elser was an enigma.

He became a cabinetmaker, a job at which he excelled. Yet he also remained an itinerant and, almost inevitably, during the economic woes of the early thirties, had to return home as he ran out of money. Soon believing that only communism would ever look after workers like himself, Elser turned against the Führer when trade unions were banned and wages frozen. Fat cats were milking the system. So when a Nazi parade traipsed along a route where he was standing in his home town, he made a point of not saluting. When a colleague suggested he perhaps should, Elser's reply was illuminating.

'You can kiss my arse,' the carpenter declared.

In the aftermath of the Bürgerbraükeller explosion, the Munich police were astonished to discover he had taken a year to meticulously plot, plan and execute the assassination attempt. Georg Elser stole gunpowder from an armament factory where he worked. He also acquired some more from temporary employment in a quarry, along with explosives and a detonator. He experimented far from prying eyes and, after a little research, realised where the kill should take place.

It was a pre-war version of *The Day of the Jackal* – or, at least, *Rogue Male*, then published to great acclaim about the killing of an (unnamed) dictator.

The Führer would never miss the opportunity to rouse with his rabble, swap stories and let them get blind drunk. So Elser made his way to the Bürgerbraükeller and started taking measurements and weighing up where best to place his bomb. The ideal detonation point, he worked out, would be behind the dais where Adolf Hitler would give his speech. There he had noticed the thick stone pillar which acted as the supporting structure for the upper gallery ran all the way around the wall and above the stage. It would be an ideal place to cause maximum destruction. The gallery would be forced to the ground, killing anybody who was unfortunately underneath.

Throughout the summer of 1939, Elser refined his work. Though he kept quiet about his plans, his characteristic devotion in collecting all the disparate parts needed to assemble a time bomb attracted attention. Another colleague became intrigued by some of his tinkering. One day, noting him messing with an alarm clock, he wondered if it was going to be used in activating a light to speed up his getting up in the pre-dawn quiet.

'Yes,' Elser replied, 'something like that.'

That August he travelled to Munich, where he obtained work as a carpenter and was employed to help renovate the beer hall for over a month. Returning to the Bürgerbraükeller each night at nine o'clock, he took his evening meal in the bar, then sneaked up to the gallery, hiding in a storeroom and waited for the place to close. When the staff had finished up for the evening, he started to assemble the bomb and hid it within the supporting column by the dais. In the quiet and gloom he would work by flashlight. He needed to excavate a cavity – which he lined with cork – in which to hide the bomb.

Georg Elser could hardly miss the fact that the pillar had been clad in wood. As a result, he had to fashion a secret door in the panelling which would not be noticeable. Then, eventually, when he was ready to loosen mortar, he prised out bricks and made sure no debris was left by use of a cloth sack. The beer hall was indeed cavernous: an expansive space which could hold up to 3,000 drunken revellers. As a result, every hammer blow 'echoed like a gunshot', writes Roger Moorhouse, 'and to escape detection, he had to time his blows to coincide with external sounds, such as the passing of a tram or the automatic flush of the toilets.'

Each morning he would leave via a side exit. One day, Elser was nearly caught when a waiter found him inside the building. He blithely told him he was an early customer, ordered a coffee and drank it in the garden.

Alarm clocks would be the key. Elser realised he would need a timer to allow him plenty of time to set the bomb and leave. So he created his own clock mechanism with extra cogs and levers: he also added a second timer as a failsafe. The clock could run for six days before triggering the explosion. A system of sprung weights would detonate a lone rifle round embedded inside the explosive. He placed both in a box to muffle their ticking. He added a sheet of tin plate in front of them to absorb any telltale sound of hollowness should anyone tap the wall.

Two months after starting work, he was ready. After setting the alarm and placing the bomb inside the false door, Georg Elser left the empty bar with the bomb in its place, on the same day that Karl Krafft had written his warning, Thursday the 2nd. Without his ever knowing it, fate – and what has been termed 'perhaps the most disastrous covert operation in the history of British intelligence' – were racing together to collide in a surprising denouement.

Venlo is an otherwise bucolic border town nestling in the south eastern border of Holland with Germany, just an hour's drive from nearby Düsseldorf. It was here at the start of November 1939 that the two most senior secret service men on the continent came to meet emissaries of the gathering conspiracy against the Führer. They had already met a pair of representatives of the German General Staff, and now the two MI6 officers were to meet the mysterious general behind the *Schwarze Kapelle*, the so-called German resistance.

The two British agents, sipping coffee in the Café Bacchus, were 'both slightly parodying what they purported to be', one contemporary would write, 'with monocle, trimmed grey moustache, club tie, touch of the Raj, whence in fact they came'. Ironically, they didn't particularly care for each other. Captain Sigismund Payne Best was a larger-than-life character, who always wore spats and a monocle, whom another MI6 colleague later termed 'an ostentatious ass blown up with self-importance'.

The other MI6 man, Richard Stevens, was a former Indian Army Intelligence officer who later claimed he was never ideal for the work he was doing. He was quite happy to confess that he was out of his depth, for he had 'never been a spy, much less a spymaster'. A brilliant linguist and excellent raconteur, Stevens was nevertheless ambitious and saw the meeting in Venlo as a way of ending the war before it started.

As befitted someone who had been personally recruited by Mansfield Cumming, Best was something of a scoundrel in the mould of the old man who had also married well (the daughter of a Dutch general). Stevens had only recently arrived as passport control officer: he had been briefed before he left that Best was something of a ne'er-do-well who worked for the Z Network, the 'other' side of the secret service. So the dual MI6 networks, supposedly operating independently, were now aware of each other's representatives in The Hague. Worse, they were working together.

It was a recipe for disaster.

A few days before, their German informants had told them at a meeting in Amsterdam that units of the Wehrmacht would be more likely to resist Hitler if an invasion of France was thwarted. All in all, this preliminary exchange had gone so well that their next meeting in Venlo would see the participation of the Army general behind the conspiracy.

Only one minor mystery remained from their previous encounter.

'Tell me,' Best had asked of his friendly contact, 'do you always wear a monocle?'

'You know,' the German replied with a perfectly straight face, 'I've been meaning to ask you the same question.'

Without their ever realising it, Best and Stevens had actually been talking to a rising star of the SS, Walter Schellenberg, later chief of the foreign intelligence service of the *Sicherheitsdienst*. Then working as head of the group defending the Reich against foreign espionage, as 'Major Schammel' he had been quietly pulling strings behind their back. Aware of the considerable anti-Nazi sentiment within the Abwehr, Schellenberg had brilliantly played upon wishful thinking in both Berlin and London.

Then in his late 20s, Schellenberg was the coming man of the Nazi espionage world. Recruited after graduation from law school by Reinhard Heydrich, the younger man would become close to his chief – and even closer to his boss's wife, Lena. Schellenberg was pliable and persuasive, traits noted from his time at university onwards. Never a brawler, many brown-shirts considered him effete: but in his own mind, he set great store by nuance. 'He believed not in force, nor in nonsense, but in subtlety,' considered one underling, 'and he believed he was subtle.'

In the words of another later assessment, Schellenberg was nothing less than 'a blue-eyed boy'. After linking his star to Heydrich, he had rapidly ascended the hierarchy of the SS in a rise several termed meteoric. A fellow SS myrmidon, Wilhelm Höttl, later told Allied interrogators that Heydrich 'soon accepted Schellenberg into his inner circle, in order, as he put it, "to train the youngster himself"'.

With a face scarred by duelling scars, the two often fenced and socialised together. Schellenberg often had to endure another form of fencing as he was hardly immune from Heydrich's Machiavellian posturing. Indeed, Schellenberg would later record that his mentor perennially engaged in what he termed 'a sort of cat-and-mouse game, played in terms of trickery and deception'.

What really does seem like a tale from a bad thriller actually had taken place a couple of years earlier. Walter Schellenberg had spent a night drinking and whoring in the company of Heydrich and Heinrich Müller, head of the Gestapo (a lugubrious detective of the plodding variety who, in keeping with the pretensions of a comic book villain, actually kept a machine gun hidden in his desk). Far into the night, Heydrich suddenly wanted to know the truth: what was the basis of Schellenberg's relationship with his wife?

He protested his innocence. Heydrich smiled and pointed at Schellenberg's drink. If it tasted bitter, that was because it contained poison. Only if Heydrich was satisfied with the answer would Schellenberg be given the antidote. He was and, no doubt due to such bizarre incidents, the younger man soon suffered a breakdown thanks to nervous exhaustion. Ironically, thanks to his overwork, Schellenberg's own marriage failed' and, for obvious reasons, he stopped seeing Frau Heydrich apart from on formal occasions.

Somehow, he survived to not just live another day but also remarry someone whose mother's sister was married to a Jew, a fact that Reinhard

Heydrich was sure to hold over Walter Schellenberg. With that, his boss seemed happy and allowed his protegé to prosper in the dark and dangerous currents within the intelligence apparatus of Nazi Germany. Schellenberg soon found he had a natural aptitude for espionage and intrigue.

He later wrote to Heydrich:

> In Secret Service work, one must never be rash. The careful selection and developing of above-average collaborators is decisive. In order to work in a foreign country they must be virtually natives, and must acquire a 'valid' profession unless there is some other natural explanation for their presence in the country in question.

Given his starring role in what was about to unfold on the Dutch border, it was something the British secret service operators he was about to meet should have taken to heart. What really happened at Venlo was more cock-up than conspiracy, an event which showed, in one assessment, 'that fatuous over-confidence in British superiority which was endemic on other parts of the imperial structure at the time'.

Georg Elser himself did not return to the Munich Bürgerbraükeller for another five days. On Tuesday, 7 November, he put the final touches to his mechanism. With the ceremony only a day away, he wanted to make sure that his bomb would actually work. At dawn on the Wednesday – the day of the visit by the Führer – Elser then set the bomb, replaced the false cladding and pressed his ears to the pillar make sure the bomb was still working. A faint ticking was discernible only to someone who knew there was a bomb there. Security was in the hands of a corpulent, corrupt former nightclub bouncer who indolently did very little and would hardly have even noticed the ticking.

All was set – literally – in the quiet of the beer hall.

When Hitler claimed he had the luck of the devil, he wasn't far wrong.

Heavy fog had pressed down all night and the golden pheasants had decided to take the train back to Berlin rather than fly. Had Georg Elser read the newspapers he would have learned that because of the expected bad weather, the Führer had cancelled his speech, then reinstated it – but then, to make the train, decided to start half an hour earlier. In the event, he finished thirteen minutes earlier than Elser had anticipated.[2]

The Führer's entourage rushed out so quickly that one waitress was amazed at the large, unpaid bar bill they had run up – though not quite as stunned as when she was thrown the length of the hall and through a doorway when the bomb exploded. Everyone else who happened to be on the stage of the Bürgerbräukeller when the supporting column – which had been draped with a vast swastika – crashed down on them was killed. Sixty-three others had to be helped out, and many of the victims of the blast who survived were certain that they had been bombed from above.

Around this same time, Georg Elser had taken a ferry across the lake to Constance, for Switzerland was his ultimate destination. Elser had reconnoitred the border the year before but now, aware that the bomb was about to explode, he was horrified to find things had changed dramatically.

Security at the border was intense. A war was on.

Guards and fencing were everywhere. Fairly quickly, his nervous pacing as he looked for somewhere to cross the border meant that he was picked up by a couple of patrol guards. Accompanying them to their post – Elser claimed he was looking for a friend – he was searched as a matter of routine. Coming as it did after the news of the assassination attempt had broken, even the most dim-witted of guards would have found a postcard of the Bürgerbräukeller and a Communist Party badge of interest. Even more incriminating were pliers to cut the border fence and a drawing of the design of the bomb, possibly to ingratiate himself to anti-Nazi elements across the Swiss border.

Georg Elser was handed over to the Gestapo. Word spread, by telephone and teletype, throughout the Third Reich.

It is doubtful whether Schellenberg's own cat-and-mouse game with the MI6 men would have reached such a swiftly executed climax were it not for that same explosion. Even though the Führer survived, the blast was not confined to the hall. 'There is no doubt that the British Secret Service is behind it all,' Heinrich Himmler told Schellenberg in an early morning telephone call the next day. '[The Führer] now says – and this is an order – when you meet the British agents for your conference tomorrow, you are to arrest them immediately and bring them to Germany.'

That same morning, Captain Best had fleetingly glanced at a 'stop press' item concerning the Munich bomb. 'Very curious,' he would later write, 'and I wondered whether this attempt had anything to do with our people and, if not, what effect it would have on their plans.'

Astrological significance or not, the Venlo meeting went ahead the next morning, Thursday, 9 November 1939. Exactly on time, Schellenberg and Alfred Naujocks (whom the former termed 'very shrewd'), an SS man posing as a fellow conspirator, made their way across the Dutch border to the Café Bacchus. Along with another seven intelligence staff, they had travelled in civilian clothes and made their way from Düsseldorf the day before.

When their blue Buick stopped in front of the MI6 men, three black Mercedes suddenly smashed through the border post. Shots were fired and, within seconds, Stevens and Best's Dutch liaison officer was shot dead when he went for his gun.

Only too well aware of what was happening, Stevens shouted: 'Our number is up, Best.' In the blink of an eye, the two MI6 men were hand-cuffed, kidnapped by the SS and soon found themselves on the front cover of German newspapers, having confessed to the crime of attempting to kill the Führer the night before by setting off the bomb in the Bürgerbraükeller.

British newspapers, too, were up in arms. Terming it 'the impudent and brutal kidnapping incident at Venlo', *The Times* subsequently noted that the juxtaposition of the two MI6 men was 'so placed as to suggest to uncritical readers that the two Englishmen are on a par with the hapless Elser in the crime'. The same newspaper had also noted that what the Germans called a British 'terror centre' in The Hague had been uncovered by the SS – in truth, both the MI6 men had been shadowed and their offices monitored.

By sunset, the two Britons had been spirited away to the basement of SS Headquarters on Berlin's Prinz Albrechtstrasse. Walter Schellenberg and all the others who had helped in the kidnapping were handed Iron Crosses by an appreciative Führer in person. To begin with, Best and Stevens were treated well, separated and occasionally saw each other on their way to the exercise yard. The mood changed when a young and 'resplendent officer' – whom Best recognised from photographs – came into his cell.

'So far, you have been treated as an officer and a gentleman,' Reinhard Heydrich imperiously declared. 'But don't think that this will go on if you don't behave better than you have done. You have two hours left in which to confess everything.'

When Heydrich threatened him with torture courtesy of the Gestapo, Best turned to his normally friendly German liaison officer.

'Who is this excitable young officer?' he asked.

At this point, Heydrich was consumed by histrionic fury and started shouting at the Briton at close range, spraying him in saliva. By comparison, all the others – including 'Gestapo' Müller – treated the two Britons with punctilious courtesy. Eventually, Best and Stevens were transported to Sachsenhausen Concentration Camp, where they were joined in early 1941 by Georg Elser, with whose name they would be forever associated.

In time, Elser told the camp guards that Best had paid him 40,000 Swiss Francs to do the bombing, although they didn't seem to believe him. Both bomber and secret service man later exchanged letters and became only too aware that another far more pervasive myth had sprang up: that Venlo was all a diabolical plot which had been orchestrated by sinister occult influences.

It was obvious where this rumour came from.

From his own precarious perch within RSHA Headquarters, Dr Heinrich Fesel was terrified after the explosion in Munich. Understandably, he had taken care to hide Karl Krafft's letter, pretending that he had never received it. Characteristically, the Swiss-born astrologer would not let matters lie. The same day as the Venlo incident, Krafft dispatched a telegram to Rudolf Hess at the Chancellery, which proclaimed that Adolf Hitler was still in danger.

Fesel soon had no option but to produce the original letter, which was shown to the Führer himself. Not surprisingly, Krafft quickly became the subject of a Gestapo investigation, was arrested and brought to the very same prison where the actual perpetrator of the attempt on Hitler's life (Elser) and its supposed architects (Best and Stevens) were also incarcerated.

Karl Krafft somehow managed to persuade the Gestapo he was on their side and that, under some conditions, astrology could indeed become a great tool. After all, hadn't he predicted that the great leader was in danger? When it became abundantly clear that Krafft wasn't remotely party to the plot, the astrologer was released to work for the Propaganda Ministry. His letter of warning certainly gave him the very notoriety he craved.

'This is the man who accurately predicted the attempt on the Führer's life!' exclaimed one high-up on meeting him. But in Nazi Germany such infamy worked in other, invariably malign ways. Unbeknownst to him at the time, Josef Goebbels had a plan for Karl Krafft that would bring to life yet another curious mystery, about which much myth has been spun in the years since the war – what is usually known as the Tilea affair, supposedly involving hidden knowledge and intelligence shenanigans which have yet to be resolved completely.

Momentous events in history invariably require momentous explanations.

Such a rationalisation satisfies some sort of psychological need for many people. Perhaps that explains the accumulation of mysteries since the deaths of JFK and Princess Diana. Adolf Hitler was hardly immune. When the Führer – who demanded daily briefings about the ongoing investigation – was handed the file of the Gestapo investigation of Georg Elser, he was stunned.

'What idiot conducted this investigation?' he asked.

The reasons were simple: why was there no conspiracy? There had to be something more behind such a momentous occurrence. Yet Georg Elser was clearly a solitary animal. In truth, he was one of those solid working men who formed the core membership of the Nazi Party. Such upright citizens were not perceived as a threat and it made no sense to the golden pheasants that Elser was – as would be later said of Lee Harvey Oswald – a lone nut.

Foreign or enemy involvement was taken as a given. After all, as the bomb ticked away in silence at the beer hall, Adolf Hitler had railed against the British and their treachery. Here was the ultimate proof of his omniscience. In the immediate aftermath came the curious concatenation of themes which run through this narrative, for as Roger Moorhouse has amusingly written, that same first winter of war 'the 'perfidious English' were portrayed as being behind every 'kitten stuck up a tree' in Nazi Germany.

When Walter Schellenberg returned to Berlin that same evening of the Venlo incident – just twenty-four hours after the explosion in Munich – he found the RSHA headquarters 'like a hornet's nest into which someone had poked a stick'. The Gestapo soon got the unpalatable truth out of Georg Elser. Beatings and torture – which included the insertion of metal rods under his fingernails and being fed excessively salty herrings – culminated in a personal kicking and whipping by Heinrich Himmler.

Yet the carpenter still stuck to his story that he had acted alone.

In Walter Schellenberg's own account, a complete replica of his carpenter's workshop was later placed at Elser's disposal while he was in captivity. He was allowed to make a complete reconstruction of the bomb and the wooden pillar.

But that still wasn't enough.

'I want you to use every possible means to induce this criminal to talk,' the Führer said to Heydrich. 'Use hypnosis, give him drugs – everything that modern science has developed in this direction. I've got to know who the instigators are, who stands behind this thing.' According to Schellenberg, four of 'the best hypnotists' in Germany attempted to hypnotise the carpenter. 'Only one of them succeeded,' he noted, 'but even under hypnosis, Elser gave exactly the same testimony as before.'

Though Schellenberg thought connecting the events with the two MI6 men was ridiculous, that soon became the official party line. In the hands of the propaganda machine, the supposed involvement of the British skilfully inflamed the prejudices and excitements of the *Deutsches Volk*. Divine providence – supported by telegrams of support from the Pope and services of thanksgiving in German churches of many denominations – had saved the Führer.

And that was what Adolf Hitler had started to believe himself.

'I had the most extraordinary feeling,' he later told his personal photographer, 'and I don't know myself how or why – but I felt compelled to leave the cellar just as quickly as I could'. His messianic fervour now tipped into the further reaches of megalomania, but quietly, behind the scenes, the industrious Heydrich would reassess security measures: the Führer would never come so close to death again from a random act by a member of the public. All future attempts on his life would come from close associates, all the more remarkable for having fomented within a growing conspiracy in which members of the Abwehr figured highly.

So far as the real life British secret service was concerned, when the news of the Venlo incident came into Broadway Buildings, in one account, C was ashen-faced.

'What the devil are we going to do now?' Sir Stewart Menzies exclaimed.

The capture of Best and Stevens would colour Whitehall's dealings with the various German resistance organisations in the years to come. It hardly helped that the new C had believed – and continued to do so – that Stevens and Best's negotiations had been genuine. Coming directly after Menzies had assumed acting custodianship of the Secret Intelligence Service – the previous Saturday, 4 November – it severely limited the new C's own room for manoeuvre. A Cassandra-like chorus started up as soon as it was clear what had happened. 'Every sort of intrigue is going on by those who want to take over the organisation,' Menzies lamented to an MI5 colleague. 'Criticisms are being made from every quarter by ignorant people.'

Like the Abwehr at the time of Canaris's appointment, the Royal Navy did not want any other service putting its own man in place. The two previous Cs had been admirals and there were those who wanted to recruit another naval man.

Foremost among them was the First Sea Lord himself.

'According to custom,' Winston Churchill had minuted, 'his appointment should fall to a naval officer.' As a direct consequence, Admiral John Godfrey had been proposed rather than Colonel Menzies, whom Churchill had happily endorsed despite their sometimes rocky dealings. There was a wide-spread perception that Menzies was a higher Tory better suited to hunting, shooting, fishing or, at the very least, propping up the bar of White's Club – in one estimation, within the service, he behaved as 'a selfish feudal land-lord, living comfortably at court on income from serfs and lands that he had never visited'.

Sir Stewart himself was only too well aware that his appointment – con-firmed at the end of the month – was controversial. As a result, it made him act with uncharacteristic caution, making many of the criticisms almost self-fulfilling. There were those who felt he was an Edwardian anachronism. Yet as his later wartime assistant Robert Cecil pointed out, in the run-up to war there had been little change in the way spying was carried out. '[I] nvisible inks and false beards were still standard issue,' he noted.

Given that the war would usher in immense technological change, others felt that some sort of intellectual giant – or at least a technocrat – would be better suited to leading the secret service. 'But this is not the attitude of those who worked with him in the stress of war,' Cecil wrote, suggesting that it was essential to have a man of integrity and cool courage. 'Menzies was the right man in the right place at the right time,' he concluded, and for all his faults, the new C was the only service chief to remain in post by the end of the fighting in 1945.

In the years since the Bürgerbraükeller explosion, any number of weird and wonderful myths and rumours have been put forward for its cause. As with all conspiracy theories, they have their basis with that hardiest of perennials: that a lone figure could never have been equal to the task. Payne Best, also at Sachsenhausen, claimed to have heard that Elser had been removed from Dachau to place the bomb, while other variations suggest similar complicity. Pastor Niemoller heard that Elser was an SS sergeant who had been put up to it by Adolf Hitler himself.

In Best's post-war memoirs, the MI6 man tells an odd story about having dealt with an astrologer, whom he does not identify, some time before the explosion. Somehow, the Gestapo had found out. Why, one interrogator in Prinz Albrechtstrasse wanted to know, had the Briton told this seer 'not to return to Germany until after the change of the Moon'? As Best later wrote, he had vaguely recalled it was a spot of leg-pulling.

During the subsequent investigation, Heinrich Himmler himself summoned a Viennese seer who underwent a trance to determine the identity of the potential assassin. Both Müller and Artur Nebe, chief of the criminal police, watched the medium writhe on a sofa. Nebe termed Himmler 'incurably credulous', though nothing further was revealed.

Within the Abwehr resistance it was felt that Heydrich had put Elser up to it; that was why there was never a formal trial. Another important player developed his own personal view which is, to say the least, surprising. 'Schellenberg puts forwards the suggestion that the Munich attempt was deliberately staged and designed to establish Hitler's popularity beyond question, at this early stage of the war,' Allied investigators later determined. In a post-war interrogation, the counter-intelligence chief was relieved that both Best and Stevens were still alive, fearful that he might be implicated in war crimes had they been killed. '[Schellenberg] claims that it was he who saved the lives of both Englishmen,' a summary from MI5 notes. Unarmed, he had kept in the background while the gun battle raged, terming the subsequent propaganda exploitation as 'ridiculous' with its linking to the Bürgerbraükeller explosion.

In reality, both events hardly derailed his career. Walter Schellenberg's general urbanity meant that unlike many of his fellow officers, as David Kahn has written, he 'could lunch smoothly with foreigners and befriend young officials in the Foreign Office and Propaganda Ministry'. Soon he would be attracting jealousy and the spite of others who wanted him to fail.

Intriguingly, in later years, when Walter Schellenberg was asked about the difference between British and German espionage, his response to a fellow SS official was equally revealing. In Britain, espionage was regarded as an occupation for 'gentlemen of high social standing', whereas in Germany 'the worst and most corrupt elements are recruited as agents'. This, Schellenberg said, was a deliberate policy of Admiral Canaris. At the time, as he tried to navigate the dangerous shoals of intrigue, Schellenberg took care to call the admiral Germany's greatest spy and, when further prompted, that Wilhelm Canaris 'was an extremely shrewd man who could be trusted in any direction'.

The first that the canny Abwehr chief heard of the Venlo incident was two days after the explosion on Friday, 10 November. On the Saturday, Canaris called his Dutch experts together in Düsseldorf. 'What are your friends Stevens and Best up to these days?' he asked Richard Protze, an old crony from the Great War who now worked in Abwehr counter-intelligence.

'They are under constant observation, Herr Admiral,' he lied.

Canaris saw through that.

'At this very moment, they're both in Berlin, closeted with the Gestapo at Prinz Albrechtstrasse.'

It was, the admiral said, all Heydrich's doing and, in the recollection of a secretary, left them in no doubt that they should be wary of dealing with Schellenberg.

In several accounts, Canaris was disturbed by the Venlo incident. Aware that the Gestapo might indeed find links with the German resistance, his repeated requests for information about the interrogation were turned down. Quite why the SD did not make greater capital remains unknown, with Heydrich referring to Canaris at one point as 'an old fox with whom one has to be on the watch'.

It was around this time that the wily spymaster's own character changed as he became only too well aware of the true nature of the Nazi regime. 'For though he detested Hitler, he loved Germany,' notes David Kahn. 'Working for Germany, however meant furthering the Führer.' This growing dilemma caused anguish, transforming Wilhelm Canaris's sociable, affable exterior into a depressive wreck. 'I have just seen a madman,' he reportedly said to a colleague after one meeting with the Führer. As a result, the admiral would escape – both physically and psychologically – by leaving the hornet's nest of Berlin and travel, most often, as we will see, to Spain. To some, these journeys were akin to those of Odysseus, but as several people have pointed out, the Abwehr chief was more like another figure from literature. Wilhelm Canaris was the Hamlet of conservative Germany, not only fomenting anti-Nazi sentiments but actively encouraging opposition while at the apex of the Führer's employ.

Much of the enduring enigma of Wilhelm Canaris coalesces around the murky yet growing anti-Hitler sentiment within the Abwehr and Canaris's involvement – however tenuous – opening conduits to other secret agencies, particularly the British Secret Intelligence Service. Yet too much can be read into these various approaches. With the Third Reich triumphant, there would be little public support: and thanks to the Venlo incident, the British treated all subsequent approaches with severe caution.

Several of Canaris's underlings also took care to reiterate his reticence at conspiracy and how he recoiled from outright treachery. Yet he allowed his deputies to organise and strengthen anti-Hitler sentiments under cover of the Abwehr's secret activities (both would eventually be arrested by the Gestapo). His executive officer, Erwin Lahousen, would refer to his approach as 'fabulous, tantalizing and sometimes incomprehensible'. When Lahousen joined the Abwehr, Canaris specifically asked him not to bring in any of his 'damned' Nazis with him (as he, like many of the true converts to Nazism, were Austrian). 'I don't want any of these swine – or at least, as few of them as possible in the Abwehr,' Canaris said.

Lahousen, in his post-war testimony at Nuremberg, noted that Canaris 'hated violence as such and therefore hated and abominated war, Hitler, his system and particularly his methods'. On this, Canaris was unequivocal. 'War means a catastrophe far greater and beyond comprehension for Germany and all material in the event of this Nazi system,' he said in the hearing of his executive officer.

Ultimately, blood was thicker than water. Wilhelm Canaris's nephew, SS Colonel Constantin Canaris, told interrogators after the war that his uncle 'was working against Hitler since the beginning of the war: he intended to do all he could to stir up trouble against him and undermine his influence'.

By the end of the month it was reported in newspapers around the world that Georg Elser had been executed. He wasn't. Though treated well at first – after all, a show trial would have had him as a star witness against British politicians in the event of a German invasion – the carpenter effectively disappeared from view. Amazing as it may seem to posterity, it was as late as April 1945 that Georg Elser was taken from his cell and shot in the head. A week later, his death was reported in Germany as due to an air raid.

Why, many have wondered, did vengeance come so late?

In the last days of the Third Reich, the Führer – consumed by the furies of his own making – made sure all those who had attempted to destroy him were themselves avenged. Perhaps the simplest explanation comes from Oliver Hirschbiegel, the director of the recently released drama about the events, *Thirteen Minutes*. When publicising the film in the summer of 2015, he said:

The Third Reich is the worst example of how methodical the German people are. If we do something we do it thoroughly and never stop. There was no way that the system would go down and the war would be lost with Elser remaining alive. Besides, Hitler took it very personally.

Georg Elser's activities have proved controversial in another arena, not least when, in 2000, an academic at the Hannah Arendt Institute called his actions immoral, starting a fury of criticism for that assertion and the fact they would not have stopped the war in its tracks. 'Elser should have either stayed in the Bürgerbraükeller and warned the innocents or chosen a method that would only have killed Hitler,' said Lothar Fritze.

Even today – as it was in 1939 – the jury is still out on what exactly Georg Elser achieved.

A different duel to the death now played out against the backdrop of the heavenly firmament. The instrument which would, over the first few months of 1940, link both Karl Krafft and Louis de Wohl – an unlikely pairing of the cosmic yin and yang – was an equally improbable, often impetuous and yet eternally jovial figure by the name of Viorel Virgil Tilea. Controversy would eclipse his relatively minor role as the Romanian minister in London. One historian who knew him well has termed him a pallbearer to appeasement. To others, he was a puckish bit part player who, in a peculiar way, helped ensure that European countries went to war[3] by lending his name to what became known as the 'Tilea affair'. Even today, historians debate whether his issue of a warning or ultimatum about German intentions was crying wolf or provocation. Famously, A.J.P. Taylor termed it 'a mystery', others preferring the word 'bombshell' and, in prompting the guarantee to Poland by Britain and France, led another participant to term it 'one of the maddest acts in our history'.

Much of the mystery surrounds the unlikely diplomat himself.

The mercurial Tilea was an unlikely choice as a representative of King Carol's government. A football fan who studied at the London School of Economics – and a key figure in the Anglo Romanian Cultural society – the ambassador was pro-Allied, despite a wife whose utterances were supposedly anti-Semitic.

'He is not really a professional diplomat,' MI5 later recorded, 'but is primarily a businessman.' In March 1939, Tilea had visited the Foreign Office in London with some startling intelligence: that his native government had received an ultimatum from the Germans that they wanted to take over the Romanian economy. It seems reasonably clear that Viorel Tilea's warning was neither a grand conspiracy nor a unilateral ultimatum, as several writers (the Romanian himself among them) have suggested. Over the years, various people claim to have been involved – with a princess who seemed better suited to a drawing room melodrama, broken ciphers, an early morning telephone call and one of Churchill's cronies.[4] All culminated with a meeting with Lord Halifax in March 1939 – after he had seen the Polish, French and Turkish ambassadors – as matters were coming to a head.

Coming three days after the occupation of Prague, there was a great deal at stake. Romania was being forced into a corner, as were most of its neighbours. The Chamberlain government could hardly stand by as country after country fell victim to Hitler's aggression, and so offered a diplomatic bulwark in the form of a guarantee.

When reported as fact in the London press, there were furious denials from Berlin, Bucharest and the Romanian Legation in London. Tilea had, in a later Romanian account, been overzealous. The Propaganda Ministry took up the cudgels and noted that the idea that Romania should only be a supplier to Germany was, as one report had it, 'alleged to have been the invention of Sir Robert Vansittart', a notable hawk who did his best to arrest appeasement. What followed was an international incident which led to trade negotiations and, as Tilea himself put it, 'the signing of the Anglo-Romanian Treaty by which Britain gave a guarantee of sorts' to his country.

But Goebbels' propagandists went further. Tilea's actions were designed, they said in one report, to hold Germany down, to destroy its friendships 'and to hold positions or establish new ones for the war desired by the Jews against the Reich'. And, according to the London correspondent of the *Völkischer Beobachter*, it was an attempt to repeat 'the game the British secret service had played' in May 1938, to claim that Germany had mobilised, yet another attempt to blame things on their favourite bogeyman.

There is a whiff of intelligence intrigue surrounding the Romanian ambassador's activities at the time, with claims that a radio signals unit of the Wehrmacht had been listening in to calls and had broken the ciphers of several Balkan countries. It has also been alleged that Romanian diplomatic bags were being opened. In his memoirs, Tilea says that when he met his staff at the London Embassy, he was shown a safe that could have been broken with a hairpin. 'We must have another one,' he said. 'I have bought a new cipher with me and I do not want it to be broken immediately.'

In fairness, Romania was caught between the German devil and a deep red sea of communist influence. 'One Romanian bird in the hand,' Adolf Hitler later said of Russian claims to the region, 'is worth more than two Russian birds in the bush.'

Mineral reserves, oil and transportation – of materials from Germany to the USSR, which Britain also wanted to stop – all played into the mix. The fate of Romania was, inevitably, linked to its oilfields which, at one point, were even suggested as a target for capture. As an MI6 assessment noted, with complete control over the oil wells, 'we do not think Germany, and less still Germany together with Italy, could obtain enough petroleum to carry on far more than a year'.

But in the first year of the war, British efforts to deprive Germany of Romanian oil continued in the same hopelessly amateurish vein that had been evident in Sweden. Everything Section D touched had turned to disaster. They used King's Messengers to deliver explosives to British Embassies in Eastern Europe, which upset both the Foreign Office mandarins in London and the ambassadors themselves. An initiative to block the Rhine by blowing up oil-carrying barges was thus stopped in its tracks, and things carried on much as before.

When Viorel Tilea had arrived in Britain in January 1939, he lived in great style and comfort in an Oxfordshire mansion. For the rest of his stay, especially when hostilities were declared, he would spend a greater part of his time plotting against the fascist regime which would take over his native country in the autumn of 1940. In a posthumous appreciation of his virtues, one obituarist regarded Viorel Tilea as quixotic, lively and mentally most agile – and a very good friend to the British. That this assessment came from the Earl of Lonsdale speaks volumes, too, of his ability to make friends at the apex of the Establishment. His social circle was wide and another friendship would lead to – so far as British Intelligence was concerned – rather more surreal ramifications.

The Romanian ambassador, though an ardent anglophile, had always been peripatetic. While passing through Switzerland in the spring of 1937, Tilea had met some Swiss Germans who were obviously pro-Nazi. One of them was Karl Krafft, whom the ambassador recalled had 'very good connections in influential circles' despite an obvious flaw. He, like most people, found the astrologer mildly repulsive.

Oddly, Krafft did seem to be aware of some past aspect of Tilea's life which he could not possibly have known about. Mildly intrigued, Tilea met with the astrologer again in Zurich and reluctantly agreed to take part in an astrological experiment.

Characteristically, Karl Krafft used the opportunity to expand some of his stranger theories about racial purity and the inevitable growth of the Third Reich (which had been codified in his masterwork that was nearly ready for publication). Tilea queried such bold assertions but was sufficiently intrigued to leave behind the dates of birth and sample writings of two prominent Romanians.

The ambassador thought nothing more of it.

For the rest of 1938, Tilea and the Swiss astrologer maintained an intermittent correspondence which culminated with a request for more information on the ambassador's background. Karl Krafft dutifully made some predictions – 'out of curiosity' on Tilea's part – about Corneliu Codreanu, the Romanian fascist leader. Krafft predicted that he would be unlucky to survive beyond November 1938 (and he was indeed shot on the last day of that month) as well as that King Carol would suffer a disastrous reverse in September 1940, the date of his eventual abdication.

But what would come to concern the security forces across the fighting came out of the occasional correspondence between these two unlikely characters – the astrologer and ambassador – which would culminate in an even more opaque mystery which one participant has justly referred to it as a 'bizarre incident'. It showed the Nazis would leave no stone unturned in trying to gain any form of advantage. What became known as the 'Tilea letter' – the first ever of its kind in the prosecution of astrological warfare – would convince British Intelligence that not only was Adolf Hitler consulting his own seer, but that his identity was none other than the mildly repulsive Karl Krafft.

Viorel Virgil Tilea was a marked man.

Because he had leaked the German demands to Romania, Tilea had not only been attacked by name in Goebbels' broadcasts, he had soon become an obvious 'person of interest' to the German intelligence services. A far more subtle attack came courtesy of the ambassador asking Karl Krafft for his horoscope to be cast. The Reich Main Security Office now became involved. At the start of 1940, the Swiss astrologer had shown a draft of his astrological study of Viorel Tilea to his sponsors in Prinz Albretchstrasse.

When Krafft went to collect his next paycheck, Dr Fesel pulled him to one side. His forecast, he explained, wasn't sufficiently pro-German. Krafft, true to form, puffed himself up by saying that the contents were a private matter and stormed out of the building.

A number of drafts were then worked on by unknown hands.

At the end of February, a horoscope was finally dispatched to Virgil Tilea with a handwritten note that it had been sent by 'a friend going to Romania'. Agents from the *Sicherheitsdienst* had sent it by diplomatic courier, where it was then mailed from Brasov.

Ambassador Tilea himself happened to be in Bucharest when the letter showed up – his mother had just died – and was astonished. Karl Krafft's letter informed him that he had deliberately been completely left out of the loop by his own government regarding foreign affairs. Both Romania and Germany, the letter suggested, had 'good aspects'.

The Third Reich, Krafft also explained, was on the ascendant, for if a 'totalitarian ruler had good aspects, his whole nation benefited from it'. In his memoirs, the ambassador suggests that Krafft was also trying to get him to resign by predicting Germany's successes. Tilea also suspected he was on the receiving end of some non-too-subtle propaganda and a power play courtesy of German Intelligence.

Around this time, Dr Heinrich Fesel had supposedly invited Karl Krafft on some sort of intelligence mission to the Low Countries. When he had heard of the letter, Tilea seems to have been delighted with the 'cloak and dagger' aspects of the affair. He decided to stay in touch with the astrologer on the 'assumption that Krafft would sooner or later be bound to give himself away'. He had, as the ambassador explained to several people, seen through that one alright, but wondered what might also result.

The fact that Karl Krafft had apparently relocated to Berlin that spring of 1940 confirmed all of Viorel Tilea's suspicions. So far as he was concerned, the truthfulness of Krafft's predictions had been compromised by his proximity to the Führer himself. When a second letter – identical, but which had passed through the German censor – turned up, the Romanian ambassador realised they were trying to crack a nut with a sledgehammer.

'This purposeful duplication of the message confirmed all his previous suspicions,' writes Ellic Howe, the late British propagandist who discussed the matter with Tilea after the war. 'Furthermore, since Krafft must be working for Hitler, it only remained to persuade the British to take the necessary countermeasures.'

And there was no mystery as to who might spearhead such an effort.

Here was Louis de Wohl's moment of glory.

If there was ever going to be any sort of countermeasure to any German astrologer, he should be the one. Yet despite his uncanny ability to land on his feet, the Hungarian astrologer was encountering suspicion in a London that was hardly disposed to mystics or mountebanks, especially those from Eastern Europe. By his own account, de Wohl was 'suspect as a foreigner, while astrology was no better than tea-leaf-reading and crystal gazing"

Once again, Viorel Virgil Tilea would be crucial in getting him taken seriously. Sometime in 1939, the ambassador was introduced to Louis de Wohl via a Romanian banker. Tilea later received a half-hearted endorsement from the astrologer. An MI5 report notes of the astrologer's attitude to his excellency:

> He is a man who expects a quid pro quo for anything that he does, he has excellent manners and in Louis's opinion might be extremely useful provided he is approached in the proper manner. Louis thinks he might be usable at present especially in the United States where the handle 'His Excellency' would count for a lot.

In other words, they were similar peas from a pod, their vanity invariably knowing no bounds. 'Louis describes Tilea as certainly the most trustworthy of all the Romanians he has met,' a military liaison officer noted later that year, 'though this does not necessarily mean a lot.'

The MI5 files show that Viorel Tilea was in some sort of financial straits. According to de Wohl, he had asked for £3,000 – 'a fantastic sum of money to ask for', the Romanian had claimed – to return home. Apparently, the government had sent him £2,000. He used that money to pay off his debts to someone called Levi. A short while later, Tilea dutifully informed de Wohl about Krafft's letter which predicted German victory (in time, de Wohl, too, would create horoscopes for the Romanian ambassador). Tilea took it upon himself to discuss the Krafft business with Sir Orme Sargent, an undersecretary at the Foreign Office. Discreet enquiries were made within Whitehall about countering this use of astrology. Ironically, Sargent reported back that most of the astrologers in the country were rather pessimistic and would not make the best propagandists for the British cause.

'I know an astrologer who is not pessimistic,' Tilea replied. 'His name is Louis de Wohl.'

Like a light – or possibly supernova – flashing on, the Hungarian astrologer realised here was his main chance. If he could make the same calculations as Hitler's astrologers, they could provide great advantages for the British government. This part of the story – which de Wohl repeated and embellished over the years – is confirmed by the records. 'Recently Tilea showed Louis a letter he had received from a Swiss astrologer called KRAFFT,' MI5 noted later that same year of 1940. 'Louis says that Kraft (sic) is one of Hitler's astrological advisers and that the letter contained a great deal of very skilful propaganda.'

Indeed, de Wohl soon became rather adept at spreading rumours that Hitler was under the influence of a mysteriously malign astrologer. This was soon picked up by the press such as, for example, the *Daily Mail*'s Berlin correspondent was reporting that Adolf Hitler was paying 'great attention to the advice of his personal astrologer'. Louis de Wohl made sure that his own special insights would prove to be of great advantage to the British, although nobody, at this stage, could be sure what 'technical' methods would be used by this mythical astrologer (if he indeed existed). In his own mind at least, Louis de Wohl envisaged himself in a *mano à mano* struggle with the Führer's astrologer.

'I realised the danger,' the Hungarian claimed after the war. 'Hitler now had first rate astrological advice. This man Krafft had to be fought.'

From the very beginning, a certain airy wackiness informed the British approach to countering the supposed German obsession with the occult and black magic. Nowhere was it more notable than in the first desperate days of the blitzkrieg against France. In the spring of 1940 came the serious notion of building an apparatus which could project (propaganda) images on clouds over enemy lines. Amazing as it may seem to posterity, both sides then decided to harness the mystical powers of a sixteenth-century mystic as a secret weapon.

Michel Nostradamus and his impenetrable quatrains provide anyone who wants it with the vaguest reading of a future malleable enough to suit their own purposes. Whether it is the rise of Hitler, the assassination of John F. Kennedy or, no doubt, the point at which One Direction will split up, the medieval seer, of Jewish descent and Provencal birth, has cast a spell. 'During his lifetime and afterword, his words have fascinated and flummoxed the West,' writes Stephane Gerson in a recent study. Nostradamiana, as the cognoscenti call it, is an obsession with many curious cheerleaders.

There is something for everyone in the vagueness of his writings. Every generation sees something of relevance. Oddly, most of the true believers in the predictions of Nostradamus always seem to forget that the seer himself thought that most astrologers were incompetent. 'Let the profane and ignorant herd keep away,' he had warned. 'Let all astrologers, idiots and barbarians stay far off.'

And perhaps Karl Krafft should have heeded Nostradamus's own warning.

For him, the Tilea business had been terrifying. Far from being manipulated by unknown spiritual forces, Krafft never really saw what was happening to him. For the next five years of war, he would predict endless victories for the Nazi regime, believing he was inching ever closer to the orbit of his hero – the Führer – to assume pole position: Adolf Hitler's own astrologer. In reality, he became a prisoner trapped in a gilded case of his own stupendous arrogance.

Nostradamus's fellow citizens were equally susceptible to his mysterious quatrains.

In pre-war France, as in Berlin, a rising tide of fortune tellers plied their trade and, as one recent chronicler has noted: 'In the early 1930s, a Parisian could begin his day with an astrological consultation at the Nostradamus Institute, located on the rue de Fauberg Saint-Honore.' After lunch, he could attend a public talk or purchase a magazine devoted to those quatrains. *The collapse of Europe according to Nostradamus's Prophecies* was one of more than twenty books published between 1937 and 1939 as the political situation with Nazi Germany worsened.

When war came, French newspapers were soon reporting that citizens were looking to Nostradamian prophecies for insight. A communist poet, Louis Aragon, later complained that his fellow countrymen were making the seer 'their shadowy, stupefying refuge'. With war looming, government officials asked one particular astrologer called Martin Privat – a journalist who, like Louis de Wohl, found casting horoscopes more profitable – to look into the matter. Monsieur Privat soon published *1940, Year of French Grandeur*, which predicted forthcoming misfortunes for Franco, Stalin and Goebbels. Ultimately, the astrologer claimed, *les français* would prevail. 'The West will not kneel down,' Privat promised. 'France and Great Britain have no reason to worry.'

During the successful invasion of France that May, the German Propaganda Ministry disseminated specially written threatening quatrains which were then dropped via leaflets from low-flying aircraft. The verses suggested that south-east France would not be affected by the carnage, thus encouraging civilian populations to move in that direction. These dozen lines of specially written doggerel were used to seemingly little effect. Ironically, after the occupation of France, the French authorities actually banned Nostradamiana so as not to give offence to the Occupying Powers.

Yet Britain, too, was interested in Nostradamus.

A strange pamphlet, *Nostradamus predicts the course of the war*, would appear a few years later under Sefton Delmer's inspired guidance. The text was ascribed to German academics but came from someone who liked to be seen as a Nostradamian figure, a seer and towering giant of prophecy. The ultimate irony was that this was a future that the author, Louis de Wohl, could never quite envisage.

Nazifying Nostradamus was almost inevitable.

A postal official who claimed to have discovered the 'numerological key' had predicted in the twenties that Nostradamus predicted 'a prophet with a raging head' who would transform the world. In one story that partisans of the occult like to tell, it was Magda Goebbels who woke her husband after being hooked on this same book. Although viewing astrology as some sort of medieval throwback, the Propaganda Minister asked Krafft for help.

Because he had already declared that Nostradamus had predicted that the Third Reich would ultimately be victorious, Karl Krafft was given some latitude by the Gestapo. He could continue publishing on Nostradamus with the understanding that he would not discuss his findings (or astrological predictions) in public. Within a year, Krafft's own *How Nostradamus Perceived The Future of Europe* predicted a collective nervous breakdown in London, world domination for totalitarian states and the reign and glory of Great Germania.

Yet a mental collapse took place somewhat nearer to home. From the start of 1940, Krafft worked with an old colleague who was distinctly frightened by what they were doing. 'During those weeks we both had one foot in a concentration camp,' his friend George Lucht would write. Their every move was watched by the Gestapo, and Lucht, more so than the gullible Krafft, was aware that matters were moving far beyond their control. Within a month, his reluctant colleague wanted to leave because he and Krafft were not getting on – exploiting and perverting Nostradamus was, in Lucht's opinion, shameful. Calling it all a load of nonsense, Lucht left to work in an aircraft factory.

Krafft, indefatigable to the last, continued his work and distributed a limited number of facsimile editions of *Les Prophéties* (a work on Nostradamus which was only ever available to his friends). Yet the RSHA was worried. They wouldn't let his work appear until the end of the year because it appeared to predict an attack on the Low Countries, which was then being planned. And despite later claims of conspiracies involving the manipulation of the French seer's words, it was always limited in scope.

The biggest problem – as with all Nostradamian predictions – was in bending his opaque prognostications into something that fitted contemporaneously. 'What Goebbels called "occultist propaganda" could both deny human powers of decision making and at the same time spur people to action,' notes the academic Stephane Gerson. 'It could provide authority and at the same time discredit.' And in this regard, there was a later irony that, in one account, when newspapers – in Spain, Sweden and Britain – followed up some of the Nazi propaganda by posing the question 'Who is Nostradamus?', the answer was, ironically, suggested to be Adolf Hitler.

And so all the various strange themes in this chapter – astrology, the occult and intelligence would come together – with the desperate situation Great Britain found itself in the early summer of 1940. It would be feared by various arms of British Intelligence that astrology might become a powerful weapon for the less mystical but equally malign purposes of propaganda. This would be the genesis of perhaps the most peculiar efforts ever attempted in the secret war whose protagonist, as we will see, was none other than Louis de Wohl.

This would be one of his greater achievements in working in tandem with British Intelligence, the unlikely genesis of perhaps the most peculiar efforts ever attempted in the secret war. 'Because it is claimed that astrology is an exact science and leads reputable astrologers to the same conclusions,' one wartime report for the normally staid Naval Intelligence Division states, 'it seemed possible to ascertain what advice was, in fact, being offered to Hitler.'

Foremost amongst them: when was the invasion going to land?

6

DESPERATE MEASURES

If we can avoid defeat this summer and stabilise, we still have to find some way of winning the war. We are certainly not going to win the war by offensives in mass and the only way of success is by undermining Germany internally and by action in the occupied territories. German aggression has in fact presented us with an opportunity never before equalled in history for bringing down a great aggressive power by irregular operations, propaganda and subversion enlarging into rebel activities ... Seen in this light, the war may be regarded as an inter-connected series of wars of independence ... It must be recognised as a principle that not only are these activities part of the grand strategy of the war, [but] probably the only hope of winning the war.

Briefing by Director, Military Operations, Sir John Kennedy,
to Chiefs of Staff, 7 June 1940, HS 8/259

The glorious weather that Whitsun (the traditional Christian holiday which fell on the last Sunday of May) was strangely balmy and peaceful that early summer of 1940. Despite the horrifying circumstances of war, most holidaymakers attracted by the traditional seaside delights of Southend looked like they didn't have a care in the world. But two men, one in naval uniform, the other in army fatigues, certainly did. Even the most casual glance would have shown them to be brothers. As they strolled along the seafront deep in conversation, they betrayed none of the suppressed hysteria which had propelled them here.

In Whitehall a letter had arrived, supposedly written by a German agent – all the more authentic, so it was believed, thanks to misspellings and grammatical inaccuracies – which suggested the German attack was imminent. That the blitzkrieg would be unleashed upon the Essex town that was disparaged for its whelks and cheap entertainments was just one of the more bizarre rumours which had gathered like so many distraught seabirds all along the shore on that fine afternoon. Yet the veracity of the warning was vouched for by the Joint Intelligence Committee, where, in the secret world at least, the buck came to a resounding halt.

Which was why Ian and Peter Fleming were there.

Older than his brother by just a year, Peter cast a long shadow in which the younger Ian had grown up. Equally effortlessly charming and confident, they had, as children, fought continually and, though still close in adulthood, were very different. Whereas the younger Ian had been a Sandhurst dropout with a somewhat raffish reputation, Peter Fleming was serious, more handsome and certainly the more accomplished with his bestselling pre-war travelogues. His contemporaries at Eton had considered him the most charismatic man of his generation and, in his long marriage to Celia Johnson (of later *Brief Encounter* fame), by far the more illustrious.

Now the brothers relished any time they could spend in each other's company. 'They were an attractive pair, amusing, good looking, sure of themselves, and devoted to each other,' recorded their good friend Joan Bright. 'In detachment from his surroundings which was part of Peter's character was also present, in a different way, in Ian's.' The invasion, it was confidently expected, would come at one o'clock the next morning. For now, the Fleming brothers encountered a distinctly carefree afternoon. 'Bands played in Palm Court lounges, courting couples strolled along the front, queues stood outside cinemas,' one of them later wrote. 'Phlegm, we felt, was being carried a bit too far.'

If the blitzkrieg was shortly to be unleashed, these two gentlemen – both former *Times* correspondents – would act as official recorders, reporting on what actually happened as opposed to what Josef Goebbels' propagandists would undoubtedly claim. They spent the rest of the evening on the roof of their hotel, alert for any signs of impending enemy activity. Scanning the horizon and the skies, the invasion never came. '[As] the night wore on,' Peter would later write, 'we found it increasingly difficult to take the whole business seriously.'

In this regard, other such rumours were not isolated and it was clear – despite the muddles that were still taking place in the corridors of power with regard to propaganda – that the only way to fight rumour was with counter-rumour. And in this regard, both Fleming brothers would come to play their own unique role in what was sometimes disparagingly called 'attacking Hitler with your mouth'. Within the Naval Intelligence Division, the future father of James Bond had settled on 'Rumour As A Weapon' to give greater prominence to rumours in the media. 'It is submitted that there is no lack of suitable "rumour information": it is an effective "rumour gun" which needs to be devised.' In time, Ian Fleming would liaise with MI6 and the somewhat confused set-up for the prosecution of propaganda. For now, Lieutenant Fleming RNVR was enough of a realist to know that the scope of these activities was small beer.

The same would go for subterfuge, sabotage and guerrilla operations, which as noted before, had been wrapped up with propaganda. Peter, in his guise as Captain R.P. Fleming, had already been recruited to elevate 'special means' into a viable weapon of war. As with the farcical situation concerning propaganda, subversion and sabotage would continue to be mired in personal animosity, duplicity and bureaucratic incompetence for the next few months. Unusual forms of warfare would need to be transformed from a popgun to a howitzer to have any kind of impact, and the Fleming brothers would play a central role in that transformation.

Sometime in the late 1950s, when the James Bond novels were being published to growing acclaim, Columbia Pictures in Hollywood decided to investigate the background of their author. After all, his publishers claimed, he had been a special assistant to the Director of Naval Intelligence. But research threw up only a further puzzle.

'This Fleming seems only to write travel novels,' one of the researchers found.

Right surname, wrong sibling. We must marvel at the way in which they got the Fleming brothers mixed up, but the moguls of Hollywood would have been surprised e'er yet at the achievements of Ian Fleming's elder brother. Superlatives had attached themselves to him throughout his life with the adjectives 'imperturbable' and 'buoyant' most often associated with him.

'Peter Fleming was a very agreeable man,' said one colleague from the early part of the war. 'He had a brilliant brain, was a quick thinker and a wit with a keen sense of humour.' There was a serious side, too, perhaps the result of losing their father during the Great War, which in the way of all older children, propelled Peter to assuming the mantle of responsibility. After going up to Christ Church, Oxford, in the autumn of 1926, he developed a habit that would astound people who met him for the rest of his life. Billowing in his wake was what one colleague memorably called 'an odour reminiscent of motor tyres burning in syrup'. Childhood illness had destroyed his sense of smell so he was often hardly aware of the effect his pipe-smoking ever had on his surroundings.

Like his brother, people always warmed to Peter Fleming.

'Unlike many authors of travel books who turn out to be pale, bespectacled little men,' Dennis Wheatley famously remarked, 'his bronzed tight-skinned face always gave the impression that he had only just returned from an arduous journey across the Mongolian desert or up some little known tributary of the Amazon.'

Southend, then, had hardly been a stretch.

As the author of *Brazilian Journey*, he had written with typical insouciance that 'São Paulo is like Reading, only much farther away'. By the time he and Ian had travelled to Southend at the end of May 1940, Peter Fleming had been effortlessly commissioned into the Grenadier Guards after having worked in that curious, rarefied branch of military intelligence, MI (R). That Whitsun, the Fleming brothers spent a quiet, ultimately pointless evening, enjoying each other's company and catching up on family news. There was a certain symbolism that on the holiday weekend which celebrated the ascension of Jesus into heaven, Peter Fleming, too, had recently returned from the dead.

In recent weeks he had been reported missing after the disastrous Norway campaign, where Captain R.P. Fleming had been the first British serviceman to land in the fjords. Peter subsequently had the equally bizarre experience of reading his own obituary. Swedish newspapers had reported the rumours that he had been killed and, to the chagrin of the family, a flurry of headlines in the London tabloids resulted, along the lines of 'AUTHOR KILLED IN NORWAY'.

Taking it all in his stride with his usual aplomb ('We Flemings are a hard-boiled lot,' he would later say, 'but even so …'), Peter Fleming returned to Scotland and made his way south. 'Hitler had missed the bus in Norway,' was how he wittily recalled it in a later broadcast. 'I had missed the train at Inverness; but it didn't seem to have made much difference to Hitler.'

Norway had been a disaster. The British response to the Norwegian invasion was muddled and the Chamberlain Cabinet was, in one general's later recollection, 'a bewildered flock of sheep'. Worse, its most vociferous hawk – Winston Spencer Churchill – had simply failed to recognise that the Royal Navy was not ready to engage the Germans in a fight. Oddly, on his return to London, Peter Fleming had been treated to a remarkable show from the First Sea Lord, whose own resurrection, politically speaking, would result from the very same disaster of which he had been a key architect.

As the first son of a banking dynasty, it had been expected that Peter Fleming would carry the torch for the family business. But in every sense of the word, the eldest son took a very different route. 'He was the writer in the family,' Ian would later declaim. At Oxford, Peter had been editor of *The Isis* magazine and a member of the Bullingdon Club. He had also trodden the boards, but it was quite some time later that Peter met up with an actress who had just made her stage debut and was already well on her way to stardom. Ironically, they didn't make any impression on each other at that time. But his later marriage to Celia Johnson was very important to him, the rock on which his life was anchored.

Yet Peter Fleming remained peripatetic. After leaving Oxford he travelled across Spain, then to the United States before working at *The Spectator*, where he arranged sabbaticals so that he could go on further adventures. In April 1933, he saw an advert in *The Times* which, as his biographer remarks, was 'just far-fetched enough to appeal to him'. 'Exploring and sporting expedition, under experienced guidance, leaving England June to explore rivers central Brazil,' it began. This strange blandishment led to the book with which he would be forever associated – *Brazilian Adventure* – and which established his name. He also developed a professional proximity to *The Times*, in whose name he travelled around the Far East in the 1930s as a special correspondent, reporting on the fighting between the nationalists and the communists on the Chinese mainland.

He loved China – and adventure. In 1936, he travelled from China to India on foot. That sometimes gruelling trek of 3,500 miles between Peking and Kashmir ('with many dangers, hardships and hold ups' as his entry in the *Dictionary of National Biography* understates it) would lead to his incomparable *News From Tartary*. For the rest of his pre-war career, Peter alternated travelling and writing, both allowing him to chronicle the experience of war, folly and misfortune with characteristic verve and wit. After marrying Celia, he took her with him on his fourth trip East and followed the progress of the Sino–Japanese War in 1938.

This added another important ingredient to his métier: intelligence, especially about the mysterious East, was badly needed. His travels gave him a unique understanding and experience of foreign military powers. Unlike his brother, of whom it was said could suffer anything but discomfort, Peter Fleming could easily adapt to unusual surroundings in the harshest of circumstances. Given his knowledge of exotic and far-flung places, it was almost inevitable that, with the onset of war, Peter Fleming would be called upon for 'special services'.

As with the secret service, other branches of British Intelligence were looking to expand. The War Office, as already noted, was distinguished by having a small, self-contained research department known as Military Intelligence (Research) – MI (R) for short – which, as one who knew its work put it, 'always seemed oddly named for it had been more concerned with operational ideas than research'. Its staff were assiduously combing Army reserve lists for writers, explorers and experts on foreign countries who could be put to better use than just ordinary conscription. Someone of Peter Fleming's calibre would surely have been near the top of anybody's list of potential recruits. Clever, well-travelled and self-confident officers were at a premium, not least, as one MI (R) report noted, 'if war breaks out early'.

So, as Peter Fleming's biographer attests, that same month of August 1939 he was telephoned by a shadowy colonel and asked if he could leave for China straight away. By now MI (R) had started to look at 'what is loosely-termed guerrilla warfare' in central Europe, North Africa and the Far East. As a well-known traveller in Asia, it was no wonder Captain Fleming had already been identified as a possible expert. 'Peter Fleming is remarkable and a useful contributor,' the Deputy Director of Military Intelligence noted in August 1939.

His specialist knowledge, it was explained, meant he could train Chinese insurrectionists against the Japanese. Though busy with his journalism, Peter Fleming swiftly penned a paper for MI (R) innocuously termed 'Notes on the Possibility of British Military Action in China' which, as he noted, 'are based on a fleeting and picaresque experience of the foreign communities in China'.[1]

In an interesting foretaste of his approach to warfare, Captain R.P. Fleming suggested that British officers should not just send advisers but act as insurrectionaries and establish cavalry units to impress the local Chinese. In the event of hostilities, he emphasised, all this disparate attrition activity should be accelerated and intensified. To turn it into an effective weapon of war, what was needed, above all else, was to define its scope – and, of course, finance.

Peter Fleming was preaching to the converted.

Subversive and guerrilla tactics had been used at various times to quell restlessness in the near and far reaches of Empire, particularly in Ireland and the Palestine mandate, with varying degrees of success. Now they would be expanded and built upon. In each territory, there would be preliminary reconnaissance, a mission headquarters and propaganda which 'should be laid on at an early stage'. Even a handful of British officers (on night patrols and raiding parties) would have a considerable impact as guerrilla leaders. Any obstacles, from a logistical and diplomatic point of view, could easily be overcome.

In the end, for reasons which remain unclear, he wasn't posted to the Far East. Peter Fleming would thus spend the rest of the Phoney War in London, continuing his journalism and eventually having to consider some of his guerrilla techniques in more familiar territory.

The issue which had so exercised the First Sea Lord – and would shortly cause embarrassing headlines – was increasingly looking like a busted flush. The fears about Swedish iron ore seemed to have evaporated with the return of spring. At the start of April 1940, newspapers were reporting that exports had been a fraction of what they had been in peacetime. In other words, the essential supplies to feed the German war machine no longer seemed to matter so much.

But Adolf Hitler had thought otherwise.

The Führer would lavish extra special attention on the Norwegian ports and harbours, whose seizure, he believed, was crucial. Capturing Norway would restrict Britain's mercantile fleets to ensure they would not have freedom of the seas. That way, unlike the previous naval engagements in the Great War, the Führer believed he could deny total victory to the Royal Navy.

As a result, the Norwegian port of Narvik would become crucial. As Norway's only all-weather port, it could feed Germany's voracious war machine all year round. So when, on 10 April 1940, the Luftwaffe landed on Norwegian airfields, it was obvious why. It took the Wehrmacht just three days to capture all the country's ports (including Narvik) cities and airfields.

The British response, as Peter Fleming reflected long afterwards, was a mess.

He was hardly alone in being sickened by the chaos and sheer inefficiency. 'The errors were so gross,' he would later lament, 'the muddles so pervasive and the whole affair over so quickly that there weren't really a great deal to be learned from it.' And yet when he arrived back in London, he was treated to a breathtakingly bizarre spectacle, that of the First Sea Lord parading around his inner sanctum at the War Office in his silk dressing gown and about to smoke a cigar.

Peter Fleming asked his lordship if he would mind if he lit his own pipe.

'Yes,' came Winston Churchill's considered reply, 'I bloody well do!'

Captain Fleming was left with the distinct impression that here was someone who could win the war almost single-handedly. Despite pushing for the Norwegian campaign, Winston Churchill survived the political fall-out which subsequently saw the House of Commons in uproar. Parliament's debate over the fiasco in the fjords on 7 and 8 May 1940 was querulous. After a tired and defensive speech by Neville Chamberlain, various speakers heaped scorn on the lacklustre prime minister. Leo Amery would serve the most devastating broadside, ending with a Cromwellian flourish: 'Depart, I say, and let us have done with you. In the name of God, go.'

Two days later, he did, as events accelerated.

On Friday, 10 May 1940, the Germans invaded the Low Countries. That same morning, when Neville Chamberlain called in Winston Churchill and Foreign Secretary Lord Halifax ('that slope-shouldered scarecrow in a derby hat' in Andrew Roberts's pithy phrase) it was clear that his lordship was the prime minister's chosen successor.[2] But Halifax wanted to recuse himself and, as Churchill would note, 'by the time he had finished it was clear that the duty would fall on me'.

Winston Churchill's elevation to the premiership would not be universally applauded, not least by many in the military establishment and the body politic. Everyone, as his private secretary famously remarked, was more than a little frightened of him. 'The mere thought of Churchill as P.M. sends a cold chill down the spines of the staff at Number 10 Downing Street,' Sir John ('Jock') Colville would famously add. 'The country had fallen into the hands of an adventurer.'

Outnumbered, outmanoeuvred and now outflanked, Great Britain would stand alone at this most perilous phase in its history. German victory was yet another foregone assumption. As the Luftwaffe prepared to fight the Royal Air Force, with German aircraft outnumbering British ones nearly three-to-one, there was little left in the British arsenal to counter the supremacy of the Führer's forces.

Desperate times would call for desperate measures.

In the absence of real forces, the British would have to rely on bluff, bluster and more than a little surreal effort. They were all the country had. Salvation would come from the cast of characters already noted in this narrative so far. At the apex of this new structure came the politician whose restlessness would, it was feared, 'get up to the most extraordinary things and undertake astonishing adventures', in his assistant private secretary's estimation.

Despite Jock Colville's sense of foreboding, extraordinary adventures and astounding things would transform the secret war. It would be Winston Churchill's presiding genius that special means, stratagems and unorthodox forms of warfare would be transformed into a potent weapon of war. The new prime minister would develop – almost overnight in his urgency and attention to detail – acts of clandestinity and terminal violence which, oddly enough, he turned first on the secret services themselves.

Within nine days, even the critical Colville had changed his mind, noting in his diary that despite the prime minister's shortcomings, he was the only man for the job. Churchill's own devotion to the secret world, as one historian has written, 'while often dismissed as Boys' Own romanticism, was also hard-headedly pragmatic and could on occasion be ruthless'. Nobody would be safe from his gimlet gaze, not even long-serving denizens of the secret world who had served him well, but whose more recent performance had been seen as severely lacking.

The farcical situation in Southend in which the Fleming brothers had found themselves was just one symptom of the spy fever that was now running rampant after the invasion of continental Europe. 'Fifth column' paranoia became a new national preoccupation, with the notion of behind-the-scenes saboteurs and quislings a constant topic of speculation. 'There is a fifth column in Britain,' one official booklet announced. 'Anyone who thinks there isn't has simply fallen into the trap laid by the fifth column itself. For the job of the fifth column is to make people think that it does not exist.'

And there were still the persistent rumours that fifth columnists had opened the doors for the invaders in mainland Europe. The security authorities had to investigate each and every whisper. 'It was a time when stories of German parachutists dressed as nuns,' one secret servant would write, 'Charlie Kunz, the bandleader passing information to the enemy through broadcast foxtrots and Lord Haw-Haw's infallible knowledge of when the town hall clock had stopped found easy credence.'

Rumour and counter-rumour mingled in the lingering summer twilight: of fireworks being used to guide German bombers to their targets; of farmers mowing fields and deliberately leaving behind chevrons of arrows to point towards cities; or the signalling of illicit messages from formations of suspicious patterns in the ground, such as arrows pointing from Snowdonia to Liverpool Docks, a story which even today is more than likely an urban myth despite claims for its veracity.

It was an alarming time, which Peter Fleming recalled involved 'aliens being rounded up, signposts taken down, milestones uprooted, street-names obliterated'. With the outbreak of war, all German and Austrian nationals who were resident in Britain had to report to local police stations. Some were immediately detained, while others had their movements severely restricted. After the invasion of France, the situation changed drastically. Internment orders were extended overnight on the direct order of the prime minister. Chief constables were given the power to intern anyone deemed 'suspect'. The influx of dispossessed émigrés from all across Europe made matters even worse. From May to July, roughly 22,000 Germans and Austrians, as well as 4,000 Italians, were interned.

It was hardly Winston Churchill's finest hour, for there were, as one later enquiry declared, 'gross mistakes and pathological stupidities' in rounding up the suspects. In some case, Jewish refugees were herded together with Nazi sympathisers, who continued to taunt them. Certainly the perceived threat from enemy agents, and the flood of enquiries to government departments which resulted, burst the registry of the Security Service, MI5. Ramshackle card indexes of information on potential subversives or known troublemakers could not keep up with the sheer volume of information being reported.

The Security Service was completely overwhelmed.

As a result, the new prime minister's first act was one of terminal ferocity. General Vernon Kell was brought into Downing Street and summarily fired. Though he had served Winston Churchill well in the First World War in rooting out German spies, there was no sentiment in the prime minister's precipitate actions. Now aged 67, Kell was in poor health, often plodding and increasingly out of his depth.

Both he and the organisation he was directing were perceived as failing. As the official in-house history notes, 'the Security Service as a whole was in a state which can only be described as chaotic.' Kell was called into the Treasury, told by the head of the civil service that changes were needed and was dismissed straightaway. It was obvious who was behind it. A few days later, Lady Kell gathered MI5 staff in the canteen and announced,

'Your precious Winston has sacked the general.' Both the general and his formidable wife would be bitter that the prime minister didn't have the common decency to do it in person.

The Chief of the Secret Intelligence Service wondered if he was next. When Colonel Stewart Menzies was called in by the prime minister himself, many presumed he too would have a rough ride. The pre-war disbelief that invariably accompanied CX reports was hardly helped by the fact it had reported – the day before it happened – to the Foreign Office on 9 May, 'there was no chance of an invasion of the Netherlands'. As the acerbic Colville noted in his diaries, 'so much for our renowned foreign agents'.

Similar disbelief hung over Whitehall like a noxious cloud. At one of their first meetings, as the authorised MI6 history notes, Churchill 'dressed [C] down roundly for his failure to produce more information from German-occupied territories'. But as Menzies argued, the failures at Venlo had 'badly dislocated the organisation' and after the occupation, they had lost most of the mainland networks. But, as the official Foreign Office historian has noted, 'it was not a situation to inspire Whitehall's confidence in MI6's capacity either to meet an invasion threat or to engage in counter-espionage.'

Though some high-level sources in Berlin, Scandinavia and the Baltic provided useful information, the problem – as with all human sources of intelligence – was picking up the wishful thinking of the émigrés. At least the PM had faith in the current C, and despite the perceived failures, Menzies was the only service chief to start and end the war.[3] There would be other wholesale changes, so much so that with the apotheosis of Winston Spencer Churchill, 'the hope was beginning to form by June 1940 that, before too long, the gap between the German success and British failure, in intelligence as in the field of strategy would be reduced'.

Above all else there remained pressing questions which only the secret services could answer.

When would the invasion come?

And where?

Clearly, by the summer of 1940, enough was enough so far as sabotage was concerned. There would be no more room for amateurishness, not if Winston Churchill had anything to do with it. As the authorised MI6 history notes, Section D's incompetence meant C would 'wash his hands of Grand' for Sir Stewart could see that General Lawrence Grand had too much responsibility, often represented his own views as those of C and – as he admitted at a ministerial discussion – even he couldn't control him. Taken together, the lingering failures cast a baleful shadow along with the 'multiplicity of bodies dealing with sabotage and subversive activities', as one report has it.

All would be replaced with a new agency dedicated to mayhem, destruction and the prosecution of propaganda. The politician chosen to handle this new agency was, in his own estimation, known as Dr Dynamo, an economist by training who had shaped Labour Party foreign policy in the thirties. Dr Hugh Dalton was convinced of his own importance, able and restless. Thanks to what one political biographer has termed his own paranoia, 'most of the sabotage and subversion took place in Whitehall'.

Yet Dalton – for all his bombast and bullying, which masked his insecurities – was a power within the Labour Party and had, as several people have noted, a pathological hatred of the Germans. The Special Operations Executive (SOE) would use acts of clandestinity and violence to 'set Europe ablaze', in the prime minister's apposite phrase. Winston Churchill had made it clear he wanted greater control of the resistance movement in Europe, and Dalton was his chosen representative on Earth. Section D would be hived off into this new organisation, though that summer of 1940, after the various disasters across the English Channel, the SOE couldn't set anything much afire. It also took over the various half-hearted attempts at propaganda and soon found itself immersed in even greater infighting.

Over the next few months, SOE spent a great deal of its time bickering with MI6 for resources and transportation. Worse, it was widely seen as an upstart, 'inevitably viewed with suspicion and jealousy by all existing departments', as one member presciently noted. Where the secret service operated by stealth, the SOE literally wanted to blow things up. Indeed, Sir Stewart Menzies came to view the Special Operations Executive as 'amateur, dangerous and bogus', hardly helped by the location of its new headquarters close by the fictional residence of Sherlock Holmes.

These Baker Street irregulars were suspect because of their lack of security and swashbuckling disregard for safety. Menzies was happy to let them do what they wanted, providing they didn't compromise MI6 operations. In the longer term, as C noted, 'the grave dislocation running two sections of the secret service with intimately interlocking interest under two masters' would have to be resolved. And watching with interest over his various charges, Dr Dalton, who knew a thing about political infighting and where the power lay, would note that by the following spring

Churchill considered C a wonderful fellow, was always calling for him and noted, significantly, that 'we must not have quarrels with C, who has become so invulnerable'.

If there was a German invasion it was most likely to come ashore in the Garden of England, Kent, and at least one secret servant manqué saw that rumours could be used to unnerve potential invaders.

> Come to England this summer and sample the fun we have prepared for you. Try bathing in our barbed-wire enclosures … Try jumping in our ditches and get burnt alive. Come by air and meet our new death ray … England or Hell – it's going to be just the same you in either.

So wrote Dennis Wheatley in a paper he prepared for the War Office.

Now in his early 40s, he was finding it hard to find a proper berth. He would publish nine books during the war, all bestsellers, but was still having a hard time convincing the authorities that he could make a valuable contribution. What is puzzling is that he was constantly overlooked by the secret services even though most of his immediate family were in the employ of MI5. Somehow he managed to slip through the net.

Towards the end of May 1940, a delicate, charming captain attached to the War Office was being driven by a female driver after a meeting with the Security Service. Hubert Stringer was preoccupied with a depressing, sadly inevitable task: how to resist the invasion in the face of far stronger forces?

'Apart from routine stuff,' he lamented to his driver, 'I don't seem to be able to think of much we can do.'

His driver smiled. 'Why don't you ask my husband?' Joan Wheatley asked.

And in extolling her husband's virtues – 'his specialty is original ideas,' she said with understated firmness – Captain Stringer saw the point. Dennis Wheatley jumped at the chance of contributing to what would be a new form of warfare. That same evening, he wrote nearly 7,000 words by working flat out through the night. Two nights later, Captain Stringer visited the Wheatley home in St Johns Wood and knocked back some drink. After a cursory glance (complimenting him that 'it seems full of good ideas'), the captain didn't want to disabuse the best-selling author of their importance.

'The trouble is that the machinery creaks so,' he lamented.

So with Stringer's blessing, Dennis Wheatley forwarded the material to 'friends' in the various service ministries. At least being a best-selling author had its advantages. People would take notice of the name, if not the contents. His timing was propitious. France had now been overrun, and as the British forces were being removed from Dunkirk – 350,000 well-trained men reduced, in Wheatley's phrase, to 'a rabble, which had to be taken off in its shirts' – many were convinced there would be an invasion within two weeks.

Wheatley's genius was to suggest nothing beyond the realms of possibility, defences which would hardly have been out of place in far earlier threats to the British Isles. Wheatley envisaged the use of floating flares, fire ships and the spreading of flaming oil across the Channel. If they came ashore, he then advocated a low-tech approach. Beaches between Beachy Head and Cromer should be covered by beacons built by civilians to illuminate the landings. Nails and broken glass embedded in concrete would impede the invaders: so would barbed wire 'borrowed' from farmers; fishing nets would foul propellers; rowing boats should be filled with explosives; shallow trenches should be gouged out and filled with oil and smoke bombs. As the enemy came inland, trees should be felled upon tanks, petrol stations would be mined and, in their pumps, water should be mixed with petrol. To further disorientate the invaders, all road and rail station signs were to be removed, a suggestion which Wheatley believes he originated. Writing years later, the removal of place names, he confessed, 'put a lot of people to a lot of inconvenience and all for no purpose'.

The *coup de grâce* was producing the pamphlets which suggested that hell awaited the Wehrmacht. 'If we can get the enemy scared before the start,' he wrote to Captain Stringer, 'we have already half won the battle.' Written just two weeks after Churchill's elevation to the premiership, his words were an inspiring call to arms. Perhaps the strongest weapons, though, were fellow scribes. Intriguingly, his 'Resistance to Invasion Paper' suggested the defensive forces be leavened with a deliberate selection of civilian liaison officers who were fellow writers, including Leslie Charteris, Peter Cheyney and Evelyn Waugh.

Dennis Wheatley wrote:

All of these are brilliant speakers. They are mostly ex-officers of the last war who would work easily with the military: most of them have names already known to a large section of the public and many of them are professional writers capable of drafting concise publicity material or instructions for swift issue.

Captain Stringer was impressed.

'Come along any time after eleven o'clock,' he said, 'and we'll talk about your paper.'

The prime minister may have promised to fight on the beaches and in the hills, but there would have been few – let alone sufficient – forces to repel the invaders. So under the greatest secrecy, Winston Churchill ordered the formation of stay-behind units, with the intention of resisting the expected German attack and harassing the Wehrmacht once it had overrun the Home Counties. While the Royal Air Force prepared to fight in the air, this hastily created nucleus of a secret underground movement would come under the prime minister's direct command. Hiding from the invaders, in a variety of weird and wonderful hideouts, they would be, as one who prepared for the invasion noted, 'a monument to the ingenuity of Peter Fleming'.

The Auxiliary Units, as they were known, would become his own finest hour.

Based on his work for MI (R), they would use guerrilla tactics to disrupt any German invaders. The units were organised into small, localised groups of marauders, who would menace the enemy before disappearing to hide in the shadows: in woods, cellars and fields or whatever subterranean hideouts they could find. Nobody in the network knew other members and their life expectancy was, at most, a couple of weeks.

Once the Germans invaded, the cells would meet in churches and apportion work as spies, assassins, saboteurs and radio operators. They would fill milk churns and sewage pipes with explosives and wire up booby traps in country houses where the Germans might base themselves. At their head would be Captain R.P. Fleming himself, for whom, as his biographer attests, 'his own long training as a small game hunter in the woods round Nettlebed [the Fleming family home] fitted him particularly well.'

Peter Fleming was the obvious choice to actually establish the resistance organisation ahead of an expected German invasion. Kent was expected to be the likeliest area for a landing and it was here that Fleming established his first headquarters in an old timber farmhouse that was christened The Garth. His first task was to identify the houses which the Germans would take over and then surreptitiously mine them or fill milk churns with explosives and fuses. Even more remarkably, nobody was ever maimed at this time for this work was carried out under the greater strictures of security.

Another group of Auxiliary Unit saboteurs set an elaborate series of traps at the far end of Brighton Pier. A seagull inadvertently set one off, which threw up planks of wood that crashed on to other trip wires that set of greater numbers of explosions.

It was a lot quieter over the North Downs, where Fleming and his men developed hideouts in which they would patiently wait for the German invaders. One was established in an engorged badger sett on the edge of a chalk pit 7 miles south of Faversham: another was built in an elongated depression, which had supposedly been excavated to allow airships to land in the First World War. With characteristically brilliant thinking, Peter Fleming realised the Germans wouldn't think that a secret hideout – a collecting point for up to 120 men – would be a hole hidden beneath another hole.

Equal ingenuity came in the hiding of another hideout in the gnarled, ivy-covered roots at the base of an ancient tree. Anyone wishing to enter it had to first find a marble that had been hidden in some nearby leaves. This would then have to be inserted into what appeared to be a mousehole. The marble would roll down a pipe about 12ft long and plop into a tin can, a signal to the men inside that they should open the trap door.

It was, one colleague who inspected the result noted, pure 'Boys' Own Stuff'. As a result, many different legends have developed about Peter Fleming's work at this time. One was that he and the first cells of resistance fighters could kill deer with bows and arrows at a hundred paces. While he did acknowledge that it was his idea to use bows and arrows, Peter Fleming's own hunting prowess was questionable. Most would have been fired by gamekeepers and foresters who already had sufficient experience of game hunting.

How successful would they have been? Perhaps in the first stages of an invasion, Fleming suggested, they might have been, but as he reflected long after the war, 'reprisals against the civilian population would have put us out of business before long'.

Perhaps the most enduring legacy of his work came from the fact that one particular underground hideout had been excavated from out of that old badger sett. It gave Peter Fleming the notion for a story that he never quite completed. The fragmentary chapters of this unfinished novel, *The Sett*, are remarkable only for a character's name which his brother later appropriated for his own brand of fiction. For reasons which he could never quite articulate, the name Moneypenny struck a chord in Ian Fleming's mind.[4]

The notion of chemical warfare hung uneasily in the air at the time. Nobody in London would put it past Adolf Hitler to break the terms of the Geneva Convention, which specifically banned them. 'If Germany attempts to invade this country,' wrote one assessment for the War Office looking at German intentions, 'she will be undertaking the most hazardous operation for which the prize will be world domination.' And it was clear, with that in mind, that Adolf Hitler would show no hesitation in their use.

Newly released files show that intelligence in early 1940 had revealed a new range of weapons were being considered by the Germans: anthrax, foot and mouth, and sleep and paralysis-inducing agents. There were rumours of 'fire rain', made from a 'tarry liquid sprayed from aircraft and ignited by incendiary bombs'.

The Luftwaffe, it was feared, could drop over 2,500 tons daily. Yet, Germany knew that Britain, too, was involved in such weapons of mass destruction. The previous October, the War Cabinet had agreed to the secret ramping-up of production of mustard gas and phosgene. 'Press on,' the prime minister had minuted, 'we must have a great store, as they will certainly use it against us when they feel the pinch.'

And that was something, no matter how unthinkable, which Dennis Wheatley acknowledged in a subsequent paper looking at the invasion from a German perspective: 'I advocate the use of poison gas and bacteriological warfare if our troops can be adequately protected from the latter: but this is a matter for the chemical section and the final decision in both cases lies with the Führer.'

Here was something about which the thriller writer was deadly serious. What seemed to impress the powers that be was that he had got into the mind of the Nazi invaders. 'Not until British women lick the boots of German soldiers while British men look on,' he would write of Teutonic motives, 'can we be certain that we have achieved our final objective and that Britain will never menace us again.'

And yet, he also realised that the simplest way to destroy the country was not to destroy it, but to *épat les bourgeois*. The complete and utter destruction of the middle classes would ensure that Britain would be subdued forever. The Germans, he pointed out, might consider a determined bombing of public schools and universities 'because these contain Britain's officer class of tomorrow'.

In an odd act of synchronicity, more or less the same task had been given to be compiled by one particular intelligence officer who regularly went horse riding through the Tiergarten each morning with Admiral Canaris. According to his memoirs, Walter Schellenberg was asked to write a report to help the invaders: rooting out troublemakers at the end of June 1940. The *Sonderfahndungsliste* GB (or Special Wanted List) is, by anyone's standards, an extraordinary piece of work.

The 'star' of the Venlo incident had been given the task of reorganising the Counter Espionage department of SS Intelligence, the *Sicherheitsdienst*. In the late spring of 1940, he was, as a matter of routine, given an urgent task to write a guide to the country the Wehrmacht was shortly expected to take over. Schellenberg was asked to detail some of the foibles of the peoples who would soon come under the command of the Führer. Though he claims he was the sole author, it is obvious that many hands came to pull the text together.

Informationsheft 1940 is unintentionally hilarious while remaining horribly sinister. Once the Wehrmacht got ashore, the SS administrators in its wake planned to single out subversives and arrest them. Most of the report is actually a long compendium which would have been invaluable in this most urgent political task. It was supposed to describe all of Britain's important political, administrative and economic institutions and their leading players.

In other ways, it is an astonishing piece of work.

For example, Schellenberg dismisses the International Boy Scout movement as 'a disguised instrument of power for British cultural propaganda' which was party to 'important anti-German material which is politically and historically significant'. Perhaps subconsciously echoing Dennis Wheatley's own class prejudices, the invasion guide went to great lengths to describe the invidious influence of the public schools. They were, it was noted, specifically designed to perpetrate the 'traditions of the ruling class'.

Though less than 1 per cent of all children would attend a public school, its graduates would take up roughly 80 per cent of all politically and socially important posts. 'It is here that the future English gentleman is educated,' the report says, 'the gentleman who has never thought about philosophical issues, who has hardly any knowledge of foreign culture and who thinks of Germany as the embodiment of evil, but accepts British power as inviolable.' Eton, it was noted, was 'sold out until 1949', and government ministers Hankey, Halifax, Eden, Oliver Stanley and Duff Cooper were all old boys.

In other respects, Schellenberg's book was handy.

The *Informationsheft 1940* alerted the invading forces to the identities and last known addresses of all potential troublemakers. When its existence was revealed publicly in 1945, one couple in particular were amused at their inclusion. Indeed, Rebecca West cabled Noël Coward: 'My dear, the people we would have been seen dead with!' Indeed, other names included socialists and social luminaries such as H.G. Wells and Nancy Cunard, respectively, as well as politicians like Richard Crossman, who were expected to create trouble but who, ironically, would become involved in Britain's first attempts at anti-German propaganda.

It is perhaps significant that one name is notable by its absence: Aleister Crowley.

After a surfeit of every ritual, perverse sexual practice and mind-addling stimulants, by the time that war had come, Aleister Crowley was literally spent, in both his impotent rage and declining financial fortune. When Anthony Powell met him around this time, he encountered a man who was positively jaundiced in appearance, his face looking more like a horrible baby, 'the skin of porous texture, much mottled, perhaps from persistent use of drugs'.

Abandoned by old friends for his persistent poncing of money, The Beast was by now a hopeless heroin addict, living in a tiny flat in Jermyn Street. The world had passed him by and, though prodigious, his diaries were his greatest occupation at the time. They are filled with the self-pitying symptoms of decay along with desperate sexual encounters with prostitutes and bus conductresses. Yet notoriety of a very different complexion had attached itself to him thanks to another guest at one of Dennis and Joan Wheatley's pre-war parties.

William Joyce was an oddball whom several people thought certifiable. Max Knight for one considered him a crank, a former leading light in the British Union of Fascists, not least because as a later MI5 file shows, he 'could never come within reach of a pencil and paper without drawing a coronated devil's head'. By now transplanted to the Third Reich, William Joyce would become infamous as Lord Haw Haw, whose crowing propaganda broadcasts were cherished for their comic value. Yet some time that summer of 1940, he name-checked somebody who could help reverse the terrible British losses. Lord Haw Haw suggested over the airwaves that Aleister Crowley should be invited to celebrate black mass in Westminster Cathedral.

Small wonder that some believe the defenders took guidance from the supernatural. Witches, it has been suggested without any confirmatory evidence, were employed so that their magic skills could be cast to prevent an invasion as well as psychically neutralising the Nazi menace. Over the years, Lord Haw Haw's facetious suggestion has transformed into the 'fact' that he took part in a black mass ceremony in Ashdown Forest for much the same purpose (this, as we will see in a later chapter, seems to have been a more recent invention and given the name Operation Mistletoe).

Intriguingly, early on the morning of 2 June 1940, two RAF fighters were scrambled to chase a German aircraft which jettisoned a pair of bombs. Several houses close by the forest received slight damage. 'Tattered frocks from one bedroom were strewn across the lawn,' according to one account. In another, garage doors were blown out and boys at a nearby prep school were unharmed, while a lone aircraft was caught in searchlights. 'We heard the drone of a plane just before and soon after the explosions,' noted one resident.

In the fevered spirit of the time, that too – like the notion of Aleister Crowley or witches being employed to ward off the Germans – is more likely to have been wishful thinking.

Though the glorious weather continued well into August, the skies over Southern England that long hot summer of 1940 occasionally darkened thanks to another form of aerial bombardment. No greater measure of the desperation felt by the British authorities came than in the deployment of unsung heroes of a distinctly feathered variety. Strange as it seems to posterity, MI5 set up its own dedicated section to monitor the movements of carrier pigeons as part of the expected onslaught from the Hun.

There should be no surprise in the use of the genus *pipio*, for pigeons have always been used in wars for sending messages. In the First World War, the Germans prevented Belgians from breeding them in case spies used them to transmit secret messages. Before the start of the Second World War, the Abwehr realised that the birds could be vital in the transmission of secret information, 'particularly in the wilder countries where communications were difficult'. Pigeon sections were routinely attached to its intelligence units in the field.

The SS, too, had its sights on the birds.

Himmler's men had commandeered all privately owned pigeons in Germany and intended to use them for the prosecution of war. Perhaps this explains why MI5 had also compiled files on 'German pigeon person-nel' (probably captured Wehrmacht signallers). It was also noted that the *Reichsführer-SS* himself had 'been a pigeon fancier and enthusiast all his life, [and] is the head or President of the German National Pigeon Society'.

To stop this expected onslaught, a Falcon Interceptor Unit was set up within MI5, with two falconers (Viscount Tredegar and Wing Commander Walker) and trained falcons. One hitherto secret report remarks: 'Whilst they never brought down an enemy bird – probably because there never were any – they did demonstrate that they could bring down any pigeon that cased the area they were patrolling.' Something approaching panic occurred when two pigeons of 'unknown origin' were found amongst the MI5 coops that summer. 'Both birds are now prisoners of war,' a report remarks with a perfectly straight face, 'working hard at breeding English pigeons.'

If there was one man who was born to talk to pigeons, it was Evan Morgan, the Second Viscount Tredegar, around whom so many more mysteries swell thanks to his occasional friendship with Aleister Crowley. With the outbreak of war, the viscount was put in charge of a Home Guard unit and then joined the Royal Corps of Signals, where his skills were put to obvious use: training pigeons to carry secret messages. As a result, he was the most exotic employee for MI8, one of the secret departments within the War Office.

Perhaps it was inevitable that he would end up doing a different form of 'bird'. Viscount Tredegar actually spent time in the Tower for an indiscre-tion that he always claimed came about thanks to Lady Baden-Powell. In many accounts, it is stated that he was arrested after talking about his work to Lady Baden-Powell over lunch and was overheard.

Ironically, he actually found himself behind bars thanks to an indiscre-tion – thankfully, an innocent one by today's standards – to a group of Girl Guides. A couple of years later, Evan Morgan was giving a group of Guides a tour of his office when he showed them various items from his safe which he shouldn't have done. Only Evan Morgan would get caught talk-ing too freely, hardly helped by having a gigantic map of Europe (Bomber Command-style) with pins which indicated where pigeons were being dropped, which also, in another account, revealed where the Dieppe landing was being planned.

There is also a suggestion that he revealed far too much about his war-work during a talk he gave at a hotel in London. And for reasons which remain unclear, Lady Baden Powell was indeed something of an enemy to Evan Morgan. After the Girl Guides incident, she pressed, most strongly, for a full court-martial. She succeeded in this attempt. Quite how Tredegar managed to escape serious punishment is still something of a mystery (he was found guilty of two of the three charges against him but he was severely reprimanded and others in the establishment intervened on his behalf).

It was agreed it might be best if he retire to his country seat. There he returned for the rest of the war, never to work on military matters again, and died in the late 1940s, though not before one final mystery involving his old friend Aleister Crowley.

Despite Evan Morgan's often bizarre activities, active measures involving pigeons were also being developed to fool the Germans. So, for example, pigeons were released across the Channel with fake identities to confuse the enemy by filling the skies with bird of unknown origin. Pigeon fanciers were asked to send birds at staggered times of the day to 'decoy' tired birds into following them back to British lofts. Abwehr-bred pigeons in Belgium and Holland were targeted by 'contaminating their lofts'.

False rings written in German were attached to batches of phoney birds, dropped from aircraft. One MI5 report concludes:

> Far from home they would find their way – as homing pigeons always do – to some loft, and as all lofts were enemy-controlled it would be a German loft. There they would be taken in as one of their own pigeons, and if used for message carrying, would, of course, go astray. Sooner or later the Germans would discover they had been fooled and they then would have to call in all their pigeons to check which were the imposters.[5]

However, the first attempt at dropping dummy pigeons out of an RAF plane failed when they were sucked into the slipstream and de-feathered. Later in the war, it was also decided that pigeons should be sent to occupied countries for use in reporting the military situation. Dead pigeons were also dropped with the answers to questions already scrawled on their tags. That way, the German security forces would think the famous British Secret Service remained active in the Fatherland. Famously, one tired pigeon returned home to an MI5 loft with a polite message attached. 'I had the sister of this one for supper. Delicious! Please send us some more.'

Under the direct supervision of the Joint Intelligence Committee, the carrier pigeon sub-committee continued to meet for five years after the war. A strange plan was then developed as the Cold War started. Fitted with lethal bacteria or explosives, it was suggested the pigeons could 'home' in on enemy targets. Though these ideas were taken seriously by Sir Stewart Menzies, there were internal disagreements which meant the plans were 'continuously forced to swim in a sea of pigeon politics'.

The fate of the invasion would ultimately rest with some stool pigeons who were, thanks to Abwehr incompetence, more like sitting ducks. Though it had seemed to many of its opposite number that German Military Intelligence was 'a first class organisation', over the spring and summer of 1940 it appeared as though it was employing some sort of secret gag writer to plan its operations. Battalions of spies would be needed to prepare for the invasion of Britain. Acting as pathfinders, they would warn the Wehrmacht about the lie of the land in the Garden of England, helping guide the forces through the quiet (but now signpost-less) country lanes and picturesque villages up towards London and beyond.

'Where on Earth are we going to get hold of that many of would-be suicides?' Admiral Canaris is known to have remarked as the plans developed.

For that he turned to a man with the prominent gold tooth, a friendly, full-faced countenance and a patter that seemed to have seeped in from a B-movie. Major Nikolaus Adolf Fritz Ritter had spent much time in the States and had supposedly escaped from one tight spot in the Great War by stealing a biplane. Though clearly a fantasist, Ritter's rise had been bestowed with the avuncular blessing of 'Father Christmas' himself.

'I got a note from Canaris telling me that I was one of his best officers,' Ritter later told one interviewer. 'All he could say was that I was better than excellent.'

Based in the Abwehr's large Hamburg outstation which directed operations against Britain (and later the United States), Major Ritter later maintained that he could never fathom out anything about *der Chef* whenever they socialised together. 'Unlike most Germans who tell you their life story within five minutes of meeting them, the admiral was always closed,' Ritter would write. 'We never got anything out of him.'

Ritter always maintained that he hated both the backbiting atmosphere and office politics within the Abwehr. Now, in the summer of 1940, an air of fatalism permeated the Hamburg offices with regard to its plans for supporting Operation Sea Lion, the planned invasion of the British Isles. Vast scepticism accompanied Ritter's plans, with one mission, in particular, termed 'Himmelfahrt', a journey to heaven, as in wishful thinking.

With the occupation of Europe, there were plentiful supplies of potential agents who could pose as refugees, but they were all recruited too late and without sufficient screening for suitability. They had either been blackmailed or attracted to espionage by greed, thrills and a sense of misplaced patriotism. What would be known to the Abwehr as 'Operation Lena' and, more prosaically, to the British as 'The Brussels Four'[6] seemed to have drifted in from cloud cuckoo land.

They were a ragtag bunch, in MI5's later estimation, which led to an episode that was – with typical British understatement – 'rather falsely alarming in its local magnitude'. The only thing they seemed to have in common was a staggering lack of ability to make themselves inconspicuous. One spoke no English at all, the others, fleetingly; including one, Sjoert Pons, whose supposed superiority as an English speaker may be gauged from how he described his mission: 'How the people is living, how many soldiers there are, and all the things.'

At the start of September, each of them had been led to believe the invasion was coming very soon. When the Wehrmacht followed, they were instructed to signal by handkerchief any approaching forces. 'Ich bin hier mit einem Sonderauftrag der deutschen Wehrmacht,' ('I'm here on a special mission for [on behalf of] the German armed forces') they would say, followed by the password 'Elizabeth'.

Their dispatch from France, in keeping with the conventions of a childhood adventure, could best be called Four Men in Two Boats. In the still of the pre-dawn darkness of the first Monday in September, they came across the Channel in fishing boats on a perfectly dark, moonless night. At daybreak, one of them, Carl Meier, made his way towards the nearby village of Lydd. As he was thirsty, he walked into a pub (literally so, for as he later told MI5, 'I stepped into the room and hit my head on the lamp.') He drew attention to himself straight away in demanding cigarettes and cider. It was just after 9 a.m. and the bar would not serve alcohol for at least another hour.

The landlady – 'Mrs Cow', he recalled – was suspicious.

'I went out and walked round the town,' Meier recalled. At some point, he got into conversation with an Air Raid Warden and, as the official MI5 report on his activities notes, 'somewhat ingenuously over-zealous, he soon began to make enquiries as to the disposition and number of British troops in the case.' When the Dutchman admitted he had no identity card, he was arrested and taken to a nearby police station. After three hours of prevarication, he finally revealed where his friend Waldberg was hiding.

The remaining spies – Dutch Army buddies Pons and Van der Kieboom – had landed a few miles away down the coast. Within an hour, they too had been questioned at Seabrook Police Station.

Though the mission of the Brussels Four may have been over before it had even started, it did prompt an atmosphere of feverish speculation. The Saturday after they had been apprehended in the Kent marshes, the code-word 'Cromwell' was dispatched to all units of the Home Guard, meaning an invasion was imminent.[7] The Joint Intelligence Committee assessment which prompted it was 'a significant item of intelligence' – most likely the confessions of the Brussels Four.

Certainly, much mystery surrounds the role of Admiral Wilhelm Canaris at this time. Did the Abwehr chief actually go so far as to leak material to the British government? After the war, when the diplomat Michael Soltikow asked Winston Churchill about how he had been so well informed about the German plans, he pointed to Ian Colvin's post-war biography of Canaris. Another intriguing vignette of Wilhelm Canaris's duplicity survives from this time. A young Luftwaffe pilot happened to say in the admiral's hearing that the Royal Air Force would crumple within six weeks. Somehow managing to keep a straight face, Admiral Canaris said: 'The Führer is said to give them only fifteen days and the Führer is always right.'

The Abwehr eventually abandoned sea landings and concentrated on dropping their agents in by parachute. Two nights after the Brussels Four came ashore, the agent codenamed Summer by the British fell from the skies over the Northamptonshire countryside. He was the itinerant son of a Swedish parson who had married a German girl, had crossed the Canadian Rockies by foot and his first job, running a silver fox farm in Uppsala, had ended in disaster.

So too did Gösta Caroli's mission to Britain.

During his descent in the middle of the night, Caroli had been dragged forward by his extremely heavy radio equipment, then the strap snapped and he somehow managed to knock himself out. When he later awoke in complete darkness, Caroli was able to cut himself free from the radio but was rather badly concussed. He was later found in a shed by a farmer's boy and was arrested. A few days later, he was driven down to London and taken to MI5's dedicated interrogation centre at a former lunatic asylum in Richmond.

It was clear he was distinctly ambivalent about how and where the Wehrmacht would come ashore.

'You haven't much faith in this so-called invasion of England?' he was asked.

'No.'

The Germans would land, so Caroli had been led to believe, in about a fortnight's time once the RAF was destroyed (estimated to take place on 15 September).

'I was told [to] come first to the South Coast and find out about the fortifications on the South Coast,' Caroli added. But perhaps the oddest detail was something which he had picked up from the Germans he had dealt with, justifying the sense of disbelief that had prompted the dispatch of their agents.

'It is impossible, of course, but I have heard about a pontoon bridge over the Channel ... '

'A pontoon bridge over the Straits!'

For just about the only time in his wartime secret service, the hard-charging MI5 interrogator – famously termed 'a devil in a monocle' – was rendered, albeit temporarily, speechless.[8]

With the onset of the autumn storms, it was clear that Britain would, for the moment, survive. The Brussels Four and Gösta Caroli were not alone. They were the first of a total of fourteen enemy agents who attempted to land in Britain over the next three months of 1940. All were apprehended in a matter of hours. Ten came by sea and four were parachuted; nine surrendered to the authorities straightaway; twelve were interned, one committed suicide and three would eventually be turned against their German masters.

At this stage, the prevailing wisdom was that anyone found to be an enemy agent would have to be executed to make sure others would not be encouraged. And so with a wearying sense of inevitability, the Brussels Four were brought to trial at the Old Bailey at the end of November 1940. Even though she was a spiritualist, Carl Meier's mother would have been hard-pressed to predict the contents of a letter her son had written in Pentonville Prison hours before he met his end.

'I know that it will be a shock for you to hear that I have passed away when you receive this letter,' he wrote. 'I certainly believe that you will understand that it is better for me to die for my ideals.'

At this stage of the fighting, what was later known as political warfare did not exist as a concrete concept. Though the notion of fighting war without weapons was an old one, in the first few months of its existence attempts by the new kid on the block, the Special Operations Executive, to create and execute propaganda were equally flawed. For some, the SOE's creation and the dispatch of its planning personnel to a variety of old mansions in the Home Counties led to its disparagement as the Stately 'Omes of England.

To many, they remained the disparate bunch of hopeless and helpless time-servers who were incompetent, and that included the former head of subversion who was finally sent into the wilderness. That September, Hugh Dalton sacked Lawrence Grand (whom he termed King Bomba, after the quixotic Sicilian King Ferdinand) who returned to the army, but not without kicking up a fuss. Dalton didn't care where he went so long as it was 'some distance off' (preferably Hong Kong or Ireland), but was beside himself with rage when he heard that Grand wanted a position in the War Cabinet secretariat.

By now, it was clear that something more dynamic than broadcasting and leaflet dropping was needed to turn the *Deutsches Volk* against their masters. What was really needed was a catalyst, and that would come in the corpulent form of someone who knew Germany, and indeed had walked through the smouldering remains of the Reichstag with the newly elected Führer himself, to take mendacious and misleading half-truths and lies into a new realm.

Denis Sefton Delmer.

7

Darkness and Light

A report has reached us today from a Swiss informant who has for many years had close connections with the English Secret Service to the effect it is the plan of the English Secret Service, by sending the Duke to the Bahamas to get him into English power in order to do away with him at the first opportunity.

July 1940 telegram to SS Intelligence from Lisbon

Since the collapse of France, Lisbon has been the principal and at times the only place through which the Germans could pass agents through this country or where they could meet them on their return.

'The German Espionage Organisation in Lisbon',
summary from the summer of 1941 (KV 3/170 52B)

Waiting and watching.

That's all anybody could really do and now, scanning the French coast through the early morning autumn mists,[1] a large, untidy figure was looking for tell-tale signs that the invading forces were ready to embark. It was a measure of some later pride to Tom Delmer that his name had already been added to the SS Wanted List. As soon as the Wehrmacht came ashore, he would be instantly arrested. Not that he knew it at the time, but the former Berlin correspondent had made high-powered enemies in Nazi Germany.

By the second week of September, it was make or break for the enemy across the Channel. The day before, ferocious air battles had climaxed with the most prolonged and fierce day of fighting – now commemorated as

Battle of Britain Day – over southern England. And now, at 8 a.m. on Monday, 16 September 1940, Tom Delmer was watching and, as he reported the next day, fifty aircraft were met with a 'barrage of fire as I have never seen anywhere before'.

It was, he thought, akin to a wall of fire as the sky filled with shrapnel.

'The explosion of shells was one continuous roar,' Delmer reported in the next day's *Daily Express*. The enemy bombers were forced to turn back as they came in under the clouds. Further bad weather but no more aircraft rolled in that same Monday. By early evening, when Delmer had filed his story, there would be no further onslaughts thanks to 'what sailors call dirty weather over the straits of Dover tonight'.

Trying to lift 'the veil of the unknown', as Winston Churchill referred to the Channel, would hardly be easy. And yet, trying to not just discern what the enemy was doing, but somehow influence its people would be something to which Tom Delmer knew he could make an important contribution. Ironically, floating above him in the early evening mists was a large blimp that had been shot down and then patched up after an attack on the port of Dover. The RAF soon christened the unfortunate dirigible Sefton, after the man himself. It was joined by a pair of large guns named Winnie and Pooh, a pointless political gesture by a prime minister, for they would hardly be sufficient to repel an attack.

Now, as he scanned the Pas-de-Calais, Tom Delmer knew there was a certain irony that the politician named for the gun was never particularly impressed by official misinformation. With Winston Churchill's general lack of interest in propaganda, similar bemusement had accompanied its development to date. One parliamentary undersecretary was genuinely perplexed by the academic abstraction and almost tortured intellectuals who had been employed in the Ministry of Information.

Many writers simply stayed clear. Dennis Wheatley had been one of them.

'Don't take it too badly that the Ministry of Information had ignored your offer of service,' one MI5 officer told him, referring to the fact the set-up was a hopeless mess. 'It would break your heart to be mixed up with such a crew'. What the successful prosecution of propaganda and psychological warfare needed, another participant later wrote, were people 'caddish and ignorant enough to tell dynamic lies.'

The efforts to date were too decent and honourable. What was needed were people who were neither. 'We need crooks,' was his simple request.

Earlier that same fateful summer of 1940, Adolf Hitler had, publicly at least, acted magnanimously towards the British people. The German leader raised the issue of ending the fighting with Churchill's government in the most dramatic terms. On Friday, 19 July, he had stood at a lectern at the Kroll Opera House wearing his simple uniform and the Iron Cross he had won in the Great War at Ypres. Appealing to reason and British common sense, the Führer offered an olive branch towards the king's subjects.

'I consider myself in a position to make this appeal since I am not the vanquished begging favours, but the victor speaking in the name of reason,' he said. 'I can see no reason why this war must go on.'

Within an hour, Tom Delmer had taken to the airwaves on the BBC German Service. His was a fiery riposte which had begun: 'We hurl it right back at you, right in your evil-smelling teeth.' The golden pheasants were so shocked at his vehemence that his name was swiftly added to the SS Wanted List. So, too, were some members of parliament, led by the Labour politician Richard Stokes, who wanted to know why 'a person of no importance' had been allowed to answer the Führer's offer.

The relevant minister replied that the right to grumble was part of the democratic process. 'We are fighting to preserve our liberties,' he loftily declared. 'If you call that fighting for nothing or fighting for something negative, I do not.'

Indeed, it was largely due to Tom Delmer's efforts, and his alone, that political warfare would be miraculously transformed as a viable weapon of warfare. Yet for him personally, the line between truth and misinformation remained precarious. Another government minister advised him to carry on working as a reporter but carry out the occasional broadcast on the BBC German service.

One thing which nobody could stem that autumn were the incessant rumours that the invasion would come any day. To combat them, Tom Delmer started to promote his own: that the British Government had imported 200 man-eating sharks from Australia. They had, he would claim, been released into the English Channel to eat even the most unappetising of invading Wehrmacht troops.

On another occasion, he travelled with a convoy through the Channel, when he gave a language lesson for potential invaders on the BBC German Service. Here, verbatim, is a transcript, done in the style of an enthusiastic language instructor:

For your first lesson we will take:

'*Die Kanalüberfahrt* ... the chan-nel cross-ing ... *das boot sinkt* ... the boat is sin-king ... the boat is sin-king.'

And then, after repeating this, Delmer added a verb declination which would come in useful:

'*Ich brenne* ... I burn.

'*Du brennst* ... you burn.'

He ended with:

'*Der SS Sturmführer brennt auch ganz schön.*'

'The SS Captain is also burning quite nicely.'

Yet it would hardly be a vintage time for Tom Delmer.

As the autumn of 1940 progressed, his was a time of uncertainty, boredom and waiting to find a niche somewhere in the secret world. Too old for regular employment (then in his mid-30s) and most likely too heavy (17 stone), Tom Delmer kicked his heels, often frustrated at the bureaucratic delays he encountered. At first he seems to have been rejected by MI5 and was later employed, peripherally at least, by MI6 on a strange mission that for all its fiascos, would lead him directly into the propaganda war.

For all the fears of invasion, there is much evidence to suggest Adolf Hitler wanted to neutralise Britain without a fight. Certainly, the Führer hoped that he could broker peace and, in any case, had made it clear that unless the Wehrmacht's invasion strategy had come together by the start of September, 'other plans' would intercede – namely, the invasion of the Soviet Union and what he termed 'the final showdown with bolshevism'.

In this regard, a destroyed Britain would only really benefit the United States and Japan with the dissolution of the far reaches of empire. 'He thought Britain would be mad or stupid not to ask for some kind of compromise peace,' Romanian Ambassador Virgil Tilea later correctly diagnosed in a newspaper article.

Yet the Nazis remained fearful of the British Empire and were envious of both its prestige and resources. The golden pheasants were also fascinated by the Crown and, in particular, the limited powers which the monarch exercised over the Houses of Parliament. They could never completely understand its honourable members' constant vigilance for any kingly incursions on the due processes of democracy. Indeed, many high-up Nazis speculated that this might have been the real cause of Edward VIII's abdication. Now, four years later, the Nazis desperately wanted to contact this same member of the Establishment, a curious, self-centred man for whom fate and a certain ignominious hubris had seen him abandon the crown for the love of a woman.

To understand how the Third Reich wanted to make contact with the Duke of Windsor involves another theme which will come to engage this narrative: Adolf Hitler's innate ability in making sure his fingerprints were nowhere to be found anywhere near any controversial actions which might backfire. This stemmed not just from the *Führerprinzip*, the fundamental underpinning of the Third Reich that his word was above all written law. Most famously, Adolf Hitler never put his signature to any written instructions for the Final Solution. Nor had his name ever been associated with an earlier peace effort about which he is known to have approved. Ultimately, Hermann Göring's approach in the late summer of 1939 to the Chamberlain government via his Swedish businessman friend, Birger Dahlerus, to try to stop the outbreak of hostilities had failed.

And now he would do the same in behind-the-scenes brokering of peace with the British. Publicly, the Führer was generous and magnanimous, as in the Kroll Opera House speech, which had prompted Tom Delmer's vitriol. After all, as he somewhat ridiculously claimed, his own generosity had extended to allowing Vichy to govern half of the conquered French nation. But behind the scenes that summer of 1940, he called in his keeper of the faith, Rudolf Hess, who would now be tasked with looking at the issue of finding peace in broader terms.

There were, Adolf Hitler told his deputy, a group of British aristocrats who were keen to circumvent the belligerent Churchill. The king would listen, Hitler claimed. 'What do I have to do?' the Führer had asked in exasperation at one point. 'Do I have to go over there myself and talk to them?'

Those very words have been a wellspring of much peculiar speculation.

Already, one of the Führer's intelligence services was working on a backup, a convoluted tale that would prompt two of the more farcical operations of the secret war, both linked to the possibility of exploring peace. The first involved the recent escape of the Duke and Duchess of Windsor to Iberia, where they were believed to be under the gimlet gaze of one of the golden pheasants' favourite bogeyman.

'The crux of the matter is that since his abdication, the Duke has been under the strict surveillance of the British secret service,' one German diplomatic report noted that summer of 1940. 'We know what his feelings are, it's almost as if he were their prisoner.' An American diplomat had also chimed in: the duke and duchess were indiscreet and outspoken against the British government.

And out of this notion came a plan to kidnap His Majesty's wayward brother to leverage peace with the British Government. What followed was another bizarre enterprise with unforeseen consequences, not least for the author of the *Informationsheft 1940* report with whom it would be inextricably linked. Walter Schellenberg's attempts to kidnap the former Edward VIII read more like a cross between *The Prisoner of Zenda* and a Whitehall farce, in which, as noted one historian, 'nothing was too fantastic to happen'.

Tom Delmer's blackly humorous broadcasts aside, these first few months of what came to be known as political warfare had also been farcical. The whole approach to propaganda had been characterised by false starts, petty mindedness, vindictiveness, amateurishness and stupidity. It was not simply a case of trying to find the right approach to political warfare, but developing any sort of approach at all. Though the formation of the Special Operations Executive had been intended to galvanise unconventional forms of warfare, it had had quite the opposite effect so far as propaganda was concerned. Various bailiwick disputes and political infighting were the immediate result.

Threaded throughout this story are the political ambitions of a generation of public-school educated socialists who could not happen upon a ribcage without wanting to stick a knife in. Dr Hugh Dalton's first act on taking over the SOE was to split propaganda from sabotage. As his firing of 'Grand Bomba' had shown, Dalton could be Machiavellian and difficult, and was, in one recollection, 'a great booming bully; and even at breakfast time, his manner was horribly hearty'.

Although impressed by 'black' propaganda, Dalton spent the first few months of his tenure fighting with Duff Cooper (nominally the Minister for Information and a crony of the prime minister) as to who should take the lead in prosecuting propaganda. A singular question remained: was its distribution overt or covert? If the latter, it would come under the SOE which, because of its very secrecy, meant that no questions could be asked in parliament. Fairly quickly, the first battleground concerned printed material: 'an impudent attempt by the Ministry of Information to steal leaflets from me,' Dalton recorded in his diary that November. Around the same time, when Tom Delmer arrived in Lisbon, there was so little activity going on that he met a Belgian émigré who asked a question that he himself would soon ponder.

'Why don't the RAF drop more propaganda leaflets?' he moaned. 'We want all we can get.'

Cooper's snoopers, as the information ministry was invariably known, worked for one of the most unpopular departments of state. 'It would take hours to describe the perfection in which this piece of chaos has been organised,' noted one politician. To be fair, the Ministry of Information's purpose was positively schizophrenic: as well as disseminating information from all government departments, it was responsible for censorship. It employed, by repute, 999 civil servants who all had one overarching aim – to argue and infight, not just with rivals but with themselves too. 'The presence of so many able, undisciplined men in one Ministry was bound to lead to a great deal of internal friction,' Cooper himself noted years later. Having taken over the capital's first skyscraper, the Ministry of Information was rapidly expanding in ways that caused much puzzlement for the people who worked there. Senate House just off Russell Square would act as a curious magnet for writers, iconoclasts and malcontents who would come to deride their own work. George Orwell would famously base his Ministry of Truth in *1984* on the situation he encountered there (a particular library office may well have been the inspiration for Room 101).[2]

Graham Greene became, much to his own astonishment, head of the writers' section based in a Senate House, which he termed 'a high heartless building with complicated lifts'. Supposedly there to 'commission and stimulate the writing of books and pamphlets', Greene was soon bored by the pointlessness of it all. He satirised the general atmosphere in his short story *Men At Work*, which he wrote that same hot summer. It tells the story of Richard Skate, an official in a Ministry of Information who spends all his time drowning in paperwork. Every effort was superseded by events and the building was full of self-important, pompous idiots.

'Propaganda was a means of passing the time: work was not done for its usefulness but for its own sake – simply as an occupation,' he wrote. Scathingly, Greene felt the accumulating staff were akin to a kind of fungoid life, growing and self-replicating to no apparent purpose. 'To send a minute to anybody else in the great building and to receive a reply took at least twenty-four hours,' Greene noted, 'on an urgent matter an exchange of three minutes might be got through in a week.'

Greene lasted six months, before finding more gainful employment. 'I loved the Blitz,' he later said after becoming an ARP warden. 'It was wonderful to wake up and know you were still alive and hear glass being swept up in the streets.' Thanks to his sister, Elizabeth, who was already working within MI6, Graham Greene was recruited into the secret world. He was later dispatched to Sierra Leone, where he became known as Officer 59200, based in Freetown. Despite his own later claims of unsuitability – most famously with the comedic possibilities of having to arrange for a blowtorch-wielding technician to open his safe after he had locked its code and codebooks inside – his job was to keep an eye on ships docking from the neighbouring countries of Vichy France.

His later dismissive attitude to the secret world came from various other comedies of errors which provided the germs of plot devices and ideas for his own books. Perhaps the most famous concerned his trying to recruit a brothel madam who, as he reported, had 'earned her living on her back for a good many years'. Greene suggested running her brothel with government backing. But after careful consideration in Broadway Buildings, he was informed there was a greater worry that she might employ whores who were already in the employ of Vichy France (as, by repute, the best-looking ones from neighbouring countries were).

It always started with a phone call to the top floor of the Madrid Embassy.

A bright female voice announced '*El tío está aquí*' ('Uncle is here') and within minutes the message would pass down to the head of the Abwehr station in the large building on Calle Castellana. It needed no further elaboration. Admiral Wilhelm Canaris would be expected shortly after having flown into the Spanish capital using one of his many aliases.[3] The admiral would find any excuse to visit the country to which he was sentimentally attached, where he had established a vast network of watchers in the Great War. Most recently, he had created an espionage organisation to specifically help Francisco Franco during the Spanish Civil War. It was significant, therefore, that a signed photograph of *Il Caudillo* hung on his office wall in the Fuchsbau. Canaris had made himself indispensable to Franco, so much so that the Abwehr was far more pervasive than even the Spanish secret police, the DGS (Direccion General de Seguridad).

Spain, then, represented a release valve.

With increasing frequency, Wilhelm Canaris returned to the peninsula to rejuvenate his often flagging spirits, finding a 'constant exhilaration' in one recent account. The admiral had a marked empathy with his Spanish hosts. With the appointment of a manservant named Mohammed and the ferrying of military aircraft to Spain to fetch fresh strawberries, he certainly enjoyed the distractions of a sybaritic lifestyle.

Significantly, his station chief in Madrid was a former naval officer, Wilhelm Leissner, who in some accounts has been called the admiral's 'alter ego', though widely seen as pedantic and over formal. But Canaris needed someone he could trust as the Spanish capital was an important centre for the Abwehr. Its Madrid station would become one of its most heavily manned. Roughly half the embassy staff were genuine diplomats and support staff, and eventually expanded to take over the uppermost floor and the basement.[4]

A similar encroachment occurred throughout the country, where nearly fifty Abwehr outstations covered the country like a spider's web of inter-connections. Yet all seemed to act independently and without reference to Madrid. 'They corresponded with Berlin, described what they were doing and sent in their agents's reports,' one MI6 hand later noted. In other words, chaos was set in from the beginning, something which would have a significant impact on the secret war.

This vast trawl of information was forwarded to the Fuchsbau with little regard for filtering. The intelligence trawl from Spain was invariably contra-dictory or defied common sense, a situation which became more acute as the war went on. Partly it was because he who made the more astonishing claim was likely to be believed, but also because of bureaucratic incompe-tence. Names were routinely misfiled or lost altogether. Not only did staff within the central registry have no language training, but as a post-war interrogation of one Abwehr officer who regularly visited Iberia noted, they had 'no experience with foreign names with the result that persons were often classified under the Christian name or, as often happened with long-winded Spanish names, under the mother's family name'.

One person who always used his family name was the Duke of Windsor.

Since the outbreak of war, the former Edward VIII had been kicking his heels in France looking for a more meaningful role than the pointless liaison job he had been handed with French Army General Headquarters. When *la patrie* had fallen in June, the former monarch had fled first to the

Riviera and, characteristically, demanded that a warship pick up him and Mrs Simpson from Nice. His request fell on deaf ears. Sulking and moaning followed, which prompted his various comments that only a negotiated peace with Hitler would end things.

As with many other refugees that summer – a vast tsunami of them – the Windsors had headed over the border to Spain ahead of the German forces. Even without the added complication of their royal personages, Madrid was already a crucible of intrigue, rumour and shifting allegiances. Though supposedly neutral, Franco's ministers could be characterised by their various competing and virulent strains of pro- and anti-British feeling, which rose and fell like Atlantic swells. The generalissimo himself had hedged his bets by declaring his country a non-belligerent as opposed to completely neutral. He had sacked his pro-British foreign minister and replaced him with his pro-Nazi brother-in-law, Serrano Suñer.

Add to that extensive German commercial influence and a primal fear of a powerful Royal Navy, the situation was potentially combustible. A further flashpoint for Spanish public outrage was Gibraltar. On his arrival in Madrid that June, the new British ambassador, Sir Samuel Hoare,[5] was greeted by a well-organised demonstration that had been looked on favourably by the police.

'Gibraltar is Spanish! Gibraltar is Spanish!' came the cries.

Staying at the Ritz, Hoare found it full of aggressive Germans and was convinced all his conversations were being snooped upon. 'You can imagine the state of nerves in which Spain and Madrid find themselves after the German arrival on the Pyrenees,' Hoare wrote to the prime minister at the end of June 1940. 'I try to keep an appearance of calm but it is not always easy in face of a completely germanised press and many germanised departments of state.'

The Spanish press were being expertly fed by the Nazi propaganda machine. In time, the British Embassy itself would be stoned by a Falangist mob, attentively photographed by German intelligence staff.

Three weeks later, the Duke of Windsor had shown up at the same hotel.

Now the rumours surfaced that both the duke and ambassador were negotiating with the Nazis for peace to stop the death and destruction. 'In London, hostility towards the duke and duchess was growing,' writes the academic Neill Lochery, a recent chronicler of these times.

For the newly formed administration of Winston Churchill, the situation was more than embarrassing. What followed next was a series of events, in the recent words of a German historian, which involved 'aspects bordering on the ridiculous and not totally free of a certain operatic quality' that played against an impending sense of catastrophe.

Throughout the summer of 1940, Admiral Wilhelm Canaris travelled to Spain to lay a false trail that, even today, remains murky and mysterious. 'If for any reason "Sea Lion" would have to be postponed,' the Führer had supposedly said to him, 'I want to seize Gibraltar.' When he arrived at Calle Castellana at the end of July, Wilhelm Canaris soon confided to his crony Leissner the real reasons behind his visit.

In Berlin, the eyes of military planners alighted on the craggy rock and its important military facilities. What became known as Operation Felix was distilled through the late summer and autumn of 1940, which would have seen a German occupation of Spain as well as its ports in Morocco and the Canary Islands. The proposed onslaught would be a variation on blitzkrieg, its details dictated by the unique topography of the target as he would now determine.

'Uncle' himself then drove down to Algeciras and watched the shipping which passed through the Straits of Gibraltar. The Abwehr maintained a constant watch on convoys and cargoes and, as a post-war examination noted, for all its shortcomings, Canaris's men gained significant information from the monitoring of the various vessels and crews which passed through the straits. They also obtained information from bribing officials, something which the British also did. A game of cat and mouse was played by enlisting local police, stevedores and clock-watchers for intelligence purposes.

Admiral Canaris then moved to a nearby hotel where he listened in to British naval officers chatting at a nearby table before visiting a Spanish army officer with whom he discussed the colony. Across Algeciras Bay and along the spit of land which formed the isthmus of La Línea, the Abwehr gazed longingly and at times forlornly at what a later MI5 security officer correctly termed the showpiece in 'an immense military tattoo' for which enemy agents had a ringside seat.

Nobody could turn an appropriately Nelsonian blind eye to the dangers facing Gibraltar from across Algeciras Bay. A later analysis for MI5 records:

> From these observation stations, [The Abwehr] received constant and valuable information on Allied convoys and cargoes. The KO [Abwehr station] also sent people on board ships calling at Spanish ports to question the crews on what they had seen at sea or in Allied countries. Employees

in shipping offices were also bribed to pass on information to make an extra copy of shipping and cargo lists.

Indeed, watchers were chosen either for their linguistic ability or their knowledge of shipping. Worse was an almost primeval fear that the Spaniards were also refuelling and revictualling U-boats.[6]

On this visit, the admiral's 'associates' were in reality engineers, paratroopers and artillerymen who would shortly stake out the Rock (all with the blessing and complicit military assistance of the Spanish). Their microscopic evaluation of the giant rock led Canaris to envisage what one biographer calls 'a three day military operation resembling a game of cowboys and Indians on the grand scale', a major assault on the Rock with crack Wehrmacht units storming in under Spanish command.

Yet, as several commentators have noted, Operation Felix only ever fed that most arrogant of follies within the secret world: self-deception. An invasion force could hardly remain incognito to spring a surprise attack. From high above, the defenders would easily spot the oncoming forces. Even if they could somehow camouflage their presence, there was only a single road leading towards the colony. Steep slopes, turbulent winds and limited landing grounds would preclude a parachute or glider attack.

For most of 1940, Adolf Hitler had a bee in his bonnet about this most potent symbol of British power. Whoever controlled Gibraltar essentially dictated naval access to and from the Mediterranean.[7] Ironically, both the head of the Abwehr and the British prime minister would come to share the same view of the colony that summer of 1940: that it would save the British Empire. And in this regard, Canaris marvelled at the survival skills of a fellow great intriguer.

'What can I do against the great W.C.?' he once said in front of his underlings. 'I am only the little W.C.'

The great W.C. made sure that a gimlet eye was kept on the Duke of Windsor.

With the growing heat, both physical and political, upon them, he and Wallis would go on to Lisbon, where the thrice-weekly BOAC flying boat would return them to London. That was the last place His Royal Highness wished to go but their stay in Madrid had, as Hoare noted, 'stimulated pro-German propaganda'.

Even at his best, the duke was temperamental, self-absorbed and expected to be treated like a king, though his mood swings were hardly helped by

the demands of a difficult wife. And now, with his enforced isolation in
Iberia, he was even worse. Behind the scenes, the oily Suñer consulted with
Franco. There was enough evidence where the duke's sympathies lay. It was
obvious to everyone that he could be used as some sort of instrument for
peace. But what exactly?

The answer to this question in the years since has veered anywhere from
honest broker to puppet king. Certainly, the Royal Family in London were
convinced that he simply wanted to avoid the Blitz, for he had always shown
a marked aversion to suffering. When, in a strange coincidence, his brother
the Duke of Kent was about to make his own official visit to Lisbon and
asked if he would await his brother, his reply was simple: 'Good god, no.'

And behind the scenes, something was afoot.

The German foreign minister, the pompous and self-important Joachim
von Ribbentrop, thought he could use this situation to curry favour with
the Führer. A former ambassador to London, Ribbentrop acted upon all
the diplomatic gossip. The foreign minister pointedly excluded the Abwehr
and Canaris, who was, as we will see, in Spain at the same time. He knew
exactly what kind of game the admiral might play. In Walter Schellenberg's
recollections, von Ribbentrop had a peculiar vision of what was going on:
'The crux of the matter is that, since his abdication, the Duke of Windsor
has been under strict surveillance by the British Secret Service.'

And every attempt to get him from under its wings had failed.

He wanted to mount a secret operation to bring the duke over to the
German side, but for what exact purpose was never abundantly clear. For
this, von Ribbentrop bypassed Canaris, Himmler and Heydrich and went
directly to the coming man of German intelligence. Walter Schellenberg
was surprised at the summons to the Foreign Ministry, the more so for what
he was being asked to do: to negotiate with the duke but to make sure they
avoided their favourite bogeyman. 'If the British secret service should try
to frustrate the Duke [then] the Führer orders that you are to circumvent
the British plans, even at the risk of your life.'

The great W.C. had, cannily, ensured that a swashbuckler was in place to
keep his eyes on Spain. Commander Alan Hillgarth had a significance far
greater than his relatively lowly role of naval attaché based in Madrid, which
for historical reasons was far more important a posting than it first appeared.
Hillgarth was just the sort of buccaneer who appealed to the prime minister.
He had been wounded at the Dardanelles in the Great War, had prospected

for Bolivian gold and written the kind of adventure novels in which he alone could so easily have been the star. He had impressed both Churchill and Admiral Godfrey, and was appointed as joint representative of MI6 and the Naval Intelligence Division.[8]

Almost inevitably, Hillgarth made enemies.

Given his closeness to the new prime minister, some felt both succumbed to a *folie à deux*, each feeding off the other's natural tendency to self-importance and grandeur. Yet a swashbuckler was needed because the intelligence structure in Iberia was weak, the result of what an official history acknowledges as long-term inactivity in the Mediterranean.

'I had, in fact, to create a sort of substitute MI6,' Hillgarth would later write.

It hardly helped that the new ambassador had developed an antipathy to the existing MI6 Head of Station, Leonard Hamilton Stokes. He was very quickly sidelined by Sir Samuel Hoare, who also ensured that all his other intelligence staff 'were in competition with each other for his favour'. The ambassador tried to rise above it by insisting that the service 'must not fall foul of the Spaniards' and not get involved with anti-Franco supporters.

The day after Sir Samuel had taken up his post, Commander Alan Hillgarth sent him a memo: 'The British Embassy in Spain, as a whole, has until recently refused to take into account the fact we are at war.' To Hillgarth's astonishment, there had been no effective control of the entrance to the building, no night watchman and no specially secure safe for holding secret material. 'One cannot be too careful,' he recorded of the situation he found. 'In Spain no one was watched all the time, but everyone was watched some of the time.'

There was little room for manoeuvre. Plenty of Spaniards, he later wrote, were known to be in the pay of the Germans. 'Though they were by no means as inventive or as enterprising as they might have been,' Hillgarth noted, 'they were not inactive and they had some ingenious ideas.' Rumours were not only the stock in trade of the diplomatic community, for, as he noted, 'the country lives on word of mouth stories'. By choosing friends who were 'inveterate gossips' and held great influence, Hillgarth could keep his ears to the ground in full view of the enemy.

They were helped as there had been a virtual famine in the Spanish capital for most of 1940, the result, another MI6 officer noted, of the lingering effects of the Civil War. 'People in the streets looked cowed and half-starved,' Kenneth Benton recalled. 'Those who had been on the wrong side could not get jobs, and many were shot every morning at dawn.'

In his New Year message, the generalissimo had acknowledged the hardships – the shortages of wheat, petrol, meat and sugar were acute – but knew he could do little.

When the Duke of Windsor arrived in Lisbon in July 1940, it was an even more seething cauldron of intrigue, awash with tittle-tattle, gossip, fear and an endless sea of refugees streaming in from all around the occupied European territories. 'Lisbon was the bottle-neck of Europe,' wrote Arthur Koestler, 'the last open gate of a concentration camp extending over the greater part of the Continent's surface.'

Grimness and seediness contrasted with the grandeur and brightness of the Portuguese capital. The lack of blackout (not for nothing was Lisbon known as the Cidade da Luz, city of light) contrasted everything that was happening behind the scenes all the more starkly. Gossip grew out of control as people of all nations came to chat and socialise over drinks. 'Rumour, counter-rumour and tales of fantasy dominated the conversations in these bars,' Neill Locherry has written. 'British and German spies told tales to enlist or frighten the clientele.'

A surfeit of suspicion descended thanks to the all-watchful eyes of a Gestapo-trained secret police. Even if you weren't a spy, an innocent visitor would frequently be believed to be one. Informers loitered everywhere in the hope of picking up tips or spotting something which could be traded with the highest bidder. The docks were the most obvious location. Ships were logged, supplies were disrupted and rumours were spread by using the disaffected lower ranks, especially the seamen who could hardly resist the beautiful women who mysteriously appeared like Sirens of old.

Simply stated, they were on the waterfront and on the game.

The naval branch of the Abwehr had set up and also financed its own brothels down by the docks so the women could obtain information about ships and intelligence about convoys. In its less salacious way, British Intelligence had officials pretending they needed similar information for newspapers, *Lloyd's List*, jealous wives or even Interpol. As one Abwehr officer noted, the stricter control of the Portuguese made their work very difficult. As a result, the Salazar government could not afford to antagonise the Germans. Gamblers were not restricted to the Estoril casino, for as Neill Locherry writes: 'It was a policy of knife-edge neutrality, a poker game for the future.'

But the problem was that nothing was as it seemed. Lisbon was full of refugees, hotel rooms were at a premium and so was mischief – not least with such shady clientele. 'Lisbon is completely covered by a German espionage net,' a report for MI5 by the embassy military attaché noted, 'There are no hotels, restaurants, cafés, etc, of the slightest importance where there are not many German agents. In the more popular hotels, the head waiters are often German agents.'

Against this backdrop, the Windsors didn't want to be the lesser bargaining chips. 'I won't have them push us into a bottom drawer,' he said to Wallis. Only with the offer of a sinecure in the sunshine as the governorship of the Bahamas would the duke leave Iberia. They arrived where he wanted – and expected – to stay: at the glamorous Hotel Palácio in Estoril, where, amongst other things, the barman was reputed to make the best Manhattan in Europe.

It was a curious fact that the Duke of Windsor ended up at the Mouth of Hell where, even stranger, his host was the Holy Ghost. As with some vaguely biblical parable, there was literally no room at the inn. Of all the Portuguese hotels, the Palácio was the most glamorous – and expensive. With all hotel rooms at a premium (the influx of refugees had increased costs so that only kings could probably afford them) both the hotel and the nearby casino, the largest in the country, were, as Neill Locherry has written, Rick's café on a grander scale. The clientele of both were aristocrats, expats, spies, smugglers and diamond traders. At the Palácio, even the chambermaids were on the payroll.

The Boca do Inferno was the name of the region up the coast at Cascais where the duke stayed courtesy of the well-connected and effortlessly charming private banker Ricardo Espiríto Santo. His two-storey house on the edge of Cascais was well hidden, looking out over the crashing waves of the Atlantic. As a confidant of the German ambassador, he was an odd choice to host His Majesty, a cause of much concern to the British, a private banker with many dealings with the Germans. Yet it was abundantly clear that Santo was pulling the strings. The PVDE, the Portuguese secret police, would learn exactly what was going on and the Duke of Windsor would be clearly looked after.

Yet the Holy Ghost was hardly the stooge that the British feared. With the banker's Jewish wife, Edward VIII made an uneasy accomplice. With dinner parties, gold and visits to the casino at Estoril, the former playboy prince was trapped in the gilded palace of his own pomposity, not least when a telegram arrived from the prime minister demanding that he return to Britain. It is said that the Duke of Windsor was so upset that he drafted a telegram where he petulantly resigned all his military commissions. Various German officials in Portugal continued to report gossip that the duke wanted to end the war.

The villa where the duke stayed was guarded – at Sir Stewart Menzies's insistence – by the local police. A king's ransom would have been little more than an extortion for peace had one of the murkier episodes of the secret war been successful, around which so many rumours still swirl. Given the appropriate name of Operation Willi, one of the stranger episodes about which even odder rumours have surfaced.

Foremost amongst them was Walter Schellenberg himself who added some curious details such as his supposed attempted poisoning by the British. Operation Willi was hardly ever a prolonged operation by German Intelligence.

The Reichsminister wanted the duke back in Spain where he could be better reasoned with. Von Ribbentrop gave Schellenberg the authority to offer 50 million Swiss Francs to the duke as an 'inducement'. 'Hitler attaches the greatest importance to this operation,' the foreign minister said. What happened next is unclear – one version has the duke meeting Heydrich and Hess – but Schellenberg flew to Lisbon to oversee all the spying operations around the duke's villa. Operation Willi was always half-hearted and in his memoirs, Schellenberg took a weary, pessimistic tone, not least with the idea to use force if necessary. The duke, indolently playing golf or visiting the casinos, seemed to be bored in the sunshine.

For anyone wanting a proper game of poker, the large, round building at the end of the Palácio's gardens was the obvious place to visit. The casino in Estoril is the largest in Europe and has attained a far greater significance in the mythology of Second World War espionage than anywhere else. Full of fat cats, the Riviera set and rich émigrés who had money to escape to the United States, it also had its fair share of hustlers, smugglers, diamond thieves – and spies. And, thanks to his own later visit there, the Estoril Casino would attain a far greater significance surrounding Ian Fleming's wartime experiences. In the company of Admiral Godfrey, he spied some sinister-looking players who wore dark glasses.

'What if those men had been German secret service agents?' he asked in a moment of fanciful whim. 'Suppose we had cleaned them out of their money. Now that would have been exciting.'

It would be another regular *habitué* of the casino who would come to attract the attention of British Intelligence. The problem with all foreigners who made contact saying they wanted to work for Britain was that they could rarely be taken at face value. The Venlo incident showed how careful they had to be. What made it exceptionally difficult was that Portugal was being flooded with refugees of one sort or another, so when just before Christmas – as crowds shivered in the streets – MI5 heard a new agent was coming, they were on high alert.

'The German secret service is very active at Lisbon and dispatching agents to this country,' a review for the security service would note during the second week of January 1941. And in the case of this fellow who made contact at the end of October, everything about him seemed to set off alarms and prejudices: by his own confession, he was an unlikely spy and playboy with slicked back hair, bright green eyes and what MI5 later called 'the appearance of being a Mongolian-Slav type with rather high cheek bones'.

And so Dusko Popov entered the secret war.

Earlier that summer, the SS Head of Counterespionage quickly came to the conclusion that the once King of England would not want to be a future monarch under a swastika. On 31 July, a message was delivered to von Ribbentrop that Germany was about to invade Great Britain. The immediacy of the duke's possible role in brokering the peace increased dramatically. So Schellenberg ordered the continual harassment of his royal highness – including the throwing of rocks through the window and the telephoning of anonymous threats – which he hoped would be attributed to the British Secret Service. And then, after more frustrating days of inaction, came the final order of all: grab the duke at any cost. Schellenberg wisely decided to ignore this last-ditch madness on the part of the foreign minister. 'Since the Duke has so little in sympathy with our plans, an abduction would be madness,' he later wrote.

Schellenberg flew back to Berlin, where he was warmly congratulated by Heydrich.

'I feel that you shouldn't have accepted this assignment in the first place,' he said. 'Obviously you realised from the beginning how it would probably end. I must say that you carried it off shrewdly.'

The same could never be said for the object of all the manoeuvring. Now en route to the Bahamas, the Duchess of Windsor thought it an amusing example of how the Germans horribly misunderstood the British character. And in Wallis's recollection, when he later heard about what had been planned after the war, the duke was stunned.

'But how could we possibly be of any use to them?' he asked.

Perhaps inadvertently, the Duke of Windsor had provided his own epitaph.

The key to understanding the character of Dusan Miladoroff Popov, several of his handlers noted, was his charm, a joyous playfulness that attracted people from all walks of life. In every sense of the word, Dusko (as he was usually known) would lead an enchanted existence with what one recent chronicler had termed 'all the charm, sexual energy and vigour which is the hallmark still of a true Ragusian squire'. Famously, he would be spotted dancing in nightclubs with the most beautiful women.

On one notorious occasion he bought a whole horse-drawn cart load of flowers on the spur of the moment to give to his latest (however fleeting) inamorata. From the moment of his entry into the secret world, he grasped the essential absurdity of the situation. A highly developed sense of humour, it was clear, would be needed to survive the dangers and rigours of deceit.

The Popovs were a well-established and well-to-do royalist family who lived well in the ancient port of Dubrovnik, and ('by Yugoslav standards', as he later put it) were wealthy. Despite the various upheavals of his native land throughout the early years of the century, they were well connected, too. A foreign education at a lycée in Paris, an English public school (from which he was expelled) and university in the German city of Freiburg followed.

By the late thirties, the clouds of war overshadowed his studies. Dusko took care to play sports and pursued pleasure in equal measure. To his delight, in Freiburg the prettiest girls were to be found in the Aüslander Club, for students who were foreign, like him. The president of which was Johann 'Johnny' Jebsen, who adopted an aristocratic standoffishness, emphasised by his wearing of a monocle and assuming the supercilious demeanour of the frosty hauteur.

Dusko Popov, however, could see through the act.

The pair bonded through a shared capacity for fun, which usually involved women and sports cars. Soon he learned that his new fast friend had managed to avoid military service by joining the Abwehr thanks to the patronage of one of Admiral Canaris's deputies, Hans Oster. Johnny Jebsen too was already exhibiting the anti-Nazi tendencies which were now fomenting in the uppermost reaches of the Fuchsbau. In the spring of 1940 came another twist in Popov's native Belgrade. A friend of Johnny's – a pompous German who turned out to be the chief recruiter for the Abwehr in Central Europe – asked Dusko to work for Germany.

'I can't really say that I was shocked,' Dusko later recalled, 'or that surprised.' If anything, he was angry with his old friend for putting him in such a position. To his slight puzzlement, Johnny Jebsen said that there were distinct benefits of opposing an organisation from within. The next day, Dusko went to the British Embassy to report this approach from the Abwehr. There he was introduced to the Passport Control Officer, the MI6 resident in the Balkans who used the unlikely name of Fickis. In time, after checking with London, Dusko was encouraged to join the Germans. A certain amount of circumspection was inevitable after the Venlo incident the previous autumn.

By now, the Abwehr wanted Dusko Popov to be inveigled into the higher reaches of the British Establishment in London. Over cocktails in the summer of 1940, Johnny Jebsen elaborated the reasons why. 'They have been desperately looking for a man who can move in the upper stratum of British society,' Jebsen said. 'The man was to have other qualities as well, as you can imagine. In essence, he has to have the makings of a superspy.'

That October, Tom Delmer had flown to Lisbon, where he filed a heavily trailed series of articles for the *Daily Express* about refugees from Occupied Europe. They were designed to – and did, indeed – present a vivid picture of what would happen if the Nazis ever invaded Great Britain. It was vintage Delmer stuff, appealing to his vast readership in a newspaper that was then in its heyday, his own experiences informing much of the narrative. The first, on Tuesday, 24 October 1940, referred to his interpreter who had helped him escape the bombing in Warsaw just over a year earlier.

Now, according to a note smuggled out of occupied Poland, she and countless others had been drafted into manual labour for the Third Reich. The whole series was aptly termed 'The Slave States' as an antidote to pervasive German propaganda. Warsaw was but a shadow of itself, an agricultural wasteland whose industrial might had been destroyed, not just by the bombing but the wholesale looting and shutting down of manufacturing.

It was, Delmer claimed, a pattern repeated all over Europe.

There were shortages of food all over the occupied territories, not least in Norway and Denmark, where, according to another informant, there was so little fuel that rugs were being knitted to keep people warm in offices. All this information came from the refugees with whom he was able to meet and discuss freely. Importantly for the future, there were stirrings of the resistance in the Low Countries.

'In a thousand ways, Dutchmen and Belgians are carrying on the fight against the intruder,' Delmer wrote, 'encouraging their own people, who rejoice in passing from mouth to mouth, news of the latest exploits of the freedom fighters.' Certainly, what had been trumpeted across the Low Countries as Hitler's New Deal – inevitably termed the 'Raw Deal' – had seen endless suffering. In his final article that week, Delmer noted that although the psychological scars remained, not least in France where the population was 'still too exhausted to fight even a war of sabotage', hope was springing that salvation would be delivered.

'All our reports agree that there is much greater popular confidence today in Britain's ultimate ability to conquer Germany than there was four months ago,' Delmer concluded from the émigrés to whom he talked. He ended with his own emotional appeal. 'I look forward to the day when the passive resistance turns active,' Delmer wrote of the slave states. 'That day is coming as sure as time goes on.'

Ironically, his own deliverance was upon him.

Over the next few weeks, Tom remained in Lisbon, from where he filed other reports with further information from the ceaseless flood of escapees. Some were, to say the least, surprising. By early December, he had met a party of 200 Jews who, it transpired, had been bribed by the *Sicherheitsdienst* to escape from Nazi Germany. 'You have no idea what it feels like to be out after the seven o'clock curfew hour for Jews,' one of them told him. In Berlin, she said the main topic of conversation was about RAF bombing. And later, when he was asked to pass on a letter for a teenage refugee – later printed in full in the *Express* – Delmer reported that on one train passing through France, this poor girl had seen some sailors. 'They said the [Royal] Navy would never surrender to the Germans and that England was sure to win the war.'

It was all good, stirring stuff and, by the end of the year, in his guise as a *Daily Express* correspondent, Tom Delmer was only too well aware of the great disparity between intelligence work and journalism. His articles for the *Express* were read by 12 million people, where his reports to MI6 were, as he acidly recalled, only ever seen by a few people, largely unread and then incinerated.

While visiting the Portuguese capital, in Delmer's memory, a rabbit-toothed Old Etonian invited him to lunch, where matters of intelligence were discussed.

'You have been working in England for MI6,' this supposed businessman told him.

'I work for no-one but the *Daily Express*,' Delmer replied.

There was a smile and an entreaty to cut the comedy.

'I represent MI6 here,' the Etonian said. 'You were told in London, I believe, that we might be getting in touch with you?'

And soon, much to his surprise, they were.

For all their fears, none of the British informants in Iberia – and that included Alan Hillgarth's extensive and usually well-placed agents – had picked up any hints of transit rights or plans prefacing an invasion of Gibraltar. After seeing London survive the Blitz, the Spanish were impressed. 'General Franco has lost almost all his prestige,' Hillgarth had written in September. 'He is regarded by everybody as being asleep and under the thumb of his brother-in-law.' This was Suñer, the Minister of the Interior, who vied for the title of most hated man in Europe.

Bribery and corruption was occurring and the Spanish Army was ill-equipped and hardly mobilised. With British resolve, many Spaniards believed the British would prevail. But more than that, as Winston Churchill had perceptively noted earlier that year, he suspected Franco 'only thought about keeping his blood-drained people out of another war'.

And that informed the discussion between the Spanish and German leaders, *mano à mano*, at the end of October 1940 about the fate of Gibraltar. Adolf Hitler wearily complained that he would rather have 'three or four teeth extracted than to go through that again'. The conference at Hendaye on the Spanish border did not go well. Neither side was willing to accede to the other. The Führer was unequivocal. Spain should enter the fighting in January 1941, starting with an attack on Gibraltar. Operation Felix needed to be in motion before the Third Reich could invade Soviet Russia. Franco, though seemingly friendly, was intransigent.[9]

Behind the scenes, Wilhelm Canaris had met with the generalissimo privately and warned him that he should not do as Hitler wanted. The admiral confided that Barbarossa was already in the planning stages and that the Führer had no intention of invading Spain should *Il Caudillo* prove too truculent. 'Franco's position,' said one who was party to the discussions, 'was totally influenced by Canaris.'

The clock was ticking. German troops would need to enter Spain by 10 January 1941 for Operation Felix to have any chance of working. But *Il Caudillo* stood firm, insisting that Spain could not join in the fighting because of military unpreparedness and lack of food supplies. What Canaris had grasped – and Hitler never did – was that the window of opportunity so far as an invasion of Gibraltar was concerned had closed.

Soon the Joint Intelligence Committee was reporting in London that Franco would not co-operate with Hitler, nor would Germany now invade Spain. Some have speculated that Admiral Canaris himself was the source of this information. Yet, despite Adolf Hitler's growing preoccupation with lands to the East, British Intelligence remained worried about his capriciousness. 'If Spain were dragged into the war by Hitler,' another MI6 officer based in Lisbon later wrote, 'there would be nothing whatever to stop the latter from occupying Portugal.'

The long-term fate of Iberia would come to loom large in the secret war for nobody wanted to leave Spain or Portugal in the hands of fate. Given his increasing waywardness, Adolf Hitler might suddenly demand precipitate action. What would happen if the Germans seized Spain and Portuguese ports? Worse, suppose blockaded Spanish and, indeed, Portuguese and neutral merchant ships were forced to fly the swastika? Who knew what whim might prompt him to occupy Spain and/or Gibraltar for himself? And in case that happened came an operation with a name that appealed to one of its unrepentant partisans: Goldeneye.

Every so often, the gaiety of the nation is immeasurably enriched when some newspaper or writer claims that they have found the 'real' James Bond or at least the real-life inspiration for 007. One name features repeatedly on the list and, with his various claims of weekends with C, evenings drinking champagne in casinos in the company of statuesque blondes, scars earned to assuage insulted honours in obscure duelling societies, bumping off chauffeurs or surviving exploding cars and the injection of truth serum in interrogations, Dusko Popov sounds all too plausible a candidate. Given that Popov also himself claimed he was followed by Ian Fleming around the Estoril casino a few weeks later, the pedigree of his claim does seem impeccable.

Yet Fleming himself always insisted that 007 was a figment of his overactive imagination. Significantly, another of the author's wartime colleagues would later note that Popov 'exhibited a basic common sense that James Bond never displayed'. If anything, Austin Powers was nearer the mark. Dusko was a hedonist, an accomplished embellisher of tales and a serial seducer of such assiduity that there still lingers today the rumour of an alleged predisposition to threesomes. As a lawyer negotiating import-export deals from his native Yugoslavia, it was imperative that he travel freely and live the kind of carefree life expected by both sides. He could only do that if the British believed that he was bona fide, and soon he passed muster. 'He is courageous, discreet and has great charm,' an MI5 assessment records. 'Accustomed to the good life, he spends money freely.'

In other words, he was everything a putative playboy should be.

He was self-confident, handsome, witty and completely charming. Most of the people he came into contact with – either male or female – were instantly beguiled by his charisma. Though not exactly good-looking (he was slightly hunchbacked, though few ever seemed to notice), his charm attracted people, and that certainly included more mistresses than most Britons could ever understand. Unlike most agents dispatched to the British Isles, Dusko was hardly a social misfit on the make.

British Intelligence now had to decide whether he was genuine or not. After the Venlo incident, there was a sense that nothing could be taken for granted. For his part, Dusko was impressed by the great resilience of the native Londoners. And now he would be afforded the red carpet treatment for he would become a key element in pulling the wool over the Germans' eyes for the rest of the fighting. In the luxurious manner to which he was accustomed, Dusan Miladoroff Popov had, in every sense of the word, arrived in the secret war after his visa had been approved at the start of December 1940.

After arriving in Britain, as one architect of what followed noted, he was 'a new agent of high quality who could plausibly meet persons in any social stratum', mixing in the rarefied upper circles close to the top. As a result, his conquests – in every sense of the word – included a relationship with a striptease artist and, more importantly (though not carnally), her brother-in-law, who just happened to be Sir Stewart Menzies. Fairly quickly, that would involve a unique experience for a double agent: he was allowed to meet the most mysterious and influential figure behind the scenes, the Chief of the Secret Intelligence Service himself.

As the shouting crowds had shown, the great fortress of Jurassic rock that flew the Union Jack was a festering sore so far as the average Spaniard was concerned. Yet for servicemen stationed in Gibraltar there was another form of bellowing that they enjoyed, usually at closing time, where they would sing at the top of their voices:

Symbol of the British Empire
Haughtily Gibraltar stands
Never will this proud erection
Be reduced by Axis hands

If the colony was invaded, which at various times seemed likely, then steps
would have to be taken to maintain essential communications with London.
The rudiments of a sabotage network would have to be put in place to
subvert the country from within. So a sophisticated plan was developed
by the Naval Intelligence Division which, if word of it had leaked, would
have led to the summary ejection of British diplomatic officials from Iberia.

What was given the name Operation Goldeneye was expanded under
the influence of Lieutenant Ian Fleming RNVR. The future creator of
James Bond spent much time shuttling between Britain and Iberia working out the physical details. As Fleming's most recent biographer, Andrew
Lycett, has put it, Goldeneye 'proved a cauldron for inter-service rivalries'
between Naval Intelligence and MI6, as well as their respective sponsors,
the Admiralty and the Foreign Office.

Fleming travelled to Lisbon, then Madrid, where he stayed with the
Hillgarths. In Ian's recollection, they went by road to Gibraltar where
Mary, Hillgarth's wife, attached a white ensign to the radio antenna, but as
Hillgarth's biographer has noted, 'her opinion of his efficiency as a secret
agent was undermined when he left his wallet behind on the table in a
restaurant'. On his return, he wrote Alan a most secret letter to say 'how
much I appreciated being "under your wing".'

In those same early months of 1941, Commander Alan Hillgarth spent
much of his time assessing the mood of the country. 'Spanish susceptibilities
would in all probability preclude sailings en bloc to United Kingdom at any
rate until the extent of British action crystallizes,' he concluded. Another
option was to dispatch Royal Navy ships into ports like Vigo and unload
demolition parties. Yet the sabotage to be carried out by H section of the
Special Operations Executive was vehemently opposed by the ambassadors
in both Spain and Portugal.[10]

The files show the veneer of almost oriental politeness surrounding the
politicking back in London. Sir Stewart Menzies became involved – a letter
on blue parchment signed in C's green ink survives in the NID files – over
exactly who said what to whom, who was responsible for what and all the
other bureaucratic battles which a prolonged bailiwick dispute usually (and
tediously) involve.

In his usual emollient way, Lieutenant Fleming managed to cover up most of the cracks. Indeed, he was in his element, travelling on an elaborate diplomatic passport and wearing the dark blue suit and Old Etonian tie that were positively natty for the time. As one early biographer has remarked, 'he must have felt he was stepping into the pages of Maugham's *Ashenden* at last.' Though Fleming also carried a commando knife and a fountain pen fitted with a cyanide cartridge, his work was less like James Bond than that of a senior clerk in his pre-war stockbroking days. Fleming's task was literally to take stock of the situation in and around the Rock.

'I feel that if Gibraltar is lost there is no hope that Tangier could work as a separate Intelligence Centre,' Fleming later noted for Admiral Godfrey. At his suggestion, a local Joint Intelligence Centre should be formed to co-ordinate all sources of information streaming into Gibraltar to make sure nothing was missed.

On a personal level, there was also an amusing interlude which involved a man with a name that sounds like something from Fleming's imagination: Commander Greenleaves, an embassy official in Tangier who was 'a most likeable and energetic man', in the writer's estimation. If nothing else, his name appealed to 007's creator, not least because it was a *nom de guerre*.

Whether they were drunk or not, he and Greenleaves enjoyed themselves. Their high spirits spilled over into their daubing a large V for Victory sign on the runway at the airport, for which Fleming was later carpeted, though at the time he referred to it as 'the unfortunate incident' in his writings to Admiral Godfrey and left it at that.

Another purpose for Ian Fleming's journey south to the Rock at the start of 1941 was to meet a silver-haired American divorce lawyer who was an intimate of President Roosevelt. Called 'my secret legs' by the polio-stricken president, Colonel Bill Donovan had already visited the beleaguered British Isles to assess a very delicate question.

Was Britain worth fighting for?

The summer before, the colonel was given a red carpet treatment throughout his time in England. First, he met the king and queen at Buckingham Palace, and then the prime minister. Eventually he met Sir Stewart Menzies and Admiral John Godfrey. Donovan couldn't help being impressed by the unwavering British resolve to keep on fighting. Britain, Donovan reported back to the president, would not succumb.

His clean bill of health would essentially underwrite increasingly close co-operation between the two countries, prompting the lend lease or 'destroyers for bases' deal which marked the start of more formal Anglo-American collaborations at the start of 1941. 'What we require are weapons, ships and aeroplanes,' Churchill himself formally told another FDR adviser. 'All that we can pay for we will pay for, but we require far more than we shall be able to pay for.'

Now, at the start of 1941, Donovan was back, touring the neutral states of Europe to assess the military situation once more. Lieutenant Fleming and Captain Hillgarth would spend an entire evening briefing this presidential envoy about the importance of the Goldeneye set-up in case of an invasion. Indeed, when Colonel Bill Donovan reported back in Washington, the president took all his findings onboard: 'It is of the utmost importance to make every practical effort to keep Spain out of the war as far as acting against the Axis Powers.'

It would lead to a lasting working together between the US and the United Kingdom. Certainly, Fleming professed himself greatly impressed with Hillgarth's work and promised to send the Naval Attaché in Madrid some long, fine Henry Clay cigars, which he should smoke himself 'and not give them to your rascally friends', as he wrote on the package he later sent via the diplomatic bag.

During those same early weeks of 1941, everything also finally came together for Tom Delmer. A few days later, when he returned home, Delmer received a telegram from Leonard Ingrams, a glamorous former Oxford Half Blue who flew his own Puss Moth aeroplane around Europe. They had known each other before the war and Delmer was amazed to find him now a star operative in the secret war. A dashing, philandering kind of financier, Ingrams – father of the satirist and recently removed editor of *The Oldie*, Richard – was well known for his imagination, insight and wit, and as a result created his own fair share of enemies.

But at the start of 1941, he sent a telegram to his pre-war friend who was still hanging around the Portuguese capital kicking his heels. Tom Delmer was delighted to read it: 'Suggest you return earliest possible and resign from *Express*, important job awaits you.'

Leonard Ingrams was as good as his word.

When Tom Delmer met him for lunch, the man who was now working in secret intelligence made him an offer he could hardly refuse.

'How would it be if you resigned from the *Express* and came in full time on this racket of broadcasting to the Germans?' Ingrams asked.

Significantly, he had obtained clearance for Delmer's recruitment from all authorities – crucially, that meant MI5, as Tom Delmer's own recently declassified files show – and now the journalist and occasional broadcaster suggested a whole new approach to undermining Hitler. 'Not by opposing him,' Delmer said, 'but by pretending to be all for him and war.'

Leonard Ingrams told him to stop gassing and get on with it. Yet turning that basic idea into a functioning reality would take far longer to achieve than anyone thought necessary.

Delmer's background was of paramount importance so far as his future political warfare work was concerned. He perfectly understood the Nazi mindset, something which had previously counted against him. As a result, he could skilfully counter the increasingly insidious nature of German propaganda. Delmer was to become something of a presiding genius in sensing the potency of 'black propaganda' and, around this time, was given the nickname 'Seldom Defter' by some, for he would turn a popgun into a howitzer. This change of fortunes would be accompanied by an extraordinary character who came into his orbit, whom Delmer later described as walking down Piccadilly looking like an unmade bed, and who now predicted an invasion would come in 1941.

The stars, it seemed, foretold that it was inevitable.

8

THE STARS FORETELL

[The] magnetic power of this man must be broken. To break it, we must not only influence the peoples all over the world: we must also influence the centre from which the magnetism emanates: we must influence Hitler himself. This is not at all beyond our power. For, although obsessed, Hitler is still a human being, and as such subjected to certain hopes, and certain fears. We must therefore disappoint and destroy these hopes. And we must increase, and a hundred times increase those fears. These two are the main themes of the campaign I suggest, the campaign I have called 'The Orchestra of Hitler's death'.

'The ouverture', introduction to a campaign proposed
by the astrologer Louis de Wohl for MI14,
Spring 1941 (WO 208/4475)

When, many years later, Admiral John Godfrey was asked about his similarities to the fictional Admiral Sir Miles Messervy – better known as James Bond's boss, M – he was aghast. The creation of his real-life assistant was nothing like his own character, so he thought, although several recognised aspects of the crusty, demanding fictional head of the secret service had been lifted wholesale from 'Uncle John's' personality.

Though some found him hard to take, for all his steely, heavy-handed ways (the Director of Naval Intelligence always seemed to run on a short fuse) Godfrey's fearsomeness was tempered by his flashing a demonic smile 'at the end of a grilling', as one subordinate remembered, 'that could make a strong man wet in the palms and weak in the bowels'. Beyond the stereotype of an irascible, salty sea dog were glimmerings of an intriguing personality. As his sympathetic biographer has noted, 'the paradoxes and contradictions of John Godfrey's career were only equalled by the quirk and complexities of his character.'

Uniquely for his time and position, Admiral Godfrey engaged a wider social circle than most men of the services, for as one of his obituaries from 1968 pointed out, the wartime DNI 'enjoyed greatly the company of scholars and artists, men of affairs and journalists'. His underlings within the department were a similarly glittering collection of minds, with men who had been barristers, dons and even graphic designers.

Perhaps such eclectic interests explain the DNI's amazing ability at intellectual abstraction. For someone who had been considered the best navigator in the service – traditionally employing the sextant and ephemerides – it was a further mystery that John Godfrey advocated using the stars for other purposes. At the start of the war, Godfrey had suggested to his underlings that they should avoid 'crystal gazing', yet fairly quickly turned to astrology in the hope of prosecuting a very different form of warfare. As the admiral himself explained it, 'under certain circumstances, it is what people believe that matters, not what it is.'

Later he said:

> If one's opponent is known to be a man who places faith in horoscopy and if, as we are assured, it is an exact science, based on the date, time and place of birth, it would surely be unwise to neglect the existence of any advice being tendered to him if, as we believed, our own people knew who were giving the advice and could say what it was.

Quite why someone as strait-laced and no-nonsense as 'Uncle John' was so minded to consider such hocus-pocus has itself caused endless speculation. Though there was the trace of the 'academic manqué' about the DNI, another obituary noted that Admiral Godfrey 'was appalled at any suggestion that he was even by naval standards an "intellectual"'.

Whatever else people thought of the boss, all agreed that Godfrey was a genius in intelligence work. 'The tribute is the more sincere as, in most ways, I disliked him as a person,' his underling Ewen Montagu later wrote. Indeed there was something of a potential personality clash with this scion of the banking dynasty, headed by his father Lord Swaythling. Many found Montagu hard to take, yet even he was dazed by this, the boss's most peculiar contribution to the secret war.

'It had occurred to that ingenious mind that Hitler was believed to have an immense faith in his pet astrologer,' Montagu later recorded in his memoirs. 'If you could predict when Hitler was going to be lucky, then it would indicate he might take a risk.'

Even more remarkably, waiting in the wings was someone who could do exactly that. What happened next would be very hard for anyone to predict, let alone a cross-dressing Hungarian astrologer who would now come to make his most singular contribution to the secret war; the result, no doubt, of it being written in the stars.

So far as Louis de Wohl is concerned, the story would now come full circle – a complete astrological one, in fact – in the autumn of 1940. With his typical devotion to duty, the Hungarian had diligently made it his business to let as many people within the corridors of power know about his work. It was never entirely clear how, in a matter of weeks, he came to the attention of the Director of Naval Intelligence, the Director of Military Intelligence, a leading international financier then working in subversion and, if his claims are to be believed, His Britannic Majesty's Foreign Secretary in the company of the Spanish ambassador.

But somehow he did and, so he sincerely claimed, they were interested in what he would have to tell them about 'where the next attack would come from'. With the onset of autumn, the immediate threat of invasion receded (temporarily at least), which meant that nothing remained beyond the realms of possibility. Strange as it may seem to posterity, the Hungarian émigré was no longer being fobbed off by various branches of intelligence.

Or rather that was how he chose to recall what happened.

The stars, he was at pains to point out, did not foretell an invasion of Britain.

The first grand opportunity for an island invasion would come a year later, he claimed. When Crete was subsequently invaded the following May, de Wohl took credit for having seen Hitler's only air, sea and land invasion of the war. And, without the astrologer ever knowing it, Admiral Räder had actually suggested the British landing be put back until May 1941, to allow for a wider front for the attack. When de Wohl subsequently announced the first grand opportunity for an invasion of southern England that same month, there was much scepticism within official circles. By then, given some of his more obvious eccentricities, Louis de Wohl's MI5 handlers would note, with classic understatement, that he would need 'careful and tactful handling'.

While most of Louis de Wohl's claims about the interest of various branches of British military intelligence in astrology cannot be taken at face value, it is a matter of record that six months earlier – in late March 1940 – the Hungarian had been, in every sense of the word, a star attraction at the annual meeting of British astrologers in Harrogate. In view of the claims which he would make exactly a year later (in March 1941, he would completely contradict his earlier views) it is worth noting what he was quoted as saying at the time.

'Astrology can be poison of the worst type in the wrong hands,' Louis de Wohl publicly declared to the press. And, for good measure, he added that anyone who used the stars to predict death was nothing less than a criminal. At that same meeting, another astrologer, Charles Carter, was noting that there was already a widespread belief in astrological circles that Hitler was being advised by astrologers: 'He would scarcely have made war with his own horoscope in such an unfortunate condition.'

This, too, was echoed in Louis de Wohl's later fanciful account, where it was clear 'that Jupiter was in conjunction with his Sun' so the Führer would invade Western Europe in May 1940. Behind the scenes, the records show that three weeks earlier the Services Consultative Committee – a War Office 'think tank' aiming to think outside the box – had also noted that a large number of Germans were superstitious and that 'it is believed that a good deal of interest is taken in astrology. There was a rumour that Hitler himself believes in astrology, and had employed the services of an astrologer.'

The committee suggested that they should obtain from a well-known astrologer a horoscope of Hitler, predicting disaster for him and his country and putting it into Germany by secret channels. This, certainly, was the general approach which Naval Intelligence eventually took in this rarefied form of psychological warfare. From the outset, though, it was recognised that each astrologer would come up with a different answer: the result, therefore, was to work out whose prediction would be the most useful for propaganda purposes.

Fairly quickly, the authorities had zeroed in on the most vociferous.

Given some of the security scares emanating from the Spanish Embassy in August 1940, of fellow travellers and agents of undue influence, perhaps it is stranger still that Louis de Wohl was invited for dinner there, where he was introduced to Lord Halifax, the Foreign Secretary.

Or this, at least, is the astrologer's claim.

In his version of the story, Louis de Wohl was intrigued to meet such a grandee. The various attendees were enthralled as the Hungarian émigré told some of his stories. They sat in a semi-circle of chairs over port and cigars as the astrologer spoke for an hour. According to the spate of near contemporary reports which he had been issuing at the time, de Wohl explained that Hitler's advisers had told him his aspects were bad until November. 'I explained all this to Lord Halifax, then his Majesty's Foreign Secretary at the Spanish Embassy on the 28th August 1940,' he later claimed.[1]

Louis de Wohl had come into the orbit of such influential people thanks to the Romanian ambassador, V. V. Tilea, who had taken it upon himself to introduce the astrologer to various influential people. A society hostess had introduced him to the Duke of Alba, the Spanish ambassador, and things moved very quickly after that. In his memoirs, de Wohl believes that Lord Halifax was instrumental in opening doors for him behind the scenes. Six days before the meeting, his lordship had apparently written to him to suggest he come along for a chat. Even so, the Hungarian was self-aware enough to realise that it would be hard to find someone with his skills a berth.

'The very idea that one fine day a member of the House of Commons might get up and ask whether it was true that His Majesty's Government was employing a stargazer, made many of my new friends shudder,' he recalled. Yet some unlikely champions were listening. To say that Louis de Wohl was tickled pink by Admiral Godfrey's interest in his work is an obvious understatement. It gave him a certain cachet and, indeed, credibility which had been lacking in his efforts to date. By the end of the year, his cup overruneth: the Hungarian was being regularly consulted by Naval Intelligence, the War Office and, shortly, by his most amused and assured patron in the fledgling political warfare establishment, Sefton Delmer.

Never one to hide his star-crossed lights under any inconvenient bushels of truth, Louis de Wohl always claimed that the admiralty became interested in his work because of the startling accuracy of his predictions.

The truth is slightly different.

Naval Intelligence files show that in September 1940, Louis de Wohl had sent a note to the DNI called 'The Astrological Tendencies of Herr Hitler's horoscope', in which he claimed that the Führer had waited until April 1940 to invade Denmark and Norway as he preferred to begin action under a new moon. Hitler's current aspects, which de Wohl claimed would 'influence the

Führer for the next six months', contained the curious observation that 15 September 1940 was an ominous date for Adolf Hitler. 'On that day,' a note on the file says, '185 German aeroplanes were brought down over southern England.'

Suitably amended, the astrologer suggested many of these prognostications could be forwarded along the chain of command. As Admiral Godfrey later noted, 'the significance of Hitler's astrological researches was not whether they were predictive of the truth but that Hitler believed in them.' And so on Tuesday, 1 October 1940, Admiral John Godfrey minuted his immediate superiors (the First Sea Lord, Vice Chief and First Lord of the Admiralty) about the possible uses of astrology. They doubtless wondered if the steely martinet who was their intelligence chief had somehow taken leave of his senses. Trying to 'sell' his new idea to his superiors, Godfrey stressed this approach was unusual but if carried out in the spirit in which it was intended, would result in significant strategic advantages.

The study, Godfrey advised, would analyse 'the horoscopes of [Hitler's] principal advisers, Generals, Admirals and of the Statesmen, such as Mussolini, with whom he has had dealings'. The Director of Naval Intelligence took care to acknowledge that 'the formation of a group of sincere astrologers prepared to work on these subjects is by no means a fantastic idea'. He added a ten-page 'explanatory note' that had been written by de Wohl and explained that Adolf Hitler had, for quite some time, had his own penchant for astrologers. Given that astrology was supposedly an 'exact science', then all reputable astrologers would come to roughly the same conclusions.

'This being so,' Godfrey added, 'it is not a science which lends itself to deception as in astrological circles the deception would soon be bowled out.' The DNI insisted that the notions which were being fed to Hitler would be checked by reputable astrologers. As ever, the name of Karl Krafft was given as this mysterious, behind-the-scenes influence on the German leader.

Doubtless Admiral Godfrey's superiors wondered if something had been accidentally slipped into their coffee when they read the full memorandum that autumn. Certainly, their lordships were bleakly unimpressed. The Vice Chief of the Naval Staff replied – somewhat tongue-in-cheek, one cannot help from thinking – that if such studies were carried out, 'we might have a new department of NID'. Dudley Pound, the First Sea Lord under whom he had served, thought the proposal 'interesting', but that he would want the admiralty to base its appreciations on 'something more solid than horoscopes'.

Yet the story did not end there. By October 1940, even the Joint Intelligence Committee set up to provide one coherent source of information collated from all secret services was considering the need to consult the stars to predict the invasion. For the period beginning 19 October, its minutes note: 'The moon and tides were suitable, the incidence of fog likely, and Hitler's horoscope, a sign to which he was reported to pay considerable attention, was favourable during this period.'

They were not alone. Another peculiar form of insurance was available.

Louis de Wohl's guesses were as good as anybody else's. Within weeks, Commander Ewen Montagu and Admiral Godfrey's secretary in Room 39 carried out the task of finding the most amenable of seers. 'So Ted Merrett and I were sent round to a vast number of astrologers,' Montagu recorded. 'The results were very entertaining but useless.'

As Montagu reflected, it might have worked.

The denouement was something none of them could predict. It seems that one of their Naval Intelligence colleagues became rather too zealous in his interest in the subject, and ultimately this unspecified gentleman, in Montagu's understated phrase, 'was speedily posted a few thousand miles away from London when it was discovered that he was actually beginning to believe in astrology'.

The full figure, 'dressed in a splendid officer's uniform' in one recollection, 'complete with a Sam Browne, an expensive leather-covered cane [and] an enormous beautifully tailored greatcoat', was a sight that very few of His Majesty's secret servants would ever forget. Yet in those ominous autumnal days of 1940, Louis de Wohl was oblivious to any and all brickbats that swarmed, like so many meteors attracted by his bulky frame. Louis de Wohl didn't care; recruited, so he claimed, by a government which, by his own account, was so grateful it made him 'a British officer with the rank of Captain'. Indeed, his autobiographical *The Stars of War and Peace* carried a frontispiece showing 'Captain' Louis de Wohl decked out in just such a uniform. By September 1940, de Wohl claims, he had formed the 'Psychological Research Bureau', which was based at Grosvenor House, Park Lane, ostensibly, he claims, to look at the psychology surrounding Hitler's men.[2]

What does sound suspiciously like a typical piece of his self-aggrandising braggadocio is actually more interesting. Bizarrely enough, it even has a ring of truth. The Special Operations Executive – then more interested in performing small-scale hand-to-hand combat with its political rivals than enemy forces in Occupied Europe – did indeed put de Wohl on its payroll. It underwrote his expenses in moving from the Esplanade Hotel to a block of unfurnished suites attached to Grosvenor House, where he set up shop.

Sir Charles Hambro, scion of another illustrious banking family and then a director of SOE, seems to have been the first to recognise the Hungarian's value in 'black' psychological operations. In Sir Charles's eyes, Louis de Wohl could do no wrong. As the acerbic former codebreaker Leo Marks recorded, Hambro was known by his Baker Street Irregulars as CD, 'a tiny symbol to embrace so vast a man'. Ironically, the codebreaker was a near neighbour of the boss and had an excellent view of his bathroom. 'We frequently had the privilege of watching the oversized banker wedged in his undersized bath,' he later recalled.

Thanks to the release of the astrologer's files, the full story of his recruitment and the granting of his right can now be told. 'De Wohl was employed personally by Sir Charles Hambro to work for SOE,' a note for MI5 records over two years later:

> In the fullness of his wisdom, Hambro arranged that he would become Captain. On de Wohl enquiring when he would be sworn in I gathered that a ceremony [was] staged at Horse Guards in which Brigadier Gubbins swore him in, following the wording of an ordinary recruit's Attestation Form. Even apart from this farce, de Wohl had every reason to believe, and still believes, that he is a Captain in the British Army. Indeed, as he has never been told he is not, I presume technically he is still, in fact.

Many of the exact details of Louis de Wohl's early contacts with other branches of British Intelligence remain sketchy because of a firestorm that took place in a prison in West London. For those who regularly took the Number 12 bus from central London in the autumn of 1940, they soon became used to upper-class 'gels' – invariably pretty ones, often giggling and walking off together – travelling all the way to that particular route's terminal stage outside Wormwood Scrubs. If it struck anybody as odd that such a ravishing array of debs and 'twinsets and pearls', as they were later termed, were spending their working days in a prison, nobody said.

In wartime, many secrets were compromised by self-evident absurdities.

In time, even the conductors were emboldened to shout 'All change for MI5' when the Number 12 bus reached the end of the line. Because of fear of bombing of Central London, most of the Security Service had been moved lock stock and barrel to the spectacularly inappropriate surroundings of the Scrubs. It had been a chaotic move, not least with the firing of General Kell at the start of the summer. Many of the women who worked for the agency as secretaries (and as noted earlier, all from 'top drawer' backgrounds) found some consolation that during the extended good weather that summer of 1940 they had could sunbathe on the scrubland outside.

As the headquarters of a security service, the prison was distinctly lacking.

Working in the former cells, there were never enough telephones and each door had to be opened from the outside. When the Signal Corps came to rectify the situation, they left behind a spaghetti of wires that dangled dangerously on floors and landings. Many MI5 staff were accidentally locked in their cells and had to wait until someone came to see what had happened to them. Four-foot-thick walls meant that not only were cries for help unheard, but conditions within the cells were either too hot or too cold depending on the outside weather.

On the evening of Thursday, 3 October, 1940, things became even more unbearable. An incendiary bomb landed and burnt off most of the roof of C Wing. With an even more curious irony, this was where the famed MI5 Registry had been located. That meant that thousands of personal files on suspected agents, saboteurs and ne'er-do-wells literally went up in smoke. Though some had been photographed as a precaution, many of the results were over-exposed. Indeed, General Kell had so balked at the huge cost of copying the files (£4,000) that he had decided the whole process was too expensive.[3]

Though the Blitz continued, many within the Security Service felt that the changes since the firing of General Kell were not for the better. Behind the scenes, an unholy jockeying for power was taking place and another recruit to the service, who delighted in wordplay and doggerel, would pen a suitable ditty to record the fact:

> What of the gaol, now cleared of scrubscious youth?
> At once there occupies its cells and towers
> A corps of para-military sleuths
> Whose devious minds divide the working hour
> Between re-numbering their divisions
> And making even more obscure decisions.

That reference to renumbering may seem obscure, but what prompted it was the root-and-branch reform, particularly within B Division, which dealt with counter-espionage. And that included a former leading light whose star was now waning as much as those which guided Louis de Wohl were clearly in the ascendant.

On the face of it, 1940 should have been a good year for Max Knight.

His work had helped uncover many agents in various organisations whose sympathies were quite suspect. These included members of the Right Club, a fascist organisation, and the American Tyler Kent, who worked as a code clerk at the US Embassy. Yet Max Knight's autonomy was starting to cause concern, not least his uncanny ability to get up people's noses and his inattention to detail. Worse, he had usurped his authority and provided false information in a case that reached the High Court. Even today, the details of how one of his contacts essentially perjured himself by creating false evidence, remains unclear.

What resulted was a dreadful mystery – of the gothic and overwrought variety in which he specialised – and shows just how far Maxwell Knight would go to get his man. The object was a misguided pacifist called Ben Greene, who in retrospect was a harmless, gentle giant of a man. Friedle Gärtner was involved too and, watching aghast, MI5 management took against him. His career suffered and Knight left London, banished to a house in Camberley, where, with his marriage to Lois long finished, he turned his attention to his menagerie. Pride of place was a cuckoo called Goo. It was obvious why such birds appealed to him: they were both subversive – infiltrating their eggs into other birds' nests – and ruthless in evicting the original occupants. By the end of the war, Knight's counter-subversion department was disbanded and he left the agency if not in disgrace, then certainly with an appropriate wing down.

If there was one issue which would come to perplex, annoy and exercise virtually all the participants in the secret world with whom he ever came into contact, it was Louis de Wohl's psychological need to wear his ornate captain's outfit. 'He is an exceedingly vain man,' MI5 noted sourly for the files, 'with all the Germans' love of uniform and rank.' Indeed, the astrologer's continued bleating about his military garb was just one manifestation of his incessant demands that soon started to alienate his handlers. Louis de Wohl never seemed to appreciate that his commission as a captain appears to have been a ploy to get him off their backs. 'I cannot give you anything in writing as it's much too secret,' one senior official had told him, 'and of course, you cannot use the rank.'

But this didn't stop Louis de Wohl getting his own captain's uniform made up. One friend who knew him well thought that he was like a little boy who had just received his Christmas presents early. 'He stood up, he sat down, stood up again, walked around the room and looked into a large mirror in silent admiration,' Dr Felix Jay recalled when he happened to have visited him when he was trying out his uniform.

At least now, by the autumn of 1940, his dealings with the various intelligence agencies had been streamlined. Louis de Wohl would now be handled by a hale, well met kind of fellow with whom he felt some kinship for being a fellow scribe. Now in his early 50s, Major Gilbert Lennox had achieved some pre-war success as a playwright after retiring early from the Indian Army. In his role as a military liaison officer with the Security Service, at times he no doubt felt that he was now starring in a bizarre cross between a drawing room comedy and farce.

As a foreign national, there were many in London who wondered if it wouldn't just be simpler to intern Louis de Wohl as an enemy alien. That September, the Iron Guard, a far-right movement that regularly employed death squads, forced King Carol to abdicate. As a result, Romania became aligned with the Third Reich, enacted stricter anti-Semitic laws and, almost inevitably, unleashed a reign of terror.

As a precaution, over the next few weeks in Britain, many Romanians were interned. That same month, MI5 vouched for Louis de Wohl's character, finding there was nothing to justify adding him to the Hungarian blacklist. Nor did the agency have any objection to his naturalisation as a British citizen. Over the next few years, as he came to exasperate his handler, internment hung uneasily as a possible solution to Louis de Wohl's various antics. But Gilbert Lennox always considered it would be a gross miscarriage of justice to intern the Hungarian astrologer. 'After all, he seemed to have done a good job of work, and as far as I know, there have been no complaints,' Lennox would write. 'If, on the other hand he is just dropped, I think the situation would be very different.'

For Louis de Wohl personally, the fate of Romania would come to have greater impact in his dealings with V.V. Tilea, the ambassador who had acted as his social secretary in the early part of the war. According to the astrologer, 'No 4' (a name that sounds suspiciously like a SPECTRE henchman in an early Bond film but was in fact one of Sir Charles Hambro's liaison officers at the SOE) had asked him outright whether he and Tilea were thinking of going back to their own country 'or break with their government and stay here'.

They both decided to stay. It was also clear that if it was announced that Ambassador Tilea had 'defected', it would certainly help in undermining both the German and Romanian governments. Such an act – which followed a few days later – revealed, as Louis de Wohl noted, that 'the atmosphere' in London was that there would definitely be a British victory in the end'.

Thanks to such public displays of loyalty, it was agreed that after five years in the country his British citizenship should be expedited. And accompanying this, the files also show that the astrologer thought he should be entitled to yet another strange sartorial recognition. 'I am only sorry that Louis's own heart's desire of giving him a commission and appointing him to a Highland regiment cannot be granted,' Gilbert Lennox noted. 'The sight of Louis in full Highland dress would have been the most cheering spectacle.'

Curiously, around this time the astrologer came into contact with an officer of genuine Scottish origins, a subtle and clever official in yet another branch of military intelligence. The only thing regimental about him, as one of his admiring subordinates put it, 'were his tartan trews' and soon, like many others, he wondered quite what the curious Hungarian astrologer was trying to achieve.

By now, to his obvious delight, Louis de Wohl was pushing at an open door.

Others in Whitehall were also being sent examples of his work, and for one branch of the War Office it was an element of faith that any insight – no matter how obscure or surreal – could help face off the enemy. MI14, the branch of military intelligence that was trying to understand the German military's strategic intentions, was headed by the former assistant military attaché to Berlin. When Lieutenant Colonel Kenneth Strong had returned to the War Office in the spring of 1940 to head up this new department, he was looking forward to it.

Fairly quickly, he was astounded to find just three officers assigned to him and they were soon overwhelmed as problems showered down all around them. Their task was gigantic, not least after the fall of France, when the German Army tended to use landlines. That meant they could no longer assess the strengths and deployments of the enemy across the water from monitoring telltale radio transmissions.

But Strong could tune into the German mindset – and that was important.

Like so many others, the pre-war assistant military attaché's voice had been one in the wilderness. By talking to his opposite numbers in Berlin, he got a glimpse of how blitzkrieg would be unleashed. 'You need three British battalions to equal one German one,' he would say. 'When will people learn this?'

In later years, it was always said that Kenneth Strong's department was set up to read the mind of Adolf Hitler. The man himself always denied this. 'The idea of having a group of people put itself in the place of the enemy is an idea [that] is constantly recurring and dies slowly,' he remarked. In other words, such an aim was wishful thinking. Yet, despite this, as *The Times* noted at the time of his death in 1982, under Strong's guidance, MI14 'produced a brilliant and accurate picture of the complicated order of battle and the Reichswehr and of the intentions of the German High Command'. Unlike much of the pre-war MI6 CX material, it was said that his reports from Berlin were so impressive that they had persuaded Chamberlain to introduce conscription.

The only son of a rector of the Montrose Academy, Strong lived up to the promise of his surname in terms of his mental agility. After Sandhurst, he had been appointed defence security officer in both Malta and Gibraltar, and after returning to London was promoted to lieutenant colonel. Thanks to his attention to detail, MI14 very quickly became renowned for the accuracy of its analyses. Lieutenant Colonel Strong's rise thereafter was meteoric and he would end the war as General Eisenhower's senior military intelligence adviser. The Allied Supreme Commander, like many others, appreciated Kenneth Strong's clear-headedness in times of turmoil.

'He looked like a beaver,' the later principal of University College London Noel Annan, who worked with him in 1940, would fondly recall, 'an eager beaver bursting [out] of his uniform, with dark hair, a fine forehead, clever, shifty eyes and so chinless that he came to be known as the hangman's dilemma.' Strong's section soon established a reputation for what today would be known as thinking outside the box.

Nothing was beyond the remit of 'The German Section' and that came to include the consultation of a water diviner whom Strong christened 'Smoky Joe'. There was also a disturbing incident with a man – who was thankfully, well meaning – who had escaped from a mental asylum and somehow managed to find himself in the lieutenant colonel's office in Whitehall. 'As always at such times we found we were plagued by all sorts of people,' Kenneth Strong later wrote of that fateful summer of 1940. 'Some of the cranks who felt they had a definite contribution to make to winning the war.'

Amongst their number, almost inevitably, was Louis de Wohl.

The Hungarian astrologer had continued to send his various assessments on German generals and admirals to anyone who might care to read them. Gilbert Lennox noted approvingly that this would keep his otherwise 'idle hands occupied – or rather his brain'. That was one way of putting it. When Kenneth Strong came to meet the astrologer in person, he was too diplomatic to say what he really thought. Though told his work was invaluable to the war effort, in his memoirs Strong never mentioned the astrologer by name but was in no doubt about his usefulness. 'I never discovered the slightest justification for paying heed to this gentleman,' he lamented, 'but I was overruled and the astrologer continued to receive support and to live in a comfortable flat in a fashionable London district.'

At this stage, it is as well to consider some of the weirder and more wonderful views of those at the top – then, and in more recent years – for all leaders set great store by prescience. That partly explains the devouring of secret intelligence by politicians, but also other forms of information. In some accounts, Winston Churchill's own superstitions had led to his consulting a clairvoyant called Reginald Hickling in the Great War as well as a psychic American, Shirley Carson. Sir Stafford Cripps, Churchill's wartime ambassador to Stalin's Soviet Union, was a devout Christian who believed in what a later ministerial colleague called 'mumbo jumbo'.

Despite Kenneth Strong's scepticism, there were those in the military who set great store in the supernatural. Lord Dowding, who had directed Fighter Command during the Battle of Britain, believed in elves. His opposite number in Bomber Command, Air Chief Marshal Harris, sometimes consulted Lyndoe, *The People* newspaper's astrologer, to determine the best time to carry out raids on Germany.[4]

In more recent times, astrologers have taken up their place in the corridors of power. In 1997, the French were stunned to learn that their recently departed president, François Mitterand, had consulted an astrologer during important decisions. Elisabeth Teissier had, it seemed, predicted the fall of the Berlin Wall as well as another international crisis which revealed, so far as she was concerned, that history seemed to be repeating itself thanks to a leader 'with the same astrological cocktail as Hitler – a Taurus with Libra ascendant'. This was Saddam Hussein's invasion of Kuwait in August 1990. There was also a surprising lack of Gallic gallantry in some of the other whispers that surrounded Mme Teissier's work with the late president of the Republic: 'I acted as his adviser and nothing more,' the astrologer imperiously declared. 'It's dreadful what some people have been saying.'

But far more notorious was the interest in the stars of a First Lady.

As the former chief of staff to the Reagan White House, Don Regan, famously recorded in his memoirs while the president was still in power, every major decision 'was cleared in advance with a woman in San Francisco who drew up horoscopes'. Joan Quigley, who died in October 2014, confirmed her role despite furious denials from the Reagans at the time. Quigley claimed she was responsible for the timing of all press conferences, speeches (including the State of the Union address) and when Air Force One took off. 'I picked the time of Ronald Reagan's debate with [Jimmy] Carter and the two debates with Walter Mondale,' she later told one interviewer, 'all extended trips abroad as well as the shorter trips and one-day excursions.'

Intriguingly, she always maintained that Ronald Reagan's horoscope was brilliant. 'His stars are very lucky for a country,' she told the *Washington Post* in 1988, explaining that what she did was 'technical work, not crystal ball gazing'. A columnist on that same paper had noted in the forties that Vice President Wallace, who served under FDR for a term, was 'a stargazer of many cults'.

Other significant political events seem to have been triggered by the heavenly runes. As the journalist Woodrow Wyatt noted, when the post-war decision to formally separate Pakistan from India was made, astrologers were consulted. Then working as a civil servant, Wyatt recalls that one particular day in August 1947 was chosen thanks to the stars to keep both sides happy. 'So Pakistan began its independence in the morning and India in the middle of the night,' he later wrote.

Various intelligence agencies in the Cold War were mindful of the stars. According to the late Miles Copeland, father of rock drummer Stewart and a former high-ranking officer of the Central Intelligence Agency, agents were planted on Kwame Nkrumah of Ghana, Sukarno of Indonesia and Mehmet Shehu of Albania in the sixties who were well versed in astrological techniques. In February 1966, Nkrumah was visiting China – the timing having been prompted thanks to a horoscope – when a military coup deposed him (which, with a certain symbolism, had been engineered by the CIA). Around the same time, Sukarno was handed a doctored chart, which the CIA's 'Cosmic Operations Section' (which Copeland headed) used to help predict his movements. A month after the Ghanian coup, the Indonesian leader was also deposed thanks to machinations that had been engineered by both the CIA and MI6.

A few years earlier, in Copeland's account, when the Director of Central Intelligence, Allen Dulles, learned that these doctored charts were being used ('bootlegging certain charts to certain members of our own White House staff' was how Copeland recalled it) outside normal channels, it was stopped. At around the same time, according to the Bulletin of the Federation of American Astrologers, the Kremlin had reinstated one Yuri Yamakkin, an astrologer whose own fortunes rose and fell after having failed to warn of the US reaction to the Korean War. Stalin sent him to the Vorkuta gulag, but according to this account he was rehabilitated by Khruschev, to allow the Praesidium to study 'the movements of the Red Star in the heavens', as one newspaper account concluded.

At the start of 1941, Louis de Wohl began sending what he classed as 'elaborate astrological analysis, month by month' to Kenneth Strong's department, MI14. Their value can be gauged from an anonymous comment in the margins of the relevant file in the UK National Archives: 'Of no value – one of MI's stranger sidelines … all 1940/1941 vintage, I think.'

It is also equally obvious that nobody quite had the heart to tell de Wohl that his work was more or less irrelevant. Following on from his earlier reports to Naval Intelligence, de Wohl had already submitted one report on the astrological 'aspects' which had been influencing the Führer's more recent decisions. According to de Wohl, Adolf Hitler would be 'lucky' from the end of October 1940 'until the end of the first week of March'. It was then, in the spring of 1941, that the runes suggested there would be a grand opportunity for an island invasion.

When Crete was subsequently taken by the Wehrmacht, de Wohl took credit for the accuracy and acuity of his work. But now, at the end of January 1941, came his *pièce de resistance*, a series of predictions about the various leaders (political and military) on both sides of the fighting. For the most part, Louis de Wohl's self-proclaimed psychological pen portraits are sometimes unintentionally hilarious. The astrologer drew up a table with the kind of information which he believed would be exactly the same as that being given to Adolf Hitler by Herr Krafft. Again, the Hungarian took care to note the significant observation that Adolf 'has never undertaken a major action unless he had "good aspects" at that time'. As a result, the Führer's 'luck' was being ordained by the stars.

From March 1941 up to the middle of May 1941, 'Hitler's aspects are bad. So are Göring's, except for a short period from April 30th. So are Admiral

Räder's. The aspects of Keitel and von Brauchistsch [sic] are not too good.' By comparison there were 'excellent aspects' in British leaders, but the strangest aspect of the Hungarian's report was to recommend a combined 'naval and military' action against Germany's military ports. It would give the Führer the shock of his life, 'to see British uniforms appearing on German soil'.

Not everybody was convinced by de Wohl's psychic powers – to create, as he saw it, a storm of occultic vengeance – though they were obviously happy to hear that it was clear 'that Germany would be defeated'.

To many, the subject of stargazing seemed like so much nonsense. Around this time, the first condemnations of Louis de Wohl as a charlatan appear. When Colonel Lennox referred some of the astrologer's predictions to Dick White, the rising head of counter-intelligence within the Security Service, he noted: 'I don't like decisions of this kind made by reference to the stars rather than MI5.'

Louis de Wohl remained indefatigable.

His next suggestion, even by his standards, was equally peculiar and came from his own background as a dramatist within the movies. He suggested that a film on the Anti-Christ be made via the Christian League, where parallels with a certain Austrian-born dictator would commend themselves. For that, there should also be an equally weird tie-in with branding and artefacts.

'There should be a symbol, equivalent to "the mark of the beast" (the swastika),' he suggested, to market the film. Louis de Wohl suggested this real cross, of metal and of artistic design, 'to be worn in the same way decorations are worn, but also in the form of tie-pins, brooches etc.' As well as funding and producing the film, the Christian League should also produce a special brochure of about ten to twelve pages. 'This should be printed in this country as well as in the United States,' de Wohl suggested. 'I shall be delighted to complete it and I consider it a grand task.'

Only Dusko Popov might ever be introduced in person by the chief of the British Secret Service to a striptease artist with whom he would almost inevitably have an affair. In those first few weeks of 1941, the charming Yugoslav had fallen – not for the last time – desperately in love with his latest inamorata. Appropriately housed at the Savoy, his handlers had asked him how he wanted to spend his first New Year's Eve in England. Entirely characteristically, Dusko had replied he wanted the company of either a good book or a temperamental popsy.

At a Georgian mansion in the Home Counties he would shortly find both in abundance within a library and drawing room. To his utter delight, the women were as decorative as the expensive chandeliers and ostentatious ornaments. Here was, exactly as his Abwehr handlers suggested, a suitable entrée into the upper echelons of society courtesy of Sir Stewart Menzies. Little Bridley in Surrey was home to C's mother, Lady Holford, who in the years between the wars had become a noted hostess.

As a lady-in-waiting to Queen Mary, she still mixed in exalted circles.

It had struck her son that here was a golden opportunity for the latest recruit to the 'great game' to join such a grand set to see in the new year. Sir Stewart Menzies had met Dusko a few days earlier in the bar at White's Club, where, C's critics always complained, he spent far too much time. Menzies suggested Dusko come along to his mother's, not least because he suspected he would enjoy meeting two of the most beautiful women in the country. Early that Tuesday evening in the drawing room at Little Bridley, Dusko was introduced to Sir Stewart's brother, Ian, and his Austrian-born wife, Lisle.

Next to her was her sister, described by Popov's most recent biographer as 'a singer who regularly appeared in cabaret in London nightclubs'. Actually, Friedle Gärtner was something more: whilst MI5 officers later called her a 'super high class mannequin' who had the mentality 'of a night club hostess', others considered her little more than a glorified stripper. It was something which even Max Knight had not mentioned in his own files when she had gone to work for Dennis Wheatley.

Popov was immediately hooked: women and wealth were his abiding wartime passions. As he related, he found her manner, at first, puzzling. So engrossed was he in her beauty, he had to be taken away from her by C himself. 'I think you will have many opportunities to see her,' the chief of MI6 said, knowing full well what the service had in store for him.

They then retired to a drawing room where Sir Stewart Menzies got the measure of his latest recruit. If Dusko's account is to be believed, the conversation smacks of James Bond, for not even the chief of MI6 in the comfy confines of a club-like atmosphere would bandy around secrets. But it was clear the country's leading spymaster drew the Yugoslav into his confidence, despite one or two reservations.

'You have too many devices on your banner for my taste,' Sir Stewart told him. 'You have the makings of a very good spy except that you don't like to obey orders. You had better learn or you will be a very dead spy.'

After her various escapades helping Dennis Wheatley and Maxwell Knight, Friedle Gärtner would now devote her considerable energies towards Dusko Popov. She would be used 'to simply entertain him and keep him out of trouble' in the strait-laced words of one security review. Perhaps she took the 'entertaining' part a shade too literally in view of what transpired. Nevertheless, Friedle Gärtner became Dusko Popov's first recruit in what he subsequently claimed to his German controllers in Lisbon was a network of spies in the making. Friedle would be used to send purposefully confusing pictures about the political situation in Britain. As she still had family in Germany, it added to her bona fides that her motivation was to ensure that no harm would to come to them.

When Dusko was told that Friedle would be taking part in this real-life game of charades, his handler Billy Luke smiled salaciously. 'Congratulations,' he said. 'You got yourself the most beautiful social mistress in London.'

Friedle provided perfect cover. It was entirely natural that she would be able to take him to all the best homes in the land. Luke added that she wasn't really a member of the 'old firm'. 'Does an odd chore for us now and then,' he said. To the Germans, Dusko explained she had introduced him to the cream of society. And, as he further elaborated, she 'specialised in using her social contacts to gather political news and secrets and information about new army commands, nominations and the like'.

Yet beneath the beguiling beauty was the omnipresent lure of danger which added a frisson to their burgeoning relationship. It was a dangerous addiction as Dusko followed her around the various parties 'like a goggle-eyed fish who sees nothing but the bait'. Their passion was consummated early in the new year of 1941 when she answered her front door dressed in a short terry-cloth robe, with her blonde hair still freshly wet. As Dusko noted, after spending the rest of the day in bed they became more than a team. Given the codename Tricycle[5] by MI5, Dusko Popov would set up a highly placed network of agents in Britain for the Abwehr which was under complete British control.

Given the peripatetic nature of his import/export business, Dusko did have good enough reasons to visit London regularly. As a result, at the start of 1941 he was able to begin an important collaboration with Naval Intelligence and the NID's point man who had investigated so many of the country's astrologers. Now, as the Right Honourable Ewen Montagu would later note, he 'fell under the spell of [Dusko's] personality, his sincerity, his gaiety and his courage'. Together, they created one of the most important naval deceptions of the Second World War to stand off the omnipresent threat of invasion.

In some ways, Commander Montagu was the very epitome of the Establishment. The eldest son of Lord Swaythling and thus an heir to great monetary fortune, he had studied law at both Harvard and Trinity College, Cambridge. Small wonder that his finely honed legal skills smelled a rat. Aware of how ridiculously the Abwehr seemed to react, Montagu soon started to wonder if they were not being taken in by some sort of elaborate deception operation.

'As the war progressed,' he would later write, 'no degree of incompetence by the Germans surprised us.'

Doubtless puffing on his pipe one day as he read through the first questionnaire the Abwehr had provided Dusko, he noticed something remarkable: that it looked as though the invasion of Britain had been delayed (but as Montagu noted 'there was no real evidence that it had been abandoned for good'). When it did happen, from the questions Dusko had been provided with, it appeared as though the Kriegsmarine would make its way through the East Coast minefields that had been set up.

Montagu provided a suitably doctored chart – that would raise no suspicions from aircraft patrols or the monitoring of routes of fishing trawlers – which would, as he later explained, 'encourage as many German ships as possible to steer into the east coast mine barriers'. This would be handed over to his handlers the next time Dusko returned to Portugal. But for this ruse to work, they would need a plausible explanation as to how the information had been obtained.

'An English barrister, a naval reserve officer who happens to be a Jew, is scared stiff that the Germans will win the war,' Montagu later explained to his agent. 'He's heard horrible tales about concentration camps and death ovens and wants to take out some insurance.'

Yet for all this ingenuity, Dusko expressed disbelief that such a person existed.

'Sorry, I thought you understood,' his naval handler said quietly. 'His name is Ewen Montagu.'

Astrology, for all the lure and promise of seeing into the future, always remained a double-edged weapon. The flipside to manipulating the German mind via the stars was that the cottage industry of newspaper horoscopes in Britain could also accidentally make predictions which would be too close to the bone (and reveal secrets) or else undermine morale from its sheer and utter pessimism. When, in the spring of 1941, the head of MI5's counter-espionage section learned about the employment of Louis de Wohl, he said that this 'whole business seems to me to be highly misleading and dangerous'.

Indeed, there was a feeling that horoscopes generally could have a detrimental effect on the populace. In July 1941, the Ministry of Information considered the matter in detail. Cooper's snoopers examined the various astrological prognostications which had been made over the previous few months. The ministry study found that two-thirds of the adult population read astrology columns. Only four out of ten people gave them any credence while, at most, 'one in ten, and [those] probably of a neurotic type make astrology a major interest in their lives and allow it to play some part in forming their conduct'.

The report looked at the predictions of Sunday newspaper astrologers and observed that of the four, none had actually predicted the outbreak of war. Many had predicted the recent (and swiftly reversed) British campaign in Libya while a couple had foreseen the German attack on Russia. By far the most accurate was R.H. Naylor in the *Sunday Express* whose column had transformed him into a power in the land.

Richard Harold Naylor had essentially invented the modern horoscope in the *Sunday Express*. By the end of the thirties, a social research organisation had noted 'nearly two-thirds of the adult population glance at or read some astrological feature more or less regularly'. Naylor had correctly foreseen the explosion of the Hindenburg, as well as the German invasions of Norway, Greece and Crete. Later in the war, Sir Peter Tennant, the wartime press attaché in Stockholm – in reality, the SOE representative there – recalled consulting him. Would Mr Naylor be amenable to tailoring some of his own predictions to help the Allied cause? 'He was scornful of any suggestion that his art should be debased in the service of propaganda,' Sir Peter recalled many years later. 'And even if he did, there would be no joy in it.'

Ironically, whispering of another variety would continue against the astrologer who seemed to be causing a great deal more chaos. That spring of 1941, Naylor had 'grassed up' Louis de Wohl. In this way, MI5 learned that the Hungarian had 'under an atmosphere of great secrecy been publicising a claim that he has been appointed official astrologer to the British War Office'. As a result, Major Lennox was asked to have 'a word' with him and, from the files at least, there seems to have been no more breaches of security.

For now, at any rate.

They were always newsworthy – as on the occasion three years earlier when it was reported weather forecasts should be banned – and, as a result, the annual meeting in Harrogate of British astrologers was a regular fixture of the calendar in the popular press. A year previously, in March 1940, Louis de Wohl had related the story of a woman who had been told that she would pass away on a certain date. 'The men who dare to say such things are criminals,' he announced. 'It is impossible to predict deaths. We can predict dangers to life but even this can be difficult.'

And yet now, in the spring of 1941, that was exactly what Louis de Wohl would do about the Führer himself as part of an ongoing effort to destabilise the Third Reich. Predictions about Adolf Hitler's demise now formed part of a greater, more coherent campaign, about which only a handful of secret servants were aware. Publicly, it provided a coda for the conference; when it concluded, the *Daily Mail* noted that 'our astrologers are unanimous that the stars are very bad for Hitler'.

At face value, the various prognostications emanating from Harrogate were often cheery, light-hearted stuff. 'One thing is certain,' another *Mail* columnist noted, even though he took care to claim astrology was useless, 'Britain wins through to victory with the help of other countries, but fighting the actual battle on her own.' On another day, it was reported that Charles Carter, 'a London ARP official', predicted that he and his fellow astrologers 'now expect peace, or the end of actual fighting about December 31 1941'. Another well-known amateur astrologer, Mr Mauby Cole, predicted 'a momentous historical event' rather sooner. This would take place, he said, on 11 May due to a major planetary conjunction. Ironically, Mr Cole was eventually killed the day before that in the last major Luftwaffe raid on London that destroyed most of the House of Commons.

At the time, it was never clear why all these predictions – especially concerning Hitler's demise – were rising to a crescendo. This planetary alignment and the dangers it posed formed the central tenet of a curious article written by a Walter Tschuppik twelve days later in the weekly *Die Zeitung*, a newspaper almost exclusively read by émigrés. 'One must remember that the ingenious Dr. Goebbels had very quickly realized astrology's propaganda value,' the author attested a while later, virtually the same words as an hitherto secret document entitled 'Propaganda: Use of Astrology'.

Amazing as it may seem to posterity, they formed the basis of a worldwide conspiracy involving astrologers (many of them unwittingly so) in predicting the death of Adolf Hitler. But perhaps the greatest surprise of all was the identity of the person who was manipulating things behind the scenes and had proposed the campaign in the first place.

Louis de Wohl always liked to view himself as a virtuoso.

That spring of 1941, he had proposed an 'orchestra of death' which he would conduct to play on Adolf Hitler's supposed primal fears about dying. It would be the first ever attempt to 'psych out' a foreign leader by use of both political warfare and astrology, thereby affecting the Führer's ability to make decisions, making him doubt his own intuition and agitating him so badly that he would make the wrong ones.

But it would hardly be an easy task, as the astrologer warned his various handlers within the disparate secret services. 'We are up against a formidable adversary,' Louis de Wohl began. 'His personal magnetism is so strong that its emanations can be felt in all countries of the globe.'

Even by the standards of the stories examined in this book, it is one of the most peculiar campaigns ever sanctioned during the Second World War. Yet that is precisely what took place, with the indefatigable Louis de Wohl manipulating the news agenda. He wrote on the eve of the astrologers' conference:

> I shall undertake as soon as possible to win the collaboration of the British Astrologers; Carter, Robson, Glewso, Lyndae, Bailey, Murray, Burnell etc. At the Easter convention of British Astrologers in Harrogate (an assembly of about 300 people including 50–60 astrologers, and always visited by the Press), I shal [sic] disclose the sensational news that Hitler's astrologer himself believes in the imminent death of the Führer.

Oddly, it was clear that such claims would have an appreciative audience.

'Hitler fears death,' de Wohl noted in his proposal. 'I know his character well enough to describe exactly what sort of fear it is.' The Führer's ultimate demise would, de Wohl insisted, be Neptunian, that is 'mysterious and strange', something which better describes the astrologer's own work that spring. Ultimately, the timing would be propitious, for the very Ides of

March, when the Harrogate conference had begun, would prompt singular changes in the German leader's luck. From the middle of March 1941 to the middle of May (in retrospect, a crucial time period so far as astrology, misinformation and black propaganda are concerned) Adolf Hitler would be enveloped in bad aspects.

'Therefore we must begin to play the symphony of his death in the first week of March and go on playing it for at least ten weeks,' de Wohl noted. 'From all parts of the world our instruments must play the melodies of his approaching death.'

It is clear that the opening notes had been played out at the Harrogate conference. De Wohl confidently announced that Hitler's astrologer, Karl Krafft, now firmly believed in the leader's imminent death. 'By then the orchestra of Hitler's death should have reached its *forte fortissimo* in the world,' he wrote, 'and especially in the United States.'

Indeed, Louis de Wohl proposed that on Good Friday, 11 April, mass meetings of the 'Lord deliver us from Hitler' variety should be encouraged all over the Union. Lest it seem too ludicrous a proposition, de Wohl helpfully provided names, addresses and details of astrologers all over the world – including Egypt, India, Ceylon and China – who could play their part. If promoted, it would mean that Hitler's death would be commonly anticipated all around the globe. 'It is impossible that the whole world speaks of the death of one man,' de Wohl concluded, 'without this man becoming aware of it. It will haunt him.'

Louis de Wohl wasn't the only scribe who was sending reports into various places in Whitehall in the hope that the high-ups might pay attention. Around this time, Dennis Wheatley was highly prolific, working up to fourteen or fifteen hours a day. In the spring of 1941, his latest work, *Strange Conflict*, appeared. 'As long as Britain stands, the Powers of darkness cannot prevail,' came a piece of oration from within it. As his biographer has noted, of his eight occultic novels, seven had a distinct time of propaganda; and as Phil Baker also notes, 'propaganda and magic both involve the manipulation of reality by means of words and images'.

Strange Conflict was a good read with a familiar theme: that Hitler dabbled in black magic. 'I haven't the least doubt that he does,' one character says, 'everything that is known about him indicates it.' As one reviewer said, it was obvious that Mr Wheatley is perfectly serious and deserves serious consideration.

Dennis was perfectly serious in his other work. He estimated that he created half a million words for the various ministry officers that same year. Considering them his most satisfying work, they were addressed, so he liked to claim, to a 'small select readership of four – King George VI and the Chiefs of Staff'. Their range and diversity were amazing. Wheatley wrote papers on the importance of keeping Turkey neutral, maintaining morale within the population and keeping an endless supply from the US across the Atlantic by the use of crude wooden rafts (perhaps explaining why many had what he later acknowledged a comic opera aspect). Intriguingly, in view of the worries about Iberia at the same time, he suggested swapping Gibraltar for Tangier, for 'the Rock has already lost much of its potency, and looking ahead it is obvious that its days are numbered'.

But more than just writing reports, the bestselling author could play upon his fame to his best advantage. Dennis Wheatley was not shy in inviting important people out for drinks and dinners to further his wartime career. By the middle of 1941, he was regularly lunching members of the Joint Planning Staff, who worked closely with Winston Churchill at the heart of the Whitehall war machine.

Much as he expected, the writer started to be sounded out for the possibility of his joining the secret world. Clearly, being a best-selling author had its benefits. Wheatley's writing skills and fertile imagination could help stamp a unique imprimatur on the covert battles ahead. Lunching provided him with the way of seeing the men at the top; and one paper in particular, 'After The Battle', which looked at what might happen in the future, a notion suggested by Winston Churchill, was well received.

'Whether the war is brought to a conclusion in the spring of 1941,' he optimistically concluded, 'or whether it drags on for several years, there can be no question about our final victory.'

After all the various false starts, around this time the Special Operations Executive was starting to get its act together in doing its part to achieve that goal. Another high-up also noted that the propagandists were no longer squeamish about violating peacetime morality involving 'untruths, deceptions, briberies, forgeries of passports, permits or currencies, acts of violence, mayhem and murder'. One key player had already emerged, a major whom Dennis Wheatley termed 'a cloak and dagger chap with whom I had numerous friendly dealings', who had developed his own special plans for a birthday surprise that would be very, very different.

Celebrating the Führer's birth would provide a suitable starting point for Louis de Wohl's ouverture of death. Rumours of Adolf Hitler's untimely demise would start that same spring of 1941. The Führer's impending 52nd birthday would act as the catalyst for just such an astrological opportunity. Sir Charles Hambro, the deputy director of the Special Operations Executive, was now also alert to the fact that both the Führer and his deputy, Rudolf Hess, might be influenced by the often malign influence of the stars.

As already noted, Sir Charles's office had originally been behind Louis de Wohl's move the previous autumn to Grosvenor House. While the files remain opaque, it is clear where his information was coming from. And now, six months later, as part of SOE's lingering involvement in propaganda, Hambro was instrumental in convincing his colleagues that 'all astrological angles were worth exploring'.

Louis de Wohl was clearly in his element.

Predictions of Adolf Hitler's demise would get back to Berlin, Hambro reiterated, possibly affecting his judgement by making him doubt his own ability to make decisions in the face of the overwhelming certainties of celestial malevolence. 'I am always asked to do curious things,' Sir Charles wrote in April 1941, 'and this is probably one of the most curious I have ever been asked to arrange but nonetheless most important. The whole subject has been carefully discussed and is being done on a worldwide basis according to a definite plan.'

One of his underlings, Leslie 'Sherry' Sheridan – an army major who, as the files note, 'also does curious things sometimes' – was the chosen instrument for selling de Wohl's plans. A former night editor of the *Daily Mirror*, Sheridan later became a barrister before joining the Special Operations Executive. He never emerged from this oddly twilit world and would achieve a greater notoriety as a post-war 'cold war warrior', heading the Information Research Division which supported the publication of *Animal Farm* in the Islamic world (where the association of pigs and communism need little elaboration).

Though he had a temper, caustic wit and clearly didn't suffer fools gladly, Sheridan's efforts beheld what one obituary termed 'the sureness of his professional approach on a subject like propaganda, befuddled as it was by a crowd of amateurs, gifted perhaps but certainly scatterbrained'. In fact, he became the lynchpin for Louis de Wohl's ouverture of death, silently and secretly helping pull the strings.

'Starting in the Balkans and using his widespread contacts with Fleet Street journalists and foreign correspondents, Sheridan built up a network of agents that, by 1941, covered the principal neutral capitals of the world,' as one SOE document notes. Some were placed under cover as hacks, while others worked for a news agency, Britannia Ltd, which had been set up on the Strand in London by Leslie Sheridan.

In other words, he was well placed to take de Wohl's exotic prognostications and extend their tendrils all over the world. For that he would need diplomats and administrators who no doubt wondered if he had taken leave of his senses. That early spring of 1941, Sheridan arrived at the Colonial Office with Hambro's blessing and supposedly 'accurate' astrological data with which to predict the dictator's downfall.

Major Sheridan visited an assistant secretary at the Colonial Office, whose global remit would allow the full symphonic range suggested by Louis de Wohl's ouverture of death. Certainly, the assistant secretary then covered his own back by sending his own memo to his colonial colleagues: 'The idea behind this strikes me as fantastic. Major Sheridan (who has no personal belief in astrology) meets all such criticism by admitting it but asking why we should not make such use as we can of the credulity of others.'

The information Major Sheridan brought with him revealed that Adolf Hitler was born at 6.30 p.m. on 20 April 1889, making him a Taurus by a few hours. Others clearly suspected a very different form of bull. Rather like the high-ups in the Royal Navy, the pukka fellows at the Colonial Office wanted to make sure they wouldn't be considered nutcases themselves before they would do anything. A number wanted reassurances that the topic had been discussed at Cabinet level (it hadn't, though individual ministers had been informed about the work).

Soon, the work began in earnest.

As Louis de Wohl had realised, in the run-up to Adolf Hitler's birthday that April, Neptune would be in opposition to his birth sign. 'Neptunian fate is always mysterious,' Sheridan wrote, following on from his master's voice, 'usually violent and full of conspiratorial danger from closest associates.' Intriguingly, the SOE major recorded for the files that 'Hitler maintains astrologer Krafft' and also feared an untimely demise before he had completed the work of the Thousand Year Reich. 'His decisions are reported to be influenced by portents in the stars.'

If nothing else, a whispering campaign involving his supposed malefic aspects would destroy the idea that the Führer was possessed of superhuman powers. The orchestra of astrological deception would include music which 'may be heard within Germany, where astrology is now a recognised science, and even reach the ears of Hitler himself, with unsettling effect on his judgment'.

SOE dispatched information to spread the word of Hitler's impending doom in places such as Turkey, Egypt, Singapore and West Africa. Perhaps the most remarkable involved the governor of Hong Kong, Sir Geoffrey Northcote, whose work came under the aegis of the Colonial Office. He briefed a Chinese contact who arranged for a suitably diabolic prediction to emerge from a planchette message (a type of séance) at a Chinese temple in Macao. This was then passed to the Reuters news agency, which dutifully filed a dispatch which reported the predictions that not only would Hitler suffer a great reverse in the second half of 1941 but also die in 1942.

But perhaps the most curious statement within Whitehall – that subversive warfare was being carried out – came on 1 May 1941. 'An attempt is being made to exploit astrological credulity to our advantage in view of the fact that astrology is now a recognized science in Germany and that Hitler himself [is] understood to believe in it.'

What happened next, though, nobody could predict.

By the early spring of 1941, there was a certain breathless expectancy surrounding the possible uses of astrology in the war effort which, with the skilful prompting of Sherry Sheridan, had become part of a concerted effort in using black propaganda and the insertion of bogus horoscopes in newspapers around the world. 'According to the stars,' *The Observer* later reported of the Harrogate conference in the middle of April, 'Hitler will try to invade Britain next month during a "blitzkrieg" which will break out in all its fury between 9 May and 11 May.'

Fury was a splendid word to describe what happened slap bang in the middle of those dates. Instead of needing to look up to follow the stars, something would come down, falling out of the sky in the form of a parachutist – and with him a veritable shower of conspiracy theories. Although the official MI6 history notes that there is no real mystery about the affair, the arrival of Rudolf Hess in Scotland remains one of the stranger episodes of the Second World War. It was an event that would electrify many observers thanks, in part, to the rumours of astrology being involved. But as is now also clear, much more of the egregious misinformation which later resulted came thanks to a rather different malign influence: the most treacherous spy of his generation, later to be elevated within MI6 to head all Soviet counter-intelligence, who was actually a Soviet agent himself.

9

Magical Mystery Tour

In the early days of the war, particularly when Britain stood alone in 1940 and 1941, the British had little with which to oppose the Germans except deception. They resorted to every type of subterfuge … in order to confuse the Germans as to the amount of military strength (they had) and, more important, its disposition. Out of this was born a habit that was later difficult (for them) to discard.

Eisenhower, *Crusade in Europe*, New York (1968)

All warfare is based on deception. Hence, when able to attack, we must seem unable; when using our forces, we must seem inactive; when we are near, we must make the enemy believe we are far away; when far away, we must make him believe we are near. Hold out baits to entice the enemy. Feign disorder, and crush him.

Sun Tzu, *The Art of War*

Of all the organisations to wage secret war against Nazi Germany, none had a more exotic – or indeed protracted – provenance than the Political Warfare Executive (PWE). In the spring of 1941, the PWE was the new kid on the block so far as the British secret services were concerned. Amazingly, it had taken eighteen months of another form of political warfare for everything to come together. In fact, the ongoing 'spat' between what one official history terms 'two combative and influential ministers' – of Information and Subversion, in effect – would not actually be completely resolved until that summer of 1941.

The PWE could call upon some illustrious members. With a Bloomsbury group novelist as its official historian, nowhere else in Whitehall could have ever employed talents as exotic and diverse as those of Noël Coward, Freya

Starck, Jock Bruce Lockhart and Joanna Scott-Moncrieff at various times in the fighting. Fewer still secret agencies would ever have found their staff mingling with the animals at the zoo attached to Woburn Abbey, where one recorded that a visiting Member of Parliament had been 'butted by a llama and bitten by a rhea'.

Opinion was divided as to quite what it all actually achieved.

One former political warfare practitioner famously declared it was 'a gigantic waste of human effort and public money which could have been better employed in other ways more conducive to winning the war'. But for all the dithering, infighting as well as personal and political bickering, in the spring of 1941 the organisation went into overdrive with the arrival of a genius who had been tasked with broadcasting to the enemy. Almost straightaway, Sefton Delmer recognised the need for something radical and innovative, and took care to upset the cosy uncertainties which had hitherto infected the subject.[1]

Tom Delmer became a skilled practitioner in the arcane arts, of what he later christened 'black propaganda'. At its heart was the notion that the Germans were never to know that such propaganda was British, and later Allied, in origin. And though it took a while to establish, Delmer eventually employed many methods of getting his message across. Leaflets, pamphlets, spurious broadcasts and a concerted effort in infiltrating banned documents into Nazi Germany were all used. And rumours – the full range of gossip and odd reports – known as sibs (from the Latin word *sibilare*, to hiss or whistle) were spread by any number of sources, agents amongst them.

Sefton Delmer understood the German mind and effortlessly worked to exploit its weaknesses. For all his Falstaffian bonhomie, Delmer was shrewd and ingeniously subverted the enemy. 'But above all Delmer possessed a true modesty and humility of soul,' recalled one of his colleagues, Robert Walmsley. 'He believed, certainly in his own power, but never in his own infallibility.' As he had been a pre-war correspondent in Berlin, where he had made it his business to get to know all the Nazi leaders, Tom Delmer was, as a later Foreign Office mandarin and wartime colleague recalled, 'the nearest thing to a genius which PWE produced.'

By the time Sefton Delmer joined the fledgling propaganda effort in the spring of 1941, the organisation which had been split off from the Special Operations Executive (and would shortly be renamed the Political Warfare

Executive) was ready-made for a surreal, circus-like atmosphere given its location next door to the Duke of Bedford's zoo. 'If the Department's installation at Woburn resembled scenes from the Beatles' comic TV Magical Mystery Tour film,' one of its earliest recruits recalled without need for exaggeration, 'the early annals of its sojourn there also had qualities which were sometimes more akin to surrealism than reality.'

And, in the propagandist Ellic Howe's estimation, nobody expected Sefton Delmer to transform it into a genuine weapon of warfare. The atmosphere, when he arrived, was 'heavily charged with personal rivalries'.[2] Delmer's most immediate difficulty came in yet another bailiwick dispute – this time with the British Broadcasting Corporation and a rapidly developing personal animosity with its then head of German section (who later rose to become its Director General).

Then, as now, the BBC considered that nobody had any business encroaching upon its territory. The Corporation was already responsible for what was termed 'white' propaganda – that is non-subversive, signed broadcasts – which now led to yet another pointless dispute over which much time, energy and vitriol was expended. Who exactly should be responsible for broadcasting propaganda to the enemy? The debate sometimes burst into public view, with Cabinet discussions as well as bitter rows which erupted in the House of Commons.

Technically speaking, all forms of radio communication came under the ministerial purview of a forceful, fast-talking Oxford philosophy don whose capacity to quarrel was well known. Richard Crossman, a Labour politician who was invariably too clever by half, was responsible for both the BBC overseas broadcasts and what came to be known as the PWE's 'black boomerang'.

His own Machiavellian posturing led to an obvious nickname as 'Double Crossman', and Tom Delmer would mildly note that his new boss overstepped his authority and was difficult. Yet even the minister couldn't help from marvelling at Delmer's work. In Crossman's recollection, he happily carried out 'any form of subversion, however odious', likening him to 'a chief who not only ate, drank and looked like Henry VIII but equalled that monarch in the genial absolution with which he ran his kingdom'.

Most of the time, Tom Delmer's ire was reserved for the former *Daily Telegraph* correspondent in pre-war Germany – whom he had known and not particularly warmed to – the tall, shambolic grandee from the well-known brewing dynasty whose younger brother was Graham Greene. Hugh Carleton Greene was responsible for the BBC's German Service and was never remotely convinced about the very value of black propaganda. It put the two former rivals on a collision course straightaway. Richard Crossman observed that Delmer and Greene detested each other and, in his own underhand way, exploited their hatred to the full.

'For deception purposes there was so-called "black broadcasting" – mainly a tactical weapon,' Greene would write many years later, 'whereas "white" broadcasting was essentially strategic.' Such circumspection was for his memoirs. In 1941, however, the fights between the BBC and PWE, not just restricted to Greene and Delmer, rumbled on for the best part of the year.

'It was not our job to persuade the enemy that, however gloomy our immediate situation might be, we were confident of ultimate victory,' Hugh Carleton Greene would write, 'and that there were very good reasons, historical, psychological and material, for this confidence.' It would be a long-term job, he decided. For this Greene was certain that the truth had to be told, no matter how unpalatable. If the BBC was frank about British, and later, Allied, losses, then claims of victory would be that much more believable. 'It is essentially an auxiliary weapon,' Greene would say of Delmer's own version of black propaganda. 'It cannot achieve victories on its own.'

As an instrument of policy, however, it only ever became useful after what Richard Crossman termed 'a departmental war in which no holds were barred'. To Tom Delmer's ears, the BBC German Service's broadcasts were run mainly by disgruntled émigrés who seemed to be appealing to the Germans' better instincts. That, he knew, was doomed to failure. Delmer instantly dismissed most of the BBC's output as spinsterish and narrowly focussed, far too sophisticated and metropolitan for the average German, which he characterised by their intolerable 'dullness and sanctimony'.

The broadcasts were, in Delmer's later phrase, rather like Maida Vale calling Hampstead (not London to Berlin). Even worse, it sounded like propaganda. Such broadcasts clearly did not appeal to the majority of Germans 'but to the infinitesimal few who wanted to lose [the war]'.

His pleas to change the tone of the BBC's white broadcasts fell on deaf ears. The fanciful, intellectual broadcasts continued. Sefton Delmer realised that trying to induce any sort of rebellion was a waste of time. Fairly quickly it was clear that precipitate action would be needed.

'Delmer had an unusual, indeed phenomenal capacity for "tuning in" to, or penetrating the German mind and its mental processes, almost as if he himself resembled an ultra-sophisticated radio receiving set,' one colleague would write, while another would simply note that he was 'indefatigable'. Even so, the various arguments with the BBC continued and it would not be until the first week of May 1941 that the first radio station dedicated to black propaganda would be ready. Even then, as an official PWE minute noted, 'Mr Sefton Delmer was choosing the necessary team, the necessary accommodation would not be available for two or three weeks.' When he did, as another record notes, he would produce talks of a 'comic, racy narrative', which were soon a hit, simply because Tom Delmer 'was able to speak Berlin slang, and was capable of introducing comic songs into his talks where suitable'.

If the propaganda effort left a lot to be desired, at least the business of running the double agents was now firing on all cylinders. By the start of 1941, British Intelligence was now orchestrating a dozen or so odd characters who had landed over the past few months and turned them against the Germans. Now, with the threat of invasion receding, they could be used for a more subtle form of warfare.

The Security Service had finally stepped up its activities to a war footing. A new influx of staff, a deliberate leavening of a debilitated service with a few home-grown intellectuals, had been brought in. Their number included academics, teachers and even a circus owner. Many were lawyers and, indeed, half a dozen would become judges in the years after the war. They formed the nucleus of a new department which would lead to the greatest intelligence triumph of the war.

Its titular head was called, disparagingly at first, 'the Oxford don': a bone-dry ascetic of a man who had been commissioned in the Intelligence Corps because he spoke German fluently (the only benefit from his internment in the Great War, a source of much personal distress for him). John Cecil Masterman was not only a leading member of the British Establishment, he had almost single-handedly created it. A governor of half a dozen of Britain's most eminent public schools, his fame as an amateur athlete and cricketer was legendary.

'He was,' recalls Sir Michael Howard (a later pupil and historian of Second World War deception), 'the Greatest and Best of the Great and Good.'

Masterman would come to chair the ad hoc committee that would disseminate misinformation via the double agents. To many he was an odd choice, for 'the Oxford don' was not universally popular. Behind the clear blue, almost Gladstonian eyes, some detected priggishness, others a gaunt humourlessness, a kind of desiccated intellectual superiority that grated on some and terrified others. Many of the double agents themselves came to appreciate the icy calm of his deliberations. Others thought him wise and tactful.[2]

It is thanks to J.C. Masterman and his report on the Double Cross System that we know how it all came together. On the cold, featureless first Thursday of 1941, a group of men met in the incongruous surroundings of Wormwood Scrubs. All represented different branches of the military, and in time their number swelled. This would be the first of weekly meetings of what became known as the XX Committee or, to those initiated, the Twenty Club, which continued right until the end of the war.

In the years since, a mythology of sure-footed genius has accompanied its successes. As the files show, it only seemed tentatively so at the time. 'Dimly, very dimly we began to guess at the beginning of 1941,' Masterman noted, 'that we did, in fact, control the enemy system.' Given the chairman's sporting prowess (he was a cricketing 'blue') it is no wonder that he likened the whole system to an elaborate Test innings. He wrote:

> Running a team of double agents is very like running a club cricket side. Older players lose their form and are gradually replaced by newcomers. Well established veterans unaccountably fail to make runs, whereas youngsters whose style at first appears crude and untutored for some unexplained reason make large scores.

In time, the Twenty Club members would be astonished at some of the whimsies of the players. 'It is not always easy to pitch the best side to put into the field for any particular match,' Masterman would add. The problem was that the nature of many was such that they were hardly trustworthy, some needed better handling 'requiring a great deal of net practice before they were really fit to play in a match', and had no idea when they would have to be retired or pulled out.

To continue Masterman's cricketing metaphor, its members never knew when they would need to bring out the best player on to the pitch. Clearly, trying to fool the Germans would be a far more complicated enterprise than anyone dared imagine. Many near misses stalked the whole enterprise, particularly as it grew in size and complexity in the later years of the war, when there would be upwards of a hundred important agents all over the world (and at most a dozen, including Dusko Popov, who were vital to the return to Europe). And yet, as they planned to manipulate the enemy, not even J.C. Masterman would equivocate. In 'communicating with the enemy almost from day to day,' he wrote, 'we were playing with dynamite.'

In all its subsequent endeavours, though, the XX Committee had a wholly unexpected ally. Time and time again, the British secret service couldn't believe how amateurish its opposite numbers were. Certainly, the sea change in British attitudes towards German Military Intelligence came at this time. Everything that Admiral Canaris's staff did seemed so unbelievably idiotic and incompetent that it looked for all the world like some sort of elaborate deception operation was being staged against the British. Surely nobody could be that useless?

In the estimation of Ewen Montagu of Naval Intelligence, 'after we had experience of German Intelligence, no incompetence would have surprised us' for virtually every attempt at foreign espionage from 1940 onwards ended in failure. All its agents who were sent to Britain – and later the United States – were captured.

The Abwehr, by any rational estimation, was severely handicapped.

Firstly, there was little understanding of the qualities needed to recruit successful agents. Secondly, Canaris's men were never able to find the best people at all. What one of its officers later referred to as the abnormal growth of the agency had a lot to do with it. There were not enough officers with the special abilities needed to run an espionage agency efficiently. There was also too much transfer between the office and the field. Nobody was ever able to actually bed down for long enough to make any difference.

'The Abwehr in the field was very poorly equipped with personnel,' one officer recalled during a debrief at the close of the war, by which time those very deficiencies had long since been apparent. And worse, the Fuchsbau was never able to evaluate the right sort of material; there was simply too much junk clogging the system.

'The trouble with the Abwehr archives was always that they contained too much information,' the officer recalled. 'The really valuable stuff was completely lost in the mass of absolutely useless junk.' Admiral Canaris would increasingly become the scapegoat for each and every disappointment. As one perceptive British Intelligence officer lated noted, it was as though the Abwehr believed the more agents their officers could add to their tally, the better they would be perceived.

'The whole organisation was permeated with "pins-in-the-map syndrome",' said Brigadier Raymond Maunsell, who ran security operations in Cairo. This, more than anything, made the Germans susceptible to deception as they were reluctant to remove these pins. Quantity rather than quality meant that Abwehr officers defended their agents – most of whom were under British, and later Allied, control – to the hilt, even when it would have been obvious that they were either lying or under enemy control.

Keeping an eye on enemy aliens meant that sometimes the funny people, as the spooks are often called, had to keep their eyes on some very funny people indeed. At the start of 1941, the MI6 representative in Montevideo had come across some odd-looking letters which had been dispatched from Nazi Germany to a female émigré who had relocated to Uruguay. Even stranger, this woman had exchanged a series of telegrams with somebody who lived at 2 Warrington Crescent, London W9, which MI6 clearly didn't seem to realise was a hotel.

The name was unfamiliar to the Secret Intelligence Service. Fairly quickly, this minor mystery was cleared up when Gilbert Lennox later reported, with crisp British understatement, 'We know all about him and then some.' Similar irony was apparent in his later report that the correspondent was 'one of the other funny people who report to me'. Others, he was certain, may have heard of Louis de Wohl, whom he described as 'a tame astrologer of German upbringing, who is employed by SO2 for their own fell purposes' in a note to the Honourable Kenneth Younger (first cousin to Dennis Wheatley's stepson, Bill, who also worked for the Security Service). Lennox continued:

> He also carries on his private practice as an astrologer and he numbers among his clients a great many interesting people, including some of the good and the great. As it is often of considerable interest to know who is consulting an astrologer and for what reason, and it is sometimes even more interesting to hear the advice which the Stars give, I have made a private arrangement by which I get reported to me the names and details of Louis's clients.

The interception of his mail came from the fact his wife seemed to be on her uppers. Alexandra de Wohl was in desperate financial straits because of her husband's lackadaisical attitude to money. As the MI6 representative in Montevideo noted, it looked as though she might well be 'hard up for money as her telegrams appear to indicate but there may be something more in it'.

Captain 'Rex' Miller, the civilian assistant to the Naval Attaché, had, in the meantime, heard about someone known locally as 'the baroness'. As she seemed to be in contact with a lot of known Nazis émigrés and employed German domestic staff, she was of obvious (though low-level) interest. As a result of all that airmail from Germany, British Intelligence was keeping a watchful eye on her.

By the start of 1941, what had started to intrigue them most was the regular remittance of money from Warrington Crescent. A couple of cables chiding her husband for not having contacted her were also worthy of investigation. What is not said in the files is the obvious notion that Alexandra de Wohl might be some sort of front, though quite what she might have been fronting would be hard to imagine.

As time went on, her tone became desperate. In one telegram, she complained that she had had to move because Louis de Wohl hadn't sent her any money as he promised. A few days later came another more urgent cable: 'FRIENDS CANT POSSIBLY HELP FURTHER CABLE DATE AND AMOUNT REMITTANCE PAST OR FUTURE COMPLETELY AT A LOSS.' Alexandra, it seemed, had gone to South America for the duration of the war. Gilbert Lennox had met her and was puzzled about her supposed baronial background. 'She is a very pleasant person,' he wrote, and whether his story about ancestry was true, it didn't seem to matter. Unlike some of the people security officials often had to discuss, her 'morals are of the highest and I have never heard anything suggested against her'.

Her own pretensions seemed to match those of her husband. 'To the best of my knowledge she is German by birth,' Lennox discovered, 'the daughter of a banker but the story is that she is of Hungarian origin and has royal blood!' Despite what he termed Louis's amatory adventures and habits, they seemed to be very fond of each other.

She treats him as a small boy and he sometimes forgets to write to her. Louis is supposed to have some arrangement for sending her money and has cabled her about this. Obviously, she has been hard up and the cables are about money. I have myself seen some of the more recent cables and I am quite certain there is no more in it than appears on the surface.

Enquiries in January 1941 via the Bank of England, Louis de Wohl's own branch of the Westminster Bank and their branch in Uruguay showed the monetary remittance was all above board. 'Our friend has apparently been doing this since March 1939 without any trouble,' wrote June Bainbridge, one of the astrologer's handlers at SOE. She noted that there had been a gap of three months when he had hadn't sent money, where it was more likely he too was on his uppers. As this coincided with his work for Naval Intelligence and MI14, no doubt he wasn't able to concentrate on commercial clients.

For the files, further investigation revealed that Alexandra was described as his loving wife and though clearly fond of her husband, 'I should describe her attitude as more motherly than wifely'. There was another dimension as to how exactly his wife was being used. Further enquiries by an SOE official called Captain Hope noted that in 1938 Louis de Wohl had been involved with the Bata shoe company, and had been trying to set up an agency for selling their wares in the United States. Such 'unmanly' interests beheld something else.

'Hope said that de Wohl was a homosexual and it therefore becomes rather difficult to explain his interest in the woman who helped furnish his flat in Grosvenor House,' the files note. This transpired to be June Bainbridge which, as another file noted, neatly 'disposed' of the theory that Bainbridge was de Wohl's mistress. In fact, somebody else who knew the astrologer when he roomed at the Esplanade had been picked up by the Security Service. 'This woman seems to be involved with some mystery in view of the fact that de Wohl who rather blatantly flaunts his effeminate inclinations and habits, has of late made rather a close companion of the woman referred to above.'

An intriguing snippet of his contacts concerns a half-salvaged letter to Dick White, the overall head of counter-intelligence within MI5, which had been written at the start of October 1940. 'I asked him for the names of any German harlots who he had ever met in this country,' a file notes. As is clear, the rising star of British counter-intelligence, like many of his colleagues, was never convinced about all the effort with their so-called 'tame' astrologer. Dick White simply came to class him as more of a pain in the backside. 'I have never liked Louis de Wohl,' wrote White a year later, 'he strikes me as a charlatan and an impostor.'

The problem for all the secret agencies was that many of the people they came into contact with overseas were not just charlatans or impostors, but most likely dedicated provocateurs. As a result, security was always a thorny issue. For the wartime Secret Intelligence Service, charged with ensuring the safekeeping of the information emanating from Bletchley Park, any hint that German agents had been doubled (or, worse, that their greater communications were being read) would bring down the whole edifice.

For MI6, the notion of counter-intelligence became paramount, and none took it more seriously than the senior officer responsible, the son of a missionary, whose own zealotry extended to not wanting to share any information with anyone if he could help it. Within the corridors of the secret services, he became viewed as an unpleasant megalomaniac.

Yet Colonel Felix Cowgill couldn't care less.

Around his slender shoulders rested the greatest secret of wartime intelligence, the lifeblood of the XX Committee in turning the enemy's agents against their masters. With good reason, nothing was more important than this electromagnetic manna from heaven. Generically known as Ultra, 'the extremely tight restriction which [Cowgill] imposed on its distribution,' one historian has noted, 'caused some friction, both within the service and in its relations with other bodies, MI5 above all.'

Here was another bailiwick dispute which stemmed from the ultimate 'need to know' basis. It centred on what had become the fastest-growing part of the British secret service which Major Cowgill now commanded. On the face of it, Section V of MI6 sounds anonymous, dull and without merit, which was exactly what it was designed to be. It was, in effect, a secret service within a secret service, an acknowledgement that counter-intelligence – and in particular its handmaiden, counter-espionage – needed to be isolated and insulated from the rest of the organisation.

With the loss of its European networks, and indeed the Venlo incident, MI6 had had to build up everything from scratch. Section V had originally been created and run during the twenties by 'Vee Vee' Vivian, the deputy chief who was better known as a fastidious fellow with a monocle, with just a couple of fellow officers. As a former Indian policeman, Vivian knew the well-known yet eccentric Arabist, Harry St John Philby[3], a strange cove by anyone's estimation. It was a friendship that would have many serious repercussions, not least when Vivian became Vice Chief to Sir Stewart Menzies shortly after war broke out.

Section V grew, like Topsy, to become as large as the rest of the organisation. Far from now just dealing with counter-espionage, it became the keeper at the gate for what is today known as signals analysis, the secure and timely exploitation of the decoded German radio traffic. At this point, British Intelligence could observe messages sent by the double agents as they passed along the system, which allowed them a 'crib' into the Abwehr's communications.

In time, there would be a Section V sub-section for every geographical area of the fighting, and by the end of the war it employed roughly 4,500 people. In particular, Iberia remained a seething labyrinth of spies, intrigue and suspected provocations. On his return from Sierra Leone, in the time-honoured way of the British Establishment, Graham Greene would be given a plum job in the Iberian section. Though he knew nothing about Spain or Portugal, their languages, their people nor their history, this was not perceived as a handicap at all. Yet, in time, working for Section V, Greene and his colleagues were more than up to the task. 'By the end of the war,' Greene would write, 'those Abwehr who were not working for us, we knew were working with completely imaginary agents and receiving pay to give to their agents, agents who did not exist.'

Iberia itself would become, in the grander scheme of things, the eye of the needle so far as Abwehr-related espionage directed towards Great Britain, and later the Americas, was concerned. For now, and for the rest of the fighting, Iberia would become the focus for the secret war. The game of the foxes, as it has been called, was helped by a certain Teutonic thoroughness. 'We were immensely helped by the fact that the Abwehr officers were a gentlemanly organisation,' recalled one MI6 hand. 'They believed in treating their spies well, accommodated them at good hotels and sent them on sleepers or first class reserved seats.'

By 1941, Section V's driving force was Felix Cowgill who, as one of his colleagues noted, was 'combative in his work, always prepared to challenge an office ruling'. To others, he was nothing short of a tyrant, a bureaucratic bugbear who was completely paranoid on the subject of security. Cowgill, as another with whom he dealt later complained, had 'a pathological inability to inform anyone of anything that he can possibly avoid'.

In fairness, Cowgill had a very difficult job of it: the secret of Bletchley Park lay within his remit. Yet this great success was also the point of its greatest weakness. Any hint to an outsider, let alone the agents themselves, that their hand encoded ciphers were being systematically read, monitored and lovingly transmitted with 'chickenfeed' (as false information was known) would see the whole elaborate edifice come tumbling down. By common consent – though there are the usual questioners – the use of Ultra and the double agents foreshortened the war by at least a year, possibly even two.

Understandably, Felix Cowgill wouldn't share Ultra with anyone.

He hadn't want MI5 officials allowed to see any Ultra material as part of the XX Committee operations. When they were, he still refused to let representatives from the Home Forces and Home Defence Executive see it. Reference to any MI6 agents was always removed from the distribution lists. Major Cowgill also believed the rubric 'most secret sources' (a euphemism for the decoded signals) was also too revealing, even in reports that had a restricted distribution.

'Cowgill was so imbued with the idea of security that when he was put in charge for C of this material he was quite willing to try entirely to prevent its use as intelligence lest it be compromised,' concluded Commander Ewen Montagu (who, as the Naval Intelligence representative, had also been allowed to see some of the decrypts) in a post-war summary of wartime intelligence. 'These views inevitably caused friction.'

Wearisome bureaucratic battles continued for quite some time.

For all his desire for utmost security, the most horrible irony of all was that Felix Cowgill inadvertently allowed its greatest ever liability to literally walk in through his door. In September 1941, nemesis literally arrived in the form of a new recruit to Section V itself. This new fellow, whose fluency in Spanish, French and German commended him, had been a journalist (rare in MI6) and a graduate (even rarer). And though he appeared to be a shy yet personable member of the Establishment, fate had very different ideas for Harold Adrian Philby, better known as Kim, when he took the reins of the Iberian Section of MI6's own counter-intelligence department.

The instrument which would allow Tom Delmer to extend his reach in broadcasting propaganda right into the heart of enemy territory had come about thanks to an arbitrary ruling by the US Federal Communications Commission. The limit to the transmission power of any formally licensed radio station in the United States had been set at 5 kW. So when the New Jersey Station WJ2 ordered a 500 kW transmitter in late 1940, the Feds stepped in. Its greater transmission power would have allowed the station to reach a wider audience and generate greater advertising revenue. This would now have important ramifications in the secret war.

In May 1941, the Political Warfare Executive bought the mothballed transmitter, which had already been built by the Radio Corporation of

America. In the words of the brigadier who conveyed it across the Atlantic, the huge device would now become 'a raiding Dreadnought of the Ether, firing broadcasts at unpredictable times at unpredictable objectives of the enemy's radio propaganda machine'. The transmitter itself was established at Crowborough in the Sussex Downs, while the broadcasts were recorded at the Political Warfare Executive's headquarters at Woburn Zoo.

Given the codename Aspidistra, after the music hall song (about the biggest aspidistra in the world), its transmission power was bumped up to 600kW so that it could reach deep into the Third Reich and far across the Atlantic. Incredibly, though it was ready straightaway, regular broadcasts were delayed by nearly eighteen months thanks to the usual interdepartmental squabbles. The BBC, the Ministry of Information and Wireless Telegraphy Board all bickered as to who should actually 'own' the transmitter. At one meeting, Dick Crossman would note his repulsion at the 'atmosphere of club chat and unconscious incompetence'.

A station manned by German Marxists was already being supervised by Crossman, who exercised no control over the content. He felt that Tom Delmer should do something similar with a more right-wing bias. Many years later, Crossman claimed he was inspired by a curious conversation with Leonard Ingrams. A German propaganda station called *The Workers' Challenge* was broadcasting in English every taboo under the sun. 'Old Ladies in Eastbourne and Torquay are listening to it avidly,' Ingrams told him. 'They enjoy counting the f's and b's.'

Delmer replied in kind. His first innovation was Gustav Siegfried Eins (George Sugar One) which started broadcasting on Friday, 23 May 1941. Using a character known as Der Chef – in reality a German-born corporal then working in the Pioneer Corps – he sounded like a crusty Prussian general. Delmer's genius was to recognise that he should appear to be a patriot, a supporter of Hitler, who could nevertheless be used to undermine the listeners.

Gustav's overarching aim was to make the listener think he or she had stumbled across a military organisation that was sending out messages and ciphers. During its first broadcast, Der Chef wanted to make contact with Gustav Siegfried 18. There was a message about an agent who should meet at the Union Theatre on an upcoming day at 'row five, parquet stalls, second performance'. Given that there were innumerable Union theatres across the Reich, Delmer knew the Gestapo would run around in circles trying to find out where this person really was.

The station was also subtly anti-British, which made it sound even more plausible. A month after it started broadcasting, Delmer was about to head to London when he learned of the German attack on Soviet Russia. A debate followed on how this news would be broadcast by Gustav Siegfried Eins. 'Der Chef is all for Hitler and his war on the Bolsheviks,' Delmer told his bemused staff. But, in subsequent broadcasts, Der Chef recognised that there were middle-ranking officials (known as the *parteikommune*) 'who were feathering their own nests in the soft-job billets far from danger and privation'.

Such attacks became part and parcel of the propaganda that was broadcast over the next two and a half years. 'While our brave soldiers are freezing to death in Russia because of the corruption of this *parteikommune* crowd,' Der Chef later railed when the offensive stalled in the snows, 'who delayed getting the Army's winter clothing ready in time because they were out for bigger profit?'

To add verisimilitude, Delmer's team eavesdropped on prisoners of war and interrupted correspondence: in one famous case from the wife of an industrialist, which revealed there had been parties for high-ups where the tables groaned with food despite rationing for everyone else. This, too, appeared in a subsequent broadcast. By the time of the final transmission in late October 1943, accompanied by the sounds of the Gestapo storming the station and shooting Der Chef, Gustav Siegfried Eins had clearly served his purpose.

Kim Philby casts a long shadow over many of the stories which follow thanks to his deliberate muck-raking, deceptions, fun-poking and what one eminent colleague called the 'poisoning the well' of the historical record. So it continues unabated today with a highly hyped book about his influence and friends in high places. Various exaggerated claims have been made for the Section V supervisor, not least with the inevitable comparisons with the most famous fictional agent of them all. His friend and fellow MI6 recruit Malcolm Muggeridge considered Philby to have been nothing less than a real-life James Bond.

'His boozy amours, his tough postures, his intelligence expertise, are directly related to the same characteristics in Fleming's hero,' Muggeridge wrote many years later.

Yet the notion that Kim Philby was some sort of masterspy who some-how masterminded all Section V's Iberian counter-intelligence operations is nonsense. He only ever visited Lisbon once and travelled through the Mediterranean stations at the end of the war. Far from being a glamorous job, his – like everybody else's in Section V – was tedious desk work that needed painstaking (and at times painfully boring) analysis of signals.

Yet Philby fitted in straightaway. He was a good boss to work for thanks to his agreeable nature that was occasionally leavened by an acerbic bon mot. Boyish, almost naive, with a soft spot for ne'er do wells and womanisers, some detected a controlled hysteria, a hint of suppressed violence 'which manifested itself in the often infantile plots his Section V work involved', in another colleague's estimation.

Yet people warmed to this stuttering Englishman of the old school. He was tremendously good company. In the estimation of another school friend who later joined him in Section V, nobody seemed able to pin him down. The fact Philby was supplying information to the NKVD, the forerunner of the KGB, was never even suspected. When Kenneth Benton (the MI6 Section V officer based in Lisbon) was experiencing difficulties obtaining an official car, Philby laughed. 'If you were working for the NKVD,' he said derisively, 'you'd get whatever car you wanted at the drop of a hat.'[4]

Philby's recruitment had come about thanks to his father, who had known 'Vee Vee' Vivian in India. After his internment, Harry St John Philby was well enough regarded to be listened to. His son's noted leftward leanings were dismissed as so much youthful exuberance. Vivian was astute enough to realise that the Secret Intelligence Service needed new, clever people and fluent linguists so his son was welcomed. There is a certain irony that in one later Russian intelligence analysis of their greatest wartime asset, Philby's father was 'an ambitious tyrant' who had caused the stammer in his son.

It also helped that Philby knew most of the people who had also been recruited into the secret services. At the outbreak of war, the former journalist with *The Times* had joined the fledgling propaganda effort thanks to knowledge stemming from the Spanish Civil War, where he had been the longest-serving correspondent during the fighting.

After being appointed an instructor in the propaganda department which was being half-heartedly run by the Special Operations Executive in Beaulieu, within a year he had transferred across to Section V of MI6 in August 1941. As many German intelligence operations against Britain were being mounted from Iberia, he seemed an ideal choice to ramp up counter-espionage against the Abwehr. With virtually just a handshake, he was in.

If there was one adjective that came to describe Ellic Howe, it was impish.

Yet that could never quite convey the quicksilver glee of the dark-haired printer, 'cosily rotund, quick witted and quick moving' in the posthumous assessment of Robert Harling, himself a fellow devotee of design and print-work. Harling, who also worked closely with Ian Fleming, considered Howe a splendid chap who 'looked more akin to a bohemian circus tumbler' than a leading typographer. But as the head of what was known as Mr Howe's Department within the Political Warfare Executive, he came to have a sin-gular impact on the prosecution of black propaganda that complemented (on the printed page) that of Tom Delmer's work which carried through the ether.

It is a measure of Ellic Howe's interests, not least in mysticism, astrology and freemasonry, that he was both a wry chronicler (as his notion of the Woburn activities being akin to The Beatles above shows), as well as partici-pant in the propaganda efforts. A puzzling character of Russian background, many found him hard to pin down. 'Mr Howe', as he was invariably known, deliberately cultivated an air of mystery about himself, his background and his various pre-war travels around Europe where he discovered a facility for languages. His life changed in the mid-thirties when he discovered typography and helped run a pioneering magazine on the subject.

Fairly quickly, he developed an incomparable knowledge of all fonts.

In the same way that Tom Delmer revolutionised the black radio broad-casts, Ellic Howe would do the same with officially sanctioned forgeries. As the official history of the Political Warfare Executive notes, the earli-est attempts at forging leaflets – supposedly written by opposition groups behind the lines – were simply not good enough. It was only when Ellic Howe took over their production later in 1941 that they passed muster.

Like so many in the secret war, it took Mr Howe some time to find his métier. With the outbreak of hostilities, he had been recruited as a sergeant in the Anti-Aircraft Command, where he was trained in using ack-ack guns. Like so many others with unusual skills, Howe had diligently submitted papers to Whitehall on how to forge material. As with Dennis Wheatley, he was either overlooked or would be turned down for more gainful employ.

In the summer of 1941, his luck turned with a submitted paper. 'The Documentary Weapon', as he termed it, had been forwarded via MI5 to the Political Warfare Executive, where he was recruited by Leonard Ingrams to work on a small postal unit. Ellic Howe's first work in black propaganda was to create more realistic stamps and envelopes that could be used to cause mischief behind enemy lines.

In propaganda circles, though, Ellic Howe's own sense of fun was infectious.

Howe got on with everybody and did a superb job. As the official history of the PWE notes, his work was so vital that he was allowed to set up his own independent unit, 'the most important member of which was Miss Elizabeth Friedlander, a typographical artist and consummate forger'. They both consulted widely. Mr Howe seemed to know every printer, foundryman and compositor in the industry, so much so that as his friend Robert Harling later noted, the result was 'far more sophisticated forgeries to undermine the finances of the Third Reich'.

It helped that Howe worked brilliantly in harness with Tom Delmer, who recognised something of a fellow spirit. 'After Delmer had taken over the provision of Black Texts, the Howe Unit began to operate on a large scale,' the official history adds. And by 1943, the unit was so prolific that Howe became more of a production organiser than printer or designer. Miss Friedlander sweated over the details while Howe outsourced the actual production to various printers and paper makers. At any one point in the later stages of the war, as many as seventeen firms ('with night shifts at two of them') might be working during peak periods of activity.

The range of this output was extraordinary.

Mr Howe's unit could forge batches of 5 million German ration cards or print just one single, though extremely important, official letter. Of the mid-war output of Mr Howe's Unit, the official history notes that some 10 per cent were straight forgeries (of stamps and ration cards) while the rest were supposedly clandestine. About three-quarters were aimed at the German audience. Most famous was the appearance of stamps within the Third Reich that carried the images of Himmler and Hans Frank, Hitler's former lawyer and unspeakably cruel Governor General of Occupied Poland, instead of the Führer. As well as causing chaos in the Greater German postal service, the stamps added to the discomfiture for the golden pheasants that the British secret service was everywhere.

Another important recruit at this time was a one-eyed Canadian lecturer from Cambridge University who was employed to look at inducing mental illness in the *Deutsches Volk*. Dr John McCurdy would write a malingering handbook which Howe's unit produced. It would be later inveigled into the Third Reich to induce, so it was thought, even the most loyal of Germans to get sick leave from their doctors. As the official history of the PWE puts it, the malingering guide was 'produced in many different editions bound up in fifteen or more different forms such as books on physical culture etc.'

No wonder Ellic Howe's printers were busy; batches of 16,000 were printed off at any one time with the aim of being disseminated by balloon. This was a work in progress as, eventually, upwards of a million were produced by the close of the war. And yet the malingering guide showed what a double-edged weapon political warfare could ultimately be. McCurdy's guide was very subtle and clever. A potential malingerer was never supposed to tell the doctor that he was ill, rather describe the symptoms and make sure that he came across as patriotic. 'One single symptom which the doctor has discovered by his own questions is worth ten which the patient has volunteered,' the text describes.

The irony came with what Delmer called 'The Black Boomerang' – how the best intentions came back to hit you – when the Germans retranslated this malingerer's guide and dropped it over Allied lines later in the war, in the hope of turning it against the forces who had landed to liberate Europe.

Towards the end of 1941, Kim Philby had already begun his ascent within the Secret Intelligence Service (MI6). Though it was routinely (and erroneously) later said that he could easily have become the next C, he was certainly one of the most important agents ever to be recruited by the NKVD. Philby provided his handlers with advance warning of the German invasion of the Soviet Union as well as Japanese intentions to invade Singapore rather than joining the German attack on the USSR.

Philby was soon well placed to learn many of the more sensitive secrets of the Second World War. As head of the Iberian Section, his 'beat' was a large one, covering Spanish North Africa, Spain and Portugal as well as the Azores and the Canaries. 'We were six officers working in what had been a spacious drawing-room,' Philby recalled for Graham Greene's biographer, 'so our paperwork was interrupted by much shop-talk – little of it memorable.'

Indeed, it was dull and painstaking work.

The fruit of the labours came with the inevitable bureaucracy of the old school. Everything ran on cross-referencing of names and identities mentioned in the Abwehr radio traffic. Every time a new name was mentioned, a new card was created within the office. These would be cross-referenced with other cards from other signals, specifying the details and dates of operations. This eventually provided a 'lead' for the relevant Section V officer in Iberia to follow up. Gradually, a priceless picture of enemy agents and case officers would be built up and updated as and when necessary.

By the time Philby joined, Section V was based at Glenalmond, an Edwardian mansion close to St Albans, one of three buildings on Lord Verulam's estate which all formed an MI6 outstation. Given the special nature of its work, Glenalmond was oddly without obvious protection. 'I recall no security guards or showing of passes,' recalled Philby's old school friend, Tim Milne, about his first visit. 'Somebody – probably a passing secretary – directed me to a door [which] opened into a large room with unbarred windows on two sides and a view of the garden.' The mansion was surrounded by a well-kept lawn, through which a path wound between some chestnut trees. In the distance, an old lily pond could be seen in front of an overgrown rose garden.

Its bucolic appearance was misleading: this was British Intelligence's main bulwark against its enemies in Iberia, building up a complete picture of the enemy intelligence set-up in both Spain and Portugal. Kim Philby was, according to Milne, unfazed by the complicated nature of their work. Philby knew everybody and everything. His attention to detail became what his friend called one of his weapons as 'he was always well informed on the subject he was talking about'.

In time, Philby used that skill in siding against everyone else's favourite enemy within. Oddly, though most of his underlings seemed to like working for him at Glenalmond, Felix Cowgill's capacity to make enemies was exploited by Philby. Ironically, the Soviet Union would now learn that the former head of Section V was unable to delegate, possessed few social graces and, as they were no doubt delighted to find out, also smoked vast amounts of tobacco like Karl Marx.

Once Felix Cowgill was removed, it would allow British double agent operations to blossom on a more even keel. Even so, Philby was quickly able to consolidate his position. 'You know, I'm beginning to think we're going to win this war,' he said in Tim Milne's hearing.

By the end of 1941, perhaps the most important step, so far as running double agents was concerned, occurred when Bletchley Park broke into the Enigma traffic used by the Abwehr to communicate with the Fuchsbau. This was not just the 'chickenfeed' of its fabrications transmitted by the double agents, but all the traffic which the Abwehr and all its outstations exchanged. From the lowliest assistant right up to the higher echelons of Nazi Germany, British Intelligence now could read everything its opposite numbers were discussing. Small wonder the dissemination of this material was limited for it was gold dust, allowing the double agent operations to go up another notch.

While the work of Section V that underpinned it was hardly a laugh a minute, comedy was on the menu in some of the stranger decryptions they broke. One radio message related a tale of how Spanish communists had shot a pet parrot because it had learned from a maid the Spanish for 'I am a royal parrot and I'm for Spain and Portugal'. Another wireless operator telegraphed to Berlin: 'I ran into an oxcart while riding my motorcycle, went over the cliff and broke my arm.'

On another famous occasion, a signal was received which revealed that Axel, a German police dog, had been sent out as a guard for the Algeciras outstation of the Abwehr. 'Be careful of Axel,' ran another message. 'He bites.' A few days later came the reply: 'César (code name for Albert Carbe, head of the Abwehr there) is in hospital. Axel bit him.'

On another occasion, various Section V officers literally fell about laughing when scanning a roster for passengers from Istanbul to Madrid when they came across the name Mustapha Kunt. 'All this may seem ridiculous,' another Section V man would write, 'but there was a lot of tensions and roster checking was as dull as it was important; silly humour often kept us going.'

So it was that on the last day of 1941, wearing the uniform of an officer of the Royal Air Force, Dennis Wheatley finally entered the secret world. He formally joined the specially created secret department whose anodyne name purposefully gave no hint of what it actually did. The London Controlling Section would eventually come to have a power and remit far beyond most others in the secret war. Using the double agents and their decrypted signals, Dennis Wheatley, famed for his pulp fiction on both magic and the occult, became intimately involved in creating wholesale deceptions that would, in the fullness of time, become infamous within the shadowy world of wartime intelligence.

Paradoxically, and exactly how they had intended it, both the public and the enemy never knew about them at the time.

Dennis Wheatley's writing skills and fertile imagination could help stamp a unique imprimatur on the covert battles ahead. For all his fears that he wasn't being listened to, The Joint Planning Staff had welcomed his contributions and, as one would write, 'it still seems incredible that one brain in the tumultuous conditions of 1940/1941 could have produced so inspired, so sensible and so far-seeing [a] solution.'

London Control, as it was sometimes known, was part of a woolly area known as 'Future planning'. To lead it was a Conservative MP, a former minister and scion of a great aristocratic lineage, who once spoke for three and a half hours in one speech. The Right Honourable Oliver Stanley was an intimate of Churchill's and when he was appointed controller, from the general tenor of his notes, it is clear that Stanley didn't know what he was letting himself in for. In view of what happened, there is a curious irony that his own job description showed the reason why he would fail. 'It will not be enough for him just to read papers, as they are issued or concluded, as they are recorded,' he noted. 'He should be able to roam free, stay in contact with the PWE and other agencies.' But crucially, he would never get on to the PM's list for distribution of the Ultra material. He also wanted to expand the section. Three officers would be needed, one each from the services, who should have 'imagination, initiative and a sound administrative background'.

A measure of how important it was thought to be came from the fact the naval representative never showed up; the army provided an elderly, one-legged old cove with a saucy sense of humour; and the Royal Air Force, which knew a thing about feeling threatened, announced there was a war on and nobody could be spared. And that was how it might have ended, had it not been for a few days later when a senior planner on the RAF staff remembered the papers which had been showing up over the last few years.

'What about Wheatley?'

By now, a few months after he had joined Section V, Kim Philby was travelling into London to meet his Soviet controllers on a regular basis. Nobody suspected anything for he had legitimate business to attend to at the Broadway headquarters of the Secret Intelligence Service. 'The job was so absorbing and completely time-consuming that I would have found it almost impossible to imagine it could take second place to even more important work,' a colleague, who later joined Section V, noted many years later.

Perhaps the greater surprise is that, for all his supposed omniscience, Philby's reports, and those of his fellow travellers who are generally known as 'the Cambridge Five', were widely disbelieved in the Soviet Union. His handlers in Moscow exhibited greater suspicions about all of the Cambridge-educated spies – more to do with pervasive Stalinist paranoia than anything – suspecting they were part of some sort of deliberate misinformation campaign. It hardly helped his credibility that some of Kim Philby's material was downright peculiar, with his sometimes overheated reports of scandals, clubland debauchery and claims that RAF officers 'under the influence of drugs, alcohol or sexual orgies or Black Mass are induced to part with information'.

An obvious question is: was this some sort of reference to Aleister Crowley? The answer may never be known, but, more significantly, Kim Philby was in place within the secret world when came perhaps the single most peculiar event of the war in which many people assume Crowley was involved. Even today, many mysteries still linger about the arrival of Rudolf Hess in Scotland in May 1941. All can now be examined in the true light of themes and people already introduced in this narrative so far: astrology, political warfare, muck raking by Philby and someone who, at his best, was hardly coherent and never seemed to make any sense.

Dr John Dee, mystic and intelligencer to the court of Elizabeth I. Though it is sometimes claimed he used the symbol 007, he never actually did.

Viorel Virgil Tilea, the mercurial, anglophile Romanian ambassador. He was the victim of Nazi espionage and the instrument by which astrology was brought to the attention of the higher echelons of the British establishment.

Left: The astrologer Louis de Wohl was sent to the United States in 1941 with a licence to predict Hitler's demise. His presence was hyped up as 'The new Nostradamus'.

Below: Maxwell Knight, pre-war star agent runner for MI5, who claimed he learned everything about handling spies from his interest in animals and birds.

Commander Mansfield Cumming R.N.

Left: The Admiral. Mansfield Cumming, the eccentric, yet truly inspired first chief of MI6, whose modern-day successor calls him a hard act to follow.

Below: The other admiral. Wilhelm Canaris, the perplexing and almost mystical head of German Military Intelligence in World War II, about whom many mysteries and conundrums still linger.

Above: Evan Morgan, the Second Viscount Tredegar, with feathered friend. An eccentric, occasional occultist who was ejected from the intelligence world due to his inability to keep secrets.

Left: Smooth Operator. General Walter Schellenberg, the rising star of SS Intelligence at the start of the war, who oversaw the greatest propaganda coup against MI6 at Venlo, on the Dutch border.

The Lone Wolf. Georg Elser, who came within minutes of killing Adolf Hitler in November 1939, setting off a chain of events that the Nazis blamed on the supposedly occult powers of the British Secret Service.

Siren of the Airwaves. The teenage Agnes Bernelle, who as 'Vicky' broadcast to her 'boys in blue' – the U-Boat crews whom she undermined with her seductive and subversive charms.

D.B.E.

De WOHL is somewhat of a thorn in my side, for in at least ~~some~~ ~~often~~ circles he is regarded as a complete charlatan with a mysterious, if not murky, past, but yet he struts about in the uniform of a British Army Captain, and gives every reason for believing that he is in some secret employment. This arouses envy and dissatisfaction among some of my agents of foreign origin, who have at least equal claim to the much coveted "cover" of a British uniform, and who regard it as at least peculiar that the British should openly employ such a man and give him H.M's commission. I understand, however, that his commission is now to be withdrawn as his so-called mission is ended.

de WOHL is clearly potentially highly dangerous; there is no guarantee whatsoever of his loyalty and he is likely to be guided solely by his vanity and his idea of self-interest. There is no case for interning him, and even if he were interned he would undoubtedly be speedily released and would, moreover, have a justifiable grievance. On the other hand, if he is left at large it is essential that we should keep a close tag on him. I understand that

is no longer available.

There appear to be two possible ways of dealing with him:-

P.T.OVER.

Louis de Wohl's self-aggrandisement and need to wear a uniform was a tiresome undercurrent that ran through all his dealings with the British security authorities, as in this MI5 assessment from February 1942 after his return from the United States

The grand old man. Dennis Wheatley, who always saw the entertaining possibilities of the occult, and used his writing skills to deceive and subvert the Germans in the later stages of the war.

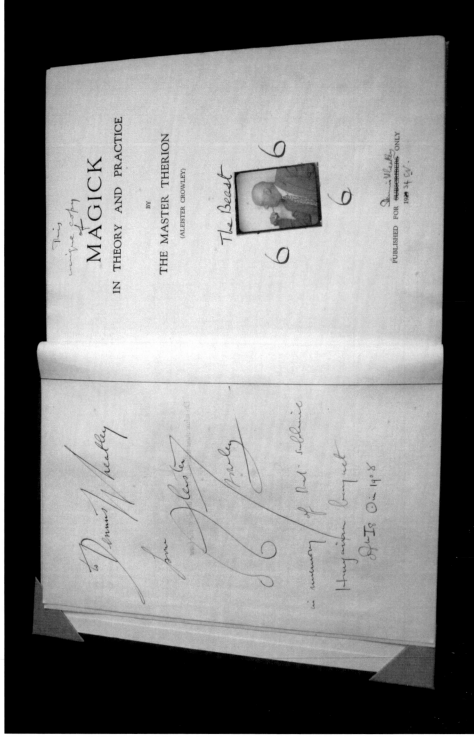

The Mark of the Beast. The inscription by Aleister Crowley on his own book on magick, which he gave to Dennis Wheatley, who always considered him a charlatan.

10

Sky Fall

Mr. Churchill made his statement. They heard him at first with incredulity, then with rapturous delight. Not a man there but assumed that the war was over, not a man but felt that Europe now to be suffused with the unearthly radiance of a new dawn, not a man but read in the fortuitous apprehension of a single mountebank, the rescue of civilization, justice and the pound sterling.

Peter Fleming, 'The Flying Visit'

Horoscope 'lured' Hess to Britain: Rudolf Hess was lured to Britain in 1941 by a plot thought up by the late Ian Fleming, then in naval intelligence involving the planting of an astrologer on the susceptible Deputy Führer.

Peter Hopkirk, *The Times*, 15 September 1969

It was a fall from the sky that should not have surprised anybody.

Several people heard the plane circling. Of this, there is little doubt. The moment its single occupant hurled himself from the cockpit, however, the certainties evaporate. Many strange and surreal discrepancies suffuse the historical record concerning exactly what happened on the late evening of Saturday, 10 May 1941 high above the lowlands of Scotland, just south of Glasgow.

It was the night of the full moon and an appropriately ghostly sheen of light accompanied the events which would shortly unfold. After flying for over four hours, shortly after 10.30 p.m. a twin-engine German fighter-bomber continued on its way westwards after crossing the Northumberland coast. Eventually circling over Renfrewshire, the pilot, it is sometimes said, was looking for some sort of landing site. In reality, he had known all along that he would have to make a parachute drop. Home defence radar had indeed spotted the enemy aircraft (but it was never followed by scrambled RAF fighters, as is sometimes claimed, defending the nearby port and city). Nor was the aircraft shot down. Nor was there a welcoming, waiting committee for the bedraggled pilot.

It was left to a handful of unprepared local Home Guard soldiers to arrest the parachutist. He didn't speak a word of English, so accounts that he told them his aim – to speak directly to the Duke of Hamilton – can be dismissed, too. In fact, it wasn't until the wee small hours of the next morning that an interpreter could be found, by which time it had slowly dawned on others that the beetle-browed parachutist was a high-ranking Nazi.

It is now that the mysteries about Rudolf Hess's unexpected arrival mushroom with myths, rumour and ridiculously silly speculation. Consider the following, for example. That Hess's arrival was propelled as part of a peace-feeling operation orchestrated directly by mysterious, secretive Establishment figures – including the Royal Family. That somewhere along the way he was replaced by a doppelgänger, or in his subsequent imprisonment he was either murdered or committed suicide. All, or variations on them, are regularly repeated as fact.

But, so far as this narrative is concerned, perhaps the most piquant of all is one that is now routinely trotted out over the Internet: that Rudolf Hess was lured to Great Britain by an intelligence sting prompted by his belief in astrology, a compulsion that had been expertly stoked by none other than a character already encountered in this narrative. Whether the newly promoted Commander Ian Fleming of Naval Intelligence had indeed prompted this real life Skyfall or not, the events surrounding Hess's arrival were such that, in the words of one contemporary newspaper, 'a man from Mars would cause scarcely more astonishment'.

By the first few days of May 1941, as noted in the chapter before last, any number of strange activities had been taking place within Whitehall with regard to astrology. With the immediate threat of invasion receding, however temporarily, Great Britain was in a far stronger position than it had been since the outbreak of the war twenty months earlier. Adolf Hitler, too, was well advanced with his plans to invade the Soviet Union, and needed some greater security before turning East. As the late historian and politician Alan Clark suggested, exploring the possibilities of a peace treaty at this time would have not been such an odd concept. Writing in *The Times* in January 1993, Clark suggested that this represented a missed opportunity.

Rudolf Hess, in Clark's analysis, came to barter just such a peace deal but his mission was hushed up by Winston Churchill, who saw what he termed 'the domestic dangers'. The prime minister would not talk to the German emissary[1] and, in Clark's estimation, 'repressed (in conspiracy with the whole Establishment) the documents' which would prove it. This is just one of many wrinkles on the theme of a cover-up which continues today.

Even allowing for such a revisionist backdrop, it is now clear that in May 1941 there were some peculiar operations taking place within the secret war. Wearing his army captain's uniform, Louis de Wohl was being consulted by various branches of military intelligence about the use of astrology in prosecuting war; the Special Operations Executive had started to place strange rumours about Adolf Hitler's own use of astrology in newspapers all the world over; but most improbable of all, there was already a published scenario which concerned the landing of a German leader in England and how such an event would be hushed up by the relevant authorities.

Even in wartime, Peter Fleming was a prolific writer.

The previous spring, after his return from Norway, he had succumbed, 'appropriately enough' as he later described it, to German measles. While recovering at home on the Fleming family estate, he penned a gloriously satirical novel called *The Flying Visit*, which, in view of events in the spring of 1941, is worthy of examination.

In so many ways, the Squire of Nettlebed was astonishingly prescient.

The novel tells an all-too plausible story of Adolf Hitler, wanting to gloat over his victory over the British, taking part in a Luftwaffe raid over London. A time bomb, disguised as a thermos flask, brings his particular aircraft down.[2]

The Führer is the sole survivor. He parachutes down into the Chilterns, the area which the Fleming brothers knew very well from their childhood, where he then tries to make contact with the various politicians who are more likely to want to sue for peace.

At first, Adolf Hitler is hopeful. After coming across a woman in a cottage who mistakes him for a peddler and sets her dog on him ('a loathsome little mongrel'), he then tries to shoot himself (with blanks) and then comes across a village hall in Oxfordshire, the kind of which the author also knew so very well.

This is by far the funniest part of the book. Peter Fleming describes completely straight-faced how Adolf Hitler enters the back door of the village hall and walks on to a brightly lit stage where he encounters a man in traditional Arab headwear, after which 'a gasp of astonishment and wonder' comes from the audience.

The Führer then tries to make himself heard above the commotion:

'English men and women!' he yelled. 'It is I, Adolf Hitler, who stands before you! I am not your enemy! You are not my enemies! We are not each other's enemies!'

The audience screams, the Arab slaps him on the back and then he is promptly handed a pound of butter wrapped in a pale blue ribbon. 'Baffled but beaming toothily,' the Führer bows his acceptance. Slowly it dawns on him that he has actually taken part in a fancy dress competition. When the clapping subsides, he notices an Ancient Briton, a pierrot and an apache and then, as he tries to make another speech, a blonde woman dressed as a Rheinmaiden flings her arms around his neck and kisses him.

'Sweety-pie!' she screams. 'You're wonderful!'

The blonde eventually takes him into custody. Like *Wag The Dog*, many years hence, what follows is a splendid piece of satire on official secrecy. The British government is thrown into absolute confusion. Adolf Hitler's capture cannot be announced as Whitehall suspects that the Nazis will have a doppelgänger ready and waiting in the wings. When an American newspaperman breaks the story, the British authorities have no alternative but to parachute him back to the Fatherland, a policy, Peter Fleming notes, 'of constructive negotiation'.

If something odd was ever going to happen involving a high-ranking Nazi leader, it would have to coincide with a full moon. On the evening of Saturday, 10 May 1941, when the lone parachutist was reported to have landed close by a farmhouse near to Glasgow, at first it seemed a curious counterpoint to the unremittingly awful news about the progress of the war that month.

Iraq had declared for the Germans; Vichy had endorsed an important agreement with Hitler; the Germans had invaded Crete and HMS *Hood* had been sunk off Greenland. That same Saturday night, the Blitzkrieg had nearly destroyed the House of Commons in one of the heaviest air raids of the war. The reports from Scotland were at first confused, but when this mysterious figure was revealed as none other than Rudolf Hess, there was general incredulity. Weekending at Chequers, the country home where he went to avoid bombing raids in full moonlight, the prime minister's reaction was typical.

'Even if it is Hess, I am going to watch the Marx brothers,' Winston Churchill said as he strolled into his private cinema.

And it is fair to say, what happened next reads like a script from one of their films. The strange coincidences and odd events have all combined to create an enduring series of conspiracy theories that refuse to be resolved even today. Many are regularly repeated in newspaper accounts and trotted out as fact in spurious interpretations of the historical record. The reality is often far more surprising than some of these more excited speculations.

Far from being orchestrated by the Secret Intelligence Service, Rudolf Hess's arrival seems to have actually raised Sir Stewart Menzies's blood pressure. Certainly, from the tenor of exasperation in the notes the chief of MI6 dispatched in the immediate aftermath, it is clear that there was hardly a waiting welcoming committee organised by 'the secret services' for the Deputy Führer. Amazing as it seems to posterity, a handful of Home Guards detained him in a number of remote Scout huts for four hours until he was transferred to the Maryhill Barracks in Glasgow.

The apprehension of Hess, then known only as Captain Horn, involved such a litany of blunders that even with the fragments of evidence available in the UK National Archives it is clear there had been one cock-up after another. Far from being on alert (as is sometimes claimed) the authorities were so unprepared that the only translator they could find who spoke German sufficiently well was a Polish official from the local Glaswegian consulate.

'It seems incredible,' C himself later thundered, 'that this should have been permitted.'

What is also clear is that the events of these first few hours – so crucial in any investigation – were woefully mishandled. The characters involved and the decisions they made put the satiric nature of Peter Fleming's exuberant fiction to shame. What is also immediately apparent is that they were far more interested in covering their own backs before they actually did anything. This partly explains why Rudolf Hess was not interrogated until three o'clock the following morning.

Later that same Sunday morning, the Duke of Hamilton was introduced to Rudolf Hess, whom the German claimed he had met before the war.

The duke – who plays a curious role in this passage – could not remember any such a meeting. In private, the Deputy Führer explained that he had arrived 'on a mission of humanity and that the Führer did not want to defeat England and wished to stop the fighting'.

C followed the case quite closely but he insisted that Rudolf Hess should be treated in a very British way. 'He will be given no mysterious drugs – if such exist – to sap his will,' Sir Stewart minuted his colleagues. 'There will be no racks, no thumbscrews, no third degree nor the threat of them.' Significantly, Hess was kept under lock and guard by military personnel, not representatives of British Intelligence as is sometimes claimed in the more febrile accounts of his time in Scotland.

Perhaps the most telling reaction took place in Cairo that same weekend.

Hermione, the Countess of Ranfurly, was working as confidential secretary to the head of the Special Operations Executive in the Middle East, where her fearsome reputation was such that, as one of her obituaries later put it, she was 'the kind of woman for whom words such as pluck and spirit might have been invented'.[3] At some point, she told an important visitor from England about the news when he happened to be in her office. He looked up, amazed.

'For a moment, I thought she was joking,' Peter Fleming recalled. 'You see I wrote a book about that not long ago,' he told her, 'it is called *The Flying Visit*.'

And in another of those strange coincidences which sometimes bedevil controversial aspects of history, Jock Colville, the prime minister's private secretary, happened to have been reading *The Flying Visit* at the same time. So when it was reported that a senior German had landed, Colville was sure, as he later recorded, 'that either Hitler or Göring [had] arrived'.

A few days later, Peter Fleming's old newspaper, *The Times*, ran an editorial called – almost inevitably – 'The Flying Visit', which mentions a literary flight of fancy, published the previous year by a well-known young member of its own staff, calling the event something which had 'staggered the world'.

And then various speculations began in earnest.

Did nature imitate art? Or was Peter Fleming party to what would happen? Had something along these lines been planned all along? Was British Intelligence involved? Though the answers to all these questions were a resounding 'no', it neither stopped the speculation then nor today as the theories became ever more elaborate. Peter Fleming later maintained the resemblance to his story was superficial and, over the years, it has become another enduring myth that his younger brother was also involved in bringing Hess over to the British Isles.

One can imagine the Fleming brothers had a good giggle about it. Small wonder that mysteries, myths and urban legends accumulated in Hess's wake, not least in Nazi Germany and the Soviet Union, where most struck a resonance with the high-ups' favourite bogeyman: the British Secret Service and its supposed occultic powers and omniscience.

Within days, the press started to speculate about the reasons behind Rudolf Hess's arrival. The same weekly publication for German and Austrian émigrés, *Die Zeitung*, which had carried the whispers surrounding Adolf Hitler's death, now pronounced on his deputy's arrival in the British Isles. Twelve days later an article headed 'Astrology in Hitler's Service' claimed that within Hess's ministerial purview was a department called AMO (concerning Astrology, Metapsychology and Occultism) from which Nazi astrologers 'sent articles to newspapers all over the world in order to prepare public opinion for events upon which Hitler wants attention to be focussed'.

Certainly, the AMO didn't exist and neither did this mysterious astrologer (nor is there any evidence of the submission of articles into the US press by German astrologers). Walter Tschuppik's report suggested Hess's flight on 10 May came from that supposedly unusual conjunction of planets in Taurus which Louis de Wohl and others had already noted. Like Adolf Hitler, the article claimed Rudolf Hess had his own astrologer, particularly because the *Führerastrologe* had disappeared – probably arrested – and had been replaced by someone of whom all that was known was he had 'daemonic dark eyes and black hair brushed back over his head'.

Though not mentioned by name, it was clear this was meant to be Karl Krafft, the astrologer who had been named in various papers as being close to Adolf Hitler. In reality, by this point in the war, Krafft had already been effectively confined for the best part of a year, though he was eventually allowed some leeway. Although Krafft had previously suggested at a public meeting there was the imminent possibility of 'large-scale military operations in the East' before the invasion of the Soviet Union, the Gestapo did nothing.

It seems they didn't have to.

Karl Krafft was soon a virtual prisoner in a Propaganda Ministry building in Berlin, where he was believed by some – expertly fed by Louis de

Wohl – to be casting the horoscopes of Allied leaders and generals. That way, his 'predictions' could be tinkered with for political warfare purposes. Sometime in 1942, Krafft would eventually suffer a nervous breakdown and refuse to do any more work, despite Goebbels's supposed enthusiasm for using the occult for various misinformation purposes.

'We are really getting somewhere,' the propaganda chief wrote in his diary for 19 May 1942. 'The Americans and English fall easily for that type of thing. We are therefore processing into our service all the experts we can find on occult prophecies etc. Nostradamus must once again submit to being quoted.'

So why had the Deputy Führer flown to Britain?

Rudolf Hess later admitted in all seriousness that 'the idea had been inspired in him in a dream by supernatural force'. Within a few days, a party line emerged from the Nazi leadership that he had been disastrously influenced by astrologers and hypnotists. 'The extent to which these people are responsible for the mental confusion that led him to his present step still has to be clarified,' the *Völkischer Beobachter* announced four days later. It was widely supposed that one or other of them had advised Hess about a suitable date for his departure.

In view of some of the later claims that the Führer had dispatched him on a peace mission, Adolf Hitler, too, was simply incredulous that his deputy would do such a thing. Albert Speer was standing outside the Führer's study when he heard 'an inarticulate, almost animal outcry'. (Hess told Speer many years later when they were both imprisoned in Spandau about that supernatural dream). General Franz Halder, the Chief of Staff of the Supreme High Command, noted in his contemporary diaries that the 'Führer was taken completely by surprise by Hess's flight', and at the time the general speculated that Hess had been driven by 'some mystical sense of mission'. Others who were staying at the Berghof that fateful weekend recorded the dismay and confusion which resulted. Hitler's former lawyer and Governor of Poland, Hans Frank, later noted that he had not seen the Führer so upset since the death of his beloved niece Geli, ten years earlier, itself a subject of much prurient speculation.

More significantly for this story, when Josef Goebbels heard what happened to Hess, he termed it 'dreadful news, a hard almost unbearable blow'. The propaganda minister also found the Führer crushed and in tears. Within a few days, an official communiqué noted that Hess had flown as part of a 'personal initiative', the result of a mental aberration prompted by 'a host of magnetotherapists and astrologers', though the original translation of the German was actually 'mesmerists'.

As a result, in Nazi Germany astrologers now became marked men.

What became known as the *Aktion* Hess now gave the Gestapo the wherewithal to arrest many hundreds whose malign influence – 'astrologers, fortune-tellers and other swindlers', in Martin Bormann's phrase – was suspected. That same day, *The Times* reported from Switzerland that 'close friends' had said that Hess was Hitler's secret astrologer. The most mystic of the golden pheasants, Heinrich Himmler, was, by all accounts, particularly bemused.

Within a month, the secret police had cast its net much wider with the arrest of Christian scientists, faith healers and even psychologists and psychotherapists without formal medical training. Most astrologers, it should be noted, were released within a few days. Particular interest was shown towards Ernst Schulte-Strathaus, who had been on Hess's staff at the Munich Brown House (the national headquarters of the Nazi Party) since 1935 and was a keen amateur astrologer. By the spring of 1941, he was actually in charge of the Chancellery's cultural/political office and not Hess's astrological adviser, as some accounts suggest.

His closeness to Hess meant that Schulte-Strathaus was one of the first to be interrogated. Yet he stated after the war that not only did he not foist his views on Hess, he never warned him that 10 May should be a suitable day for departure. Whether the Gestapo found any evidence for astrological prophecies is not known, but it seems Schulte-Strathaus had made a comment in January 1941 that the 'Major Conjunction' (the presence of six planets in one sign of the zodiac, Taurus) would take place on 10 May 1941 and coincide with the full moon.

But that was all. Schulte-Strathaus had also joked that the Earth might well tilt on its axis as a result. He would languish in prison until 1 March 1943 for this astrologically incorrect jest. Public performances or lectures on anything vaguely alluding to the occult, spiritualism, clairvoyancy, telepathy or astrology were soon banned throughout the Third Reich. By October 1941, editors were instructed not to publish anything on such topics. The zodiacal wheel had come full circle by late November, when a Party edict asked functionaries to read recent articles in *Die Weltliteratur* which described the campaign against astrologers, anthroposophists, clairvoyants and occultists.

In the immediate aftermath of Hess's flight, more than one astrologer found themselves imprisoned and incommunicado. Many were asked the

ultimate pointed question which came from SS Headquarters in Berlin:
'Suppose that a negro, a Jew and an Aryan were all born on the same day
and at the same time, would you make identical predictions?' That some
interrogators knew as much as their suspects is also borne out by the recollection of one astrologer held in Breslau by the Gestapo. It led to a farcical
exchange with his questioner.

'What are your aspects like at this time?' the Gestapo man asked.

The astrologer hesitantly replied that Uranus was close to his Ascendant
and the sun was transiting his Saturn.

'In which house?' The Gestapo man's eyes narrowed.

'The ninth.'

The astrologer detected the merest flicker of a smile opposite. 'Then at
the moment nothing should surprise you.'

There was, however, one peculiar intelligence dimension to the arrival of
Rudolf Hess in Great Britain.

It all began with a conversation that the Deputy Führer had had the previous autumn with one of his oldest advisers. Though many mysteries remain
about what had happened in Bad Godesburg in September 1940, it certainly
does point to a half-hearted British disinformation campaign that, ultimately,
was cancelled before Hess had even considered taking off. Yet it does suggest that there was some sort of back channel being established by British
Intelligence to allow associates of the Deputy Führer to communicate directly
with MI5. By any stretch of the imagination, though, it was hardly an earth-
shattering mechanism that 'lured' Rudolf Hess to Britain. It involved a strange
coincidence, a postcard and an elderly widow in Cambridge.

Professor Karl Haushofer had once been one of Hess's teachers at university and came up with the notion of *lebensraum*, the need for living space
that provided an intellectual justification (of sorts) for Germanic expansion.
Haushofer headed the Institute of Geopolitics which, in Nazi Germany,
represented a brave new world of academic self-interest. In thanks for his
support over the years, Rudolf Hess had appointed him president for life of
the council that dealt with German citizens who lived abroad. The Deputy
Führer was also close to his son, Albrecht, a scholar, musician and playwright
who spoke English like a native. Almost inevitably, Haushofer Junior became
an adviser to the Nazis about English affairs.

Significantly, Albrecht Haushofer had met the Duke of Hamilton at the
Olympic Games in Berlin in 1936. Like Hess, the then Lord Clydesdale

had been a pre-war aviator of some note. The duke's relationship with the Haushofers was unclear. And though even at the time Hamilton was suspect in many people's eyes because of his pro-peace sympathies, the fact the Deputy Leader of the Third Reich turned up in the middle of the night asking to make contact with him caused him a great deal of embarrassment. He issued any number of libel writs against journalists, the first, rarely remarked on, a few weeks later in 1941 when the Communist Party of Great Britain suggested he was behind Hess's arrival. Since his death in 1973, historians have no longer feared his litigation and, more to the point, his son James Douglas-Hamilton, himself a historian, has written extensively and usefully on the subject. Indeed, the younger Hamilton has shed a great deal of light on the connections between his father and the Haushofers.

So it was that on the last day of August 1940, Rudolf Hess summoned Karl Haushofer. This was the culmination of the discussions which had followed in the wake of the Führer's peace offering that had been roundly rejected a few weeks earlier. This, as we saw in Chapter 8, prompted Adolf Hitler to jest that he should head over to Great Britain in person. The belief that there were elements in Britain who wanted to overthrow Churchill remained potent. Its political ramifications were now delegated to Hess and the two Haushofers. The Deputy Führer confided in his mentor that Great Britain would seek peace and discussed the matter with him for over eight hours.

Both father and son became involved in the matter. A few days later, Haushofer Junior wrote to urge him to 'stop something which would have such infinitely momentous consequences'. As a result, Albrecht himself went to see Hess. Describing the Führer in British terms as 'a representative of Satan on Earth', he suggested certain Britons who would be amenable to peace. And Albrecht would know. Unknown at the time, the younger Haushofer was a member of the growing resistance against the Nazi regime. Peace, even with Nazis in power, was better than continued slaughter.

Yet from the outset both Karl and Albrecht Haushofer knew how difficult it would be to make contact with any British peace element. On 8 September 1940, Albrecht drew up a memo that he and Rudolf Hess discussed in Bad Godesberg which remains in the files: 'ARE THERE STILL POSSIBILITIES OF A GERMAN-ENGLISH PEACE.' Their discussion, too, took many hours and, at the conclusion, Albrecht suggested that he meet on neutral soil 'with the closest of my English friends, the young Duke of Hamilton, who has access at all times to all important persons in London, even to Churchill and the King'.

It was not every day that a letter arrived from England, in this case from the daughter-in-law of a former Viceroy of India, whose son had been killed in 1937. Violet Roberts was the widow of that unfortunate Cambridge professor of geography who, in the years since her husband's death, occasionally corresponded with his friend Karl Haushofer. When a letter or postcard (it is not clear which) from her turned up in the post that September which suggested he stay in contact via a Lisbon post office box, it was not just a bolt from the blue.

It was taken as a sign of providence.

In fact, the letter was most likely sent at the behest of British Intelligence.

It transpired that Mrs Roberts's nephew, Walter, worked for SO1, the part of SOE that dealt with propaganda (and would shortly be hived off into the PWE). When reference to this letter was discovered in the British archives in 1999, it suggested there had been some sort of intelligence conspiracy. The only problem with this interpretation is that the files clearly show how half-hearted it all was and went no further. Certainly, the dispatch of this letter was more likely a mirror image of what the Haushofers were doing. The British propagandists were probing to see if they could string the Nazis along. If the propaganda effort could show that there was, indeed, a sizeable peace movement, the notion would be implanted that the Third Reich would not need to invade. It would only be a matter of time before the appeasers took over again.

As always, the golden pheasants got hold of the wrong end of the stick.

In Albrecht Haushofer's recollection, his desire to make contact with his old friend the Duke of Hamilton was because the German leaders were sure he had direct access to the king, confirming that odd Nazi view which had prompted the farce in trying to kidnap the Duke of Windsor a few months before. It was agreed that in reply they would use 'the old lady with whom you are acquainted', as Hess described it. In reality, Albrecht was soon telling his father that 'the whole thing is a fool's errand'.

A few days later, a polite letter was dispatched via Lisbon by Hess's brother in which indeed Albrecht Haushofer offered to meet 'my dear Douglo' in a neutral country. When it was intercepted by British censors – ironically, in view of what later transpired – at the Ministry of Information it was, as a matter of routine, copied and sent to MI5 and the Foreign Office. Far from being orchestrated by them, both the Security Service and the FO (which had responsibility for MI6) were ignorant of who had actually sent the letter.

They let it pass, noting that 'no doubt the Duke of Hamilton will be tickled to death' to receive a letter from Germany after three months. By February 1941, the duke was summoned to a meeting at the Air Ministry in London. At first, he thought this interest referred to a letter he had received in 1939 from Haushofer warning of war, which he had copied and showed to Chamberlain and Churchill. Another meeting a month later saw MI5 representatives ask the duke to go to the meeting in Lisbon. Hamilton was very, very reluctant, even though it was pointed out to him that he could claim plausible deniability in case things went wrong. Several people who were party to this proposed meeting were sure that, as one of them later said, it was actually a non-starter.

Far from involving a high-level conspiracy, there was a farcical cock-up: after the protracted moving of files from MI5's temporary headquarters at Wormwood Scrubs following on from the fire that destroyed much of the service's archives the previous October, the original letter from Germany had been lost or misfiled. And, more germane to this story, by now it was six months since the initial correspondence had been dispatched. It was going to be very hard to explain why Hamilton had taken so long to reply. Eventually, the authorities saw sense: in a letter sent to the duke on 3 May 1941, an Air Ministry official, Group Captain Blatchford, informed the duke to stand down, noting, with masterly understatement, that sending a reply 'might not carry conviction and so have undesirable consequences'.

It certainly did a week later for the Haushofers.

Two days after Rudolf Hess's flight, Karl Haushofer was arrested. Walter Schellenberg could report to his superiors that the Deputy Führer had been 'influenced by agents of the British Secret Service and their German collaborators'. At the time, even German statements suggested that he could have been lured into a trap as 'Hess has for years suffered physically', the Nazi Party noted, 'and increasingly took refuge in various forms of hypnotism and astrology etc.'

Equally intriguing – and infinitely more revealing – is the role of another character in British Intelligence whom some have suggested supposedly inveigled astrologers into Hess's immediate circle to spread the very rumours which prompted his flight. If so, such a notion would hardly compare with the extravagant plots of his later fictional writings or their transfer to the silver screen.

Did Ian Fleming have a hand in bringing over Rudolf Hess?

Given the interest of the Naval Intelligence Division in astrology, it would hardly seem out of place. That was certainly the view of one of his post-war colleagues, Donald McCormick, who, towards the end of his life, enjoyed making odd claims about his illustrious former colleague which are also now routinely reported as fact. Writing as Richard Deacon, he first aired the theory five years after Ian Fleming's death, in his history of the British Secret Service (where he also ascribed the numerals 007 to Dr John Dee).

McCormick's suppositions in the late sixties had the advantage that most of their wartime colleagues were still alive and could comment on this new theory. All, it should be noted, denied the idea that Ian Fleming had lured Rudolf Hess to Britain. As time went on, however, McCormick continued to rehash the same ideas – even though they had been denied – and added odd flourishes and touches which he ascribed to the very same people who had dismissed his ideas in the first place.

By then, in the early 1990s, most had long since died.

Perhaps the kindest comment to be made about Donald McCormick is that he was prolific. In a penetrating, pioneering analysis of the author's way of working, the thriller writer Jeremy Duns has provided irrefutable evidence that McCormick simply made things up. In various biographies of such historical figures as Lord Kitchener and Jack the Ripper, for example, McCormick clearly peppered the narratives with 'uncheckable and bogus documents and statements'.

So it was with his various statements about Dr John Dee[4], Ian Fleming and others in his various writings about the British Secret Service. The odd thing was that Fleming clearly liked McCormick personally, for his fellow author was clearly a likeable rogue, a flavour of which may be discerned from the headline to his later obituary from *The Guardian* in March 1998: 'Spooks, bars and brothels'.

They had originally met in the Barbizon Plaza Hotel in New York. Donald McCormick later worked for Fleming as a foreign correspondent when the latter was running the Kemsley newspaper foreign news operation (during which time several others in his immediate circle still wondered if he was working as a spook). McCormick had served in the Royal Navy during the war and had been involved in intelligence, famously writing a guide to spies in Algiers which focussed on the dangers of brothels in the kasbah.

A revealing anecdote about his working methods came in the late fifties. Donald McCormick was confronted by another author about the inconsistencies and provable forgeries in the Richard Deacon book about the death of Lord Kitchener. McCormick admitted with a sly wink that whoever was behind it was 'a very clever man who enjoys his quiet fun'.

That, perhaps, is how Donald McCormick should better be remembered.

So far as this narrative is concerned, a much more malign legacy stems from his affectionate, though very peculiar biography of Ian Fleming, *17F*, published in 1993. Once again, Donald McCormick rehashed many of the basic elements of his 'Hess lured by 007 author' story from the late sixties with new, amazing twists: that Rudolf Hess was lured to Scotland by means of forged astrological charts, as well as mysterious meetings in Portugal and Switzerland, curious emissaries and a 'chief astrological adviser Ernst Schulte-Strathaus', who in 1969, the former PWE executive Ellic Howe had already clarified in a letter to *The Times*, 'merely talked to [Hess] occasionally about astrology'.

Nevertheless, McCormick's newly embellished account carries another weirdly plausible invention: that Peter Fleming's *The Flying Visit* was part of the grander deception, 'doubtless seeing it as a possible means of signalling to the Germans that the British might think if someone were lured to Britain – if not Hitler or Hess, then possibly Canaris.' For as we will see, the notion that the head of the Abwehr would also be orchestrated to meet his British equivalents is another story that has grown in recent years – and been ascribed to the literary creator of 007.

It is significant that the first public airing of the 'my brother lured Hess to Britain' story was vehemently denied by not only Peter Fleming but his brother's old pre-war sparring partner, Tom Delmer, who was also involved in trying to exploit propaganda value from the Deputy Führer's arrival in 1941. On the eve of publication of Deacon's history of the secret service, a story in *The Times* on 15 September 1969 picked up on Delmer's thoughts about Ian Fleming's involvement.

'As an idea, inducing Hess to fly to England by means of astrological hocus-pocus – and the bait of the Duke of Hamilton – was something that might have appealed to Ian Fleming or even to have been conceived by him,' Delmer was quoted as saying in Peter Hopkirk's story. 'I am quite ready to believe that.'

But crucially, he added that the details were unconvincing.

'It is all too pat and does not fit the fact that the flight on 10 May was not Hess's first attempt to fly to Britain.'

In fact, Hess had made three earlier attempts, prompted by his growing sense that he was being sidelined within the Nazi hierarchy. Many of the people interviewed by *The Times* were clearly reticent. A certain circumspection was expected with regard to the duke (who did not die for another four years), who was notoriously litigious so far as the Hess story was concerned.

Nevertheless, Peter Fleming was more succinct. Ian had never told him about such a mission, calling it 'a new legend about my brother' and leaving it at that.

But Donald McCormick was never one to leaving anything at that at all.

His later biography of Ian Fleming (dismissed in one contemporary review as 'unoriginal and inaccurate') claimed to have discovered new and exciting plots involving his old wartime friend. The reality was that many of those same new details were very silly exaggerations which took the basic facts of an already surreal story into something else entirely. Namely, that James Bond's creator didn't just approach Aleister Crowley, but together they concocted the use of both magic and astrology to lure Rudolf Hess across the Channel in the first place.

Ultimately, the conspiracies surrounding Rudolf Hess's arrival in Scotland owe much of their potency to the fact the man himself never really made much sense as to why he had done so. On every side of the fighting – in London, Berlin and Moscow – everyone in a position of power was completely baffled by his sudden appearance over Scotland. In truth, Hess rarely made sense about anything, especially at his trial for war crimes at Nuremberg after the war. Many of the rumours emanate from the immediate crackdown on public speculation about his flight on both sides of the fighting in 1941.

With characteristic boldness, Sefton Delmer suggested at the time – against the express wishes of C – that Hess should be injected with a truth drug. 'That's not done, not in this country,' said one of his superiors, who was visibly shocked. Then, as later, Delmer was puzzled as to why no greater political capital was made of the flying visit by Captain Horn, treating him as some sort of Trojan Horse.

Delmer, characteristically, decided on a far more subtle approach.

He asked for a false page from the *Völkischer Beobachter* to be made up. This, it was hoped, would make Hess reveal what he was up to, having seen the (completely false) public vituperation which had followed his departure. Even in his confused state, the Deputy Führer took umbrage and, irony of ironies, declared himself the victim of a conspiracy. In the weeks afterwards,

Rudolf Hess refused to eat or taste anything without somebody else tasting it first in his sight.

By making no statements, it seemed that the government was hiding something. In a recent review of the propaganda aspects to the story, Dr Jo Fox of Durham University also notes that 'Hess's arrival marked a deepening of pre-existing fissures between black and white propaganda units'. In fact, the ongoing struggles between Hugh Dalton and Duff Cooper (the ministers responsible for the SOE and the Ministry of Information respectively) meant that they were sidelined in the greater debate as to what to do about Hess. The Foreign Office became the preferred conduit. As Dr Fox notes, the Hess affair sealed the fate of the MOI and Cooper's ministerial career.

And so, real life imitated Peter Fleming's fiction. The British government would do and say nothing about the fate of the Deputy Führer. There was, to be sure, a delicate balance. If the British portrayed Hess as mad, then that would confirm the German propaganda. If his peace offer was genuine, it played into Hitler's hands and made the British look warmongering. Goebbels – four days later – suggested a similar almost cod-British war movie stance: he instructed the German media 'to keep a stiff upper lip, not to react, not to explain anything'.

Into this breach stepped Gustav Siegfried Eins.

Tom Delmer would never adhere to a party line. It was only twelve days after Hess's arrival that his first subversive station started broadcasting black propaganda. To make it seem as though Der Chef had been broadcasting for a while, he now implied that he knew Hess was going to do something ridiculous. His followers, he announced, should lie low, which had explained Der Chef's silence in the immediate aftermath.

The danger, it seemed, had passed.

'First, let's get this straight,' Der Chef announced about the Deputy Führer, 'this fellow is by no means the worst of the lot. He was a good comrade of ours in the day of the Freikorps.'

But soon, in Germany – as in Britain – Rudolf Hess became a non-person.

So far as the public was concerned, he had disappeared off the face of the earth. No photograph was ever publicly produced of him during his imprisonment. As with Peter Fleming's *The Flying Visit*, no evidence was ever revealed to show the circumstances in which he had arrived. There were other rumours which almost inevitably followed: that he would head up a fifth column; that he had come to assassinate the prime minister, lunging at him with a poisoned ring. MI5 also intercepted letters written to Hess

– from cranks, pacifists and religious extremists – and had to dissuade one press photographer from trying to find the elusive quarry. These rumours still persist today, but as Dr Fox has elegantly summarised the circumstances: 'Hess had come uninvited, so he was not an envoy; in uniform, so he was not a spy; unarmed, so not an assassin.'

In another story that was circulating, MI5 learned that people were saying that Hess had come with a planeload of drugs and alternative therapies. And as Mass Observation, a forerunner of today's polling organisations, noted that August, 'people want to believe in something which at least appears to interpret events in the complex and dangerous civilization in which uneducated people find themselves confused, worried, many of their certainties weakened.'

And that certainly seems to be the case in the years since.

If Hess himself thought he was the victim of a conspiracy, so do many others who have looked into the story. Any number of even weirder and more wonderful 'explanations' for why the deputy leader defected have been proposed over the years. With the passing of time, the 'theories' have become ever more bizarre: that it wasn't Hess who flew to Scotland but a double; that Reinhard Heydrich accompanied him en route in his own fighter; that the British Home Defence forces were forewarned and ordered not to shoot his aircraft down. The Royal Family has also been implicated – through the king's brother, the Duke of Kent – as have aliens. *The Omega File: Rudolf Hess and the Secret German Space Race* claims he was murdered because he knew all about secret plans for a Nazi space base in the Antarctic.

In 2013, the historian Peter Padfield suggested that far from being a lone nut, Rudolf Hess had brought with him a detailed peace plan:[5] that Britain would become neutral if Nazi Germany withdrew from Western Europe before turning east. This was the basis for recollections of an unnamed academic who helped translate the document. 'This was not a renegade plot,' Mr Padfield noted at the time of publication. 'Hitler had sent Hess and he brought over a fully developed peace treaty for Germany to evacuate all the occupied countries in the West.' As well as learning of this supposed treaty and its contents, Mr Padfield claimed that he learned salient details about the subsequent cover-up. According to his account, two inventories of items carried by Hess when he was arrested after landing were made.

Neither has, it seems, ever been released.

Padfield found witness statements from a woman living near where Hess had landed, which indicate that police were 'ordered to search for a valuable document which was missing'. The item, according to this lady, was discovered 'over near the wee burn in the park'.

Further light may be shed on all these matters when, it is believed, a number of files will be released into the public domain in 2017. While it is true that those already released have been weeded – and there are some who believe this has been done to spare the blushes of relatives of important people – Adolf Hitler's reaction at the Berghof is telling. The fact that, in the months before his departure, Hess had been marginalised shows just how unimportant he was as a figure. Yet for many he has become a symbol of the iniquities of Western capitalism, 'a tool for putting pressure at key moments in the war', in one assessment. The involvement of the Duke of Hamilton seemed to confirm an Establishment cover-up. In the late spring of 1941, the arrival of Rudolf Hess now certainly meant that he would become an unwilling – and unwitting – pawn in a far bigger game.

As is clear from the equally strange themes examined in this book – of astrology, political warfare and misinformation – it is more than likely that Rudolf Hess accidentally got caught up in a disinformation campaign concerning peace feelers and the potential removal of the king. The timing of his flight in May 1941 was clearly linked to the forthcoming invasion of the Soviet Union, which occurred just six weeks later. Lord Beaverbrook said as much on several occasions after the war: others have speculated that Hess came with the news of the upcoming Russian campaign so that the British could 'swap sides' in the battle against the Bolsheviks.

Such a notion certainly had an appreciative audience behind the Iron Curtain. Even before the invasion of the Soviet Union, Josef Stalin was alert for plots and peace talks between his two imperial foes, Britain and Germany. Soon, the NKVD (the forerunner to the KGB) was reporting what he wanted to hear. 'Hess arrived in England with the full agreement of Hitler in order to begin talks for a truce,' said one report from the United States to Moscow. 'Because Hitler found it impossible openly to suggest a truce in view of the damage this would inflict on German morale, he selected Hess as his secret emissary.'

Rumours were soon circulating around the Kremlin. The invariable party line came a few days later in *Pravda*, which noted that Britain was now 'a haven for gangsters'. In Moscow, the notion quickly became established that the British Secret Service had somehow lured Hess to Britain. When, a year after the fall of the Berlin Wall, the author John Costello was allowed to see the relevant NKVD papers, yet another variable came into play: that Hess was lured to Britain by MI6. This story has it that the Führer was only too well aware that his deputy wanted to broker peace but only without injuring German prestige. Eighteen months later, in another account, Lavrenti Beria informed Stalin that it was due to an MI6 plot; yet another account said it was 'with full approval from Hitler'; and another suggested it was a conspiracy to make peace with Britain before the invasion of the USSR.

Certainly, that was what Stalin wanted to believe.

During a later wartime visit to Moscow, Churchill was astonished when Stalin toasted the health of the British Intelligence service which, he said, had inveigled Hess into coming to England. 'He could not have landed without being given signals. The Intelligence service must have been behind it,' said Stalin.

Inadvertantly, the silence on the British side – as one historian has written – was 'simultaneously inexplicable and disconcerting to the Russians [and] provided fertile grounds for a propaganda coup'. Others suggest that more mileage could have been made. If disinformation had inadvertently lured Hess towards the UK, another disinformation campaign would now be directed eastwards. The main instrument for what had already been termed 'running the Bolshevik hare' involved a complicated game of black propaganda to have the Soviet Union alter its views.

The British ambassador, Sir Stafford Cripps, realised it was a 'golden opportunity' to play or allay Stalin's fears. '[The] Hess incident has no doubt intrigued the Soviet government quite as much as anybody else and may well have arranged their old fear of a peaceable deal at their expense,' he wrote.

Little actually came of Hess's interrogation concerning Germany's intentions towards the Soviet Union – or any other matter. Despite questions being put to him, the Deputy Führer provided nothing useful at all. At the time, though there was a growing volume of intelligence that there was a build-up on the Soviet border, it was only ever believed that this would give Adolf Hitler a more powerful hand in negotiating with Stalin.

On 23 May, MI6 was instructed via its Foreign Office masters that it should begin 'the exploitation of the Hess incident through underground channels abroad' to reiterate the folly of taking Hitler at face value. This obviously concerned the peace pact between the two countries that had been signed in August 1939.

Directives were sent to embassies in Stockholm, New York and Istanbul, to be added to by whispering campaigns set into motion by the SOE and others. As many 'whispers as possible' were to be directed towards the Soviet Union forthwith. Much of this information was already being forwarded by Kim Philby to his Soviet controllers. As a result, somewhere within this combustible brew of well-meaning conspiracy is the supposed unseen hand of British Intelligence. 'The 18,000 pages of documents on the Hess affair made available by [the UK National Archives], when read in conjunction with archival material of the Russian Security Services,' notes Gabriel Gorodetsky, 'reveal a deliberate disinformation campaign carried out by British Intelligence which misfired and led to misinterpretations both at the time and subsequently.'[6]

If it was, as several have postulated, a last-ditch attempt to broker peace before the invasion of the Soviet Union, it was a cack-handed one. In Turkey, a German assistant naval attaché told a local intelligence official (who then repeated it to an MI6 officer) that the real reason Rudolf Hess had flown was because of his disagreements with Hitler over Balkan policy.

There is certainly no smoking gun lurking in the files.

Perhaps the most revealing detail is that when a contemporary report was circulated within MI6 which had picked up the rumour that Hess had been brought over 'owing to a trap laid by the British Secret Service', somebody had written 'A new one!' in the margin.

Rudolf Hess had become depressed – in his eyes because he had been deliberately kept away from meeting the king, whom he believed was party to peace feelers – and shortly, with his move to a holding camp in Wales, his mental state deteriorated even further. One psychiatrist diagnosed paranoia with a 'morbid persecution disillusional system'.

There was clearly no way he could be exploited for propaganda purposes.

In a final twist, in official MI6 papers released at the start of 2014, there is also a sequence concerning a *Daily Telegraph* report from the time on the finances of Rudolf Hess. It was alleged that he, like all other Nazi leaders, had somehow amassed enormous fortunes in various foreign banks. 'Unless my officers have been completely deceived by Hess,' C himself recorded for the file on 6 June 1941, 'there is not the slightest probability in the story. He takes not the slightest interest in financial matters, nor does he appear to have any knowledge of business.'

Nor, Sir Stewart Menzies added, were Hess's clothes 'those of a City magnate'. In another exchange with MI6, when it was asked by the Ministry of Economic Warfare as to the provenance of the Deputy Führer's clothes

– presumably to determine how well the German cotton industry was performing[7] – Menzies noted that they 'were of the cheapest variety and might well have been purchased at Marks and Spencer'.

To add to the downright peculiarity of the mysteries, at this point the self-styled Beast now reared his head that late spring of 1941. Aleister Crowley was far from having a good time of it having washed up on the English Riviera in Torquay. His tenancy agreement was up and he confessed to his diaries that any notion of moving 'may be upset at the moment by [a German] invasion [which] completes the picture of frustration'.

Being passive, it seemed, was the only course of action available to him. He was at a loose end, not so much dallying in the diabolical, but offering his services to anyone who would listen. But at the start of March came a curious escapade concerning the Soviet entry into the war. 'The sickle and Hammer have simply GOT to come in somehow,' he wrote on 1 March. And he suggested there were astrological portents, 'moving up to May 8', which was yet another extraordinary coincidence given the arrival of Hess around this time.

The Beast's scanning of the heavens had more to do with a more pressing worry. Even the English Riviera was not immune from air raids. Crowley was more than a little put out to have suffered a bombing. As ever, a great deal of smoke covers his activities, for in several accounts he was either being watched or consulted by the secret services. There is, however, little evidence to support this. In one account, he had been making repeated 'madcap' suggestions to MI5, including the dropping of occult literature over Germany to influence the *Deutsches Volk*. According to the more febrile reports based on Donald McCormick's fabrications, Ian Fleming wanted to use Crowley (who was friendly with occultists on both sides of the fighting) to entice a leading Nazi to Britain.

As with all stories about the Great Beast, most remain speculation.

After the arrival of Rudolf Hess, Fleming did suggest that Crowley be interviewed at length. The personal representative of Admiral John Godfrey was asked to interview the self-proclaimed Beast, leading to the surreal encounter which opens this book. Fleming had been invited to meet him in a curious, handwritten letter, which had arrived on the desk of the Director of Naval Intelligence bearing a Torquay postmark. According to some others, he did visit the Beast in Devon: the evidence is not clear. Fleming certainly cherished the letter as one of the more peculiar correspondences from the whole time of his war. Ultimately, the Naval Intelligence Division, decided not to take up his offer of assistance, but that has never stopped some of the more peculiar stories from taking hold.

Amado Crowley, as he liked to call himself, claimed he was Aleister Crowley's son. In fact he was an occultist whose real name was Andrew Standish, who had, it might be said in the politest of terms, a vivid imagination and yet looked a little like the great man and suffered from asthma. Amado claimed that his father, Ian Fleming and others were involved in a strange escapade around this time. This story is worth recounting as a wellspring for later rumours and weaves in several other names mentioned in connection with Rudolf Hess's arrival. Many are all lumped together and routinely referred to in the more credulous newspaper reports.

Standish was certainly never in the immediate orbit of the great man himself. 'Amado claims in his book that Aleister taught him between the ages of seven and fourteen: i.e. 1937–1944,' notes one apologist for the self-styled Beast who was more likely to believe him. 'If so, why isn't there a single mention of this vital matter in Crowley's Diaries? There he records matters as trivial as the breaking of a tooth or the quality of his dinner: but he does not see fit to record meetings with an initiation of a son destined to be his successor.'

Here, in all its preposterous glory, is what Andrew Standish claimed.

One day in early 1940, a short while after war had broken out, three men came to visit the Beast at his London home. Their appearance scored them for comedy: one was small, another tall and a final one was fat. This corpulent fellow spoke first.

'Mr Crowley, you must have heard of me,' he said portentously. 'My name is Louis de Wohl, the astrologer.'

The world's greatest necromancer was nonplussed.

'No,' he replied, 'I'm afraid it rings no bells.'

If Amado Crowley's account is to be believed, there followed an ill-tempered exchange, the result of two immense egos not just rubbing up against each other but rubbing each up the wrong way. His short and tall accomplices, who were supposedly working for MI5, then asked Crowley what he could do for them. There followed a *Catch-22*-type riddle: unless he signed the Official Secrets Act, they wouldn't tell him; but Crowley wouldn't sign anything unless they told him what this entailed. As an expert on German occultism, they reluctantly agreed to pay him money for help.

According to Standish (who, it should be noted, was actually 10 years old at the time) both he and his father signed the piece of paper. They were then taken to a heavily sandbagged building near Downing Street in which a number of senior figures were waiting. There then followed yet another bizarre conversation where everyone was given implausibly silly codenames. And then they were addressed by someone who had genuinely considered astrology as a weapon.

'You come highly recommended by a certain Mr Maxwell Knight, an important figure in the country's secret services,' said Admiral John Godfrey. 'Mr Churchill sought his advice. Consequently, he has asked for you by name.'

In this version of the story, using his specialist knowledge, Crowley would help target a Nazi leader susceptible to the occult and entice him to the United Kingdom. It was suggested that the Beast should meet two German officers – whose participation had been arranged via the Romanian mission in London – and that one of them was none other than Karl Haushofer, one of Hess's leading advisers. Crowley *père et fils*, another admiral and Louis de Wohl then went down to Tangmere Airport[8] to meet the Germans, who had arrived by aircraft. To say it went badly was an understatement. Their conversation came to an abrupt ending that saw Crowley Senior giving a right uppercut to one of the Germans.

The conclusion to an already bizarre story gets even more peculiar. Crowley hosted a firework ceremony in Ashdown Forest, where people in occultic robes danced. Pride of place was 'a dummy dressed in Nazi uniform, being sat on a throne-like chair', which was set on fire and then launched on a cable towards Germany (it landed a few hundred yards away). The rest, as they say, is history. Aleister Crowley waited for the repercussions from this event and on 11 May 1941 was simply informed that 'the bird had flown'.

Despite the self-evidently silly nature of these reminiscences, Aleister Crowley made quite an impression on Ian Fleming for other reasons. He was to store away the memory of Crowley's gross physical characteristics – especially his hypnotic eyes – for over a decade, when they would make a dramatic appearance in the form of a high-stakes card game. A foreign spy's appearance became a metaphor for various underhand activities in the form of strange physical disfigurements, a technique which Ian Fleming would later use to great effect.

There was clearly some precedent in the stories which Fleming had devoured in his youth. Erskine Childers's *The Riddle of The Sands* tells the story of two essential duffers who somehow manage to foil a sinister German plot to invade Eastern England. Childers was an accomplished yachtsman who had made a number of journeys through the foggy, sand-banked Friesian Islands. It gave him the germ of an idea for his pair of heroes – a man from the Foreign Office and his sidekick – who come across a profusion and prolixity of small boats. Eventually they realise that an invasion is planned when these boats will 'traverse the North Sea and throw themselves bodily upon the English shore'.

Our heroes in *The Riddle Of The Sands* are alert for scars and tics which are the telltale signs of a dangerous enemy. The weal on arch villain von Brüning's forehead, for example, indicates his inner conflict. 'The Edwardian thriller creates ways of representing the spy's body that carry through the twentieth century,' notes Professor Allan Hepburn. 'Fear of invasion from without in Childers's novel marks dangerous doubtlesness within the body politic and within the body itself.' Given that Professor Hepburn's mother was Audrey Hepburn, it could be said he knows a thing or two about appearances.

Ian Fleming simply carried on the tradition.

In recent years, there has been a cottage industry of speculation about who exactly the Bond villains were based upon. Fleming ascribed a similar guise as Crowley to Ernst Stavro Blofeld, whose dark hypnotic eyes were similar to Mussolini's.

Fleming certainly appropriated that particular name from a fellow member of Boodles, Tom Blofeld, who was also chairman of the Country Gentleman's Association (and whose nephew is the noted cricket commentator Henry Blofeld). In the book of *Thunderball* where he makes his first appearance, Blofeld was described as a large former weight-lifter (whose bulk had turned to fat, now weighing 18 stone) whose sheer animal magnetism was also based on the author's reaction to Aleister Crowley.

Crowley had also provided the inspiration for a truly prototypical protagonist in Fleming's first attempt at writing a thriller a few years earlier This alter-Crowley (or überbeast) would use a carpet beater to assault the testicles of Fleming's own alter ago, the spy whom he decided to give his old wartime rank, Commander RNVR.[9] Le Chiffre and *Casino Royale* – along with all the literary James Bond adventures – would have their origins in the strange wartime world in which Fleming had worked, providing them with a certain basis of reality which others have, for other reasons, blown out of all proportions.[10]

The next step, for both Fleming personally and others encountered so far in this story, concerned the other side of the Atlantic. A few weeks after the surreal events surrounding the arrival of Rudolf Hess, the newly promoted commander and his boss, Admiral Godfrey, made their way incognito to the United States via Lisbon, where they made a visit to the nearby casino in Estoril. Much has also been made of this singular event in the life of Admiral Godfrey's fixer.

To add to its lustre, Dusko Popov (double agent Tricycle, who was regularly journeying to and from Portugal), later claimed that Ian Fleming followed him around the casino. The naval commander won a great deal of money from a foreign braggart who apparently had annoyed him. Yet Fleming and Popov were never in Lisbon at the same time, and Fleming would hardly have worn his uniform as he was en route to New York on a delicate mission to be examined in the next chapter. Dusko Popov never actually met Fleming until many years later. So how would he have known the identity of the handsome Etonian?

As with all wartime stories involving Ian Fleming, its telling and significance have become convoluted, not least with a more recent suggestion of a fully fledged 'British spy ring' in the United States which supposedly employed various unlikely Mata Haris and Hollywood stars.

Yet the real story is even more remarkable.

'The British used ruthless methods to achieve their goals,' one American reviewer marvelled when the official history of British Intelligence operations in the Americas was published, 'by [today's] standards some of the activities may seem outrageous.' Certainly, one of the more remarkable characters encountered so far would become involved in the story, that now moves across the Atlantic. A true humanitarian, of great power and energy – or so Louis de Wohl claimed – would come to understand the dangers involved. 'President Roosevelt's horoscope is perfectly beautiful,' he said that same summer of 1941. 'He towers above all others. A Yogi once told me a man born on the date Hitler came into power would cause his downfall. Hitler rose to power on 30 January, and that is Roosevelt's birth date.'

II

ACROSS THE WATER

It is unlikely that any propagandist would seriously attempt to influence politically the people of England, say, or France, through the medium of astrological predictions. Yet in the United States this was done with effective if limited results. In the summer of 1941, Louis de Wohl, a bogus Hungarian astrologer, was sent over to the United States by London. He was to be controlled by British Security Coordination, but his instructions were that he must never mention Britain or show in any way that was especially interested in her welfare. His mission was to shake public confidence in the invincibility of Adolf Hitler.

From The Official History of British Security Co-ordination,
'Propaganda by the Stars'

When the Pan Am flying boat *Dixie Clipper* arrived at La Guardia on the last Sunday of May 1941, two civilians disembarked and couldn't help looking very sheepish. To their horror, press photographers descended. The two British 'government officials', as they soon declared themselves, did their best to hide their faces to avoid being photographed. They had flown from Lisbon via the Azores in civilian clothes and were here on a most delicate mission. They didn't want anyone – certainly not the pack of snappers who had zeroed in on the celebrated fashion designer Schiaparelli – to know what they were doing.

Two weeks after Rudolf Hess's defection, Admiral John Godfrey and his fixer, Commander Ian Fleming RNVR, had travelled to New York to advise the US government on how to create its first ever overseas espionage service.

The timing was, to say the very least, propitious.

The president himself wanted to know if espionage activities could help in 'strengthening our defenses to the extreme limit of our national powers'. After the usual customs runaround, the two Britons took a cab downtown to the Rockefeller Center, where an elevator whisked them to the 36th floor and an office marked 'Rough Diamonds, Ltd'.

What sounds like something from Fleming's imagination actually did exist: it was a cover for the headquarters of the British Security Co-ordination (BSC) which, in short order, had become an umbrella for all British secret agencies in the Americas, including MI5, MI6, the Special Operations Executive and the Political Warfare Executive. Over the years, many silly stories about its omniscience, influence and the extensive reach of its spy rings have been peddled, often by people who should have known better in the first place. Alas, that includes its wartime head who, despite his own claims which are still routinely repeated, was never a global spymaster, quietly pulling the strings to wage secret war and making unpalatable decisions.

The truth was more prosaic and subtle – and to understand why, the visit of Ian Fleming and Admiral Godfrey needs to be placed into context as to what they were really trying to achieve, a subject of equally frenzied and inaccurate speculation over the years that has muddied the historical record.

If the United States was ever going to enter the fighting, the British wanted to make sure that whoever took over its intelligence service should be somebody they could trust. After his visit to Europe the previous autumn, Colonel Bill Donovan had made a good impression. The British secret services had now identified him as their preferred candidate. Donovan was already a genuine war hero, one of the most decorated men in the American military. From humble Irish origins, by diligence and a certain native cunning, the colonel had become a successful law firm partner on Wall Street. Though nearing retirement age, he soon assumed the mantle of 'the last hero'. Memorably described by the film director John Ford – with whom he later worked in Burma – as 'the sort of guy who thought nothing of parachuting into France, blowing up a bridge, pissing in Luftwaffe gas tanks, then dancing on the roof of the St Regis Hotel with a German spy', it is small wonder that legends have attached themselves to the man usually known as 'Wild Bill' Donovan.

The president realised he needed a foreign intelligence supremo, not least because the United States was becoming the focus for much espionage activity, both overt and covert. Subversion and sabotage by the Axis powers, particularly directed towards lend-lease supplies by German sympathisers, remained a major concern. Italian crime families were bribed to sweep the New York docks for any suspected influence of both Nazi saboteurs and spies. For the host country it meant learning new techniques of counter-intelligence and security which went far beyond its understanding and experience.

Unlike the British, the American government had only a fleeting familiarity with espionage. Though George Washington had been helped by Nathan Hale (who had gone to the gallows for his spying behind British lines) and Pinkerton's detectives had rounded up Confederate spies for Abraham Lincoln, there was little in the American experience concerning sabotage, subversion and covert activities. Its existing arms of military intelligence were both limited in scope and uncoordinated – not just with each other but in feeding information upwards to the apex of political power.

The very openness of US society tended to preclude the activities which the British had been practicing for centuries. 'Very few Americans knew anything about espionage outside the work of Messrs Oppenheim, Greene and Ambler,' one historian has succinctly written. And now the existing US intelligence system – 'if the jumble then prevailing in Washington may be so characterised' – would need to learn about it very quickly.

By this time, Bill Donovan had been actively wooed by a supposedly 'quiet Canadian' with piercing blue eyes and an equally legendary capacity for knocking back dry martinis, a fable eclipsed only by the myths which he peddled about himself and others with whom he dealt that have yet to be completely demolished even today.

At the offices of British Security Co-ordination, Admiral Godfrey and Commander Fleming were welcomed by its titular head in person. William Stephenson was not a particularly quiet Canadian, nor was he ever called Intrepid, as one bestselling biography once claimed. Stephenson was assuredly never the *éminence grise* who secretly pulled strings and single-handedly ran all the secret war's most celebrated coups from New York. And yet even today that remains Stephenson's legacy – which, long after the war, the man himself did his best to cultivate – aided and abetted by an offhand remark by none other than Ian Fleming.

Bill Stephenson, Fleming once said, not James Bond, was the real thing.

The historical record was hardly helped by the fact that Bill Stephenson was often highly secretive and Machiavellian, thereby allowing innumerable myths to accumulate and intensify in his wake. Most stem from two biographies, *The Quiet Canadian* in the sixties and, most notably, *A Man Called Intrepid* by his near namesake William Stevenson, which appeared a decade later (and was aptly demolished by the espionage historian Nigel West as 'hopelessly unreliable').

It is a matter of record that the man himself helped to concoct such fictions. When West met him in 1979, Stephenson was already showing signs of mental decay.[1] Yet like so many others who felt they had been underappreciated during the war, he purposefully over-promoted his record and achievements. When many inconsistencies were pointed out about his claims, Stephenson continued to insist they were genuine. At the time of his death in 1993, it prompted the official historian of British Intelligence, Sir Harry Hinsley, a former Bletchley codebreaker who was then master of St John's, Cambridge, to ruefully remark, 'the trouble is when the rumours start, you can never kill them'.

And now, thanks to the Internet, they continue to proliferate.

Even today some accounts identify Bill Stephenson as a cross between James Bond and an all-knowing member of the Illuminati. The best-selling *A Man Called Intrepid* certainly perpetuated the most preposterous notions: that he had been dispatched to the United States by the personal intervention of Winston Churchill (who told him to be intrepid). Yet there is no evidence that Bill Stephenson ever even met the prime minister. It is unlikely that his photograph was ever found in the remains of the bombed-out House of Commons the following spring (another oft-repeated claim).

As the splendidly acerbic Hugh Trevor-Roper, who had worked for MI6 during the war (and often had been threatened with court martial for his disdain for authority), noted in a wonderfully excoriating review of *A Man Called Intrepid* in 1976, Stephenson had been portrayed as a universal genius, 'the Midas who turned all that he touched into gold; the master of economic life; the prescient mastermind who directed all British and American intelligence; the secret manipulator of presidents, prime ministers and kings.'

The truth is more mundane. Though Bill Stephenson was a well connected, highly successful businessman, he had originally been sent to Manhattan in the late spring of 1940 as the ubiquitous passport control officer – under which many MI6 staff worked – and was attached to the British Consulate. His real function was to run British Security

Co-ordination, the government's intelligence 'window' on America, which had been set up, at his suggestion, 'to do a very important job'.

When Bill Stephenson arrived in New York, he did so with Sir Stewart Menzies's blessing as his personal representative in North America. 'I have appointed Mr W.S. Stephenson to take charge of my organization in the USA and Mexico,' C minuted his bosses at the Foreign Office that May. British Security Co-ordination's work was threefold: to investigate enemy activities, to stop sabotage against British supplies and to make American public opinion more favourable in aiding Britain.

It helped that the Canadian got on famously with 'Wild Bill' Donovan, for they were cut from a similar cloth. They were both self-made men, dedicated adventurers who also liked to bend the rules. 'Each is a figure about whom much myth has been woven,' warns the former Foreign Office chief historian Gill Bennett, 'by themselves and others, and the full extent of their activities and contacts retains an element of mystery.'

Bill Stephenson's wealth would underwrite the move of BSC from dingy offices off Wall Street to the prestigious locale of the Rockefeller Center. With increasing urgency, Stephenson's actual remit in 1941 expanded as an umbrella organisation to take in intelligence, contraband control and propaganda. Working alongside the diplomats in Washington, another stated aim for BSC was to cement better working relations between the existing intelligence organisations in the United States and Britain where great advantage could be gained. The vanguard for such a more formalised approach came from the Director of Naval Intelligence, Admiral John Godfrey, who had already noted: 'There is no doubt that we can achieve infinitely more though Donovan than through any other individual.'

This then was the background to Godfrey and Fleming's arrival in New York. In the Rockefeller Center they drank gin, smoked Turkish cigarettes and talked a great deal with Bill Stephenson about their main task: how to usher Donovan into the catbird seat. So far as the British were concerned, Wild Bill was the man for the job, already identified as the lynchpin of an alliance between British and American intelligence that flourishes to this day.

But first the amenities would have to be observed.

For the Naval Intelligence officers, that meant the heart-sinking prospect of a visit to the main obstacle in the way of their plans. He was a pugnacious and bulldog-faced stumbling block who had developed a terrible antipathy to anyone encroaching upon his territory – both literal and political – and that included greater co-operation between the security agencies of the two countries.

J. Edgar Hoover was a nightmare. Quick to anger, vengeful and the ultimate petty bureaucrat, the myth is that Hoover effectively ran Washington by use of dirty tricks, phone taps and blackmail. President Roosevelt, it is often claimed, was scared of him. In fact, virtually everyone in town found the FBI Director hard to take ('Very childish, petulant,' recorded the chief of military intelligence), for his methodical mindset was never particularly adept at the needs of running an effective counter-espionage agency.

Despite this, Ian Fleming – as 007 was often wont to do – took a train to the capital with the admiral in attendance in early June, heading towards the antiseptic offices of the Federal Bureau of Investigation on Pennsylvania Avenue. Against the brightness of the skies and monuments, they knew they would be entering the twilight zone of American intelligence fiefdom disputes.

Not only were there anti-British elements within the administration, but Hoover was implacably opposed to any foreign spies working on American sovereign soil. Worse, he saw Bill Donovan's increasing visibility as the president's adviser on intelligence as Roosevelt's folly. Hoover was well prepared to fight any encroachment on his territory or the prestige of the FBI.

Yet Hoover's organisation hardly commended itself.

So far as counter-espionage was concerned, Ian Fleming had already come to the conclusion that the G-Men were 'amateurs without special training'. Their natural instinct was to bust the spy rings which they came across. They had neither the experience nor the know-how to 'run' them against the Germans. The G-Men were completely at odds with the needs of wartime deception. '"Intelligence" in the United States generally means "Security and Counter-Espionage",' Fleming would write. 'The concept of "offensive intelligence" is not well understood.'

The two naval officers did at least come with a shopping list which they hoped would help build greater co-operation for the future. They wanted the FBI to be more active in stopping sabotage in naval dockyards, better debriefing of captured saboteurs and greater cipher security. They also wanted to help train spies to a higher standard and, most importantly, they were pushing for the creation of a centre to analyse intelligence which would be directed by a single co-ordinator. Fleming had certainly already formed the view that the bureau was too much of a 'small and uncoordinated force' to undertake this crucial role in shaping American foreign policy.

And so they came face to face with J. Edgar Hoover.

The men from Naval Intelligence were ushered into Hoover's spartan inner sanctum where the director – 'a chunky enigmatic man with slow eyes and a trap of a mouth,' in Fleming's later estimation – made it all too clear that he was politely uninterested. He then complained about a Nazi spy whom he suspected had been 'whacked' by British Security Co-ordination. The meeting ended far sooner than they expected. After a cursory visit to the basement shooting range, the admiral and his fixer were left blinking in the sunshine outside.

A major step forward took place a few days later when they were both invited to a private dinner in Georgetown to meet 'Big Bill' himself. Both men knew Colonel Donovan from his earlier visits to Europe. Now they pressed him to lead a unified US intelligence service. Though he had wanted to return to the fighting and be promoted to a general in the army, Donovan couldn't help being excited by the possibilities. Espionage commended itself straight away.

'Information is useless unless it is intelligently directed to the strategic purposes,' Donovan would write. Long into the night, as he listened to their spiel, those strategic purposes became abundantly clear if America was going to be prepared for the fighting which most now thought inevitable. Fleming, for reasons he never explained, remained at the general's house the next day and prepared some notes on how to create a possible overseas intelligence organisation.

An American secret service, Ian Fleming wrote, 'should not be controlled by the FBI, which has no conception of effective intelligence and is incapable of a strategic mentality'. Donovan would use some of Fleming's lapidary words himself when he wrote to Roosevelt – at the president's request – a week later. Japanese sabre rattling and Germany's unstoppable belligerence required precipitate action. On 10 June 1941, Donovan minuted that the United States was 'lacking in effective services for analyzing, comprehending and appraising information' and that something should be done about it.

And there was no doubt who he felt should be in charge of it all.

A week later, the two British naval officers visited the White House, where Admiral Godfrey spent an hour alone in the Oval Office with the president. His message was simple: make Donovan the undisputed intelligence 'master' of the United States. Roosevelt agreed with Godfrey's obvious manoeuvrings. So much intelligence information was passing through the White

House that he later acknowledged he needed a gatekeeper. After reading Donovan's paper, partly written by Ian Fleming, the president called for the colonel himself.

Wild Bill was in a bullish mood, even by his standards: he made it clear that he would only take the job of intelligence co-ordinator if he reported directly to Roosevelt, could draw money from a presidential emergency fund and that all existing government agencies would furnish him with help and information.

Franklin Delano Roosevelt agreed.

Bill Donovan's appointment, in the words of the subsequent presidential decree, would 'neither displace nor encroach upon the FBI, Army and Navy Intelligence, or any other department of government' and would lead to the creation of the Office of Strategic Services, a secret agency that reflected the image of the two-fisted Irish émigré who would run it.

On hearing the news, Ian Fleming cabled Stephenson in New York, who wired the prime minister directly: 'You can imagine how relieved I am after months of battle and jockeying in Washington that our man is in position.' Commander Fleming remained in the capital to help write memoranda on how to co-operate with the British and staff the American agency. In his clearly recognisable style, the future thriller writer waxed lyrical on potential recruits: 'Must have trained powers of observation, analysis and evaluation; absolute discretion, sobriety, devotion to duty, language and wide experience; and be aged about forty to fifty.'

James Bond – if not Fleming himself – would have been an ideal candidate.

So began a minor historical controversy over whether Donovan was a British agent or there was an overtly malign influence from the British Empire on America's fledgling intelligence activities. The colonel was certainly well aware that he had been manipulated into a position about which he had originally been ambivalent. Ian Fleming, whose insatiable desire for adventure and fantasy was only truly sated in his literary creations, later maintained that Donovan was so grateful that he gave him a .38 revolver that was inscribed: 'For Special Services'.

As a result, Fleming would facetiously claim that he had written the charter for an American secret service on which the Central Intelligence Agency would eventually come to be based. It is a statement that also seems to have been taken at face value by some journalists and writers, elevating the creator of James Bond to the very heart of the long, fruitful intelligence collaborations between Britain and the United States, and an importance that he never sought nor indeed achieved.

By the summer of 1941, British Security Co-ordination had expanded its activities under William Stephenson's benign patronage. A thousand or more regular informants would routinely help the British to prosecute the secret war in the United States. Many of these operations involved covert and overt propaganda (and if need be, its pure fabrication) as well as searching out evidence for German agents and businesses which collaborated with the Third Reich.

Its remit now took in the whole of the western hemisphere, which also encompassed offices across the Caribbean, Central and South America. There was a large censorship bureau in Bermuda, the fruits of whose labours were regularly shared with a grateful Hoover, despite his obvious disdain for Stephenson's wooing of Colonel Donovan. 'When the full story can be told,' the FBI director later wrote to the Canadian, 'I am quite sure that your contribution will be among the foremost in having brought victory finally to the united nations' cause.'

In some ways, British Security Co-ordination was less a secret agency than a glorified literary salon, for some of its most provocative operations made good use of two of the most celebrated writers of the time. Nöel Coward had been hired to report on fascist sympathisers and helped in the setting up of a 'rumours factory' which used newspaper gossip columnists, magazines and radio commentators to discredit the more isolationist of Americans.[2] When it was then suggested he take over the whole of propaganda operations back in London, Hugh Dalton minuted that Coward was 'An indiscreet stinker, off his proper beat'. As he noted in his own diaries, Dalton 'reacted violently' against such a promotion. 'The man is utterly unsuitable and attracts publicity everywhere,' Dalton wrote, believing Stephenson would go nuts when he found out.

Another writer, whom his biographer describes as 'a kind of walking magazine of stories, a conduit of numerous rumours and revelation', was also employed to great effect in the United States. After serving in fighter squadrons in Greece, Syria and North Africa, Flight Lieutenant Roald Dahl was now ostensibly working as an Assistant Air Attaché at the Washington Embassy, where he was supposed to be the liaison man for all American air forces. He also secretly worked with Wild Bill Donovan's nascent intelligence organisation and was instrumental in helping with propaganda activities. As always, given the calibre of writers like Roald Dahl and Ian Fleming, it is sometimes hard to determine what they really did and, more to the point, achieved at this time.

As a reviewer of Dahl's secret work has noted, it is hard to know what to make of many of his and others' claims – half-truths or true lies, for certain – as it was hardly a coincidence that both Dahl and Fleming became accomplished storytellers 'The BSC agents emerged from the war practiced in the arts of deception, obfuscation and seduction,' writes Jeanne Connant, also noting that Fleming and Dahl became rich and successful as fabulists.

Yet neither ever came close to some of the claims of another visitor to American shores at this time, who, with the direct blessing of British intelligence, was being allowed some latitude to finally be allowed to vanquish his foes, the Führer and his supposed malefic astrologer, in public. For once, one of Louis de Wohl's predictions had come true, that, exactly as he had identified in his ouverture of death proposal, activities should now be concentrated on the United States.

Within a month of Rudolf Hess's defection, Louis de Wohl had been summarily dispatched to the United States for the culmination of his 'astrological mission' that had started a few weeks before. His American sojourn was prompted, one colleague recalled, because he wanted 'worldwide backing' for his astrological propaganda campaign. Over the summer of 1941, de Wohl did exactly that, regularly creating horoscopes that were generally unfavourable to the Nazi leadership in the hope that they would be published in the press or highlighted in lectures.

In a sense, his American mission was to fight like with like in a country that the official BSC history sniffily dismisses as 'a fertile field for outré practices'. German-backed astrologers, it was feared, were suspected of doing the same, influencing mass circulation magazines like *American Astrology* with the inclusion of readers' letters which predicted the inevitability of Nazi victory. 'At fairly frequent intervals SOE were to send to the New York office items of black propaganda they wanted to appear in the American press, in the hope that they would go from there to Germany,' recalled one party to this antidote astrology created on the British side.

No sooner had Louis de Wohl arrived in the United States, than the BSC arranged a press conference where he talked of the 'Neptunian fate' (as he had termed it in discussion with Leslie Sheridan) which would shortly consume Adolf Hitler. His overarching mission was to disseminate information that Germany was going to lose the war, and so the stories followed. 'His latest prediction is that Hitler will be assassinated within a year,' the columnist Ruth Reynolds reported a few days later.

Indeed, the astrologer's various prognostications knew no bounds as a random selection of headlines from the US press that summer shows: 'Seer sees Nazi Doom if U.S. acts in Eight months'; 'Hitler Ill-fated'; 'Hitler's Star Is Setting'; and, most notable of all, a headline from the *New York Sun*, 'Seer sees plot to kill Hitler', below which was a strap head that the Führer would be done in 'within a year'. Noting that the Führer was a doomed man, it added de Wohl's 'talk of things to come that would be nerve-shattering in their emotional impact'. The kill, it seemed, was already under way as the Führer was slowly going insane and 'his own astrologers dare not tell him the truth any longer'.

'Hitler would be done away within a year,' it added.

At this point, Louis de Wohl was making use of a speaking agent based in Manhattan called Martin Starr. He seemed to be earning his keep. 'The learned astro-philosopher became the darling of the special feature writers,' he noted in a publicity flyer. 'Here was drama in the making.' And according to Starr, the New York papers had started to refer to him as 'the modern Nostradamus'.

Further stories followed, including the one that Karl Krafft had predicted 'Germany will not win the war'. The notion was that the *Führerastrologe* had been sugar-coating his predictions so as not to upset the Third Reich's leaders. 'If English and French astrologers put their hopes in the fact that the Führer has no more good constellations from now on, then these people overlook the fact that the work achieved in the last ten years would keep its value and vigour even if the Führer would suddenly disappear.'

By comparison, Louis de Wohl appeared all over the Union.

A certain plausible deniability suffused his work, as he had been sent as a private citizen. 'Wild Bill' Donovan's prototypical Office of Strategic Services was informed about the astrologer's activities. 'Our friends in OSS were not impressed,' recalled another of de Wohl's handlers. 'I have no doubt that they thought that the de Wohl mission was a cover story for something infinitely more sinister. Perhaps indeed it was.'

There remained a global scope to his work following on from his earlier ouverture of death. 'It was planned that the first prophecies which de Wohl would make upon his arrival in the US should harmonize with pre-arranged astrological and magical predictions of Hitler's fall which would be made in other remote parts of the world,' the official BSC history notes.

Everything came together smoothly.

From the Egyptian capital, an Arabic newspaper carried some warnings from an eminent astrologer, Sheikh Youssef Afifi. 'Four months hence a red planet will appear on the eastern horizon and will indicate that a dangerous evil-doer,' the Cairo-based seer was quoted as saying, 'who has drenched the world in blood, will pass away … this means that an uncrowned Emperor will be killed, and that man is Hitler.'

From Nigeria came a long, involved prophecy of a priest: 'The cripple stabbed the breadfruit man in the back. The long-haired one cursed the glass-eyed one and pushed him from the ledge.' Thanks to Sherry Sheridan's efforts, these stories were picked up by American newspapers and, as the BSC history notes, people began to sit up and take notice.

The coal-black eyes were burning with fire and the pug-like face was visibly snarling. J. Edgar Hoover was not happy with the latest British-sent visitor to his office. The dark-eyed man with the straw-brown hair brushed back, however, gave as good as he got. Dusko Popov smiled despite the venerable FBI director's onslaught. 'You come from nowhere and within six weeks install yourself in a Park Avenue penthouse, chase films stars, break a serious law and try to corrupt my officers.' After a few more barbs, Hoover angrily told him he was trying to teach him how to do his job. Popov couldn't help grinning as he delivered the line which saw him ejected from the FBI Director's office.

'I don't think anyone could teach you anything,' he said, savouring the moment.

This almost mythical exchange in the life of agent Tricycle – which according to FBI files never actually seems to have taken place – obscured a far more predictable official disinterest in Popov's work in the United States after his arrival in August 1941.

It was a symptom of Hoover's insistence that no intelligence operations should be carried out by foreign spy rings – as he saw them – on American soil. With heart-sinking inevitability, many on the British side thought the FBI was completely the wrong sort of agency to undertake any counter-espionage activities. Bill Stephenson, for one, thought that Hoover's personality counted against any closer working together. A federal domestic espionage agency, he noted, 'needed as its chief a man less rigid and sensitive to potential rivals'.

What seems to have caused Hoover's ire was Dusko's arrival with a *mikropunkt*, the latest marvel of German technology, a microdot machine that could hide secret information within any document. In fact, Popov would arrive in the United States with eleven microdots about his person. In vain did Dusko point out to Hoover that these had been presented to the bureau on a 'silver platter'; the director was dismissive.

'You are like all double agents,' he had said, 'you're begging for information to sell to your German friends so you can make a lot of money and be a playboy.'

It has also recently come to light that the director had a special ire for even mythical playboys. It might have come as a consolation to Dusko that Hoover's hatred extended into surreal realms with the release in December 2014 of a memo from the early sixties, that showed how out of touch the FBI remained.

The bureau, Hoover minuted, should not associate itself with 007 in any way. In 1964, the producers of the Bond films had sounded out the FBI helping them with their first film which would be shot on American soil. As they started production on their third film in the series, Hoover insisted that far from co-operating, the bureau should 'vigorously protest any mention of the FBI or portrayal of its agents in his proposed movie'.

His minions were hardly on the ball. In the memo, Hoover noted with puritanical dismissiveness that the Bond stories were 'generally filled with sex and bizarre situations'. Almost inevitably, they always seemed to present 'beautiful women presenting themselves to him in scanty attire'.

And, in an odd case of life imitating fiction, if Dusko's memoirs are to believed that is exactly what happened on a beach where, in the film that the bureau didn't want to help make, 007 and Goldfinger meet for the first time.

In the summer of 1941, while on his supposedly secret mission in the United States, the fame – and in some estimations infamy – which Louis de Wohl had craved for so many years finally now came to pass. Its apotheosis took place in early August at a meeting of the American Federation of Scientific Astrologers in Cleveland where, his agent later maintained, audiences clamoured to know more from 'one of the most informed authorities on the subject'.

Louis de Wohl remained good copy. 'Hitler's move on Russia was a great mistake,' he said on the closing day of the conference. And though the views of astrologers were supposedly banned for broadcast by the Federal Communications Commission, while in Ohio he was allowed to discuss his thoughts about Hitler and Napoleon on air. While the transcripts seem to be lost, his agent took up some of the slack. Martin Starr noted:

Because of the attempted Russian invasion of the Hitler forces has de
Wohl's intensive study of the Little Corporal and Der Füehrer become
one of the most timely subjects of the day. Yesterday's bloody pages of
history are mirrored against the tumultuous happenings of today with
ironic parallel. The subject is more dramatic than drama itself.

As ever, the astrologer could be relied on to grab attention about his certainty of the Führer's demise. 'We can't predict a date for his defeat,' de Wohl
continued, 'but if the United States enters the war before next spring, he is
doomed.' This neatly contrasted the astrological situation with a politician
rather nearer to home. 'President Roosevelt's horoscope is perfectly beautiful,' he said. 'He towers above all others.'

Louis de Wohl made sure to reiterate this same point when visiting
friends in Los Angeles – where the *Los Angeles Times* called him 'chubby,
curly-haired and bespectacled' – in early September 1941. The Führer, he
revealed, was mentally ill and could not focus during his recent five-day
conference with Mussolini. 'Hitler's horoscope shows he has not long to
live,' the paper reported, 'as he could not concentrate.' But the final word
in California was an even more astounding prediction. The astrologer also
announced that 'between now and 11 June 1942 would be the best time for
the United States to enter the war'.

Even after the invasion of the Soviet Union in the summer of 1941, many
Americans still did not want to become embroiled in the war that had
rent the whole of continental European asunder. The previous September,
America First, a vociferous pressure group, had been established in Chicago
for that very purpose. Its leading light was a genuine American hero, the
first man to fly the Atlantic on his own, Charles A. Lindbergh, whose sometimes anti-Semitic rhetoric often alienated many of those to whom he
was appealing.

As the history of the BSC notes, De Wohl attacked 'lucky Lindy' for the
fact he thought he was an exemplar which made the weak-minded believe
that a man who can handle machines well must be an authority on things
of the spirit. Clearly de Wohl was an authority: 'He said that the kidnapped
Lindbergh baby was still alive' and was one of a number of future Führers
being trained at a Nazi school in East Prussia.

'De Wohl delivered many other attacks like these upon anti-British per-
sonalities,' the history notes, 'and there is little doubt that his work had a
considerable effect upon certain sections of the people.'

It would have made a great scene from a film, exactly as it did at the start of *Goldfinger*. A foreign playboy, lounging around with a beautiful woman, suddenly looks up to see an apparition in dark jacket, white shirt, dark tie and snap-brim hat. Even on Miami Beach in 1941, Hoover's men would never relax. In Dusko Popov's memoirs, he explains that this striking scene led directly to an even more astounding conclusion: that the FBI knew there was going to be an attack on Pearl Harbor.

Variants on this theme linger today. The greater truth is that anyone who takes Dusko Popov's claims at face value has to be very careful indeed. One of the reasons for his visit to the United States in 1941 was that his Lisbon controllers wanted him to establish answers to a series of pressing military questions. The eleven microdots contained several complicated questionnaires about US and Canadian air defences, the numbers and extent of training for pilots, tank production and dispositions of the naval forces.

In particular, one questionnaire was devoted to information which could only ever have been of use to another Axis power. The Abwehr wanted to know all about the air and naval defences surrounding Pearl Harbor. Dusko says he was shocked when he saw these questions. He realised, or so he claimed many years later, that the Japanese were going to attack the United States. Indeed, once he had settled in New York, his German masters made it clear they wanted him to visit the Hawaiian base itself because their Japanese allies were having problems infiltrating native orientals anywhere on the island.

When permission from the FBI wasn't forthcoming, he delighted in tormenting his handlers by taking a trip to Florida with an English model he knew. 'It seems I have the reputation of being a playboy,' he explained to a horrified FBI supervisor, 'and taking a girl on a trip fits my cover.' According to his post-war memoirs, it was on a beach in Miami that they looked up to see a man in a hat and tie. A G-Man from central casting strolled over to tell him that he had contravened the Mann Act – it was a federal offence to cross a state line with a girl for immoral purposes – and the English lovely was forced to fly back to New York City.

According to Popov, he never saw her again. His MI5 and FBI files show that nothing so melodramatic took place: with a certain amount of reservation (the Mann Act was mentioned but only as a vague threat), the Yugoslav was allowed his 'dirty weekend' in the sunshine state. According to his FBI files, Popov met the model again in New York City, where an even stranger occurrence took place that he pointedly didn't mention in his autobiography.

When the Feds pointed out to him that this girl was suspected of having pro-Nazi sympathies and had perhaps deliberately made his acquaintance to spy on him, Popov calmly replied that he would have no compunction in killing her. His FBI contact was once again horrified: even with the bureau's protection, the young Yugoslav would not be immune from the due process of law: arrest, trial and hanging.

'I'll take her to South America, then,' Popov smoothly replied. 'I'll kill her there.'

To enhance Louis de Wohl's reputation, while he was in the United States he would have to make a prediction that would come true. For that, a French naval officer from Martinique would be involved. The colonial island was a worry for the Royal Navy because it had the only deep water harbours in the Caribbean. That gave greater latitude for Vichy and German vessels to re-victual.

So earlier that summer, Louis de Wohl had made his first public prediction that a 'strong collaborator', neither a German nor a Nazi, would go violently insane somewhere in Central or South America. Three days later, according to a later report in the *New York Sunday News* (headlined: 'Hitler's astrologer sees heavenly stop light'), Admiral Robert, leader of the Vichy French Caribbean territories, had indeed gone mad.

As the BSC history notes, Louis de Wohl really seemed to know what he was talking about:

> After all here was a prophet who had made a prediction in New York which was immediately confirmed, first by an Egyptian astrologer in Cairo, and secondly by a Nigerian priest in the jungles of Africa. Furthermore he had definitely said that within ten days one of Hitler's allies would be found to be mad.

The astrologer's supposed ability now became a potent propaganda tool.

'For the moment, anyway,' the official history of British Security Co-ordination notes, 'his reputation shone as brightly as the stars of which he spoke.'

'Few European notables ever made a more retiring entrance in to the United States than Louis de Wohl,' his agent noted in promotional literature.

Described as a distinguished author, astro-philosopher and 'exile from Hitler's Geo-Political Institute', he claimed that he 'he would have to dash off prognostications right and left'.

He went on tour and whether in private, at meetings or in widely syndiacted articles, he repeatedly declared that Hitler was doomed. He later attacked the Frency Vichy government and the isolationist Lindbergh. And for the next year, he made another curious prediction. 'If Germany is still going it may attempt to invade the US through Brazil because of its many German colonists'.

Curiously, Brazil and South America would see many strange events before the US entered the fighting. A minor squall certainly blew up in the run-up to the US election that November of 1941. Even today, it is a story mired in mystery concerning the supposed 'find' of a map supposedly taken from a German courier whose car had crashed outside of Buenos Aires. This time, though, the map's provenance was plausibly denied and nobody is exactly sure who was responsible.

The map showed South America divided into German states, each with its own identified gauleiters. It was most likely a BSC operation and, as such, a useful addition to the diplomatic bluster. 'This map makes clear the Nazi design,' Franklin Delano Roosevelt fulminated, 'not only against South America but against the United States as well.'

A few days before the election, Dusko Popov received a cable which read: 'ELIZABETH DEPARTED FOR RIO.' This was confirmation that he should travel to Brazil for his latest trawl of information about the organisation of the US Army, so arrangements were made by the FBI for his trip. Popov departed on 16 November, and so far as Hoover was concerned it was good riddance. At least the playboy would reveal who was responsible for German espionage in South America, but the bureau – from the director downwards – wouldn't like to bet on it.

In fact, the trip to Rio was equally frustrating. He had waited in vain for a week to receive instructions as to how to meet his local contact. With its usual breathtaking incompetence, the Abwehr outstation in Lisbon had failed to let its South American equivalent know where star agent Ivan was staying. Though he wrote nine letters in all to his contact in Portugal, it wasn't until October that he received a reply and was blithely told that none of his earlier letters had been received. Aggrieved, Popov wrote back straight away: 'Wonder what has happened to the radio? Have retained my radio man nearly a month ago and must sign the lease for the house outside New York. I could avoid a lot of trouble if you would act with more speed.'

With mounting frustration, Popov made his way to the German Embassy and asked to see the military attaché. Eventually, after meeting the local Abwehr officer, he was given $10,000 and more instructions and questions to resume his espionage activities in the United States. They also discussed the vexed question of the lack of communications. It was agreed that he should buy the parts of a radio set commercially and get his radio operator to assemble them when he was back in Manhattan.

After just under a month in Rio, Popov set sail for the United States aboard the SS *Uruguay*, on which, to his delight, a ballet company was returning home. On reaching Trinidad, he was fully intending to have an afternoon's illicit pleasure with one of the ballerinas whom he had befriended. When they walked down the gang plank, however, a short, freckled man who was obviously English appeared.

He whispered that he wanted a word. Walter 'Freckles' Wren was the MI6 station chief at the embassy in Port of Spain and had been ordered to debrief the Yugoslav. For obvious reason, his handlers in London wanted to know what Tricycle had been up to in Brazil, particularly because the FBI – thanks to Hoover's usual mixture of petulance and heavy handedness – had been less than forthcoming. Any disappointment Popov felt in losing the ballerina were more than made up by meeting Wren's secretary, an English rose who was 'long-legged and brainy but also sensationally beautiful', who provided him with some compensation. Neither his later memoirs nor hitherto secret files elaborate any further on this latest seduction.

The smoke and devastation over Ford Island had hardly dissipated before the conspiracy theories began. Amongst the most persistent stories about Pearl Harbor comes the agent whose own clairvoyance, if it really had occurred, must have been unique in the annals of espionage. If Dusko Popov is to be believed, he arrived in Manhattan on the day of infamy itself where he was met by an FBI man at the docks. Because of the detailed questionnaire about the Hawaiian island, Dusko claimed that he was astounded by the news of the attack.

In fact, newly released files reveal that because of worries that he might be watched by German intelligence agents, contact wasn't actually made with the bureau until later. More to the point, Popov didn't dock until the second Monday after the attack, 15 December. 'I never did get an answer to the enigma of Pearl Harbor,' he later claimed. 'Over the years I have studied the question, tried to draw conclusions, had all sorts of speculation and conjectures.'

These murky events have prompted the conspiracy theorists' smoking gun: that somehow the Federal Bureau of Investigation knew all about the impending attack and decided to ignore the warnings. Though there was a basic truth about the Pearl Harbor questionnaire, nowhere does it suggest a Japanese attack was going to take place. To be fair, the FBI Director did paraphrase its contents and had passed it on to the relevant military authorities. None of the British files released in the twenty-first century make any contemporary reference to Popov's warnings of an attack.[3]

Immediately after Popov's revelations (which came about in his autobiography *Spy/Counterspy* published in 1974) the FBI took care to re-examine its own files. Even allowing for residual reverence for 'the old Man' – Hoover had died eighteen months earlier – there is little reference to Popov's supposed warnings in the bureau's otherwise meticulous files. 'The Pearl Harbor story is a typical example of "Monday morning quarterbacking",' an unknown G-Man wrote after searching the archives, 'in that he now plays up an explanation of the significance of the material he furnished which our file does not show he mentioned contemporaneously.' Thomas Troy, a former CIA analyst who was the official historian for its predecessor, Donovan's Office of Strategic Services, flatly declared that Popov 'never personally warned Hoover about such an attack … He warned nobody.'

And even in the aftermath of the cataclysmic event that brought America into the war, the Feds seemed more concerned about butterfly trays which Dusko had seen when he visited the German Embassy in Rio. He had, he claimed to his handlers, seen a number of people in a sideroom who seemed to have been poring over what appeared to be trays of pinned butterflies. It appeared to Popov that they were going to be used to smuggle secret information into the United States as they would make a perfect hiding place for microdots. The result was that shortly thereafter 500 butterfly trays were impounded from the SS *Uruguay* and examined in minute detail by FBI forensic experts.

On his return to the US, Dusko Popov was uncharacteristically depressed and down in the dumps. So to cheer himself up, he made an extended visit to the recently opened and currently trendy ski resort of Sun Valley in Idaho, where he spent much of his time getting drunk and chasing women. 'My nights passed in a blur of alcohol and sex,' Popov would later recall.

He returned to New York in the new year to good news from the FBI. A transmitter was going to be installed in a safe house on Long Island. Popov was finally going to be allowed to earn his keep and drip feed falsified information provided by the US military. Behind the scenes a row started to simmer between British Security Co-ordination and Hoover as to why he should be allowed to do this. In the meantime, an FBI radioman sent agent Ivan's first radio message on 27 January from the house on Long Island.

It took five days for a response to be heard through the crackling short-wave. Popov wrote to Lisbon in secret ink the next day: 'Because of situation here have to be very careful. Can only transmit for a short time so I won't be discovered.' A few weeks later, he started to receive airmail letters from Portugal in which further clarifications were asked for. Yet the tenor of the letters showed that his controllers were obviously disappointed. To all intents and purposes, Dusko Popov was stranded in the States with little interest from American and German intelligence.

'Very little of consequence was developed from the time the radio was set up until Tricycle's departure from this country,' British Security Co-ordination reported a while later. It seemed that his great mission to report on the new transatlantic enemy had ground to a halt even before it had begun.

Another visitor was preparing to return home in those first few weeks of 1942. In his own mind, Louis de Wohl was always convinced that his US tour had been a massive success. 'I know from SOE that his propaganda visit to America was considered highly successful,' Gilbert Lennox noted at the end of the war, 'and both before and after that he did a lot of propaganda work which was considered very good. He has certainly done more for the Allied cause than many of his foreign brethren.'

But that was written way after the event. Whatever his US mission really achieved – and the files show there were many questions being asked – many in British Intelligence were now starting to question both his role and the astrologer's actual value to the war effort. Once again, Louis de Wohl was hardly treated as a serious participant in the fighting of the secret war. '[What] could have been an excellent piece of psychological warfare turned out, from lack of co-operation, into a fair flop,' another colleague has recalled.

By now, virtually everyone in British Intelligence seems to have been fed up of what one called this 'bumptious seeker after notoriety'. His

American sojourn was the last straw. Far from galvanising the British secret services into realising how important a weapon astrology could be, Louis de Wohl was now increasingly being dismissed as a prima donna whose Walter Mitty-like fantasies extended to some slightly peculiar, unsettling sexual tendencies which the authorities did their best to keep hidden.

The irony is that though he was being employed to create whispers, there were many more now accumulating behind his back. The security officer of the newly formed Political Warfare Executive (de Wohl's ostensible employers after the SOE) now considered him 'a complete scoundrel'. As a matter of routine, MI5, the British Security Service, was keeping a beady eye on all his activities. A number of high-ups were aghast when they found out what he had been up to.

A number of high-ups were also aghast about Louis de Wohl's work. 'I don't like decisions of this kind,' wrote the head of MI5's counter-espionage department, 'made by reference to the stars rather than MI5.' Now, as Louis de Wohl prepared to return home to London, an MI6 officer noted for the files that he could not 'believe that anyone is going to re-employ this dangerous charlatan and confidence-trick merchant'.

One person who had thought his entry into the secret world would be a cushy sinecure found that it wasn't during those first few months of 1942. Cutting a dashing figure in his scarlet satin-lined greatcoat and swagger stick – both of which were very much against Royal Air Force regulations – Wheatley found himself in an unusual position. The fact that the London Controlling Section was the holiest of holies in Whitehall counted against the work they were trying to do.

'We were regarded as the most secret section in the whole building,' Wheatley later recalled. 'We were kept absolutely incommunicado and not even allowed to tell the other members of the Joint Planning Staff what we were up to.' The first controller of deception lost heart and didn't seem to understand what was required of him – or, indeed, it.

The greater truth was: there was nothing to do.

Nobody in Whitehall understood deception, and given the secrecy, they couldn't discuss what they were doing with colleagues. A famous vignette occurred when they aimed at deception at Stavanger. When he was told that it would be called Operation Hardboiled, Oliver Stanley was aghast. 'Who was the bloody fool who chose such a silly codeword?'

In the meantime, Dennis Wheatley was determined to enjoy his food. Even during the height of rationing, the occult writer's consumption was astonishing. To the devil, a dieter. A typical day would see him consume a couple of glasses of Pimms, then a 'short one' of what he termed 'Chanel 5' (absinthe – with fine wine, ended with port or kummel). And while the country neared starvation, he would feast on whatever specials were to hand. Smoked salmon, potted shrimps, Dover sole, jugged hare, game or Welsh rarebit. When he got back to the office he would have a sleep and then there would be afternoon tea and cakes, which goes some way to explain one of his more famously strange proposals. 'Deception on the higher plane' would see the rumour of a Christ-like figure emerging to save Germany. Unsurprisingly, it got nowhere.

At the start of 1942, the balance of the war remained precarious. Even with the entry of the United States to make it a truly global confrontation, there was no certainty that the Allies would prevail against the Axis powers. It would take the tide quite some time to turn. Indeed the first half of the year coincided with a low ebb of misfortune. The miracle of Midway and the fatal attritions of El Alamein and Stalingrad had yet to come. Wherever they looked, the newly merging high command of Britons and Americans could find some comfort that all the elements of the secret war – the agents, the deceptions and the decryption of enemy signals – were gearing up for that singular and most important event: the return to Europe.

There would be no such epiphany for Louis De Wohl.

After arriving back from the United States on 27 February 1942, there was no welcome. 'I didn't expect to be met by a brass band,' he later said somewhat indignantly, 'or even one fiddler, but I did expect someone to pay at least some attention to my return.' Increasingly, he felt that he had been left in the lurch. Miss Bainbridge returned before him and soon became his sounding board for a litany of complaints. As always, something insignificant managed to annoy him.

He had returned to Grosvenor House but it seemed that all his furniture had been kept at his old apartment, to which he did not expect to return. 'It is not an inexpensive flat,' a note in the file records, 'and I think this rather surprised de Wohl, although his own ideas are not what I should call money saving, in the ordinary case of events.' So he re-took his flat rather than move the furniture and then, as the note records straight-facedly: 'To his astonishment nothing happened at all, and no one tried to get in touch with him.'

As the report makes clear, the vain astrologer had had no premonition that there was no more work for him back in London, 'and above all, he had not the faintest notion that his temporary rank of Captain might come to a sudden end'. He also wanted access to the money he had made in the United States which had not been forthcoming.

Nor did he have any idea where his handlers had moved to. When he next went to meet Sir Charles Hambro, he discovered that his offices had moved from Fitzmaurice Place. When he later telephoned Sir Charles's secretary, the call was not returned. As the subsequent contact report notes it, de Wohl returned to the attack.

He went to Bush House, where he was shown up to the 'new people' but was rebuffed. Though he knew SOE Headquarters was in Baker Street, thankfully, from the point of security, he did not go there. Louis de Wohl, as Colonel Lennox noted, was somewhat desperate. With no money and no contracts, he was in a bind.

'It is all just as if the whole thing is a dream,' he later lamented to Lennox.

He wanted desperately to carry on his work, and work with June Bainbridge. Once again, he found it inordinately difficult to get hold of her. When he did make contact, she gently pointed out that he should go back to his life before the war. June told him that he should move into the Esplanade Hotel and set up shop as an astrologer again. But that clearly was not an option. 'He also reminded her that he was a Captain in the British Army,' Lennox noted, 'and this seemed to entirely flummox Miss Bainbridge.'

His various attempts at contacting the authorities had clearly reached Gilbert Lennox. So the major turned up and listened to the astrologer's various moans. Louis de Wohl wanted to not just do more of what he had been doing before he left for America, he wanted to do more broadcasting as he had done in the United States. 'He showed me his book of press cuttings of his trip,' Lennox wrote, 'and from these it certainly appeared that his mission had not been altogether unsuccessful.'

Behind the scenes, British Intelligence were examining what to do next with 'this troublesome case'. In March 1942, Sir Charles Hambro saw him, told him he had done 'an excellent job of work in America, that he was to go on leave on full pay until the end of April and that his future would be considered in the interval'. Nobody mentioned anything about his 'temporary commission' in the British Army because as a later note makes clear 'no one has ever told him that he does not hold it!'

It was clear his future was very uncertain, with one note recording that he 'at one time exercised some influence upon highly placed British

Intelligence Officers through his star gazing profession'. Within a few months, the authorities were simply finding it easier to ignore him. Sir Charles Hambro had alleged that his one-time golden boy was 'a complete scoundrel' and others thought he might become very dangerous, 'owing to the considerable influence which his charlatanism enables him to exert over the superstitious in high places'.

They wanted to keep him on side, but get shot of him to another department as soon as possible. But within a matter of weeks, against all the odds, he had found a saviour. 'The outcome is that de Wohl has, in fact, got a job under Sefton Delmer, in which he is to be editor of an astrological monthly paper which is being send to Germany by surreptitious means.'

Without spelling it out, this would be the last great hurrah for Louis de Wohl. The astrologer who always liked to consider himself 'the modern Nostradamus', would be employed to manipulate the sayings of the original one in perhaps the most dangerous chapter of the Second World War so far as the British were concerned.

Nothing was off the table so far as the Battle of the Atlantic was concerned.

The situation was so serious that the Director of Naval Intelligence had been prevailed upon to help fight the U-boat menace by any means necessary; so much so that, in his own words, 'an element of perfidy, verging on the unscrupulous', was necessary. Admiral John Godfrey looked no further than his special assistant to ensure that the myriad possibilities of broadcasting subversive material could be realised. Any advantage, no matter how quixotic, would be needed. By the spring of 1943, the situation had become so very dangerous that all of the people in this story – the admiral, Ian Fleming, Sefton Delmer and Louis De Wohl – were involved, but none as important, controversial or improbable as a 19-year-old torch singer whose sweet voice gave no hint, as Tom Delmer noted, that she had lost half her family in a concentration camp.

12

ZENITH

A series of meetings is taking place all over Germany to combat the growing war weariness and dissatisfaction with the Nazi party. Two slogans – 'Party and nation are indivisible' and 'the end of the party is the end of the people' are hammered into people's ears by every party lecturer … More and more is being heard of desertion in all branches of the services, but it should be remembered that the oath of allegiance to the colours binds two parties, the soldiers to serve, and the authorities to see to the welfare of the soldiers and their families. In the majority of cases, these so-called deserters are not deserters at all, but men whose minds are unhinged with anxiety about their families.

Transcript of news item, *Atlantik Sender*, broadcast 9 August 1943

The voice, even as it faded in and out of the shortwave static, was enticing, exactly as it was supposed to be. Intimacy was inevitable in the choking confines of a U-boat in the swells of the Atlantic, but this was something altogether different. When the German submarine crews inadvertently happened upon a husky-voiced, seductive female broadcasting to them directly, they could hardly believe their ears.

'This is Vicky speaking,' the sultry female voice could be heard saying, 'it shouldn't take us long to get acquainted.' And between German-flavoured jazz records, the novelty of Vicky's honeyed tones invited each of them to dance. In time, she would reveal items of news far more accurate than anything which was officially sanctioned by Goebbels's Propaganda Ministry. Generally, she made the crews feel good about themselves despite the terrible confines of their boats and the horrible conditions.

Many German submariners were hooked, especially when the voluptuous Vicky revealed other intimate details about the average U-boat man's life at home: the bars where they drank, the names of their officers, the latest gossip from the Hotel-Am-Steiphatz, where they were headquartered and even the names of their favourite whores and the addresses of their brothels. It was definitely subversive but didn't seem overtly propagandistic.

And it was, to its creators' everlasting gratitude, a certifiable hit.

The radio station formally known as *Kurzwellensender Atlantik*, but more often as *Atlantik Sender*, was the latest, greatest contribution of Sefton Delmer's continuing efforts in the propaganda war. The voice of Vicky was provided by a Jewish refugee from Berlin, 19-year-old Agnes Bernelle, whose seductive tones had come to his attention a few months before. Like her, the station was irresistible, partly because it was forbidden but mainly because its subversion was subtle. The crews knew it wasn't operating from within the Third Reich but that didn't really matter. It was entertaining and that was all that really mattered.

Unlike the sledgehammer crowing of Lord Haw Haw, whose broadcasts created derision in their intended British targets, Vicky's work adhered to Sefton Delmer's basic principle: to be successful, propaganda always had to tell the truth. In the face of their constant hardships, it was his intention that *Atlantik Sender* would become the submariner's best friend. And in time it did, even though Vicky would start to slip disconcerting details into her broadcasts, which had been gleaned from prisoners of war.

The process had been far simpler than Delmer had dared imagine. Interrogators from the Naval Intelligence Division realised that their captives might not reveal technical details in which they were really interested. But, sailor to sailor, they were keen to boast about what they had been up to on their shore leave. And as Vicky could attest, all the nice girls really did like a sailor.

This approach to subverting the German submariners had come from perhaps the most fertile imagination in Naval Intelligence. Commander Ian Fleming, with whatever reserves of inventiveness he had at his disposal, could be relied upon to come up with any number of remarkably crazy ideas that were always worth considering. 'A lot of Ian's ideas were just plain crazy,' remarked Admiral Norman Denning, a post-war Director of Naval Intelligence. 'But a lot of his far-fetched ideas had just a glimmer of possibility in them that made you think twice before you threw them into the wastepaper basket.'

As Naval Intelligence's point man for the prosecution of political warfare, Fleming had been the first to realise that U-boat crews could be targeted by another twist in the uses of radio. *Atlantik Sender* would employ a heady mix of sex and music, and team him with his pre-war compatriot, Sefton Delmer, and another Naval Intelligence colleague, Donald MacLachlan, who had also been a *Times* correspondent in the years before the war. And when the station began transmitting in the spring of 1943, it was badly needed as the fight against the U-boat menace was becoming increasingly desperate.

Nothing was considered too far-fetched in the fight against the wolf packs.

Many years later, when Winston Churchill was asked what had been his greatest worry throughout the six years of the fighting, he replied without hesitation: the U-boats. Indeed, the Battle of the Atlantic was both crucial and decisive, a relentless exchange that spanned from the first hours of the war – when U-30 torpedoed the passenger liner *Athenia* off Rockall – to the very last, when, on the same day that Adolf Hitler committed suicide in the Berlin bunker, the first Type XII U-boat – the most technically advanced submarine ever built in wartime – slipped into the cold waters off the coast of Bergen Harbour.

The fight against the grey wolves, as the U-boats were known to their crews, would involve many thousands of people, by far the more exotic of whom were propagandists and secret agents. Their unsung, yet key, role in the battle is only now being appreciated for it was, in the prime minister's graphic phrase, a 'war of groping and drowning, of ambuscade and stratagem, of science and seamanship'.

Nothing too outrageous would be rejected in the fight against the U-boats. 'The Battle of the Atlantic was the dominating factor all through the war,' Winston Churchill would write. 'Not for one moment could we forget that everything happening elsewhere, on land, at sea, or in the air, depended ultimately on its outcome.'

The combat was merciless, appalling and all the more horrifying for its facelessness. There were terrible losses experienced on both sides. Though the U-boat crews were portrayed by German propaganda as heroes who formed a swaggering elite, all were only too well aware that they were mostly doomed. A staggering 70 per cent of all German submariners lost their lives, with most only ever expecting to survive their first journeys to sea. Leading them was Admiral Karl Dönitz, a U-boat Commander in the First World War (when he had also been taken prisoner) who has been aptly described as 'one of the most able, daring and versatile flag officers on either side of the war' by the official US historian of the conflict.

Like so many others in post-Versailles Germany, Dönitz had remained in the service of the reconstituted German Navy for reasons of prestige. In January 1943, when he became Commander-in-Chief of the Kriegsmarine, his apotheosis was complete. 'I wanted to imbue my crews with enthusiasm and a complete faith to instill in them a spirit of selfless readiness to serve,' he would remark. Their behaviour at sea was uniquely informal, where the privations alone meant that they didn't have to wear uniforms; nor did they have to remove their beards (there was never enough spare water to allow them the luxury of a shave).

After the fall of France in 1940, Dönitz set up his bases on the Biscay coast to shorten the boats' journeys into the killing fields of the North Atlantic. Marshalled into wolf packs, the submarines would form a line and wait for convoys to appear after being spotted. The sheer size of the Atlantic alone made radio communications a necessity. When hunting in the packs, a U-boat – or a Focke Wulf Condor reconnaissance aircraft – would radio the position where a convoy had been encountered. In the operations room at Lorient, all the U-boats would then be directed by radio to converge in the vicinity.

Dönitz's use of signals intelligence grew out of necessity. The *Grossadmiral's* triumph led to his greatest weakness: careful control of the submarines meant they had to be in constant radio contact with Berlin. A network of Allied listening stations was thus alert for these transmissions. Triangulation allowed them to estimate where each U-boat was located. More so than codebreaking, the British use of direction finding would be the key to the Battle of the Atlantic, particularly in the period of blackouts when the German naval codes weren't being read.

Very few people appreciate that Bletchley Park was locked out of the naval Enigma code for most of 1942, and by the start of 1943, when they were back in, events were looking even more apocalyptic. The Battle of the Atlantic would reach its terrifying climax when two convoys lost twenty-two ships in half that number of days at the start of March 1943. If losses had continued at that rate, the results for the Allies would have been disastrous. Anglo-American operations in the Mediterranean would have failed, aid to Russia would have dwindled away and there would have been no possibility for an invasion of Western Europe in 1944. Indeed, some historians have speculated that Britain could well have been starved into submission.

Life aboard the U-boats was unremittingly harsh.

There were no bathing facilities, fresh air was at a premium, as was privacy, and crews constantly complained of rheumatic pains. Technically speaking, the submarines were not totally submersible: they spent most of their time on the surface, which meant the crews had to suffer endless rolling from Atlantic swells. Lookouts got very wet and very cold very quickly. And yet, despite the hardships, the crews were 'engulfed in comradeship', in the simple phrase of one, much to the chagrin of the British secret services who spent a great deal of time trying to understand why their spirits remained so high.

'The morale of U-Boat crews continues good and is not thought likely to decline seriously although since the Russian successes it may have become slightly more brittle,' one psychological evaluation records in early 1943. 'U-Boats are now being manned by younger officers and possess a high standard of personal morale.'

Given their terrible losses, no wonder so many German submariners took refuge in superstition. Fairly quickly, some boats and certain commanders were considered luckier than others. The sentimental mysticism of the *Deutsches Volk* inevitably combined with other strains of Teutonic fatalism far out in the Atlantic. Crewmen often wore 'lucky sweaters' knitted by loved ones as well as British Army apparel which had been liberated from depots in France.

Such superstitions became a more fertile ground for subversion.

To play on these fears came another remarkable publication called *Der Zenit (Zenith)*, which was aptly named. It would represent the very apotheosis of the uses of astrology in the secret war, thanks to Tom Delmer, who, by now, was, as one colleague would write, 'both inimitable and too successful to be interfered with'.

For his 'tame astrologer', it came not a moment too soon.

A certain desperation had accompanied Louis de Wohl's other work.

According to his memoirs and the interviews he gave later, the previous summer of 1942, a British officer bought him details of two birth dates and exact times. 'I cannot divulge their names,' he said, 'but we would like you to tell us what is in store for these two for this year.' That July he declared that the older of the two would triumph. 'His chart is on the rise and

success will follow him from now on.' As this was supposed to be Bernard
Law Montgomery, de Wohl took credit for seeing his victory at El Alamein.

By now, there had been official recognition that astrologers might actually tip off the enemy by making inadvertently accurate predictions. At a
meeting of the War Cabinet's Civil Defence Committee in the previous
January, the whole matter of printing horoscopes and the press was discussed. As the discussions went back and forth (against: they 'had a harmful
effect on public morale'; or for: they were not accurate 'but on the one
or two sensational instances' where true), the Principal Secretary of the
Ministry of Information was asked to investigate.

To their surprise, they found the earlier investigation from the previous July.
'The astrologers have a considerable amusement value,' the committee concluded, 'but otherwise exert very little influence in the public, except in the
case of neurotic individuals, for whom they supply a relatively harmless trap.'

Yet, oddly, the boil was broken with a discussion in that most public
of arenas, the House of Commons. When, in the summer of 1942, the
latest Minister of Information, Brendan Bracken, was asked in the House
whether he would stop astrological predictions, there was much merriment
and laughter.

'Astrologers seem to have the misfortune to be perpetually in conflict,'
Bracken noted. 'And, as no sensible person takes their predictions seriously,
I cannot ask our overworked censors to meddle in their mysteries.'

The Member for Twickenham then responded in kind. 'It is well known
that Hitler dabbles in astrology. May it not be that certain articles are written for him?' There was further mirth when he stated that there was no
monopoly on Hitler's astrologers. Manny Shinwell, an old Labour war horse,
saw a golden opportunity. The previous weekend, a tabloid had carried a
story that suggested a very different form of conflict.

'Is the Minister aware that one astrologer predicted last Sunday a government crisis this month? Is there any truth in that?'

It was typical of Tom Delmer's wartime activities that the first time he
encountered Agnes Bernelle was in the convivial social whirl surrounding
the more cultured of German-émigré circles in London. Agnes Bernelle was,
as he later termed her, just a spotty-faced teenager, hardly the siren she would
become when she took to the airwaves. In the ether, with her gravelly voice
akin to that of Lotte Lenya, it was not too hard to imagine her living in an
Otto Dix painting. Her father, Rudolf, who had been both a well-known

composer of satirical songs in Weimar Germany and a successful theatrical impresario, had long thought her voice would be ideal for broadcasting.

And when Tom Delmer heard her singing, he knew he had found the perfect instrument for *Atlantik Sender*. Like a music hall manager manqué, Delmer would transform Agnes Bernelle into a potent, alluring weapon of the airwaves. The U-boat crews would soon be taken in by her beautiful, breathy voice, leaving them hanging on for more.

Born in 1923 as Agnes Bernauer, she and her family had lived a gilded existence in Weimar Berlin. Spoiled yet playful, she grew up around the theatre and in 1930 was cast in a film playing a little boy. Hers was a comfortable, bourgeois existence and she, spoiled and indulged, liked to dress up; but then, to be fair, so did the Nazis. Her mother's family was Jewish and she was brought up a Protestant, which didn't seem to bother her family. Her father was Hungarian, which meant that she could travel on a Hungarian passport when the going got tough.

Given the political ferment of the times, she learned early the value of satire from her father, who, as she admitted, had foibles that were women and cards. Rudolf Bernauer had worked as an actor, then performed in plays and cabaret before buying several theatres. 'He was a very honest man,' she recalled, 'but at times took his honesty to ridiculous lengths.' He would never smuggle money out of Germany and had only a gold watch on him when they did eventually leave for London.

The Bernauer family knew Marlene Dietrich and Albert Einstein lived nearby. But by far the most astounding encounter came when she was older and was waiting on the Unter den Linden. She happened upon a politician in the street whom she couldn't help from noticing had interesting colouring and, much as she hated to admit it, was attractive.

'He had red hair and very bright blue eyes,' Agnes recalled many years later. She was near enough to him that 'I could kill him if I had a gun'. Fairly swiftly, this self same rabble-rouser took over the country. And with the full confidence of youth, Agnes sensed just how Adolf Hitler was going to change things. 'Whereas my Jewish relatives on my father's side were either killed or tortured in the camps,' she recalled, 'members of my mother's "Aryan" family married men in Nazi uniform.' When her mother was later asked to take some documents over the border for obvious Nazi 'goons', she knew that it was time to leave.

In 1936, she persuaded her father to move to London. Finding the repression and cold of England hard to take at first – her Mitteleuropean vulgarity, as she termed it, shocked many of her new friends at boarding school – they were able to settle in London as he had been ghostwriting films. Changing their name to Bernelle, her father once more took ownership of theatres and later directed low-budget films. While attending school in North London, Rudolf Bernelle let her daughter perform with the Free German League of Culture as a social and artistic forum.

Strange as it may seem to posterity, in all the time she worked for Sefton Delmer, Agnes Bernelle did not know his real name. He was only ever known to her as 'the beard', 'as no one in our outfit was allowed to know the identity of those above or below them'. She would be driven each day to Woburn Abbey where, as she later recalled, the studio had been 'built into the chapel in one of the Abbey's wings, which would explain its stain-glassed windows'.

As well as talking between records, Agnes would record German versions of songs in the cottage she shared with two other girls. Somewhere in the social whirl of the time, she met a dashing Spitfire pilot who, amongst many other claims to fame, was the cousin of Winston Churchill. Desmond Leslie was a composer, a collector of electronic noise and a believer in UFOs. He was entranced by the heavens, having seen 'an immense green fireball move slowly across the sky and disappear behind the Sussex Downs' as a schoolboy. As to his piloting skills, a family historian tellingly recalled: 'He destroyed a number of aircraft, most of which he was piloting at the time.'

Colonel John H. Bevan MC was a frail-looking insomniac, rumoured to possess the best polished shoes in the British Army. Memorably described as having 'sleepy, pale-blue eyes and thin fair hair which turned grey from the strain [of] work', he would turn around the fortunes of the London Controlling Section after taking it over at the end of June 1942. When he took over in the basement at Storey's Gate, Bevan – like his only member of staff before him – was amazed at how little was happening.

'Our staff duties are pretty poor aren't they Dennis?' he said one day to the occult writer.

'No sir, I'm afraid they aren't quite all they might be.'

As Dennis Wheatley relates, they had been operating in a vacuum. They needed a better sense of purpose and what that meant was, thanks to Bevan's great knowledge of the army, 'a directive'. So he and Bevan worked on the scope of the London Controlling Section.

'And from that point,' Wheatley said, 'Johnny Bevan and I went to work.'

It would be easy to over-emphasise the importance and significance of the London Controlling Section under Johnny Bevan. In a matter of weeks, the colonel recruited more members in an attempt to give the section a higher profile. Known as mysterious yet clever men, their exact duties were never quite clear, which forewent most people taking too much of an interest. They would soon famously be characterised by Dennis Wheatley as 'a stockbroker, a thriller writer, a soap manufacturer and a retired civil servant, all disguised as officers only for the purposes of war'.

They worked in what was known as Mr Rance's room, close by the Joint Planning Staff. It was subterranean and secure, covered by 4ft of hardened concrete, reinforced by tramlines, which shored up the room where they were meeting. 'This underground fortress resembled the lower decks of a battleship,' Dennis Wheatley later vividly recalled. 'It was white-painted and along the ceilings of its narrow passages ran a mass of cables carrying light, heat, telephone and air conditioning to the many rooms, most of which were like ship's cabins.'

And it was a happy ship, more like a prefect's room at a public school where, unusually for the time, everyone was on first-name terms. 'We were a team,' Wheatley recalled, 'a good team, and by and large a happy one.'

After its faltering start, the London Controlling Section would become so successful that it attracted its fair share of jealous critics. In later years, many who had served alongside them were less than complimentary. Some saw Johnny Bevan and his cronies as indolent amateurs whose greater priorities were shown by their permanent table at Rules restaurant.

Its expansion had a great deal more to do with the liaison with MI5 and MI6, helped by Johnny Bevan's membership of the XX Committee. Bevan also created separate committees which would leak information, some via the double agents but also other channels. 'Close liaison with the Political Warfare Executive was also necessary,' one chronicler of the deceivers notes, 'to make sure that propaganda did not inadvertently lead the Axis to draw conclusions with deception plans.'

If Bevan provided the cool head of the operation, Wheatley was its flamboyant heart. And in very short order, strategic deception became a well-oiled machine whose efficiency was fine-tuned by the Enigma decrypts which were streaming from Bletchley Park. With Colonel Johnny Bevan's arrival, they revolutionised the work of deception. Up to this point, most of the work had been piecemeal and uncoordinated: now it would go to the heart of the fighting of the war.

Under Sefton Delmer's equally expert tutelage, Louis de Wohl had also finally been given something useful to do. By the summer of 1942, de Wohl was holed up in Atheneum Court, a Piccadilly hotel, where he was paid in cash from secret slush funds but only as a part-time job. That explained why, in Delmer's amused recollection, his tame astrologer had been spotted 'walking down Piccadilly just like an unmade bed'.

In August 1942, despite being 'warned off' – according to a note from an unnamed MI6 officer – de Wohl had been put into contact with the PWE, who reported that he was still wearing a captain's uniform. 'Is it really possible that this man is allowed to wear the uniform of a British officer?' a senior MI6 man exclaimed when they heard. 'Surely it is time the gullible were protected from the creature.'

For most of the time, Sefton Delmer appears to have just about been able to keep a straight face when he dealt with his increasingly troublesome diviner of heavenly intentions, terming him a sinister-looking creature.

At times, the astrologer was painfully aware that he was being treated less than respectfully. Louis de Wohl became petulant. In time, he became such a nuisance that he was banned from one central London office used by his superiors. So Sefton Delmer was forced to visit him at his apartment in Atheneum Court, where he was holed up alone, 'a vast spectacled jellyfish [of] a man dressed in the uniform of a British Army Captain, puffing over-dimensional rings of smoke from an over-dimensional cigar,' the propagandist recalled. His warnings had little effect on the astrologer's general behaviour. One messenger who regularly took him his money complained that de Wohl kept gassing on for hours about his astrological predictions. But soon there was an instrument through which they could be channelled.

Towards the end of 1942, he was asked to provide copy for half a dozen issues of a black 'astrological magazine' which were squarely aimed at U-boat crews. The Special Operations Executive was then used to distribute copies of *Der Zenit* throughout the French Atlantic ports. It was later noted with some satisfaction that Admiral Dönitz himself was paying attention to its advice about when U-boats should not depart on 'unfavourable days'.

Der Zenit skilfully incorporated the dates of known sinkings. By back-dating its predictions, U-boat crews would, it was hoped, come to think of the magazine as particularly omniscient. Certain future dates were then identified with astrologically unsound conditions along the lines that some departure days were better for older vessels or that a particular captain was ill-starred. Seemingly genuine, it carried adverts for obscure medicines and genuine German astrological books. Although the stand-ard of each issue improved, by March 1943 Delmer and de Wohl made a curious mistake.

In that month's issue they identified the editor as one Dr Hubert Korsch, a well-known pre-war astrologer. In fact, by then he had been incarcerated in a concentration camp for two years. Most of the time, Delmer humoured the corpulent German to make his life easier. The astrologer refused to amend his predictions, but luckily Delmer found they often coincided with the greater needs of psychological warfare. To create even more confusion in the mind of U-boat crewmen, Delmer would turn his attentions to the same electromagnetic medium that made tracking the U-boats possible at the very moment of their greatest success.

When *Atlantik Sender* began its broadcasts on 18 March 1943, it did so at the height of the Battle of the Atlantic. Allied losses had been steadily mount-ing; 1942 had been disastrous so far as merchant shipping was concerned. In June, the sinkings were the greatest of the war – 834,196 tons of shipping – so much so that American shipyards could not replace all the sunken ships. By the start of 1943, the cumulative losses were nudging 8 million tons, much of it sent to the bottom along the Eastern Seaboard.

'Our submarines are operating close inshore along the coast of the United States,' Karl Dönitz himself would crow, 'so that bathers and sometimes entire coastal cities are witnesses of that drama whose visual climaxes are constituted by the red glorioles of blazing tankers.'

At the start of 1943, Dönitz had the greatest number of U-boats he had ever had at his disposal. German industry was producing the submarines faster than the Allies could sink them. Bad weather in January reduced the tonnage that was sunk, but the losses were gradually rising in the spring despite the inclement conditions – from 203,000 tons in January to 360,000 tons in February. It looked like March's loss would double that figure again.

So now, at the start of the month, the stakes were at their greatest.

The situation was self-evidently so bad that precipitate action com-mended itself to the men in Whitehall. Nothing less than the removal of Karl Dönitz himself, it was suggested, could solve their problems. That same month, the Special Operations Executive was asked to look at how to reduce the efficiency of the U-boats by sabotaging their fuel supplies, their torpedoes, their batteries and all the crews' 'amenities' on land.

But more terminal action might be necessary to settle the matter once and for all. 'The assassination of Admiral Dönitz and/or the blowing up of his Headquarters in Paris would profoundly affect the morale of U-boat crews and U-boat operations,' a file from the Special Operations Executive records, testimony to just how desperate the situation was.

Under Tom Delmer's benign patronage, Agnes Bernelle had been transformed into a siren of the airwaves. On *Atlantik Sender* she became known as 'Vicky', quickly becoming known as a German Vera Lynn whose signature tune was the highly appropriate *A Smooth One*. Her fame spread far and wide – not just to the U-boat crews but all over the world – thanks to the power of the Aspidistra transmitter. Agnes also broadcast on Soldatensender West, supposedly run by a patriotic old curmudgeon who subverted the Nazi regime. To her amazement, she received letters that seemed to emanate from Occupied Europe, forwarded, so she thought, by the Swedish Embassy. As Agnes relates in her autobiography, the main attraction was the constant stream of jazz, a musical form which Hitler considered abhorrent and decadent. 'This made the German forces want to listen to us,' Agnes wrote, 'and since the music was interspersed with items of news and other subtly disguised pieces of propaganda, they would invariably get the information we wanted them to have.'

The accuracy was vouchsafed by prisoners of war – often taken blindfolded to the studios as volunteers. A vast network of information was produced to target them. As a supposedly patriotic station, Vicky would criticise hoarders as unprincipled, then the audience would cause a run on certain items. 'If we wanted to lower the morale of the soldiers,' Agnes wrote, 'I would simply tell a certain battalion that although it was surrounded and trapped, all was not lost, and I would play them a cheerful tune.'

Some Germans, she hoped, would surrender while they had the chance.

Even though it was clear that the tide of war was on the turn, Adolf Hitler still had, at the start of 1943, the satisfaction of knowing that his forces were arrayed from the north of Norway to the Spanish border, across at least four time zones and three different climate regions. His soldiers were freezing in the shadows of the Caucasus and sweltering in dugouts across parts of the North African desert.

Yet now came an even swifter reversal of fortune within the tangled intelligence world of Nazi Germany. Perceptions of Admiral Canaris and the Abwehr would change dramatically. More so than the rise of the SS *Sicherheitsdienst* – temporarily halted by the removal of its former chief, Reinhard Heydrich, at the hands of Czech partisans the previous summer – the waning of Admiral Canaris's influence would come to paralyse the German intelligence machine.

The successful Torch landings, in French Vichy-held territory in North Africa towards the end of 1942, more or less set the seal on the admiral's career. When experts at the Kriegsmarine Directorate of Naval Warfare analysed the information which had been available to the Abwehr, they concluded 'in this intelligence battle, we lost the day'.

'Yet again,' fumed Hitler's chief military adviser, General Alfred Jodl, 'Canaris's imprudence and inconsistency has landed us in the soup.'

The Abwehr was supposed to provide the Führer, the Supreme Command and the General Staff with everything it needed for the successful prosecution of war. Yet it never actually warned of El Alamein nor the invasions of French North Africa and Sicily or the landings at Anzio. The Abwehr's fate would also be sealed when it singularly failed to report the Soviet build-up around Stalingrad at the start of 1943. It had already enraged the Führer by failing to anticipate the Soviet T-54 tank, the most efficient ordnance on the battlefield, which could outrun and outgun anything in the Wehrmacht's considerable armoury.

Admiral Canaris rarely visited Hitler and the Supreme Command anymore. By the start of 1943, two of his deputies were in jail, undergoing a Gestapo investigation into their loyalties and various nefarious activities against the state. More than anything else, what the admiral had feared all along would now come to pass: an extended examination of the Abwehr by Himmler's men, exposing its inefficiencies for all the world to see.

It had all started with something that was fairly routine within the Third Reich's espionage services. In the autumn of 1942, a German businessman by the name of Schmidhuber was arrested in Switzerland. Like so many other Abwehr informants, he was making a nice little packet smuggling foreign currency in and out of Zurich. The head of the Gestapo, Heinrich Müller, had him arrested as he felt there was more to what he was actually doing than met the eye.

During interrogation, Schmidhuber obligingly sang like the proverbial canary. He claimed that he had heard of a 'generals' clique' which was plotting against the Nazis to end the war as well as the extending of peace feelers towards the British via the Vatican. Even worse, a number of Jews had been exfiltrated out of Germany by enrolling them in the Abwehr and making it appear as though they were involved in intelligence operations.

Schmidhuber knew about these various intrigues as he was close to one of Canaris's senior lieutenants, a political adviser called Hans von Dohnayi, and often visited the Abwehr's chief of staff, General Hans Oster. Both, the businessman claimed, had betrayed military secrets and were personally involved in plotting against the Führer. When Canaris's men became aware that their friend had been incarcerated, it was too late for them to do anything.

After so much smoke, here was a tangible conflagration of the various intrigues which were being directed against the state. General Müller wanted to raid the Abwehr's Tirpitzufer headquarters for he believed that Admiral Canaris himself was complicit in all these treasons. Given the obvious political sensitivities, such an action had to be approved by Heinrich Himmler.

To the Gestapo chief's amazement, when the docket came back the Reichsführer-SS had written in his own hand: 'Kindly leave Canaris alone!' In all the mysteries that surround the great enigma of how the admiral survived for so long, this is by far the most curious.

Was Himmler actually protecting Canaris?

One of the Reichsführer-SS's biographers asserts that the head of the SS was 'wedded to Canaris by an almost grotesque overestimate of his professional ability'. Indeed, much of the admiral's longevity owed to the fact that Himmler viewed him as some sort of genius and, to some extent, continued to protect him.

This may partly have come from the SS leader's growing realisation that he might profit from the sorts of connections the Abwehr was trying to extend to the enemy. With the self-evident failure of the Russian campaign into the later winter of 1943, Himmler was certainly nudged in the direction of defeatism by his own foreign intelligence chief, Walter Schellenberg, which would propel them both in the most bizarre of directions towards astrology (a story told in the next chapter).

Yet nobody was completely immune from prosecution in a police state.

Early in April 1943, a surprise raid from the Gestapo descended on the Tirpitzufer. Despite a tip-off from a fellow conspirator, both Dohnayi and Oster were arrested, tortured, interrogated and eventually executed.

Canaris's almost feral instinct for survival now reasserted itself.

The admiral dropped all contacts with his deputies. Though there was not enough evidence to tie him to the conspirators, he came under increasing suspicion from his rivals in the SS and the *Sicherheitsdienst*. To add to the confusion, Heinrich Himmler himself took a great deal of personal interest in these sorts of intrigues. And, as ever in the acres of speculation concerning Admiral Canaris's true intentions, the name of someone familiar to these pages once more reappears.

That of Ian Lancaster Fleming.

So far as the prosecution of psychological warfare was concerned, *Atlantik Sender* started right on time. To date, though, most of the fighting had occurred within Whitehall over just who should be responsible for such activities. It had been a miracle that the station ever got on the air, given all the bickering about who should actually 'own' the transmitter which preceded it. By the autumn of 1942, however, Admiral John Godfrey had been prevailed upon to help fight the U-boat menace, so much so that, in his own words, 'an element of perfidy, verging on the unscrupulous' was necessary. The Director of Naval Intelligence looked no further than his special assistant to ensure that the myriad possibilities of broadcasting subversive material could be realised. Wherever there were difficulties, Ian Fleming would invariably help resolve them. His special assistant would happily call some luminary with the words 'Admiral Godfrey feels very strongly about this', and, as his colleague Donald McLachlan wryly noted, the problem would be smoothed over with an inevitable inquiry about the admiral's personal assistant, 'a giant among name droppers'.

It was worth it. *Atlantik Sender* was an unexpected hit.

Much to their amazement, the naval interrogators found that many captured U-boat crews were only too delighted to help bring down the Third Reich. Potential scriptwriters were carefully screened to ensure they provided all the latest U-boat jargon and background information to make the broadcasts seem as genuine as possible. Many captured crewmen were used for the actual broadcasts when Vicky herself was unavailable.

Thanks to the reading of Enigma, it became clear that the Germans themselves thought that the station's eclectic mix of information was coming from agents in high places, possibly including ones in the Führer's headquarters. Fleming and Delmer's work helped perpetuate the powerful myth that the British Secret Service was omniscient.

In time, *Atlantik Sender* would subtly undermine every aspect of life at sea by spreading confusion with a beguiling mix of truth and horrifying rumour which would reduce morale. Tom Delmer ensured the compilation of a huge file of gossip and personal details that had been collected from intercepted prisoner of war correspondence. This allowed Vicky to display an intimate acquaintance with her 'dear boys in blue', as she called them. Coded messages, disguised as record labels and catalogue numbers, were also targeted for resistance fighters.

Agnes Bernelle herself was in no doubt that the only way to make people listen – as she had done in her various pre-war cabaret shows – was to be funny. On one famous occasion, she announced over the airwaves on *Atlantik Sender* that by special request of the comrade 'blockade-runners who are getting awfully bored down there in the Gironde Estuary while they await orders to sail' she would play a choice selection of music 'from our brave allies in the East'. Thereafter came an hilarious cacophony of Japanese and Chinese records.

Vicky's very charm was in direct contrast to the unnerving content of many of the broadcasts. In later years, Agnes Bernelle often related how the words of Gertrude Stein stayed with her. 'Everything is so dangerous that nothing is really frightening' was a quote that could apply equally well to her own life – as well as those of the submariners to whom she directly appealed. Vicky's greatest success was in telling the captain of one particular U-boat that his wife had given birth to twins. As he had not had leave for two years, in one account he surrendered his boat straight away to be with his family. On another occasion, Vicky also caused chaos in the German post office by announcing that the Führer required all good citizens to send samples of urine to the Ministry of Health.

Humour aside, many of the broadcasts were designed to be unsettling.

Tom Delmer would ensure that information about the losses of crews and the effects of bombing on the homeland was purposefully included in Vicky's broadcasts. Truthful information about the latest allied mining operations was also mixed in with false claims. That way, the U-boat crews couldn't help but wonder if whole swathes of the Atlantic were simply too dangerous to navigate.

By August 1943, the Gestapo had become so impressed by the station that its individual claims were being investigated for how they might have been obtained. According to their best guess, the station's transmitter was based in Switzerland, from where, ironically, the MI6 station in Berne reported in February 1944 that 'despite the death penalty for listening to illegal broadcasts, *Atlantik Sender* is the most popular. The impression gained from PoWs interrogated [is] that listening at their bases to Atlantik broadcasts is now the rule for naval personnel rather than the exception.'

Did Admiral Wilhelm Canaris actively plan to actually meet with his opposite numbers in the Allied secret services? It is a stark question which several people have posed, yet another thread connected to the enigma that is the Abwehr chief around this time. It became entwined with his involvement in many murky and mysterious intrigues, many of which were further rebuffed due to the pervasive influence of one of the most damaging of spies in the history of British Intelligence.

If some accounts are to be believed, Canaris wanted to meet both his opposite numbers – Sir Stewart Menzies and 'Wild Bill' Donovan – in Portugal, an event that has been characterised as a 'clandestine encounter between three men who controlled the most powerful espionage networks in the contemporary world'.

As ever, these stories are exaggerations which result from an intriguing and, as always with Admiral Canaris, opaque reality. Because of his regular visits to Spain – and in particular, the Algeciras outstation – it was suggested that some sort of accommodation with the Abwehr chief might be considered. As ever, the more egregious claims came from our old friend Donald McCormick, concerning the recollections of a Royal Naval Attaché who picked up whispers from contacts that no less a personage than Admiral Canaris 'dropped hints that he might have talks with a certain naval person'.

Needless to say, this was Commander Ian Fleming.

'At times it seemed as though Canaris was practically inviting the Naval Intelligence Division to open secret negotiations with him,' McCormick claims that another of Fleming's colleagues recalled. 'But with Canaris one couldn't be quite sure what his motives were.'

As ever, this is just the usual kind of speculative nonsense surrounding James Bond's creator that ties various loose ends of a story into a more attractive whole. For around this time in the fighting, there was a great deal of smoke emanating from a low-burning fire connected to Admiral Canaris's intentions. In one account, Sir Stewart Menzies said after the war that attempts to contact the Abwehr chief had been overruled by the Foreign Office for fear of offending the Soviet Union. In another account, one senior diplomat was asked a pointed question by an intelligence source: 'Would you like to meet Canaris?'

Though the truth is, as ever, somewhat more elusive. There was an important change to the prosecution of the war that had prompted these overtures. By 1943, greater urgency about the resolution of the war had come about thanks to the Allied leaders' declaration of 'Unconditional Surrender' at the Casablanca conference that January. At the end of a military strategy session, Franklin Delano Roosevelt used the phrase that, he later claimed, was a soundbite that resonated in American history, originally coined by General Ulysses Grant.

The president's public insistence that nothing less than complete and total surrender of the Axis powers would be accepted by the Allies certainly caused shock. Take a look at the newsreel footage of the press conference where Winston Churchill's reaction was the same as if somebody had slapped him in the face with a giant fish. Others in the military were stunned, too. If there had been conditions attached to a potential surrender, the growing internal conspiracy against the Nazi regime – centred on the Abwehr, in particular – might have been more emboldened.

As several historians have pondered, even if an assassination of Adolf Hitler had been successful, would the rest of the German military have taken orders from the conspirators? In any case, without the remote possibility of a political settlement, why would they ever need to kill the Führer? The stage was set for what Josef Goebbels termed 'total war' in a rabble-rousing speech which induced the German determination to fight to the end. There was head-shaking incomprehension on the Allied Side. Sir Stewart Menzies himself warned the prime minister directly that the Germans would now fight 'with the despairing ferocity of cornered rats'.

Much of the confusion, and indeed misinformation, surrounding the various peace feelers supposedly emanating from Admiral Canaris himself has a human cause. Kim Philby ensured that in his position as head of MI6 counter-espionage in Iberia he would undermine any attempt to make peace. Such rumours, even if unfounded, would as a matter of routine enter his in tray, and he was in a position to do something about them.

The merest possibility of a separate Allied–German peace settlement remained high on the list of Josef Stalin's considerable collection of paranoias. As a highly placed mole, Philby was especially alert for any intrigues that might circumvent the influence or safety of the Soviet Union. In one former MI6 colleague's recollection, reports that the admiral wanted to meet were dismissed by Philby as 'mere speculation' and their circulation was deliberately limited.

More lurid stories still have emerged concerning the assassination of the admiral himself and his own role in attempting to murder the Führer. According to some accounts, Sir Stewart Menzies himself wanted to meet Admiral Canaris at a castle on the border with Portugal. Indeed, Abwehr decrypts revealed that 'Father Christmas' was going to be driving from Madrid to Seville on one particular day. This, some officers in MI6 suggested, would provide an ideal time to assassinate C's opposite number.

'I want no action whatsoever taken against the Admiral,' Philby recalls Sir Stewart writing in a memo in his personal green ink. If it survives – or ever existed – nobody has ever seen it. In another account, a British launch took the admiral to meet Sir Stewart at La Linea in Gibraltar, where they discussed ways of bringing the fighting to a close by killing Hitler.

Most of these stories can be shown to emanate from mischief-making (a great deal by Philby) long after the war. Sir Stewart Menzies did make a foreign trip to Algiers around this time, but there is no evidence that Wilhelm Canaris was in Iberia at the same time. And though the Chief of the Secret Intelligence Service would hardly write 'off to meet my opposite number' in his diary, there was no such evidence that he ever contemplated such a move.

When the late Professor Keith Jeffery came to look through the MI6 archives to write his authorised history, there was little concrete evidence to show any direct ties between the admiral and the British Secret Service. There were a handful of indirect ones, which Prof. Jeffery referred to as 'the only recorded face-to-face meeting between Canaris and anyone reporting directly to SIS'.

They concerned Hala Szymanskà, the wife of a Polish military attaché, who was now working as a translator in Berne, a sinecure which had been suggested to her by the wily admiral, who had known her before the war. 'Canaris knew that anything he told this Polish lady would be reported,' reflected another MI6 officer long after the war, 'she being a patriotic Pole. Straight to Polish intelligence, who would, of course, pass it on to us.'

Another intriguing aspect to the story – that was not referred to in the authorised history of the Secret Intelligence Service – was another salient, well-established fact: Wilhelm Canaris also had a mistress in Vienna whose sister was married to Menzies's brother, Ian. Much was made of this by Dusko Popov in his memoirs, which were written in the seventies.

According to Popov's account, British spymaster and self-styled master spy encountered each other at the start of 1943 when they separated from a dinner party under the guise of drinking whisky sodas.

Menzies, as he had already minuted the prime minister, was completely aghast concerning the merest contemplation of unconditional surrender. 'As a phrase, I personally dislike it,' C is quoted as saying. 'It means nothing.' In Popov's recollection, the Chief of MI6 thought that a negotiated peace may have been possible before Roosevelt's unequivocal pronouncement.

Sir Stewart apparently wanted Dusko Popov to be alert for any whispers of plots to bring down the Führer from his own contacts in Germany. As Popov later related, one of his old university friends who was now in the Abwehr was incredulous about the removal of the leader. 'Why the hell should the Allies want to get rid of Hitler?' his friend exclaimed on one occasion. 'He's winning the war for them!'

And the same could be said of Admiral Canaris and the agency he directed. There was certainly a grim logic behind the leaving of both the Führer and his wily intelligence chief in place. With Adolf Hitler in power, the war would continue on its wayward course: with Wilhelm Canaris remaining in office, there would clearly be no German victory in the intelligence war. Yet the dangers for the admiral now intensified in the remaining two years of the fighting. Though the Schmidhuber affair had not succeeded in landing any punches, the Gestapo already had compiled reports about Canaris's unreliability that ran to several volumes.

'Abroad he was widely regarded as the sinister *deus ex machina* behind all the crimes of the National Socialist regime,' wrote Wilhelm Höttl, a member of the *Sicherheitsdienst* after the war. 'His friends profess to see in him the spiritual leader of all the opposition movements against Hitler and a martyr in the cause of the fight against National Socialism.'

The enigma of Canaris and his true loyalties remains deep.

Even with Himmler's blessing – on one occasion the Reichsführer-SS famously remarked that 'the old man should be left in peace' – quite why or how the admiral survived has never been satisfactorily explained, even with the limited release of some diplomatic files in both the British and American national archives of their dealings with the Abwehr at the time. Rather like the Führer himself, his military intelligence chief had the luck of the devil.

As the tide of the war changed in those first few months of 1943, Louis de Wohl's involvement in the secret war reached its own high-water mark.

Many years later, the manner of his prognostications were gently sent up by Tom Delmer when he recalled his seer would often frown 'at me with terrifying ferocity as though to reproach me for my infidel cynicism'. By the late summer of 1943, de Wohl worked on a supposed 'secret' interpretation of Nostradamus's predictions with a new twist designed for the purposes of political warfare.

The results would also be inveigled into Occupied Europe by SOE-sponsored partisans to undermine the very basis for the Führer's continuing suitability to lead the Reich, as well as his health. There were fifty bogus quatrains in archaic French, whose German translation refers to 'Hister' winning more victories than was good for him and later being murdered by six men in the night ('Naked, taken unawares without his armour, he succumbs'). It bore the imprint of Regulus Verlag, a company which had produced genuine occult and astrological publications before the war.

Attached to a 100-page booklet called *Nostradamus prophecies the course of the war* was what appeared to be a secretly distributed note – supposedly written by Karl Krafft, the Hitlerian astrologer – explaining that its contents were so dangerous, it was implied he had been abducted by the SS because of the startling accuracy of his predictions. 'Here, as promised, is the carbon of my letter to the Führer,' Krafft had supposedly written as a kind of insurance policy. 'I know it is in safe hands.'

Dated 14 November 1942, the attached booklet also appeared to have been privately circulated by Krafft's friends. In particular, the supposed *Führerastrologe* had drawn attention to the leader's own doctor, Karl Brandt, whom he accused of undermining the Nazi regime by prescribing medicine that was killing the Führer. This doctor, it was suggested, was nothing less than a dangerous quack who, for good measure, was also accused of being a reincarnation of Rasputin. In reality, British Intelligence had fingered the wrong doctor. Adolf Hitler's personal physician, Dr Morrell, was already prescribing fairly dangerous drugs for his patient.

The Nostradamus booklet opened with an unsigned essay entitled 'Can humans see into the future?' along with a radical new interpretation of the great seer's predictions. These subtly altered quatrains were the obvious work of Louis de Wohl, who provided helpful 'notes' to what the various Nostradamian prognostications actually meant. For example:

A captain of Greater Germany will approach the king of kings, who justly mistrusts him with a feigned appeal for help.

Its meaning, according to the appended notes, could not be clearer. It continued:

> [F]oreign astrologers linked this quatrain to the case of Rudolf Hess, who
> supposedly flew to England to offer the King an alliance against Russia.

Other hints and helps are followed before a rousing finale:

'Jupiter in cancer – the great pocket will weep to have elected him. Hister's ruin approaches. From the heavens approaches an army so fearsome that Augsburg, Frankfurt and Berlin grow pale.'

'The great pocket' alluded to heavy industry. The rest showed that the Third Reich's days were clearly numbered as destruction would continue until the very end.

But without his ever predicting it, so too were Louis de Wohl's days working as an astrologer for British Intelligence. The records show that he was paid £70 for this booklet – three months' salary for an army captain, his MI5 files noted – and that was the final money he ever received from the British government.

Epilogue

Remembrance Foretold

Like nearly all my professional colleagues, I too was severely persecuted from 1933 to 1945. I suffered the same fate as the other German astrologers; I was arrested and taken to the infamous police prison in Hamburg-Fuhlsbüttel. [When] I was released from prison, I was anything but a free man. On the contrary, I continued to live as a prisoner on an estate belonging to Himmler's masseur, Kersten, an estate which served as a secret work camp for specialists and, as such, was affiliated with the Ravensbrück concentration camp. I was no longer physically maltreated, but I worked under the constant threat of severe punishment should my calculations prove inaccurate.

Wilhelm Wulff, *Zodiac and Swastika* (1968)

By the late winter of 1942, an air of cautious optimism hung over the capital.

London was still bearing the tell-tale scars of war, yet it had survived. The threat of the Blitz had evaporated. With the Führer's gaze increasingly preoccupied by the war in the East, raids were few and far between. By this fourth autumn of the fighting, there was some flickering hope that with the last great imperial battle of the war – the victory at El Alamein – the tide of Allied fortunes was on the turn.

And now, a very special meeting had been called in Mr Rance's room.

Some of the attendees had flown halfway around the world. Foremost among them was Peter Fleming, with the tanned countenance of someone who had been working in India doing what he termed 'this ungentlemanly stuff far from the heat and dust'. After his various earlier jobs for the Special Operations Executive, he was now in charge of creating deceptions in the

Far East. From the outset, its scope was limited and, as he would shortly explain to Dennis Wheatley, it was 'a one-horse show and I am the horse'.

Though, as the official history of deceptions is at pains to point out, Fleming 'neither achieved nor could have achieved the imposing results which [he] scored against our German enemies', he did have his successes. Many read like Boy's Own adventures. Peter Fleming developed his own agents and double agents – known as Hiccoughs or Cough Drops – along with dead bodies dropped with apparently faulty parachutes, triple agents who spent their time broadcasting insults, completely false officers drawn by an imaginative cartoonist and a real-life double agent who killed an informant by chopping tiger whiskers into a curry.

Back in England, it was time to take stock.

After taking extended leave in the company of his actress wife, Celia Johnson, Fleming had spent most of this time shooting pheasants, pondering the now global needs of warfare, which had their own special needs, not least in corroborating evidence implicit in other operations around the world. Now it was time to bring it all together into a coherent whole to create an ultimately false picture of Allied intentions all around the globe. False rumours had to be backed up with a modicum of truth and, as Peter Fleming would later remark, 'It is impossible, or at least highly dangerous, to tell a lie until you know what the truth is going to be.'

This, then, was a unique gathering of the clans, the only time these curious, secretive and sometimes mystical men ever came together in one location. At the end of October 1942, there was a sense they could achieve so much more.

'The presentations for the conference were immense,' Dennis Wheatley recalled. 'For days, all of us sweated blood getting out a vast agenda, writing long papers on the innumerable ways we might hope to deceive the enemy, upon grades of operators and spheres of influence and arranging accommodation for our visitors.'

Yet on the morning of the first day there was a notable absentee: the thriller writer himself. The meeting had started at ten o'clock sharp but Wheatley didn't show until 11.45 a.m. after sleeping through his alarm. He arrived by taxi and bounded into the large conference room as though nothing was wrong.

'I'm terribly sorry I'm late,' he said in a stage whisper to Johnny Bevan. 'I overslept.'

Everyone fell about laughing. Wheatley's faux pas was a comic counterpoint to the seriousness of the discussion in hand. It was nothing if not propitious. October 1942 saw – in Winston Churchill's apposite phrase – the turning of the tide, when finally everything came together. It was a time of new beginnings, too, and an end to the confusion that had often stymied the deceivers' works to date. That is why the gathering of the clans was so important; it marked the change from failure to success.

Without realising it, everything was now set for the final battles of the war.

In Johnny Bevan's apt phrase, good deception came from double agents, codebreaking and good planning. All allowed them to become the most artful dodgers in military history, highly adept at playing on the prejudices and curious beliefs of the German High Command. Johnny Bevan had so many responsibilities that his hair literally turned grey overnight, his sleep was disrupted into painfully recurring episodes of insomnia and he was often made physically sick with worry.

The London Controlling Section would eventually come to have a power and remit far beyond most others in the secret war. Dennis Wheatley essentially wrote the handbook which codified all the steps needed to deceive the enemy. It became a strategic masterplan for the expert deceivers. The occult writer also provided a dancing faun, a statuette that represented the trickery of the sprites, that was placed in the centre of the room along with a Persian carpet.

It seemed a suitable augury for the future and one that did not need any help from the occult anywhere around the world.

By the time the tide of war had changed, Louis de Wohl's exit from the secret war was only a matter of time. In all the surviving files on his dealings with the secret world, the issue that continued to exercise both him – and the authorities – was the small matter of his uniform, which he still felt entitled to wear. 'None of this situation is understood by de Wohl himself,' wrote Colonel Lennox after he was off the payroll. 'Indeed, why should it be? In so far as he was given a commission and was never informed that it was only for one particular purpose, and would thereafter come to an end.'

The problem was that he was starting to draw attention to himself:

Since de Wohl's return from America he has quite naturally had no ration card, for the simple reason that the Army has not issued him with one (why should it?), but he thinks he is a soldier and therefore cannot apply for a civilian card. He has repeatedly asked Sefton Delmer if the authorities will let him have his military card.

The matter came to a head because the management of Athenaeum Court were threatening to take legal action unless he handed over his ration coupons. The great fear for the security authorities was that if he ever did go to court, 'one could hardly blame him for telling all this to an astonished Magistrate and gaping reporters'.

An exasperated correspondent noted that if SOE could hand out commissions 'to all and sundry', surely somebody could find him a ration card. Equally, if his work for the PWE was worthwhile – 'and only Sefton Delmer can answer that' – they should make a card available to him. MI5 realised they needed to keep as close a surveillance over him as possible. That now involved monitoring his mail and applying for a Home Office Warrant. That way, they could keep tabs on what he was up to.

'He has a considerable clientele as an astrologer, and in view of the influence which he may well wield, by this means it is desirable to learn more of his contacts and activities.'

Indefatigable to the last, de Wohl continued to issue reports on how the war would play out. Hitler's astrologers, he claimed, would not be able to predict victory for the Third Reich. 'This is the first year of the war in which really strong aspects are shown in the charts of King George VI and of Churchill, and a few really bad ones are in Hitler's chart.' But intriguingly, at the end of 1942, he had picked up the rumour that units of the Kriegsmarine were carrying 'devices of an astrological nature' which revealed that there was one last gasp for astrology in Nazi Germany.

Mysterious, brooding and certainly paranoid, Adolf Hitler was no slouch when it came to plots and deceptions. 'He was,' as one historian has rightly remarked, 'extraordinarily quick to spot a trick.' Despite their false start, the artful dodgers of Storey's Gate would become highly adept at playing on the prejudices and curious beliefs of the German High Command. Though Hitler considered himself a strategist beyond compare, he would ultimately be defeated by tricks as old as war itself which left him 'puzzled as well as beaten'.

Just one example – for which Dennis Wheatley was inordinately proud – was when, at the start of 1944, the British military mission in Stockholm was spotted measuring the heights and widths of tunnels along the main rail routes to Oslo, they took care to let press photographers know about it. This was quickly followed by reports that Allied military engineers were making enquiries about load capacities of rolling stock and that British air personnel were inspecting Stockholm runways. There were also many rumours within the diplomatic community that the Allies were negotiating for transit rights to Swedish islands which faced the German Baltic. And when the press reported that the Swedish populace should start digging air-raid shelters and stock up on emergency supplies, it was clear that something was afoot.

Was Sweden about to ditch its neutrality?

Stockholm, like Lisbon before it, would now become the focus of a number of murky episodes in the secret war, which, in another historian's estimation, involved 'secret negotiations, trade concessions, economic pressure and financial skulduggery'. All formed part of a wave of deliberate provocation and deception that were part of a wider Allied effort to make it appear as though the Swedish government was about to enter the war on the Allied side. Known formally as Operation Graffham, its purpose was 'to induce the enemy to believe that we are enlisting the active co-operation of Sweden in connection with British and Russian contemplated operations against northern Norway in the spring of this year'.

It was also suggested that after a dash for the Swedish ore fields, the Allies would invade Norway as a precursor to the main landing. This deliberately planted notion formed part of the greater deception operation known as Fortitude North, which jacketed the real intentions surrounding D-Day in what Churchill once famously termed 'a bodyguard of lies'. It worked by playing on one of the Führer's pet fears that an invasion of Scandinavia was imminent.

'I've always told you those pig-headed British would go back to Norway,' Adolf Hitler screamed after falling for one such deception. 'Reinforce it with two divisions at once.' The result was that the Führer continued to pour more money, men and weapons into Norway than he ever would do in Normandy. Nearly 500,000 troops remained on station there, along with 90,000 naval and 60,000 Luftwaffe personnel. They were thus not available to repel the Allied assault forces when they came ashore on Normandy's beaches and were not able to alter the course of history in Adolf Hitler's favour.

In the meantime, Tom Delmer prospered, not least with another equally influential 'black' radio station, *Soldatensender* Calais (Calais Armed Forces

Radio Station) supposedly broadcasting at the most likely landing point for an Allied invasion. In reality, the station's aim was to subvert the morale of troops all along the French coast, including those who were defending the Normandy coast where the invasion would come. 'Units which show themselves smart and efficient are drafted to the Eastern Front,' the station repeatedly claimed in an effort to generate slacking. 'Promotion in France is a sure way to death in Russia.'

These and other strange but true broadcasts became part of Tom Delmer's endless fund of war stories. One colleague felt that the journalist 'had a very amusing war, but is very doubtful whether his efforts were anything like as successful as Tom claims'. But even his difficult boss, Dick Crossman, with whom he often was at daggers drawn, admitted that his underling's approach was successful for the very good reason that 'black propaganda seems to have an irresistible attraction for those in authority'.

Agnes Bernelle went on to become a cabaret singer of some note.

Perhaps the greater irony is that when she later applied to the BBC Overseas Service to work as a broadcaster, she was rejected. By then Agnes had married Desmond Leslie, and lived a bohemian – and at times trying – life in London for most of the fifties. In time, they moved to Dublin, divorced and Agnes established herself on the arts scene in the Irish capital. She died in 1999, after which one obituary noted that nobody could fail 'to be impressed by her courage, energy and dedication, qualities which she showed all her life'.

Atlantik Sender also represented the highwater mark of Ian Fleming's career as a propagandist. At the start of 1943, Uncle John, as Fleming usually referred to Admiral Godfrey when he wasn't around, had been dismissed without warning as head of the Naval Intelligence Division. Considered opinion was that the Director of Naval Intelligence had stirred up 'a pretty angry hornets' nest' thanks to his impatience and general tactlessness. When he was absent, it was noted that the deliberations of the Joint Intelligence Committee seemed to pass along more smoothly than when he was present.

Never one of the prime minister's favourites, Admiral Godfrey was dispatched – dismissed in some accounts because of his acerbic nature – to become Flag Officer of the Royal Indian Navy, where it was his misfortune to preside over a mutiny during which he went on the air with an order to 'Submit or perish'.

Uncle John's 'special assistant' had been at something of a loss since the departure of his best advocate and mentor. Subsequently, he devoted his attentions to what became known as his Red Indians (a phrase that, curiously, resonates in many of the Bond novels when 007 sometime obliquely referred to his own wartime secret service). Inspired by German intelligence commandos, Fleming became senior commander for a detachment of personnel who accompanied troops on raids to obtain ciphers, weapons and useful information. Fleming helped in the meticulous planning for what was better known as an Intelligence Assault Force.

What was also formally known as 30 Assault Unit operated under the direct authority of the Director of Naval Intelligence. Fleming's Red Indians, as they were better known, would move in with or immediately behind front line troops to secure as many secret documents as possible from naval – and, in time, other military – institutions. Its ranks swelled from the toughest of recruits who had shown that they could survive a choice selection of run marches and assault courses, as well as parachute and glider training, safe cracking and explosives training.

It was clear that James Bond would have passed those tests.

Commander Ian Fleming, however, remained resolutely based at the admiralty and again, despite specious claims, he was never at the forefront of the Red Indians in the field. So Ian Fleming had to settle for more vicarious participation in the secret war. During the final stages of the war, he watched with an almost paternal pride as his subordinates went in with the first troops to return to Europe.

Commander Fleming was still invaluable as his new boss's fixer, but as his most recent biographer has noted, 'Room 39 was no longer the buzzing ideas factory it had once been.' There he began to daydream, doodling designs for a holiday home in the sun and squirreling notes for what he called the spy story to end all spy stories. Both would be combined in Jamaica, which he would shortly visit to investigate strange rumours about Hermann Goering's Swedish brother-in-law and suspected U-boat activity.

Within a matter of weeks, Ian Fleming had bought a property on the old donkey racetrack at Oracabessa on the north coast of the island. Fleming christened it Goldeneye after the sabotage network which he had planned in the event of a German invasion of Iberia. As for the spy story to end all spy stories, Ian Fleming's wartime escapades would provide an endless well of inspiration and, seven years later, on the eve of his marriage, he sat down at his desk and started a story about a British spy set in a casino. It was called *Casino Royale* and some said he had a great future as a thriller writer.

Despite the crackdown on astrology after Hess's defection, there were still reportedly outbreaks of mysticism throughout the Third Reich. One astrologer, Wilhelm Wulff, who had been incarcerated in Fuhlsbüttel Prison after the Aktion Hess in the early spring of 1941, had been released to work in a naval institute for the strangest of reasons. Even after officially locking up most occultic practitioners, Nazi officials continued to employ mystics to help in the search for Allied submarines. In this, they used pendulums instead of dowsing rods.

By studying the way in which a pendulum swung, concealed objects such as hidden treasure or missing people, it was said, could be found. The Germans often did this over a map (which was how the Munich physician predicted the presence of Jews). The astrologer's own expertise extended to a particular Indian pendulum known as Tattua. 'Day in, day out, the pendulum practitioners squatted with their arms stretched out over nautical charts,' Wulff would write. 'The results were, of course, pitiful.'

After Benito Mussolini was deposed in September 1943 – which, oddly, Louis de Wohl had predicted ('This seems an absolutely crucial month for Italy with strong bad aspects for the King of Italy, the Crown Prince and Mussolini') – another group of German astrologers were locked into a house in Wannsee by the SS to see if they could predict where *Il Duce* was located. As late as July 1944, a secret report circulated by the SD (the SS intelligence service) noted that there had been 'a considerable increase in all possible forms of prophecy about the future course of the war'.

Clairvoyancy, astrology and numerology were mentioned.

And there now came the unexpected rise of Wilhelm Wulff.

'All intellectual, natural and supernatural sources of power – from modern technology to medieval black magic and from the teachings of Pythagoras to the Faustian pentagram incantation – were to be exploited in the interests of final victory,' Wulff would write in the late sixties.

When he was later introduced to the Reichsführer-SS, he was described as a professor of Sanskrit and, strangely, a student of poisons. Rather than helping Heinrich Himmler devise new ways of killing, the introduction had been effected so that the self-styled mystic could advise him on Indian matters and their importance in the curious genesis of the Nazi mythology.

Wulff's elevation to the inner sanctum had been dictated not by the stars but for reasons of political expediency: as an astrologer, it was hoped he would be in a position to influence Himmler to assassinate Hitler. The Reichsführer-SS, who in one historian's assessment 'seldom took any steps without first consulting his horoscope', was keen to learn about Wulff's work.

The astrologer first met Himmler in the late spring of 1944 in the horribly appropriate surroundings of a gothic castle in the Alpine mountains surrounding Salzburg. Now, in the final months of the 'thousand year Reich', Wulff would come to play a strange and surreal role in the machinations of peace feelers, which were tentatively being extended towards the Allies in the Swedish capital, a city that was 'a flypaper for peace feelers'.

By now, it was all over for the occult on the Allied side of the fighting.

At the end of 1943, MI6 learned that Louis de Wohl had played his 'usual line of mystery man' when approaching a fellow Hungarian and claimed he was an aristocrat. 'When addressed in Hungarian it was, of course, found that he could neither speak nor understand it.'

The reading of his mail revealed that he had also been in contact with other cosmopolitan émigrés of whom the authorities were highly suspicious, though they were, ultimately, pretty harmless. But in June 1943, they discovered something more worrying. He had been in contact with a member of the White Hawk Circle – a group of spiritualists who met at 72 Queen's Gate – and one member became suspicious. He informed MI5 at the end of May that de Wohl was 'an indiscreet talker and a bumptious seeker after notoriety'.

Though posing 'as a professional astrologer', it seemed that the informant learned de Wohl 'from time to time gives out he is working for the secret service'. Even more worrying, this unnamed informant feared something else: 'If not actually the same "family" as the dark man he might definitely become related to him and his business.'

Though not immediately obvious, the 'dark man' was Aleister Crowley.

'My firm think he may be very slightly mental,' the White Hawk Circle spiritualist noted, 'but the slightly abnormal are just the dark man's cup of tea.'

This is one of the few references to the Great Beast in all the haul of MI5 files which have been released in recent years. By now, in 1943, Crowley had suffered a bout of pneumonia in Torquay, recovered and, according to his diaries, on 17 and 18 June, went to visit an old friend. He entered Evan Morgan's 'magick room' and says very little else about what they did. Early the following year, Crowley moved back to London. By then, at the start of 1944, it didn't need an astrologer to see which way the war was headed. But strangely, a couple of seers were involved in fairly brisk traffic involving secret negotiations within Nazi Germany concerning the very conduct of the war and bringing it to a swift conclusion.

At the start of 1944 came an event which sent shockwaves through the secret world and beyond, when Erich Vermehren, who was the Abwehr resident in Istanbul (a scion of a Lubeck family who had twice been awarded a Rhodes scholarship to Oxford), defected with his wife. Within hours, the news was deliberately leaked via the Associated Press that they 'were disgusted with Nazi brutality'. 'He is said to possess detailed information of the greatest value.'

It was certainly the final straw for the Führer so far as the Abwehr was concerned. When Admiral Wilhelm Canaris went to visit Hitler later that same week, he flew into a rage when the head of intelligence said that he was 'only transmitting the reports of my agents'.

'Your agents?' The Führer screamed. 'Are they as trustworthy as the Vermehrens?'

Hitler was so incensed that in some accounts he actually knocked over a table. Within days, the admiral was removed, effectively pensioned off while most of his underlings were dismissed and the Abwehr itself was merged with the SS *Sicherheitsdienst*. With Admiral Canaris's dismissal, Walter Schellenberg now took the prime position as head of the Nazi intelligence apparatus. Schellenberg, in a contemporary conversation, said that eight of the best German agents had defected as they were not gentlemen.

'He proposed to train men of good repute to act as agents and announced that he would endeavour to place espionage on a higher social footing.'

As with most activities in Nazi Germany, the amalgamation of the Abwehr and the *Sicherheitsdienst* was messy and protracted. But it meant that Heinrich Himmler had got what he always wanted with his favourite, most trusted associate from the intelligence world in charge. Indeed, Walter Schellenberg now had a greater game to play in the closing year of the war: stopping the madness before it got any worse. A whole new strand of treachery would now intensify as Schellenberg himself would work to overthrow Hitler and negotiate a peace with the Western Allies. And with this would come a last gasp for mysticism and the strange role of a man who claimed he was a faith healer but soon came to be much more besides.

Once a month, Dr Felix Kersten – memorably described as a 'great giant of man who posed as a harmless masseur from Finland' – travelled to Berlin from his Stockholm practice. His healing hands had come to the attention of senior Nazis before the war. The masseur himself had concluded that 'most high-ranking Nazi officials were unstable, neurotic men, not only evil of intent but quite unfit for the duties demanded of them', as he would later write.

Intriguingly, Kersten had treated Rudolf Hess in the early years of the war and the Deputy Führer had allegedly told his masseur that he would 'make history' a few days before his departure to Great Britain. Such rumours had brought Felix Kersten to the unwanted attention of the Gestapo. Ironically, he would be protected by the head of the SS himself thanks to his supposed powers; Kersten's healing hands were used in the relief of Heinrich Himmler's chronic intestinal pain.

In time, the masseur became so well regarded that the Reichsführer-SS referred to him as 'my only friend, my Buddha'. Given this unusual position of trust, Kersten was able to discuss many matters with Himmler, such as the fate of the Jews, which were beyond the scope of most conversations.

Significantly, in the first years of the war he had also treated Walter Schellenberg, whose own health problems intensified and which he had blamed on the British trying to poison him. As a result, the good doctor now became party to the plots against the Führer and, increasingly, plans to depose him by both Schellenberg and Himmler. The various plottings of Brigadeführer-SS Walter Schellenberg thus came to fruition with the most cosmic of influences.

When Wilhelm Wulff was introduced to Felix Kersten by a mutual friend in the winter of 1942, the Finnish masseur did not strike him as a particularly benign influence. 'Greedy little eyes, which were reminiscent of a child's, peered from Kersten's bloated face,' Wulff recalled. His description of the masseur makes him sound like yet another prototypical Bond villain, for he was 'extremely passionate and sensuous, extremely lazy, extremely vain and ambitious'.

After his incarceration in a concentration camp, Wulff was understandably circumspect at this first meeting. By now, he was a dedicated anti-Nazi. Yet Kersten insisted that the astrologer could talk openly and proceeded to ask him about Hitler's horoscope. It seemed that the Führer had 'the same Saturn positions in his natal chart as Napoleon', in Wulff's recollection.

Kersten wanted him to show this chart to Himmler, which would obviously help subvert the Nazi cause.

The astrologer was understandably terrified.

'You must meet Himmler,' the masseur said in an attempt to calm him down. 'You'll like him. He is a nice man and can do a great deal for you if you want him to.'

Wulff had little desire to meet the Reichsführer-SS, but having now come into the orbit of Felix Kersten, perhaps it was inevitable that he would be introduced to the rather more subtle Schellenberg. On an ice-cold day at the start of 1944, the astrologer was introduced to Himmler's *éminence grise* in a villa on the outskirts of Hamburg. Ironically, he was handed a copy of Sefton Delmer's *Zenit*, which Wulff found extraordinarily good.

When he said that the Führer's prospects weren't quite so good, 'He will probably die under the hand of an assassin, certainly in "Neptunian" – that is, enigmatic – circumstances, in which a woman will play a leading part', Schellenberg was intrigued. Wulff's subsequent meeting with Himmler took place at the Reichsführer's Bergwald Castle in the shadows of the Alps sometime towards the end of May 1944.

His first impressions, once more, were not particularly good.

Heinrich Himmler came across as a political calculating machine, 'a robot with horn-rimmed glasses and a metal heart full of magical spells which had been put there by some evil genius'. After a lunch with some local bigwigs and a pretentious discussion about ancient India, they retired to a private room to discuss Wulff's horoscopes. Kersten had already taken care to pass some of them on to Himmler. Here was proof, the astrologer said, that the timing was ripe for precipitate action. The Reichsführer-SS should take note of these predictions and 'consider it necessary to overthrow Hitler and enter into peace negotiations'.

Without spelling it out in either of their memoirs, Schellenberg had put the astrologer up to it. Curiously, like Louis de Wohl on the other side of the Channel, Wulff maintained that he never doctored his charts for base political motives nor the needs of expediency. Though Himmler reportedly said that 'the abuses amongst astrologers are very great', it was obvious that Wulff's freedom would very much depend on following Schellenberg and Kersten's instructions, no matter what the stars foretold.

Schellenberg, it seemed, was interested in 'special astrological calculations concerning the military situation'.

Like de Wohl's later recollections, it should be noted that Wulff's memoirs are self-serving and ridiculously exaggerated with his uncanny ability to recall whole screeds verbatim twenty years after they had taken place. After a five-hour talk with Himmler – lovingly recalled in detail in his 1968 memoir – Wulff predicted that Hitler's military ventures would come to nought.

'Hitler will not be assassinated,' he added. 'There may well be an assassination attempt, but it will not cost him his life.'

They talked more – of whether Russia would prevail, what might happen to the German people – before Himmler stared at him with more than a hint of menace. The Reichsführer-SS pointedly remarked that what they were 'discussing is high treason and would cost us our lives if Hitler were to find out about our plans'. That same evening, Wulff was chauffeured back to Berlin where the silky intelligence chief obviously 'wanted to use me as a means of influencing him [Himmler]'. Indeed, Schellenberg wanted to use Wulff's horoscopes to prompt the assassination of Adolf Hitler. Himmler himself seems to have been party to this, for he later asked Schellenberg about some predictions 'and in particular the question of concluding peace with the Allies and liquidating Hitler'.

As history shows, Hitler was nearly liquidated by his own people in 1944.

Wilhelm Wulff continued to provide Schellenberg with his own special insights that were ordained from the heavenly firmament and, in predicting greater danger for Schellenberg personally on or about 20 July, he wasn't far wrong. Following the July Bomb Plot, there followed an unleashing of fury that nobody could predict, not least when, in the dying days of the war, indiscriminate revenge was taken against anyone who had sided against the Führer – and that included astrologers.

Perhaps the most savage irony was that Karl Krafft died of typhoid on the eve of being sent to Buchenwald concentration camp. Just about the only one allowed freedom was Wilhelm Wulf – who predicted a mysterious death not long before 7 May 1945, referring to the demise of Adolf Hitler. But nobody expected somebody who had been arrested in the wake of the July Bomb Plot would also be sacrificed at Flossenbürg concentration camp.

Even at this stage, there were some who thought Admiral Canaris might yet survive. In the spring of 1945, even under arrest, the old fox was running rings around his interrogators, denying accusations, destroying credibilities and dismissing the claims of other plotters as fantasies. His rhetorical skills were undiminished; his evasions masterly.

But then in early April, fate intervened.

'It now emerges from confiscated material found in an Abwehr safe that plans were already afoot in earlier years to effect a change of government by military means,' said a note that was passed to Martin Bormann by the Gestapo.

Throughout his time in Flossenbürg, Canaris had been tapping out morse messages to the prisoner in the next cell. On the evening of 8 April, came a valedictory communication. 'Nose broken at last interrogation. My time is up. Was not a traitor. Did my duty as a German. If you survive remember me to my wife.'

At 5.30 a.m. the next day, guards came for Admiral Canaris.

'Move! Out!' they cried and pushed Wilhelm Canaris into the corridor. Stripped naked, he was hanged by a noose and, along with many other Abwehr conspirators, thrown into a hastily dug hole in the ground. On that fateful Monday, the US Army was just 50 miles away and the camp would be liberated just a fortnight later on 23 April, three days after Adolf Hitler committed suicide.

'Canaris accordingly remained, until the day of his senseless death, what he had always been,' writes his incomparable biographer Heinz Höhne, 'an imperial cadet and a champion of German claims to international dominance which became steadily less compatible with the realities of the twentieth century.'

Ultimately, the peace feelers came to nought. Walter Schellenberg claimed that he had been trying to save Germany from a yawning abyss since 1940. He wrote:

> It was a long and tiring road that I had to travel, a road presumably pre-destined, and in the end without result. It was not lack of will and industry, but stupidity, vanity and brutality on the one hand (my enemies inside the RSHA) and the indecision of the Reichsführer-SS himself, on the other, which ruined all these plans.

Schellenberg gave himself up in Denmark and was interrogated by all the various Allied intelligence agencies. 'Actually, all he wanted was to save his own skin,' one MI5 official would write. 'In office, he would be a vile enemy; in captivity, he was a cringing cad. In office, he would ruthlessly cut down his opponents; in captivity, he would as ruthlessly betray his friends.'

Amongst his belongings was a volume of Kipling's poetry, including *If*, with its fateful lines:

> If you can keep your head when all about you
> Are losing theirs and blaming it on you,
> If you can trust yourself when all men doubt you
> But make allowance for their doubting too;

'Have the first four lines ever been in more bitter quotation?' wrote the MI5 interrogator who discovered the book. Schellenberg was tried at Nuremberg and sentenced to six years' imprisonment but was released early on the grounds of ill-health and died in March 1952, all his last-minute efforts to save his skin having come to naught.

That same year, Louis de Wohl had produced his memoirs which he had been talking about for years. In one of his last communications with his most wayward charge, Colonel Gilbert Lennox had had the dubious pleasure of reading drafts and, as he noted for the files, could not 'safely dismiss the book as merely drivel unlikely to come to any wider notice'. The security services feared that the public would get the impression that many important actions were influenced by 'the mumbo jumbo of astrology' but felt the best approach was to let him publish and be damned.

The latter certainly happened to *Stars of War and Peace*. When Louis de Wohl's autobiography came out in 1952, one official noted that his memories did not exactly coincide with the realities of the historical record. In the fifties, Louis de Wohl prospered as a film writer in Hollywood, but by the early sixties had settled in Lucerne, where he pursued writing about Catholic saints and died in the summer of 1961.

Just over a year before, he had visited London and made what may seem like an odd confession. 'I still believe cosmic forces can influence people,' he told a reporter, 'but I believe forecasting can do far more harm than good. I'm glad I helped to stop Hitler but now I realise how very fallible astrology is.'

In this analysis, at least and at last, he wasn't alone.

Chapter Notes

All file references below refer to documents in the UK National Archives (TNA) or else books which may be found in the bibliography below.

<small>Chapter 1 – 007 and Counting</small>

1 Dr Dee's occultic background is often at odds with his range of remarkable scientific achievements. John Dee confounds us today for he was – especially in the years immediately after his death – viewed as a charlatan. That he was also an 'intelligencer' for Walsingham there is little doubt. John Dee was extraordinarily well placed to know what was happening around 1580s Europe, through which he could freely travel. It may well be that the magician's often apocalyptic pronouncements about plague and pestilence which he placed in the ears of foreign monarchs were one of the world's first disinformation campaigns.

2 In a survey of intelligence lessons from the Great War, a somewhat tart write-up comes in TNA ADM 223/479 'Naval Intelligence Organisation – Based on an historical analysis of the 1914–1918 war'. On page 7, the reader is referred to Le Queux. 'The atmosphere is melodramatic. The ingredients are spies, adventuresses, dark alleys, passwords and crime. An Intelligence Official, like the "Secret Service Agents" of romance is something between a bandit and a detective. He is conceived as a sinister figure, in a slouch hat and cloak, armed to the teeth – a desperate fellow with a shady past and a lurid future. Such was the popular view. But it was only an exaggeration of the official conception.'

3 In several estimations, Malcolm Muggeridge was hardly a great asset to MI6 despite his vivid memoirs of his time in Lourenço Marques – now known as Maputo – in which he played up his own attempts at Bondish roguery – philandering, drinking himself silly and loafing. He was, in several col-

leagues' estimation, a failure; 'quite useless' (Hugh Trevor-Roper), 'a bit of a flop' (Graham Greene). In another contemporary estimation, although quick-witted, Muggeridge was 'quite irresponsible in action: he is unable to think out the steps of an operation and its probable results' (HS 3/84, note 25 May 1943). See also E.D.R. Harrison, 'Something beautiful for C' in *War, Resistance and Intelligence, Essays in honour of M.R.D. Foot* (Pen and Sword, 1999).

4 The first author to articulate the mood at the début du siècle was arguably the best. Erskine Childers' *The Riddle of The Sands* tells the story of two essential duffers who somehow manage to foil a sinister German plot to invade Eastern England (discussed later in Chapter 10, p. 281). Childers, at that time a young clerk at the House of Commons, was an accomplished yachtsman who had made a number of journeys through the foggy, sand-banked Frisian Islands. It gave him the germ of an idea for his pair of heroes – a man from the Foreign Office and his sidekick – who come across a number of small boats. Eventually they realise that an invasion is planned when these boats will 'traverse the North Sea and throw themselves bodily upon the English shore'. Childers also moored his boat at Bursledon, where Mansfield Cumming was based at around the same time. There is no evidence that they ever met but it is certainly possible that they would have known each other, if only from each other's reputations in the local community.

5 Very few point out that Adolf Hitler had found a more than obvious way of avoiding the cold and that he had bankrupted himself by attending various Wagnerian operas. Such musical extravagances provided the soundtrack to his self-inflicted fantasy of heroic suffering that was later incubated in *Mein Kampf* and other writings. Ostracism, it could be argued, defined the young Adolf Hitler.

6 James Herbert made use of supernatural plots and, as he said at the time, made horror accessible by writing about the working class. 'The great advantage of my field is that you can always go way over the top if you're in danger of getting bored,' Herbert noted. He claimed to have torn the horror genre from the grip of the bourgeoisie and 'upper-middle-class writers like Dennis Wheatley'.

7 Almost inevitably, some now suggest that American soldiers may not have found THE Spear at all for the good reason (sic) there has been no subsequent *Anschluss*. As a result, a spate of modern occultic apologists suggest that what was found beneath the ruins of Nuremberg by US troops in 1945 was some sort of elaborate copy. In this version of the story, The Spear which was rightfully returned to Vienna's Kunsthistorisches' Museum is nothing but an elaborate forgery. The Americans forged it – the reasoning goes – so they could keep the power of the real Spear for themselves. Or alternatively,

there are theories that escaping Nazis took the original spear to the South Pole or South America via U-boat. Quite!

8 The balance between operations and intelligence is an important distinction, the cause of much confusion in the historical record. Originally, the Security Service was known as MO5, the O standing for Operations. But in 1915, Lord Kitchener rearranged the structure of the War Office and created a separate Military Intelligence organisation that was divorced from operations. Cumming's organisation became known as MI1(c) while MO5 became MI5. For sake of clarity, the later variant, MI6, is used throughout this narrative.

9 According to the autobiography of Valentine Williams, an MI6 officer who served under Cumming, C once told his staff that he intended to publish his memoirs, *The Indiscretions of a Secret Service Chief.* 'It will be a splendid-looking publication bound in red with the title and my name embossed in gold and consisting of 400 pages – every one of which will be blank' (p. 338, *The World of Action*, Houghton Mifflin, 1938).

10 Crowley, it should be noted, was revered in his lifetime by an admittedly small number of people who recognised the seriousness with which he studied the occult. The fact that he was vociferous in his opposition to the norms of Christianity meant that he became an easy target for what would be called 'the yellow press', particularly in the years after the war. In that sense, he was a true original as he himself liked to claim. Crowley was a libertarian bohemian whose philosophical outlook in combining sex with spirituality, humour as well as mockery managed to upset many people from all walks of life.

11 The first airing of this unlikely, but actually partly true story came from Sir Compton Mackenzie in the third volume of his autobiographical writings, *Greek Memories* (Cassell, 1932). Mackenzie, most famous for the book *Whisky Galore*, became a thorn in the side for the intelligence establishment. He was the first author to refer to Cumming as the mysterious 'C', thereby creating the aura of invincibility to the anonymous secret servant whom those inclined to conspiracy thought was pulling the strings behind the power in the land. Like so many other writers, in his later life Mackenzie mercilessly poked fun at the idea of spying and was later charged with a breach of the Official Secrets Act. He satirised both MI5 and MI6 in *Water on The Brain*, describing how the two agencies spent all their time spying on each other. In the introduction to a later, post-war edition, Mackenzie tartly points out, 'during the Second World War many more people discovered that those responsible for Secret Intelligence [do] behave like characters created by the Marx brothers' (it is no accident that the writer claimed *Duck Soup* was his favourite film).

12 C's bureaucratic skills would be used to discourage the British Expeditionary Force – the army in France – from wanting to set up its own espionage networks. Understandably, the War Office wanted to subsume Cumming's work within that new effort. 'This argument did not sit well with Cumming who regretted his dimunition of his independence,' notes today's official MI6 website ('SIS or MI6 – What's in a name?', www.sis.gov.uk) 'As a naval officer, he was less than pleased at appearing under the auspices of the War Office.'

13 The 'creole' woman (as she is referred to in various files, TNA KV 2/2) born Margareta Gertruda Zelle was the original *Desperate Housewife*. Better known as Mata Hari, the reality of her life is much more mundane than the legends which have accumulated in her wake. By the time of the Great War, she was the bored spouse of a Dutch Army officer who, approaching her 40s, fell on hard times and turned to espionage to gain money and alleviate her boredom more than anything else. Born in Holland, she became an exotic dancer, her faintly erotic past as a temple dancer in Java becoming one of the first myths she created for herself.

Performing on stage and in private performances, Mata Hari travelled around Europe during the Great War – where she often stripped with coiled snakes – beguiling audiences with her charms, picking up lovers, duping some and living the life of a prototypical femme fatale: deceit, high living, an earthy sexuality for sale to the highest bidder. An overwhelming sense of doom suffused her activities as a secret agent, which were hardly earth-shattering. When the official MI5 files on her case were released in 1999 (KV 2/1), they proved anaemic, anti-climactic and more than a little pedestrian. Most Allied intelligence agencies had latched on to her thanks to contemporaneous newspaper clippings.

At various times, Mata Hari had the distinction of coming under the suspicion of the French, British and German intelligence services, often all at the same time. In 1917, the French had her arrested after she had taken a German lover in Spain. Mrs Zelle was later tried and found guilty of aiding and abetting the enemy. Strangely, she never denied what she had done, only the motivation. Mata Hari was shot on 15 October 1917, at the age of 41. There was never any unequivocally incriminating evidence against her. Three decades later, one of her French prosecutors admitted that 'there wasn't enough evidence to flog a cat'. As her most recent biographer notes, her greatest crime was independence, wealth and 'she admitted to having a lover. Women like that were immoral and not to be trusted' (Pat Shipman, *Femme Fatale: Love, Lies, and the Unknown Life of Mata Hari*, Harper Perennial, 2008).

14 Roger Casement had been highly decorated for his pioneering work in human rights – particularly abuses in the Congo and Peru – for which he was eventually knighted. But in 1913, he resigned from the Consular Service

to become a self-appointed ambassador to the Irish state. Campaigning for its freedom, he travelled to America on the outbreak of war and thence to Germany to promote the cause of Irish separatism. After attempting to recruit Irish prisoners of war to form an Irish brigade and obtain weapons, he was dispatched by German Intelligence by U-boat just before the Easter Uprising of 1916. Subsequently arrested on charges of treason, sabotage and espionage, Casement's trial was enlivened by the unseen hand of British Intelligence. Photographs of a diary – known as the Black Diary because of its binding – were surreptitiously shown to those who had been campaigning for his death sentence to be commuted. Casement was hanged at Pentonville Prison on 3 August 1916. His files may be found in KV 2/9.

Chapter 2 – Higher Authorities

1 In many accounts, German mysticism – which grew out of a twin heritage of romanticism and paganism – contributed to an occultic counterculture which was a predecessor to Nazism. According to Professor Nicholas Goodrick-Clarke, mysticism was only ever a symptom rather than a driver of Adolf Hitler's various political ideas.

2 On this same occasion at the Hofbräuhaus, Hitler declared that Jesus 'was the greatest early fighter in the battle against the world enemy, the Jews'. Here, he was referring to the battle against the power of capitalism underwritten by the Jews. Hitler, for reasons best known to himself, considered that Jesus was half Jewish – and therefore free of the 'Jewish virus' as he charmingly called it – because the immaculate conception meant he only had two Jewish grandparents.

3 Sidney Reilly, whose own life is laced with intrigue from start to finish, was an odd character for a masterspy for he was later said by his secretary to be delusional. 'Once he thought he was Jesus Christ,' she recalled. An excellent discussion is by Andrew Cook in *Ace of Spies: The True Story of Sidney Reilly* (The History Press, 2004).

4 Vernon Kell fought several rearguard actions against plans to force their extinction or a merger with MI6 – or even worse, so far as he was concerned, Special Branch. Shortly after taking over MI6, Quex Sinclair (see pp.48–53) declared that the secret service had been set up all wrong. Its various branches needed to be amalgamated and he clearly thought he should become titular head. C made the point that there was no distinction between espionage and counter-espionage and, in any case, both were needed due to the effects of foreign espionage. This would not be the last time the notion of a unified intelligence service reared its head in the twenties – or indeed later.

5 The All-Russian Co-Operative Society shared its premises with the Soviet Trade Delegation in Moorgate. The spy ring was led by yet another unlikely,

self-styled 'masterspy', Wilfred Macartney, who was famously described as 'a pink-faced, cherubic grinning youth'. Macartney was an impulsive, former Army Intelligence officer who had gambled away his family fortunes, been involved in a jewellery heist and in 1927, came to the attention of MI5 for offering to work for the communists. The Security Service planted a secret RAF manual on him which he then handed to a Soviet contact. Macartney was convicted at the Old Bailey, given a ten-year jail sentence and later served with the International Brigade in the Spanish Civil War. Towards the end of his life, several people were quite certain he was teetering on the edge of madness.

6　The most complete and well balanced account about the Zinoviev affair comes from the former Foreign Office historian, Gill Bennett, in *A Most Extraordinary and Mysterious Business: The Zinoviev Letter of 1924*, which was published in 1999. As Ms Bennett said at the time of publication, the exact circumstances of how the forgery was passed to the *Daily Mail* will never be known, though several names from this narrative are suspected of involvement. Four days before the election in October 1924, the *Mail* ran an alarming story on its front pages: 'Civil War Plot by Socialists' Masters: Moscow Orders To Our Reds; Great Plot Disclosed'. Labour lost by a landslide though Ms Bennett noted at the time of publication the impact of the letter on the Labour Party 'was more psychological than measurable'. She described MI6 as being at the centre of the scandal, although it was impossible to say whether the chief, Admiral Hugh Sinclair, was involved.

7　More on this startling link may be found in Chapter 12 (see p.325).

8　Atop Wilhelm Canaris's perennially untidy desk – unvarnished, ink-stained and looking older than its nineteenth-century vintage – was a bronze cast of three monkeys, the supposed symbols of security – minding what you saw, heard or said – which as one biographer has written, 'had a wider symbolism, with echoes of Kipling and the Anglo Saxon world of the Great Game'.

9　Wilhelm Canaris, in several writers' estimations, was a notoriously poor judge of character. He had an irrational loathing for large men and those whom he considered to have small ears. He had an insatiable interest in malicious gossip. He often favoured naval officers and surrounded himself with incompetents and largely incapable time-servers. It was often said that he preferred animals to people, and his pair of dachshunds, Sabine and Seppl (his favourite), followed him everywhere. His love of animals was so great that officers would buy pets to curry favour or else talk about them and remind him to feed the birds on his window sills. On one famous occasion, he called the Fuchsbau from Rome because one of the dachshunds was sick. Because of the intricate detail in the conversation, his Italian hosts were certain it was all some sort of elaborately coded instruction.

10 Some measure of distraction came from his marriage to Erika Waag, a wealthy heiress who was musical and sensitive, the sister of a brother officer he had met during the war. Wilhelm Canaris rarely spent any time with her during these turbulent times. She gave birth to a pair of daughters whom he generally ignored. Theirs was never a happy marriage and given his effete, lisping demeanour, various questions about his sexuality have proliferated.

11 This was Constantin Canaris (whose files may be found in TNA KV 2/3161). The Abwehr was clannish, another dimension to its officers not wanting to rock the boat on behalf of its head who was their relative. Another nephew, Joachim Wilhelm Canaris, was a desk officer in Madrid (see TNA KV 2/167). Another, Heinz Canaris, was attached to the Abwehr outstation in Lisbon and was only ever tolerated as the boss's nephew. He was 'no great shakes' according to one of his superiors. One of his nieces worked in Madrid, another in Portugal. And Colonel Waag, who was Frau Canaris's nephew, later ran the large Paris outstation of the Abwehr out of the Hotel Lutetia on the Boulevard Raspail.

12 In today's world, where complete strangers telephoning from call centres greet you as their long lost friends, the use of such nicknames is often misunderstood. Throughout the war years, it was common for people to refer to even their closest friends by their surnames. Nicknames were, as Noel Annan points out (note, p. 7 of *Changing Enemies*), 'used as a gesture towards informality, particularly in the Army and Navy'.

13 In some accounts, Stewart Menzies is said to have joined MI6 then. The confusion comes from the fact that both MI5 and MI6 routinely sent officers on attachment to the British Expeditionary Force. In Menzies's case, it was the other way around: he was a BEF officer on attachment to a collateral branch of Military Intelligence. At the time, Cumming's agency was subbranch (a) of Military Intelligence 1, one of four divisions under the nominal control of the Director of Military Intelligence. In later years, when opinion was sharply divided about his effectiveness, Stewart Menzies' bravery was never brought into question. What this citation for the Distinguished Service Order didn't spell out is that the Life Guards had been virtually decimated during the November 1914 salient at Ypres. Nearly a million men were either killed or maimed.

14 When, in the late sixties, Sir Stewart was first identified as the wartime chief of MI6, in the aftermath of the defection of Kim Philby, one of his leading critics was the Oxford historian Hugh Trevor-Roper. 'He was a bad judge of men and drew his personal advisers from a painfully limited social circle,' Trevor-Roper noted. However critical many were of the organisation ('it was not a rational extension of an efficient bureaucracy of information', in Trevor-Roper's estimation), most regarded the chief with respect. He was

personally considerate and 'patently just, patently honest' (p. 72, *The Philby Affair*, Kimber, 1968). That point was echoed in the recent authorised history which termed the new chief a fundamentally honest man 'where a dishonest one might have been disastrous'.

15 A certain scurrilousness surrounded Stewart Menzies' royal connections which he sometimes positively encouraged. There were whispers that he was an illegitimate son of the king's (because he never mentioned his father in his *Who's Who* entry) and Stewart Menzies later divorced his first wife on the grounds of adultery. After his father's death in 1910, his mother, Lady Susannah, remarried. Lieutenant Colonel George Holford was granted that most illustrious of titles, a Silver Stick, whose function was to stand close to the sovereign's person to protect him or her from danger. Dating from Tudor times, its name derives from the staff of office which had a gold or silver head. Holford – unlike Stewart's real father's somewhat raffish reputation and nickname of 'Hellfire Jack' – was solidly dependable and became an equerry to successive monarchs. Fairly quickly, his mother became a lady-in-waiting to Queen Mary and soon, on his first marriage, Stewart married into another family with connections. His new father-in-law had been an intimate of the Prince of Wales (in whose set his parents also ran).

CHAPTER 3 – THE DEVIL IN THE DETAILS

1 It is a curious fact that the undoubted maestro of British deception activities who was later based in the Middle East, Colonel Dudley Clarke, was arrested in Madrid in 1941 for much the same reasons: he was caught dressed in women's clothes. Though Clarke claimed it was part of an elaborate deception, the discomfiture from his arrest and photograph in feminine attire – which extended to his wearing of a brassiere and pants –was curiously not exploited by the Spanish security authorities who were close to the Abwehr.

2 Known as Section VII, it would form part of the Reich Main Security Office (RSHA), which had been founded by Reinhard Heydrich and now included all the various arms of the police state – the Gestapo, the Kripo and the *Sicherheitsdienst*.

3 Much of the mystery surrounding these years comes from the fact many of the sources are anecdotal. For example, a writer called Porter refers to a McGill and gets other names wrong even when mentioning Knight. John Hope in his 1994 paper veers on the side of him being fascistic.

4 In the last year of Gwladys's life, Knight had started work on a thriller, which even his sympathetic biographer calls 'a dire mixture of Dashiell Hammett and Mickey Spillane, tinged with John Buchan'. A typical passage from *Crime Cargo* (Philip Allan, 1934), reads almost beyond parody:

McGurk raised himself up on his elbow, his pig-eyes already glazing, the breath whistling in his throat.

'You've got me – ye treacherous dago,' he gasped. Then he fell back, blood running from his mouth.

Chapter 4 – From Russia, With Condoms

1 In 1961, Commander Anthony Courtney, a friend of Fleming's, was compromised in the very same room with a younger femme fatale as part of what was widely seen as a honeytrap, when he was photographed with an Intourist guide. Three years later it led to a scandal that saw the end of Courtney's political career, as a kind of curious coda to the Profumo affair.

2 Behind the scenes, the former DNI continued to give the latest incumbent good advice. Where Reggie Hall was secretive and enjoyed splendid intrigue, John Godfrey knew how to delegate and consulted as widely as possible.

3 In several accounts, Max Knight is taken to be the role model for M, a notion first aired by Anthony Masters in *The Man Who Was M*. While Knight did run what was sometimes termed M Section, he was never known as M. It is not clear how well Ian Fleming knew him and, in any case, the crusty admiral of Fleming's later creation is clearly based more on Admiral Godfrey than the bohemian Maxwell Knight.

4 Mata Hari was not alone. After the Great War, a number of women came forward who spun extraordinary tales of their involvement in all sorts of clandestine activities, all of which can easily be dismissed as fantasy. The Special Operations Executive employed any number of female agents whose various mishaps led to murders and massacres due to the Executive's almost criminal level of negligence.

In one account, when Wilhelm Canaris was told about a Second World War agent who had fallen for a Belgian woman and told her of his forthcoming mission, he merely twinkled: '[It's] what I always say: there's trouble as soon as you let women get into espionage affairs' (Wighton & Peis, pp. 76–7). Some writers have gone further to suggest that Mata Hari had an affair with Admiral Canaris, which can easily be dismissed as a myth thanks to the release of her MI5 files (see for example, Nigel West's *Counterfeit Spies*).

5 As an interesting aside, many Bond girls in the films are also fish. That was the tongue-in-cheek view of the late Alexander Cockburn in an amusing essay, 'James Bond at 25' in *American Film* in 1987. This association with the sea began with the first film in 1962 when Honey Rider (played by Ursula Andress) 'comes up out of the sea in *Dr. No* in one of the most success-

ful associations of woman with water since Botticelli stood Venus up on a clamshell'. Bond himself, Cockburn also pointed out, in subsequent films was often found in either cold water or snow. Trying to compensate for what Cockburn termed 'the distraught psychic landscapes of the books', the filmmakers often filmed underwater where the movies 'take on the surreal texture of a Max Ernst painting'.

6   In some accounts, it seems as though Admiral Godfrey and NID were running some sort of shadow secret service. From the outset, the admiral wanted to ensure that the Naval Intelligence Division extended its nominal brief to co-ordinate information about the war at sea. Yet it should be noted that Godfrey's main enemies were Admirals Räder and Dönitz, not Canaris and the Abwehr. For this, he created the Operational Intelligence Centre to co-ordinate all sources of information about the Kriegsmarine, which became critically important in the later fight against the U-boats.

7   Operation Ruthless was outlined in a memo from Ian Fleming to the DNI on 12 September 1940, interestingly at the same time as Naval Intelligence started to consider astrology:

> I suggest we obtain the loot by the following means:
> 1. Obtain from Air Ministry an air-worthy German bomber.
> 2. Pick a tough crew of five, including a pilot, W/T operator and word-perfect German speaker. Dress them in German Air Force uniform, add blood and bandages to suit.
> 3. Crash plane in the Channel after making S.O.S. to rescue service in P/L.
> 4. Once aboard rescue boat, shoot German crew, dump overboard, bring rescue boat back to English port.
> In order to increase the chances of capturing an R. or M. with its richer booty, the crash might be staged in mid-Channel. The Germans would presumably employ one of this type for the longer and more hazardous journey.

8   On 30 October 1942, radar contact was made with U-boat *U-559* by a Sunderland flying boat on patrol in the Eastern Mediterranean. After a heavy attack by depth charges, the submarine was literally hoisted by HMS *Petard*, then forced to the surface where its crew abandoned ship. Led by First Lieutenant Anthony Fasson, Able Seaman Colin Grazier and Tommy Brown, a younger lad working in the canteen, they all entered the sinking submarine. Fasson discovered some restricted documents and handed them up to Brown in the conning tower. Fasson and Grazier returned to recover

some electronic equipment when *U-559* lurched and quickly started to sink. Brown jumped clear but Fasson and Grazier were drowned. Their haul was gold dust for Bletchley Park: the German Weather Short Code Book and the Short Signal Book which enabled the codebreakers to get back into 'Shark', their name for the Naval Enigma. As discussed in Chapter 12, there had been a blackout resulting from the introduction of a four-wheel Enigma machine. Fasson and Grazier were posthumously awarded the George Cross. Brown received a George Medal.

9 An interested observer and participant to these various claims and counter-claims was Sir Alexander Glen, arctic explorer, shipping industry veteran and, so far as this narrative is concerned, author of *Footholds Against A Whirlpool*, in which he discusses some of his time as Assistant Naval Attaché in Belgrade in the first year of the war. In a letter to *The Sunday Times* in October 1975, 'Sandy' Glen also noted that he, too, had made another remarkable contribution to the literary legacy of Ian Fleming. He actually wrote James Bond's obituary in *You Only Live Twice*. 'Fleming knew I had been at Fettes and asked me to fill in that bit of Bond's life after the slight hiccup that had led him to leave Eton at a rather early age. We did this over lunch at the Savoy, a lunch which not so strangely brought out a good bit of who was Bond himself.' As for the various discussions of what may or may not have happened on the *Orient Express*, another correspondent to *The Sunday Times* noted: 'I have never seen such a window not protected by bars.'

10 The day after his appointment, Channon noted Churchill in the Commons whispering to Chamberlain. 'He is behaving well,' Chips observed, 'but their deep mutual antagonism must sooner or later flare up and make co-operation impossible.'

11 As well as saving many MI(R) and, later, SOE files from destruction, Joan Bright is often said to have been one of the inspirations for Miss Moneypenny (though C's assistant Kathleen Pettigrew has a greater claim). Joan certainly mixed in the higher circles where the Fleming brothers could be found. 'I liked Ian,' she said in one interview just before she died in 2008. 'I thought he was awfully attractive and fun, but elusive. I think he was a ruthless man – he would drop somebody if he didn't want them any more. That would be it.' After the war, she married Philip Astley, who had been involved in political warfare, and wrote some fascinating memoirs of her work during the war.

12 To feed its blast furnaces, Germany imported three-quarters of its iron ore from Sweden. After war was declared, supplies continued – 7–10 million tons per year – which in one contemporary assessment represented 'a direct act of war against Britain'. In the late sixties, a debate about whether Sweden could have stopped the war by shutting off these supplies came to exercise

various economic historians. 'If the mines of Lapland had ceased working,' wrote one, 'the blast furnaces of the Ruhr would have shut down too.' The veracity of the various discussions centred – like all economic debates – on the statistics which were used. The point is that Germany was a heavy user of Swedish ore, something that Adolf Hitler had recognised as early as 1934, and the delivery of ore represented, in one newspaper assessment, 'The neuralgic point of German-Swedish relations.' (For further information, see pp 64–65, *Nazi Germany and Neutral Europe*, Christian Leintz, Manchester University Press, 2000).

CHAPTER 5 – EXPLOSIVE FORCES

1 The former Käthe Kartekamp, a seamstress, was another victim. Walter Schellenberg complained of her carelessness, her frumpiness and – so far as an up and coming bureaucrat was concerned – the worse things of all, poor spelling, grammar and handwriting. Because of this, Schellenberg felt he was being held back in his career. Matters came to a head when she later attacked him, threatened suicide but divorced him after being offered the purchase of a well-run fashion business. 'None of you know my husband,' she later told Heydrich. 'He's selfish. He can never stick to what he says.'

2 Given some of the often repeated inaccuracies about this evening, the timings of events are highly important. Records show that Adolf Hitler finished his speech at 9.07 p.m.: he left the beer hall five minutes later at 9.12 p.m.; the explosion took place at 9.20 p.m. There were – as the title of the recent film shows – just thirteen minutes between finishing his speech and the explosion.

3 The 'Tilea affair' is enlivened by a series of often anachronistic characters, many of whom would not have been out of place in a drawing room melodrama. Chief amongst them was a woman of letters, Princess Bibescu, the Paris-based *habitué* of salons with an incomparable list of political contacts. 'The Germans are at our border,' Tilea told her. 'Give up industry and remain an agricultural country.' Behind the scenes, she alerted an MP and, in turn, Lord Halifax himself (as he explained in person to Tilea).

Where the actual warning had come from was not revealed until 1996 by Tilea's nephew during a radio interview. Reading directly from his uncle's notes, the ambassador recorded that on Friday, 17 March 1939 his phone had rung at 6 a.m. The voice belonged to Adrian Dumitescu, businessman and general manager of Malaxa, one of the bigger industrial concerns in the country. Its eponymous founder, Nicolea Malaxa, was, like Admiral Canaris, of Greek origin and close to King Carol II, the cause of much speculation at the time. Later that same afternoon, Tilea called on Lord Halifax in what might be politely termed an excitable state.

4 Churchill's crony Bob Boothby always liked to claim he was the master-mind. According to one diary account, he claimed that he had made up the story – or rather, suggested to his good friend Tilea that he pass it on to the newspapers. 'Viorel Tilea was a nice but impetuous man,' Boothby himself later wrote. 'He told me that he was determined to embark on a campaign designed to produce action.' Boothby suggested it would be foolish to provoke a premature crisis. 'His activities, however, had some effect,' Boothby noted, precipitating the guarantee to Poland, which he later termed 'one of the maddest acts in all our history'. All these themes are covered in Sidney Aster's splendid paper, *The Tilea Affair*.

CHAPTER 6 – DESPERATE MEASURES

1 As regards potential personnel, Peter Fleming suggested recruiting Britons who were already in situ, including the Keswick brothers of Jardines, his brother Richard ('The best potential leader of irregular troops I know'), and intriguingly, Roger Hollis, a later director of the Security Security (whom Fleming noted as follows: 'MI5: married: circa 34'). Hollis's work around this time has been the cause of much speculation, not least for the suspicions that he was recruited as a Soviet mole and his later starring role in the *Spycatcher* affair. Peter Fleming's pen portrait at the time notes: 'Did several years in China with BAT. Though he has not been there recently, his judgment of Far Eastern affairs has always impressed me as unusually realistic. His cooperation, or even his comments, might be valuable at an early stage.'

2 A very interesting discussion of the events of 10 May 1940 may be found in the *What If?* series of books. Andrew Roberts's essay – 'Prime Minister Halifax, Great Britain makes peace with Germany, 1940' – is Chapter 16 of *More What If? Eminent Historians Imagine What Might Have Been* (Pan, 2003).

3 Many of the stories about MI6 around this time have been distilled through the recollections of Desmond Morton, a special adviser to the prime minister and long-time crony, who had been an MI6 officer for many years. This is covered in Chapter 11 of Gill Bennett's superb biography, *Churchill's Man of Mystery: Desmond Morton and the World of Intelligence* (Routledge, 2007). What Gill Bennett aptly termed the 'Morton Myth' – that he knew far more than he ever said or did – has become pervasive, not least with his delivery each day of the decrypted Enigma material from C to the PM, which Ms Bennett calls MI6's trump card, 'the goose that laid the golden eggs as Churchill would have it'. It allowed C to be 'like a rather elegant and effective spider commanding every point of growth'. Her research has shown that the chief of MI6 'was far more dynamic and successful, in professional terms, than has often been thought', a view reinforced by the

recent MI6 authorised history which states that the wartime success of the service did not solely depend on signals intelligence.

4 It is largely due to the pen of Peter Fleming that we know what might have happened had the invasion come ashore. Given his work on the resistance networks, he was well placed to write a book about Nazi plans for the conquest of England which appeared in 1958 as *Invasion 1940!*, a spirited and lively book which became a bestseller. It was helped by the fact that various documents were found in German archives after the war, including the Gestapo handbook which was usually ascribed to Walter Schellenberg.

5 Ireland, too, would be alert to feathered friends. As late as May 1944, a meeting in Dublin revealed that 'The Eire authorities had already been warned of the possible parachuting of pigeons and special instructions have been issued for the reporting of stray pigeons.'

6 The Brussels Four were so named as they had been trained in the Belgian capital. Three were of Dutch origins, as shown in their official MI5 files. Carl Meier (KV2/12) had been born in Germany and worked in The Hague. The most exotic was Charles van der Kieboom (KV2/11), a Eurasian Dutchman who had been a hotel receptionist in Amsterdam; his friend, Sjoerd Pons (KV2/13) was an innocent naïf, who had driven ambulances for the Dutch Army during national service. Pons and van der Kieboom were army buddies. The last recruit, Jose Waldberg (KV2/107), was Alsatian, bilingual in French and German. He had never had a job until he joined the Abwehr. He had already distinguished himself in the invasion of France and Belgium as a fifth columnist, providing information on local arrays of troops.

7 Ironically, that same first Saturday of September, salvation came from an unlikely source. In retaliation, for a raid on Berlin, the Luftwaffe's attention turned to the capital and the first night-time raid. The Blitzkrieg on London began. Within hours, Surrey Docks became a vast conflagration of fire. 'Send all the pumps you've got,' one fire officer was heard to say (p. 256, Deighton, *Battle of Britain*), 'the whole bloody world's on fire.'

8 This entertaining dialogue came from the most frightening part of the treatment of suspected spies. This was the interrogation by the steely martinet who was the camp 'commandant', Captain Robin Stephens. Known as Tin Eye because of his monocle (which he was rumoured to wear in bed), he loathed all foreigners and yet loved his job. A splendid biographical portrait may be found in Oliver Hoare's introduction to the book which he edited, *Camp 020: MI5 and the Nazi Spies* (PRO, Secret History Files).

CHAPTER 7 – DARKNESS AND LIGHT

1 The *Daily Express* of Tuesday, 17 September 1940 carried both Delmer's

story and that of the US correspondent, H.R. Knickerbocker. 'Hitler's all bluff,' said one army officer to the latter, oddly echoing the rumours which the Brussels Four had picked up. 'If he doesn't come soon we will have to build a bridge for him.'

2 As befitting a ministry that dealt with misinformation, there are many legends and whispers about the building which is now the administrative headquarters of London University. That, for example, both Oswald Mosley and Adolf Hitler intended Senate House to be their respective parliaments and London Headquarters. There is also the rumour that the Luftwaffe didn't bomb it as it was a near perfect navigation aid. Finally, there is supposed to the body of one of its builders entombed in concrete or the often-stated fact that the building faces the 'wrong' way.

3 It soon became clear that the admiral had come to Spain in the company of his closest aides with the ostensible purpose of looking up old friends from the Great War. On his various wartime trips to Iberia, Canaris would use a variety of aliases, such as Ernest Volpi and, in Portugal, Wilhelm Gravig, Passport No. 1570 (TNA KV 3/3 Canaris MSS Traffic). This time, he used the name Juan Guillermo and was travelling on an Argentine passport.

4 The other half of the embassy staff worked for the Abwehr and many of them (eighty-seven officers at one point) travelled on diplomatic passports. After the US entry to the war, the addition of radio intercept staff, attaches and the rival *Sicherheitsdienst* took this figure up to 315 – nearly double the diplomatic staff of 171. In time, the Abwehrstelle would come to occupy two more houses, several apartments and employ up to 2,000 informants. By the end of 1944, there were more than 250 officers based there.

5 Samuel Hoare himself was an odd choice. London recognised that such a delicate posting would require more than a career diplomat. Later ennobled as Lord Templewood, he had been Foreign Secretary and, in one fell stroke, Winston Churchill had removed a potential political rival to a hotspot of diplomatic – and other – activity. And with regard to those unavowed, undiplomatic activities, Hoare had an unusual ace in the hole which very few of his staff knew at the time. In 1916, he had been recruited by Sir Mansfield Cumming to the Secret Intelligence Service, where he had been Head of Station in Petrograd and the first to report the death of Rasputin. Many years later, Hoare bumped into Kenneth Benton on the steps of his club in London. The older man's power of recall was astonishing. 'How are all your agents, Benton?' he asked.

6 Most of this suspected activity centred on the Galician port of Vigo in the first few months of the war. Raided by Sir Francis Drake amongst others in less recent times, Vigo was, by the outbreak of the Second World War, a thriving and busy commercial port. Yet its very remoteness made it more

difficult to monitor, not least because many Spaniards there were openly hostile to the British cause. Though he was on the alert for such actions, Hillgarth later told an American journalist: 'You can take it as a definite that no German submarine refuelled at Vigo during World War II.'

7 Because of this importance, the directive for Operation Felix envisaged German troops would seize the colony. Three weeks before they struck, the Wehrmacht forces would cross the Franco-Spanish border. Luftwaffe aircraft would take off from France and attack the Royal Navy before landing in Spain ready for the assault. Over 200 guns would concentrate around the rock, firing a barrage of 20,000 shells, followed by dive-bombers which would support the assault across the isthmus from La Línea. The rest of the forces would come ashore by landing craft at North Mole. Mountain troops would be trained in the French Alps to learn how to scale the crag-like terrain. As the Luftwaffe and the Royal Air Force battled over the skies of southern England, the Rock seemed an obvious next target.

8 More importantly, Winston Churchill had met Alan Hillgarth when he had been Vice Consul on the island of Majorca on the eve of the Spanish Civil War. When Mrs Churchill complained about the state of their hotel accommodation, Commander Hillgarth put them up for a couple of nights. During the fighting that tore the country apart, he was resolute in trying to help stranded Britons, most famously when he persuaded the Nationalists not to attack the battle cruiser HMS *Repulse* when it entered the Republican-held Barcelona to remove British citizens to safety. The ship's captain, John Godfrey, was impressed by Hillgarth's dash, daring and also his great subtlety of mind. Three years later, on being appointed Director of Naval Intelligence, Admiral Godfrey remembered him.

Both the British ambassador to Franco and the Permanent Under Secretary at the Foreign Office – who had once referred to him as a charlatan – later declared Hillgarth was effective, discreet and exhibited that most elusive of attributes in the intelligence world: good judgement. Commander Hillgarth happily filed reports to both Sir Stewart Menzies and Admiral Godfrey. And the former First Sea Lord and newly installed prime minister would refer to Alan Hillgarth as 'a great prop' (ADM 223/490). Hillgarth soon minuted that a long shadow casting over Spain was the legacy of the Royal Navy from Elizabethan times. Its modern-day representative – following on from Walsingham and Drake – would be taken seriously, because 'our prestige is still immense in Spain'. Indeed, Hillgarth's use of the codename 'Armada' in correspondence with Menzies echoed that (and to some, suggested an over-reaching grandiosity).

9 Franco's intransigence manifested itself in a series of logical but intolerable demands before he would agree to taking part in Operation Felix. Germany

should supply him with grain instead of the Allies; new weapons and materiel should be supplied so that his forces could be modernised; and large swathes of Vichy North Africa should be transferred to Spanish administration. And, most stubbornly of all, General Franco would not sanction a German attack on Gibraltar. That left the residual horror of what one biographer of the Abwehr chief has termed 'resolving it only by the Spanish themselves'. And that, unknown at the time, was their ace in the hole.

10 For the rest of 1941, Alan Hillgarth also remained worried about the invasion of Gibraltar If it did happen, he would be in the thick of it. 'I should be kept informed of every hint [so] that I can tip off the Spaniards,' he wrote to Admiral Godfrey, asking that the sabotage come under his wing. Godfrey was aghast – he didn't want his star attaché compromised – but Hillgarth put his foot down. 'If I'm not to be the head of the Naval Mission,' he wrote to Godfrey, 'please get me out of the country altogether and let me be useful elsewhere.'

CHAPTER 8 – THE STARS FORETELL

1 And, according to this contemporaneous note in the WO 208/4475 file of MI14 activities on the 'Orchestra of Death', Lord Halifax agreed with him, for in his first interviews with the US press, he spoke of 'the revelation of a well kept secret' – that Hitler had lost the war in June by going to Paris, not London.

2 A secretary to Sir Charles Hambro later told Ellic Howe: 'I'm pretty certain that we did not move de Wohl into Grosvenor House until at least October 1940, probably later. I was very often at the so-called Bureau, posing as his secretary … I had, at the time, to go there to type his "reports" to the Admiralty and War Office as his English, although good, was still a bit rocky as to grammar.'

3 The fire in the registry also means that many of the first contacts MI5 had with Louis de Wohl are irretrievably lost. For conspiracy theorists, there is a feast of detail in such a conflagration as many other files were lost, too.

4 There was a subsequent curious development in using Bomber Command for propaganda purposes. 'You have no chance. Soon we shall be coming every night and every day,' read one leaflet which was later dropped over Germany. 'We are going to scourge the Third Reich from end to end if you make it necessary for us to do so. You cannot stop it and you know it.'
This leaflet caused a 'storm in a teacup' with its political message. As Richard Crossman also noted, the leaflets were diffused as they fell to earth and never seemed to reach their target. 'It was a very wasteful way of getting information to the enemy when the radio could do so much better.' This set the scene for the work discussed in the next chapter masterminded by Tom Delmer.

5 The fact he controlled three agents led to his codename of Tricycle, not, as some have stated, because of his interest in threesomes.

CHAPTER 9 – MAGICAL MYSTERY TOUR

1 His reputation for genius was well deserved. As Ellic Howe remarks: 'Delmer was far too modest to explain that until he arrived in the spring of 1941 nobody had the slightest idea of what was possible in the black department.' (p. 8, *The Black Game*.)

2 Querulousness continued to define the various propaganda efforts. Even a cursory glance at the sub-headings in the relevant chapter in the *Official History of the Political Warfare Executive* tell their own story: 'Need to recognize the BBC overloaded'; 'Mr Kirkpatrick's Threat of Resignation'; 'PWE Executive Committee Fails To Solve The Problem'; 'Mr Newsome's Attack on PWE'; and finally 'Mr Newsome's Insubordination'.

3 To many others, Masterman's pre-eminent association was unfair because the true genius who ran the double agent system was Colonel Tommy Robertson, usually known by his initials as TAR. Masterman later agreed. 'TAR was in no sense an intellectual but he had certain qualities of a high order,' he would write. 'A born leader, gifted with independent judgement, he had, above all an extraordinary flair in all the intricate operations of his profession.'
And ultimately, it was all about his contacts. 'It's not what you know,' TAR would lament, 'it's who you know.' Indeed, such could be said of Masterman. When, many years later, he attempted to break ranks from official secrecy to publish the history of the double-cross system, his friends in the Establishment protected him. His former pupil, later prime minister and then serving as Foreign Secretary, Alec Douglas-Home, was aghast: 'Lock up the best amateur spin bowler in England? They must have been out of their minds.'

4 Better known as the father of the Kim Philby, St John, as he was usually known, had been interned as a precaution in 1940 as he had become a vociferous critic of Great Britain. Described as 'mentally deranged' in one recently declassified report, it was believed he was about to head off to India to work on anti-British propaganda. Philby had become highly critical of British policy in the Middle East after working in the civil service in India (where he met Vivian) and later the British administration of Iraq. In 1930, he had converted to Islam and become an adviser to the Saudi king, Ibn Saud. Harry Philby was interned for a year and released in March 1941.

5 Many years later, when it became clear Philby had defected to the Soviets from Beirut, a sense of delayed shock permeated throughout the hallowed halls of British Intelligence. Ken and Peggie Benton were having drinks with a former head of the MI6 Political Section. Mrs Benton suggested

Philby's defection should be made to look like a triple cross – that he was still secretly working for the British – that he was still in contact with the British Embassy. The diplomat said that the Russians would shoot him. 'Yes,' Mrs Benton replied, 'and serve him bloody right.'

CHAPTER 10 – SKY FALL

1 This discussion took place at a time when a certain strand of revisionism – called counterfactual reasoning – was then in vogue, particularly by younger historians such as John Charmley and Andrew Roberts, whose biographies of Churchill and Halifax (in 1993 and 1991 respectively) set the tone for such discussions. The Charmley biography, *Churchill: The End of Glory*, prompted *The Times* piece by Alan Clark, which was not universally applauded for, as his official biographer notes, many historians were dismissive, one going so far as to say that Clark was 'an arrogant, self-centred man who talks bollocks'.

In his commentary, Alan Clark noted that if peace had been made in the spring of 1941, then Britain's forces could have shored up the defences against Japan. An interesting discussion of what might have happened had the Nazis prevailed may also be found in Chapter 5, Hitler's England in *Virtual History*, edited by Niall Ferguson (especially pp. 291–6, Picador, 1997).

2 A later real-life plot seasoned within the Abwehr, it should be noted, used exactly this same device to attempt to kill Adolf Hitler. In March 1943, Major General Hans Henning von Tresckow decided to take precipitate action after the Führer visited the supreme headquarters on the Eastern Front. The general would place a bomb aboard Adolf Hitler's personal aircraft thanks to fellow conspirators from within the Abwehr who had provided what looked like two bottles of cognac that were actually British-made plastic explosives. But en route from Smolensk to Rastenburg, the cold in the hold of the Junker froze the timer mechanism which was set to explode in mid-flight. Adolf Hitler survived to fly again. The Cointreau bottles were retrieved on the ground by a decidedly agitated von Tresckow. Unbeknown to him at the time, a few weeks before, army officers in Kharkov had independently decided to kill the Führer on a visit there but he had changed his travel plans at the last moment.

3 Hermione had gone to war with her husband, Dan, who was now a prisoner of war after having originally been posted to Palestine with their butler/cook, Whitaker. Her reminiscences, *To War With Whitaker* (Picador, 2001) are one of the more delightful diaries published in recent years concerning sometimes otherworldly stories of how the upper classes played their part. In one senior official's recollections, the Countess of Ranfurly knew everybody, everything and was able to 'outmanoeuvre every general in the Middle East'.

4 My own researches into Dr John Dee for another project elicited bewilderment from several respected scholars about his supposed use of the numeral 007. Jeremy Duns quotes at length the academic Theresa Burns who has written about Dr Dee's life most recently. 'Yet for one who had studied much of the Dee material which has become available after 1968, Deacon's book reads like a blurred excited rehashing of ideas slightly out of focus and in the service of someone else's ego; he footnotes here and there as if for kicks, referring to letters and legend one can find no record of, but weaving a story that is almost plausible.'

5 Another 'new' theory appeared in 2010 with the claim of John Harris that Rudolf Hess was lured to Britain by MI6, using a Finnish art historian, Tancred Borenius, who travelled to Geneva in January 1941. There he convinced the Deputy Führer that members of the Royal Family wanted to broker a peace deal with the Nazi regime. Harris claimed that Borenius's son, Lars, gave him the information shortly before he died, further expounded in his book *Rudolf Hess: The British Illusion of Peace* (Jema Publications, 2010).

6 In this quote, the original text refers to the Public Record Office as it was written in 1999. Since then, all the relevant MI5 files have been released, which show the bewilderment of official agencies. There is a veritable pick and mix of theories as to which organisation was actually responsible. Peter Padfield (*Hess: Flight for the Führer*, 1991) and John Costello (*Ten Days That Saved The West*, 1991) suggested the XX Committee was behind it, while *Hess: The British Conspiracy* by John Harris and M.J. Trow (1999) suggest the Special Operations Executive.

7 There was also the related intelligence matter of the fact that Rudolf Hess's father was a retired cotton merchant who now lived in Egypt, then under British control. The relevant security authority, SIME, based in Cairo, kept a gimlet eye on him and all enemy émigrés in the country. When Mussolini had declared war the previous summer, all Italian property had been sequestrated and all Italian men interned. Their wives were left to fend for themselves, with some turning, inevitably, to prostitution. There were also perhaps 1,000 Germans in and around Egypt, with a Nazi *Auslandsabteilung* in existence. The leader in Alexandria was an elderly cotton merchant, whom in one SIME report is respectfully termed 'Herr Hess, father of Rudolf'.

8 In recent years, a curious story concerning the nearby Lympne airfield has come to light. In early 1941, it seemed that Adolf Hitler's own personal pilot wanted to defect and bring with him the Führer. The story began in Sofia, where a man who claimed to be the brother-in-law of Hans Baur, the Führer's personal pilot, told a military attaché that this would shortly be attempted. The

material in the National Archives has been weeded and contains only RAF Intelligence files. The date for this planned flight was, according to research by Andy Saunders, 25 March 1941. The salient details – aeroplane, Kent airfield and high-ranking Nazis – led the head of RAF Intelligence to term it 'a fantastic story'. The full story may be found in the chapter 'Kidnap Hitler' in Saunders' *Arrival of Eagles: Luftwaffe Landings in Britain 1939–1945.*

9 As such Ian Fleming was, as Alan Judd so accurately notes, 'a headquarters man who helped devise operations and use the intelligence from that in the field' (*Sunday Telegraph*, 25 August 2012). Bond is, his creator noted, a blunt instrument, who does not gather intelligence or ferret out secrets. But – in the books, at least – the derring-do is compensated for by the self-doubt, the vulnerability and what Fleming vividly termed the deathwatch beetle of the soul, the languorous ennui and lassitude. It is significant in this regard that the shrink character of Sir James Maloney is also absent from the films. In the books, he advises M on the state of all his 00 operatives, not least when Bond is nearly killed by Rosa Klebb in *From Russia With Love* and also when recuperating after his wife's death at the start of *You Only Live Twice.*

Chapter 11 – Across The Water

1 As Nigel West later noted, it was clear that Stephenson had been 'exploited by just about everybody who had ever met him'. The more egregious lies about Stephenson's influence are exposed in West's splendid *Counterfeit Spies* (1999), as well as his introduction to the official BSC war report.

2 In the years immediately before the war, Noel Coward had been employed in Paris in a small liaison section which dealt with political propaganda. When Quex Sinclair heard about this and was told Coward wore a naval uniform, he is supposed to have quipped: 'I suppose he had it specially designed for him.'

3 Many official records acknowledge the fact that the intelligence agencies had dropped the ball. There were, according to the Chairman of the XX Committee, J.C. Masterman, clear indications that 'Pearl Harbor would be the first point to be attacked and plans for this attack had reached an advanced state by August 1941'. One of the most perceptive American investigators after the event – Rear Admiral Edwin Layton, who had been a senior naval intelligence officer – noted that Hoover's 'failure represented another American fumble on the road to Pearl Harbor'. Colonel Tommy Robertson, who ran the day-to-day operations of the XX System, conceded that 'the mistake we made was not to take the Pearl Harbor information out and send it separately to Roosevelt'.

Author's Note

This book has its origins in my growing up in the seventies and reading all the bestsellers about wartime intelligence (and also, as was mandatory at the time, the James Bond novels). Some sort of spark was clearly ignited. Most – though not all – of those factual books can now be dismissed as fantasy. To be fair, many stories which have taken hold from that time came from people who were trying to remember events that had taken place decades beforehand, invariably without official records or contemporary notes to hand. There were others who were, alas, deliberately telling ridiculous lies or exaggerating the importance of their work. Yet deception, myth and all sorts of rumours were almost inevitable thanks to another peculiarly British obsession – that of secrecy for its own sake.

As a result, much of the historical record has been distorted. Only now, at the start of another century with the unprecedented release of many hitherto secret files, can the story of some of the stranger operations be told. Many files remain classified even today, so parts of it remain incomplete. That said, many official records, though, are often as riveting as watching paint dry. When the first volumes of official histories of British Intelligence came out in the late seventies – without names of relevant participants – they were famously described as 'written by a committee about a committee to be read by a committee'.

Thankfully, the many thousands of pages which have been released by the British government of virtually all the secret agencies' wartime records contain much more interesting material. The phrase 'British Intelligence' is one of almost infinite elasticity, but here, specifically, refers to MI5, PWE, SOE, MI (R), Electra House, Section D and MI14. The notable exception are the records of the Secret Intelligence Service, MI6, which the government – for entirely understandable reasons – has not released. What is interesting is that much MI6 CX material may be found in many other files if you look closely enough. Names have been redacted; sometimes there are tantalising references to further information. Handwritten notes to and from its wartime chief, Sir Stewart Menzies, may also be found which seem to have not been weeded.

Writing this book, then, has been akin to assembling a jigsaw with pieces that remain hidden. So far as possible, I have tried to back up any assertions with reference to official or at least contemporaneous files. Often this has not been possible. Academic papers are useful in providing both context and as an antidote to the more exaggerated reminiscences of participants. The truth, I suspect, lies somewhere in between.

As is probably apparent from the text, I am not a believer in the occult and so have not – as many have done – told aspects of this story through the prism of those beliefs. As such, I have not made use of the more partisan accounts which, as the text makes clear, often peddle unsubstantiated stories and versions of stories. In some cases – particularly concerning Aleister Crowley – that simply isn't possible. The same goes for much of the material on the occult itself.

The point here – to paraphrase Admiral Godfrey – is that it doesn't matter what I think, or what an academic researcher thinks or a reviewer might think or indeed a believer steeped in the arcane practices of the occult thinks. What matters is what the participants believed at the time. On one point I should be clear: many who did believe in the occult did so for entirely laudable reasons. Not everyone who reads (or casts) a horoscope is a gullible fool. Those who believe in other such superstitions do not walk around the house wearing tinfoil on their head. Many are genuine in their beliefs and cannot be dismissed out of hand.

It is a simply a matter of record that in the summer of 1940, the occult provided a useful tool and, in an odd way, worked. That is, fairly quickly, it showed its limitations almost straightaway. Ultimately, trying to discern the advice being given to Adolf Hitler was self-defeating. But in that strange dawn of interest in the subject against the backdrop of the greatest danger the United Kingdom ever faced, emerges a remarkable story to which I hope I have done justice in these pages.

Nicholas Booth
June, 2016

Notes on Sources

Introduction

Opinion seems to be divided as to whether Ian Fleming and Aleister Crowley actually met. The letter quoted at the start may be found in the Naval Intelligence files and the original has been located in the Crowley files at the Warburg Institute, London. The bizarre dialogue comes from p. 4 of *The Riddles* by Amado Crowley, whose real name was Andrew Standish and, as discussed in Chapter 10, was most likely not Aleister's son. This and stranger episodes about the Beast are related in Amado Crowley's three books, the middle one of which is quoted from here. The reference to Crowley's eyes comes from p. 77 of *Casino Royale*: 'the period of horoscopes, crystal gazing and guesswork' is from p. 11, Cradock.

Chapter 1 – 007 and Counting

Francis Walsingham's story is related in biographies by both Stephen Budiansky and Robert Hutchinson. Dr Dee's story has been told by many others, not least by the academics Deborah Harkness and Stephen Clucas. At various times in the last decade, I have had occasion to speak to both of them and other scholars interested in the good Dr Dee, a figure of great curiosity and mystery. The quote about Thomas Connery (later Sean) comes from p. 102 of *British Greats* (Cassell, 2000), in an essay by Joseph Connolly about James Bond. The notion of 007 relying 'on individual pluck and initiative' from is p. 47, Winder.

Material about *Kim* is taken from the standard reference by Peter Hopkirk and the background about the Boer War from David Stafford's *Churchill and Secret Service*, a superb book about the future prime minister's interest in the subject.

Background on the kaiser is from Zara Steiner's *Britain and the Origins of The First World War* (Palgrave, 2003); Le Queux is covered in Alan Judd's biography of the first C and his quote is from the *Sunday Telegraph*, 25 August 2012; 'romantic nonsense', p. 47, Knightley; William Stevenson 'spyglass' quote from obituaries in the *Daily Telegraph*, 3 March 2014 and also *The New York Times*, 1 December 2013. The quote 'diplomats and intelligence agents' from p. 149, Muggeridge.

Details on the early life of Mansfield Cumming are from his biographer Alan Judd, the authorised MI6 history by Jeffery; the 'valuable' quote about Cumming, from p. 31, West, MI6; and 'amateur improvisation' (TNA WO 106/45/525). An excellent guide to these earliest years of intelligence is David French's 'Spy Fever In Britain, 1900–1915' in *The Historical Journal*, Vol. 21, Issue 02, June 1978, pp. 355–70.

Nigel West has examined how myth and literature have intertwined in 'Fiction, Faction and Intelligence', *Intelligence and National Security*, Vol. 19, No. 2, Summer 2004, pp. 275–89. Less accurate but quite readable and entertaining is *Literary Agents* by Anthony Masters. For Graham Greene's background – and how his literature fits into the genre – see also Dennis Smyth, 'Our Man In Havana, Their Man in Madrid: Literary invention in espionage, fact and fiction', *Intelligence and National Security*, 1990, 5:4 pp. 117–35.

Literature in the field of magic, astrology and the occult contains, alas, a great deal of twaddle. One person whose writings are assuredly not and stand head and shoulders above others are those of the late Professor Nicholas Goodrick-Clarke of Exeter University, whose *The Occult Roots of Nazism: Secret Aryan Cults And Their Influence on Nazi Ideology* (IB Tauris, 1992) is a standard reference. His more recent work *Black Sun, Aryan Cults, Esoteric Nazism and the Politics of Identity*, particularly Chapter 6, 'The Nazi Mysteries', is an incomparably excellent source. Another paper which provides context is Reginald Phillips's 'Before Hitler Came: Thule Society and Germanen Orden', *Journal of Modern History*, No. 35, (1968).

The reality of Hitler's rise to power is taken from p. 109, *Black Sun*, and details on Trevor Ravenscroft and Walter Stein are covered in the same Chapter 6, 'The Nazi Mysteries', pp. 118–20 of *Black Sun*. Stein's activities in Belgium are covered in TNA KV 6/47; information about James Herbert is taken from his obituaries in the *Sydney Morning Herald*, 21 March 2013, and *Daily Telegraph*, 20 March 2013. For the general rise of mysticism see also the Blavatsky biography by Nicholas Goodrick-Clarke, the history of the Golden Dawn by Ellic Howe and *Stealing from Heaven: The Rise of Modern Western Magic* by Neil Drury, (OUP, 2011).

For the record, many of the wilder speculations may be found in Trevor Ravenscroft's *The Spear of Destiny*, Louis Pauwels and Jacques Bergier's *The Morning of the Magicians* as well as Dusty Sklar's *The Nazis and the Occult*. See also, Peter Levenda's *Unholy Alliance; A History of Nazi Involvement with the Occult* as well as Flowers and Moynihan, *The Secret King: The Myth and Reality of Nazi Occultism*.

The standard reference for the Nazi 'take' on astrology is Ellic Howe's *Astrology And The Third Reich* (Aquarian Press, 1984), an expanded version of his *Urania's Children*, an earlier look at the work. An amusing gallop through the whole subject is *The Fated Sky – Astrology In History* by Bevan Bobrick (Simon & Schuster, 2006).

The remarkable Mansfield Cumming has been examined by his biographer, Alan Judd, as well as the academic historians Gill Bennett and Keith Jeffery, in a superb biography of Desmond Morton and authorised history of the Secret Intelligence Service respectively. The speech to English Heritage of Alex Younger, the latest chief, may be found on the SIS website. The various quotes on Cumming are taken from: 'his manner of speaking', p. 35, *ST 25: Adventure & Romance in the Secret Intelligence Service in Russia* by Paul Dukes (Cassell, 1938). The unfortunately named Knoblock story is from 'MI6 used body fluids as invisible ink', 21 September 2010, *Daily Telegraph*; the whereabouts of the £28,000 is discussed on p. 32, Knightley. Biographical details of Reginald Hall are taken from the *Oxford Dictionary of National Biography*. The quote 'an inner body' appears in TNA ADM 223/479.

Tobias Churton of Exeter University – like his colleague Professor Goodrick-Clarke – has written two standard references to Aleister Crowley, a biography in 2013 and a chronicle of his time in Weimar Berlin which appeared a year later. General biographical information on Aleister Crowley is taken from two earlier biographies, by Martin Booth and Roger Hutchinson. Further information is taken from his entry in the *Dictionary of National Biography* as well as his own *Confessions*. A good starting point for studies of Aleister Crowley during the First World War is Professor Richard B. Spence's 'Secret Agent 666: Aleister Crowley and British Intelligence in America, 1914–1918', *International Journal of Intelligence & Counterintelligence*, Vol. 13, No. 3 (October 2000). There are traces of Crowley's Great War work in TNA KV 1/25 on microfiche in Kew. Related files FO/2541, 371/145230 and 371/1216 have all been redacted.

While many see a certain fire of intelligence intrigue burning behind the story, I see more smoke. Professor Spence's subsequent book, *Secret Agent 666*, is a very useful guide to the intelligence dimension to Crowley's life. Background on British propaganda in the First World War are taken from Messinger and, to a lesser extent, the classic text on psychological warfare by Linebarger, particularly p. 64; 'so blatantly extravagant only a German', p. 752, *The Confessions*; Churton, pp. 187–88; Crowley, an employee of the British government. Cross referencing of MID 9140-808, 19 September 1917; 'the traditional weapon', PWE History, Garnett, p. 2.

CHAPTER 2 – HIGHER AUTHORITIES

Further quotes here about the Nazi interest in the occult are taken from: 'faith, hope, hatred', Burleigh, *The Third Reich*, p. 1; 'surprisingly large number of Germans', p. 84, Howe; 'There is a divine will,' Donarus, *Hitler, Speeches and*

Proclamations; 'The work that Christ started', John Toland, *Hitler* (Doubleday, 1976), p. 222. Interesting details about spirituality in Weimar Germany come from Heather Wolffram, 'Crime, Clairvoyance and The Weimar Police', *Journal of Contemporary History*, Vol. 44, No. 4 (October 2009), pp. 581–601.

The authorised histories of MI5 and MI6 detail most of the convoluted history of both agencies between the wars, as does Gill Bennett in her biography of Desmond Morton. The quote 'fellow conspirators', p. 45, Orlow, *History of the Nazi Party*.

The strange character who was George Makgill is touched on briefly in Jeffrey, Andrew and Bennett, Chapter 4 of *The Occult Octopus*; see also *The Sunday Times*, 17 October 2010, 'Red Paranoia led MI6 to hire freelance spies'; Makgill's background is taken from various contemporary stories in the (then *Manchester*) *Guardian*, 15 October 1915, 'Londoners and Zeppelins'; 16 February 1916, 'Mob law and the friends'; court case on Hills vs. Makgill, see *The Guardian* and also his obituary, *The Times*, 20 October 1926.

The Zinoviev letter is discussed in Gill Bennett, *A Most Extraordinary and Mysterious Business: The Zinoviev Letter of 1924* (1999). Most of the quotes are taken from *The Guardian*, 4 February 1999, the day after the press conference where Ms Bennett revealed her findings.

The convoluted history of the private intelligence groups – more fully discussed with Max Knight's involvement in the next chapter – are covered in John Hope's excellent paper 'Surveillance or Collusion? Maxwell Knight, MI5 and the British Fascisti', *Intelligence and National Security* (1994), 9:4, pp. 651–75. Mike Hughes, *Spies At Work* (1994, available online) examines much of the evidence, with a useful analysis of the interconnection between Makgill, Reggie Hall and others.

Details on Crowley's time in Sicily are taken from Booth, Churton and Spence; 'in a period defined by' from Raymond Mortimer, 18 November 1951, *The Sunday Times*.

Bibliographical information about Quex Sinclair are from: 'the little man', Read and Fisher, p. 163; 'that you really got lost in', Jeffery, p. 226; 'As the admiral got up', Winterbotham, *The Nazi Connection*, p. 70; 'spent most of his time', p. 141, Cave Brown, *Churchill's Spymaster*. Freddie Winterbotham's meeting with Hitler is described in *The Nazi Connection*. Ropp details from MI6 authorised history; 'We all had a drink', p. 153, *The Ultra Secret*.

Nicholas Goodrick-Clarke provides the most useful summary of the Nazi interest in the occult. On various leading Nazis' odd views about the occult, see: 'The usual view of Himmler', p. 51, Cohn, *Warrant for Genocide* (Eyre & Spottiswoode, 1967); 'redeemer sent by providence', p. 157 of *Hess, The Incorrigible Intruder* (Stafford, editor); Hanussen's meeting was in 1932, not 1926 as detailed in Gordon, p. 217. The quote 'we cannot allow astrologers', p. 285, Bobrick, *The Fated Sky*; 'sidereal pendulum', p. 119, *Black Sun*.

Wilhelm Canaris has been profiled many times. I have used many incidental details from Brissaud, Höhne and Kahn. Richard Bassett's biography from 2005 is a judicious assessment. Quotes as follows: 'You can talk to the man', Kahn, p.234; MI6 assessment is from TNA KV 3/820a quoting CX-4282 dated 25.8.37; 'The room where Canaris worked', p. 103, Brissaud. An excellent assessment of Reinhard Heydrich's role comes from George Brouder, whose book on the Nazi police state is exemplary. Wighton and Peis contains much useful information; Canaris's assessment of Heydrich's character from p. 143, Bassett; further information from p. 22, Brissaud; Constantin Canaris quote is from p. 17 CSDIC/CMF/SD45 quoted in WO 204/1206.

Profiles of Claude Dansey: 'a nice man', p. 516, from paper by E.D.R. Harrison, 'More Thoughts on Kim Philby's My Silent War,' *Intelligence and National Security*, 10:3 (1995), pp. 514–25, which discusses the situation within MI6 when Philby joined; 'Alexander Got a Knighthood' from *The Sunday Times*, 16 October 1983; C's men upsetting FCO may be found in TNA FO 371 passim; Colonel Vivian's obit from *The Times*, 16 April 1969; 'such a service as the SIS', p. 190, Bennett; 'clandestine sources,' abridged Hinsley, p. 10; 'the background of many', Johns, p. 15.

Information on Stewart Menzies taken from his DNB entry, *The Times* obituary (6 June 1968) and some details from Cave Brown, *C – Churchill's Spymaster*. The quotes are: 'was exceedingly good-looking', Cave Brown, p. 47; 'Stewart was a beautiful athlete', note added to obit from Benson: Robert Cecil assessment, 'C's War', from Intelligence and National Security, 1:2 (1986), pp. 170–88; Theodor story on p. 381 of MI6 by Jeffery; background in Harrison paper, *More Thoughts On Kim Philby* (op cit); 'C rarely left his desk', p. 181, Cecil paper; 'he would not have held', from Howarth, p. 115, *Intelligence Chief Extraordinary* (Bodley Head, 1986); and the story about the king, from p. 294, Robert Sherwood, *Roosevelt & Hopkins* (Harper Brothers, 1948).

CHAPTER 3 – THE DEVIL IN THE DETAILS
Louis de Wohl's files were released into the National Archives in KV 2/2821 in early 2008. As noted in Chapter Eight, because of the fire that destroyed much of the MI5 wartime registry a great deal is missing concerning the whole process of recruitment and his first contacts with the Security Service in the mid to late thirties. The astrologer's own books contain a great deal of odd claims which cannot be substantiated. Dr Felix Jay, who was a friend of the Hungarian, wrote a charming, friendly reminiscence in 'The Louis de Wohl I Knew' in *The Traditional Astrologer* magazine, March 1998, pp. 10–15.

Background details from his various dealings with security officials may be found in KV2/2821 dated as follows plus other sources: 'a charlatan and a fake', 8 April 1941; Mucsinyi Wohl Lajos, 10 July 1945; 'he has lived', 24 September 1942;

'De Wohl does not', 8 April 1941; 'he struggled to become an author', Jay, p. 2; 'he wrote in Germany', 8 April 1941; 'an extremely clever man', 6 October 1942; 'his wife is', 10 July 1945; 'feminine attire', 8 April 1941; 'which employs 1,000 experts', *Los Angeles Times*, 9 September 1941; 'somewhat in a hurry', 10 July 1945; 'but I saw and heard stories', *New York Sunday News*, 27 July 1941.

Background details on Karl Ernst Krafft are taken from pp. 130–40 of Howe, *Astrology and the Third Reich*; 'There the SS cranks', p. 183, Wighton, *Heydrich: Hitler's most evil henchman* (Odhams, 1962).

Max Knight's career is covered in *The Man Who Would Be M* by the late Anthony Masters and Joan Miller's *One Girl's War*. While both are vivid and colourful, as several people have pointed out the intelligence background in both is shaky. In 1986, the British government tried to ban publication of her autobiography (see *The Guardian*, 'Memoirs of a MI5 burglar', 14 November, 1986) which, like so many similar accounts, is colourful, entertaining and contains a host of allegations whose veracity cannot be checked. It seems to have informed the same tone of Masters's book.

Max Knight's obits were surprisingly perfunctory: see *The Times*, 27 January, 1968.

To set his work into perspective is Chapter 5, 'God save the King and His Agents Provocateurs', of Gill Bennett's biography of Desmond Morton. Both the authorised MI5 and MI6 histories (particularly pp. 123–24 of Andrew) discuss the background to Knight's work. As noted in the text, Knight's own recollections of his work may be found in TNA KV 4/227 – Report on the work of MS (recruitment and operation of agents) during the Second World War. Canaris and women – see Chapter 2, 'Canaris, Traitor or Hero', of *Unreliable Witness*, West, 1984.

An interesting angle on the freelance activities of the private intelligence agencies and Knight was in *The Sunday Times*, 17 October 2010; as noted above, the paper by John Hope and, though quoting more secondary sources, Mike Hughes's *Spies At Work*, have much useful information. Quotes are as follows: 'he used to come round', *Sunday Express*, 22 May 2011; 'Maxwell Knight's quite clearly', Hope paper, p. 653.

Information on Esplanade Hotel from current owners and line about Polish government from Agnes Bernelle, p. 67; Klubsessel from Felix Jay article; 'Both dialogue' and review are in *The Observer*, 30 May 1937; 'gained him respect in the super', from 'Why Churchill had an astrologer', article by Christine Hotchkiss, p. 11, *Baltimore Sun*, 1 November 1959, clearly based on material written by Louis de Wohl; 'There's nothing supernatural or uncanny', *Los Angeles Times*, 9 September 1941.

The death of Gwladys Knight was reported in newspapers in December 1936, particularly *The Times* of 18 December, 'Open verdict at Inquest'; pp.

45–60, Chapter 3, of Masters; p. 45, Joan Miller for the 'occultic' circumstances. The story of Olga Gray is covered in various MI5 histories, but also see p. 48 of Masters, TNA KV 4/227 and *Daily Mail*, 10 October 1997, based on the release of her files.

Dennis Wheatley told his own story in three volumes of autobiographies, and, as to be expected from a master story teller, there are clear exaggerations in places. Here the record of his wartime papers by Craig Cabell and a recent masterly biography by Phil Baker, *The Devil Is A Gentleman*, provided invaluable background. Eric Tombe's story is also revealed in 'The Surrey Farm Pit Mystery' sequence based on the inquest which was reported by *The Guardian*; 'Missing Man In Concreted Pit', 14 September 1923; Death Caused by bullets, 17 September 1923; Surrey Farm Crime, 26 September 1923. Further details on Montague Summers, see *The Times* obituary, 11 August 1968; 'with its list of black mass' from p. 306, Baker; 'The three of us settled down' from Masters; William Younger, discussed by Knight on p. 7, KV4/227 as well as more colourful biographical sketches of him and the Wheatleys from Joan Miller. Wheatley's dealings with Crowley, Chapter 24 'Luncheon with the devil', Baker, along with Rollo Ahmed details and *The Times* Diary piece, 18 October 1969, 'Crowley novel'.

The complete story of the remarkable Evan Morgan appears in Paul Busby's *Hush, Hush: The Peculiar Career of Lord Tredegar* (2013) as well as various newspaper articles from when his MI5 files were released in 2004. These include TNA WO71/1078 and KV 4/229–231 about MI5's pigeon policies. A useful article was the *Sunday Telegraph*, 15 June 2002, 'Huntin', Shootin' – and barkin' about Tredegar House and its occupants.

For the dealings of all three, see pp. 297–305 of Baker; and Knight's involvement with Crowley is also covered on pp. 161–67 of Francis Wheen's biography, *The Soul of Indiscretion: Tom Driberg, Poet, Philanderer, Legislator and Outlaw – His Life and Indiscretions* (Fourth Estate, 2001). Quotes are as follows: 'applied to Crowley', Masters, p. 90; 'his conversation was', Baker, p. 300; the overlap of spooks and authors, p. 280, West paper, 'Fiction, Faction and Intelligence'; 'They came to dine' quote from Wheatley's last ever interview, 'That Satan Feeling', 12 January 1977, *The Guardian*; plus that same paper's appreciation after his death, 'The dean of the occult', 12 November 1977. For Wheatley's place in literature, see 'From saintly snob to savage slob,' *The Times*, 18 October 1986.

Jack Curry's history of MI5 was published in 1999 by the (then) PRO and the quote 'it was obvious that in official' is taken from p. 110. German perceptions of Britain are discussed in Irwin Strobel, *The Germanic Isle, Nazi Perception of Britain* (see p. 226 for quote).

CHAPTER 4 – FROM RUSSIA, WITH CONDOMS

Amongst all the speculation, the two standard Fleming biographies which are superb are those by Andrew Lycett and John Pearson. Tom Delmer's own *Black Boomerang* is a useful and entertaining romp through his life and times. The quotes are taken from: 'striding inexorably across', Joan Bright Astley, p. 31; 'The result was that Britain', from JFK's *Why England Slept*, p. 165; 'I am from British Intelligence', Alan Judd, *Sunday Telegraph*, 25 August 2012; 'As soon as I saw him', Pearson, p. 113; 'His creator is Ian Fleming', *Pravda*, 30 September 1965; 'Isn't that chap Sefton Delmer', p. 15, *Diamonds Are Forever*.

Admiral Godfrey has been discussed in detail by his exemplary biographer Patrick Beesley and, to a lesser extent, biographical details appear in another excellent chronicle of what the NID achieved in the war, Donald McLachlan's *Room 39*. The quote 'of the devious and unscrupulous' is from p. xix of the Beesley intro; 'with his own quick', McLachlan, p. 3; see also *The Sunday Times*, 'Churchill's Secret Battle with "M"', 22 June 1980, based on the Beesley book.

Max Knight's discussion of female agents is taken from KV 4/227, with the quotes about 'a clever woman and others', from pp. 19–20; 'We didn't lead much of a social life', Masters, p. 79. Contemporary reviews of *One Girl's War* include that of Deborah Moggach –'all the ingredients of a class yarn' – 21 December 1986, *The Sunday Times*. His intolerant attitude, West paper, op cit, p. 67.

The 'Quacker' Drake quotes are from his oral history testimony to the Imperial War Museum (Reel 6, IWM 8250, 1984, Charles Hawken Drake); Friedl Gartner's official MI5 files are found in TNA KV 2/1280 with other details in KV 2/1276; 'I can't tell you how frightful', Miller, p. 35; 'the reason for coming' is a note dated 18 May 1938 in KV2/1280; 'why are you here?' is from p. 15 of the same TNA file.

The background to the day that war broke out may be found on pp. 12–23 of E.S. Turner's *The Phoney War*, (St. Martin's Press, 1961). The quotes are taken from: 'Are you aware that it is?' Len Deighton, *Battle of Britain*, p. 61; background on propaganda from Balfour and Cruickshank; 'the results were not good', Rex Leeper comments from p. 17 of Official PWE history; 'an interdepartmental game', Cruickshank, p. 15.

The story of the NID as the 'Dirty Tricks' department is taken from Appendix G, TNA ADM 224/794; Robert Harling's recollections of Ian Fleming are taken from the 18 August 1964 issue of *The Sunday Times* (immediately after his friend's death); 'What nonsense they were', Pearson, p. 130. Merlin Minshall's book, *Gilt Edged*, appeared in September 1975. It was reviewed under the title of 'Munchausen RN' by Ronald Lewin in *The Listener* of 4 December 1975. *The Sunday Times* Insight Team looked into Minshall's claims in 'Will the real James Bond please stand up?' (28 September 1975) and 'Enter The Real James Bond (5 October 1975). Further details from Minshall obituary, *The Times*,

23 September 1987; and the phrase 'shared Bond's susceptibility to blondes' is from Foot, *SOE*, p. 12.

The story surrounding Winston's return – 'already doing the Admiralty', p. 279, 14 September 1939 entry, Channon diary; further details on Admiral Godfrey's relationship with Churchill from *The Sunday Times*, 22 June 1980, as well as details in the Beesley biography.

The entangled history of British sabotage and propaganda is covered in various books such as the official SOE history by Mackenzie, Howe, Foot, *SOE*, pp. 3 and 5. To understand the convoluted history of all three, see Simon Anglim's paper 'MI (R), GI (R) and British Covert Operations, 1939–1942', *INS*, Vol. 20, No. 4 (December 2005), pp. 631–53. Section D and Lawrence Grand are discussed in various books – notably Jeffery and Foot's SOE history – as well as Grand's DNB entry and Lampe.

The quotes are taken from: 'an organisation in which', Astley, p. 31; 'I can let you have one', Lampe, p. 79; 'I want you to do sabotage', *Black Game*, p. 33; 'Carrying an attack on a Panzer Division', Jeffery, p. 352, *MI6*. The Rickman capers, as they might best be termed, have been discussed in various SOE histories and Stafford's *Churchill and Secret Service*. The best papers on the subject are 'Iron Ore and Section D: The Oxelösund Operation', *Historical Journal*, issue 4 (December 1986), pp. 975–76; and the paper by the Foreign Office chief historian 'Gelignite In The Basement', based on the PUSD records of MI6 on the SIS website.

CHAPTER 5 – EXPLOSIVE FORCES

The events in Munich and Venlo in November 1939 have created their own myths. Several historians have noted a discrepancy in the reported dates for the two, which seem to stem from Walter Schellenberg's own memoirs, *The Labyrinth*, first published in 1952. It is a matter of record that the Elser bomb exploded on Thursday, 8 November 1939; the Venlo incident the following morning, Friday, 9 November 1939.

The most readable and useful summary of the events in Munich and Elser's life which preceded it is in Chapter 2, 'Georg Elser, The Lone Bomber' in Roger Moorhouse's *Killing Hitler: The Third Reich and the plots against the Führer* (Cape, 2006). For further background to the Elser plot, see also Michael Balfour, *Withstanding Hitler in Germany 1933–45* (Routledge, 1988); Martyn Housden, *Resistance and Conformity In the Third Reich* (Routledge, 1997). For general information on the Third Reich and the importance of the Munich event, see Ian Kershaw, *Nemesis, 1936–1945* (Penguin 2000); and Nigel Farndale's piece, 'The carpenter who almost killed Hitler', *Daily Telegraph*, 13 July 2015.

Though several people have suggested Walter Schellenberg was a compulsive liar, his various contemporaneous statements in the MI5 KV 2 files – 94 to 99 –

along with other interviews which have appeared in other archives such as the Nuremberg War Trials and in the US National Archive, broadly agree with his own account. A most useful recent account is that of Reinhard Doerries, *Hitler's Last Chief of Foreign Intelligence*, particularly 'The Formative Period', Chapter IV.

Walter Schellenberg's career is discussed on p. 260 of Kahn; TNA KV 2/95 186 pt 7, where 'meteoric rise' is mentioned; 'to train the youngster himself', 9 July 1945, NRA; 'that fatuous over-confidence', Foot, *Resistance*, p. 135. Details of the Venlo Incident and its immediate aftermath are discussed in Chapter 2 of Moorhouse, pp. 43–53 ; the Krafft elements of the story are discussed on pp. 169–71 of Howe; and Schellenberg's memoirs, particularly pp. 91–93, provide a sense of how it was playing out behind the scenes, not least with reference to the Venlo Incident.

The quote 'perhaps the most disastrous covert' is from Harrison, p. 516; further details on Venlo, Elliott, p. 103; 'One Man Against Tyranny', Mike Dash, 18 August 2011, Smithsonian.com. The astrological fallout from the Venlo incident is taken from: Bobrick, p. 286; 'There is no doubt', Schellenberg, p. 76; 'very curious', Best, p. 15. Supporting details from KV 2/94 35a; 'our number is up', Best, p. 17; how it played out at the time, see *The Times*, 24 November 1939; for their time in prison, see Best, pp. 41–42; '40,000 Swiss Francs', Best, p. 228.

The investigation is covered by Moorhouse, pp. 51–55, with quote on 'perfidious English' on p. 51; 'like a hornet's nest', pp. 81–92, Schellenberg memoirs; 'every sort of intrigue' comes from the entry of 24 November 1939 in Volume 1 of the *Liddell Diaries, Vol. 1*; 'a selfish feudal landlord', is from Adam Sisman's biography of Trevor-Roper; 'invisible inks and false beards', from Cecil, *C's War*, p. 183; Best and the astrologer, from *Venlo*, p. 57, with further details discussed on pp. 60–61, Howe; 'Schellenberg puts forward the suggestion', from p. 76, Doerries; '[Schellenberg] claims that' from KV 2/95 39a, p. 34; 'the worst and most corrupt', KV 2/94 42a; 'was an extremely shrewd' comes from the Schellenberg memo, NA T-175 quoted in Doerries.

Wilhelm Canaris's reaction to the Venlo Incident and its aftermath comes from Höhne; and further details of Canaris's growing alienation from the Nazi regime are from Best, p. 177; Colonel Z, p. 212; Kahn, p. 235. 'Fabulous, tantalising', Wighton and Peis, p. 23; 'I don't want any of these swine', Wighton and Peis, p. 20; Lahousen's post-war testimony may be found in KV 2/173 and that of Constantin Canaris in WO 204/1206. The Hirschbiegel quote is from the Farndale piece, *Daily Telegraph*, 13 July 2015. See also 'Drama celebrates man who tried to kill Adolf Hitler,' *The Guardian*, 16 February 2015; while the modern moral dilemma comes from the 5 January 2000 issue of *The Times*, with Roger Boyes's story 'Bomb attempt on Hitler immoral'.

The Tilea affair – concerning a short-term threat to Romania in March 1939 – is covered from Krafft's perspective in Howe, Chapter 12, 'The Affair of the Tilea Letter'. Viorel Virgil Tilea himself wrote of his experiences in *Envoy Extraordinary – Memoirs of A Romanian Diplomat* (Haggerston, 1998). Professor Sidney Aster, University of Toronto, who also knew him, has provided a splendidly exhaustive discussion of the whole enterprise in: 'The Tilea Affair', *Diplomacy & Statecraft*, Vol. 13, No. 3 (September 2002). Further background details are taken from Sidney Aster's book about the origins of the Second World War; Tilea's obituary, which appeared in *The Times*, 25 September, 1972; and the more recent *How War Came* by Donald Cameron Watt, pp. 169–72.

Quotes concerning Tilea and de Wohl are from: 'He is not really a professional diplomat', from TNA KV 2/2821 102a 17 September 1940; 'we do not think', Bennett on Morton, p. 195; 'We must have another one', Aster, p. 159. The various denials were reported in *The Guardian* in the following issues: 20 March 1939, 'Germany and Romania, Reported Demands'; 21 March 1939, 'Britain Trying To Hold Germany Down; 4 April 1939, 'British Inquiry About Romania's Defensive Need'. 'Overzealous' is from Keith Hitchins, *Romania 1866–1947*, p. 442 (Clarendon, 1994); the quote about Vansittart is taken from *The Guardian* of 21 March 1939; that same newspaper reported the background to various peace talks on 25 April 1939; 'one Romanian bird', Gorodetsky, *Grand Delusion*, p. 71; 'out of curiosity', Tilea's own book, p. 271; details on Krafft's work at this time from Howe, pp. 175–81; 'his whole nation benefitted', Tilea book, p. 271; 'Louis describes Tilea', note in KV 2/2821 102a, 17 September 1940; 'I know an astrologer who is not pessimistic', Tilea, p. 288; 'Louis says that Krafft' from KV 2/2821 102a, 17 September 1940.

A full discussion of Nostradamus appears in Howe and also, more recently, Chapter 11 of Stephan Gerson's book, 'Nostradamus Is Adolf Hitler'; the quote 'I realised the danger' is from Louis de Wohl's interviews with *The Palestine Post*, 28 October 1945. The French and Nostradamus, Gerson, pp. 213–16; 'What Goebbels called "Occultist propaganda"', Gerson, p. 226.

CHAPTER 6 – DESPERATE MEASURES

Duff Hart-Davis's exemplary biography of Peter Fleming is a standard reference to the life of 'The Squire of Nettlebed', with particular emphasis here on Chapter 10, 'Into Action', about his time in Norway. Hart-Davis also penned the DNB entry about his father's good friend: Peter Fleming's later role in deception work (after 1942) is also discussed in Thaddeus Holt, *The Deceivers*, Chapter 8, 'Hustling The East (1)'.

The quote 'always seemed oddly named' comes from p. 13 of Beevor. As secretary to the head of MI (R), Joan Bright (later known by her married name of Astley) wrote her memoirs, *The Inner Circle: A View of War At The Top* (Memoir Club Reprint, 2007). More famous for working within Churchill's war cabinet, she is an unsung heroine so far as the history of sabotage papers are concerned. Joan collected most of the papers which form the HS series of MI (R) papers and then the later SOE series. The details of Peter Fleming's proposed work in the Far East is taken directly from HS8/260, which contains the 'Progress Reports of MI (R)' from June 1939 to August 1939, from which his paper is taken.

The facts and figures about Swedish iron ore comes from *The Times*, 2 April 1940; Peter Fleming's conversation with Churchill is described on p. 231 of Hart-Davis; 'that slope-shouldered Scarecrow', *More What If?* (editor, Robert Cowley), p. 279; 'it was a time when stories', Milne, p. 73; The firing of Kell and changes to MI5, Andrew, pp. 226–7; background on MI6, Jeffery, pp. 341–7; 'it was not a situation to', Bennett, p. 248; Hinsley, Vol. 1, p. 164 provides a useful background.

Biographical details on Dr Hugh Dalton are taken from the *Dictionary of National Biography*, Robert Skidelsky's Dalton biography (and the review of that book in the 2 March 1986 issue of *The Sunday Times*); further details are from Beevor, p. 27, and Jeffery, p. 353; 'we must not have quarrels', Bennett, p. 252.

Dennis Wheatley's activities in the summer of 1940 are covered in Cabell, pp. 30–31; the Auxiliary Units from Hart Davis, pp. 233–8, and Lampe, p. 84; Bioweapons – December 2014 newspapers; Wheatley's discussion of such weapons is on p. 40, Cabell, and p. 400, Baker.

Schellenberg's role in the Arrest List is discussed in John Erickson's introduction to *Invasion 1940!*, reprinted in 2000 by St Ermin's Press. The story about the Ashdown Forest bombing is from the *Derby Telegraph*, 3 June 1940. The story of Morgan, pigeons and his later court martial is taken from KV 4/229–31 and WO71/1078.

Nikolaus Ritter spoke with the German author Gunther Peis for his *The Mirror of Deception* (Weidenfield, 1977), which often relied on faulty recollections. Yet his meeting with Admiral Canaris seems accurate: see p. 39, 'I got a note'. The more accurate recollections of Ritter and the spies he despatched that summer of 1940 may be found in various MI5 documents as follows: Ritter's files (KV 2/88); Carl Meier (KV2/12); Charles van der Kieboom (KV2/11); Sjoerd Pons (KV2/13); Jose Waldberg (KV2/107). Further information used here about Operation Lena, KV 2/1699 pp. 17–19; KV 2/1348a; 'we will need to', Peis, p. 33; 'Himmelfahrt', Farago, *The Game of The Foxes* (David & Charles, 1971), p. 237; Cromwell, Bennett, p. 60; the Caroli story, KV 2/60, pp. 38–40, with Straits quote from p. 39.

CHAPTER 7 – DARKNESS AND LIGHT

The story of Tom Delmer's summer of 1940 are told in his autobiographical *The Black Boomerang*. His report from Dover is in the 17 September 1940 issue of the *Daily Express*. The quote about the leaflets comes from his interview with refugees in the 12 October 1940 issue, 'Little Belgium Stirs'. Details about the reaction to Delmer's speech come from the *Daily Express*, 16 October 1940,

'Minister Defends Delmer's Speech', and in the immediate aftermath, *The Times*, 25 July 1940.

'Don't take it too badly,' Cabell, p. 10; background on Hitler's speech from Bullock and William Shirer, *The Rise and Fall of The Third Reich*; 'We are fighting to preserve', *Daily Express*, 16 October 1940; the Tilea quote is from *The Guardian*, 12 September 1965; 'What do I have to do?', McGinty, p. 27; 'a great booming bully', Balfour; 'an impudent attempt', 'Dalton Diaries', 22 November 1940; Richard Skate details from Greene's 'Men At Work'; 'I loved the Blitz', p. 289, Michael Shelden, *Graham Greene, The Man Within* (1994) and further background details from Jeremy Lewis, *Shades of Greene* (2010, Jonathan Cape).

Wilhelm Canaris's time in Spain is discussed in a number of biographies and books. The quotes are taken from: 'Uncle is here', Höhne, p. 429; Kahn, p. 238; Bassett, p. 137; and to a lesser extent, Ladislas Farago, *The Games of the Foxes* (1971), who later claimed to have met Canaris in person; 'They corresponded with Berlin', Kenneth Benton, 'The ISOS years – Madrid 1941–1943', p. 379, and *Journal of Contemporary History*, Vol. 30 (1995), pp. 395–410.

Ken Benton was the former MI6 Station Chief in Madrid and his recollections are a remarkably candid guide to what happened in the Iberian operation at the start of the war. The quotes are from: 'no experience with foreign names', KV 3/271, p. 3 118b, a later review of intelligence from Madrid; most of the Hoare quotes are taken from J.A. Cross, *Sir Samuel Hoare, A Political Biography* (1977), particularly p. 319; 'germanised press', Hillgarth biography by Hart-Davis, p. 201; 'Falangist Mob', Benton paper, p. 379; Neill Lochery quote is from p. 64 of his book, *Lisbon: War In The Shadows In the City Of Light, 1939–1945*. The broader details of Operation Felix are discussed by Brissaud on p. 191; 'sent people onboard ships', KV 3/371 p. 4; visit to nearby hotel, Höhne, p. 425; Cowboy and Indians quote, p. 429 Höhne.

The situation in Madrid is discussed in Hinsley, pp. 275–76; Hillgarth to Hoare memo, p. 331 of Cross; 'shop window' is from David Scherr's history of security on the rock in KV4/259, pp. 17–18; the observations on the Abwehr come from 'The KO in Spain', from pp. 3–4 in KV 3/271. All other Hillgarth quotes on this page are from that same document, especially pages 4 and 7.

The situation with regard to espionage in Portugal is covered by extensive MI5 files. Many may be found in KV3/170–174, the MI5 'policy' series which deals with espionage activities in Lisbon. In particular, KV 3/170 deals with Abwehr activities in the crucial 1940–41 time period when it was realised how important a springboard it was for espionage. It is not too much of an exaggeration to say that the cat and mouse games – guided by decrypted codes – provided British Intelligence with their first victories in the secret war.

The situation in Lisbon may be found in KV 3/170 81b; Lochery, p. 67; Benton, p. 386. All of the details on the Duke of Windsor are from Bloch,

Lochery and Schellenberg's memoir, as well as KV 2/95. In his various interrogations, Schellenberg was oddly reticent about his time in Iberia: as Michael
Bloch points out in his masterly study, his time there can be reconstructed
from his telegrams to Berlin (though not all have survived) and his RSHA
log – revealing movements and encounters – which as Doerries noted, p. 15,
involved 'aspects bordering on the ridiculous'.

The situation in Madrid by the end of the year is discussed in: Hillgarth,
p. 204; Benton paper, p. 379; on Gibraltar invasion, Bassett, p. 200; 'If Spain
were dragged', Johns, p. 77. Tom Delmer was in Iberia for three months, filing
stories as and when he could. His 'Slave States' articles for the *Daily Express* are
as follows: 'If they had conquered us', 23 October 1940; 'They are forced to dig
for (Nazi) victory', 24 October 1940; 'Freedom Fighters Call it the Nazi Raw
Deal', 25 October 1940; 'This is the day the real France waits for', 26 October
1940. Further details are from 5 December 1940 issue, 'Berlin's Bomb curfew',
and 6 February 1941, 'They said the [Royal] Navy.'

Dusko Popov was described as 'a new agent of high quality', from p, 56, XX
System. Of all the double agents, Dusko Popov was one of the more honest.
A cursory examination of his MI5 files are at variance with some of his more
extravagant claims in his somewhat self-serving (though highly entertaining)
memoir, *Spy/Counterspy*, which was originally published in 1974. It is clear
that Dusko Popov exaggerated aspects of the basic, often prosaic realities of his
wartime secret service and that his memory played tricks in recalling the exact
sequence of events. His MI5 files relevant to the early years may be found in
KV 2/846–850, containing a wealth of details. The more recent biography by
Russell Miller tells the more accurate story.

The quotes are from: 'The German secret service is very active', KV 3/170
6a 13.1.41; 'all the charm, sexual energy', Bassett; 'by Yugoslav standard', *Spy/
Counterspy*, p. 5.

The Gibraltar song is from Bristow, p. 50; 'How much I appreciated, Hart-
Davis, *Hillgarth*, p. 203. The various Goldeneye Files may be found in ADM
223/490; see also Stafford, *Churchill and Secret Service*, p. 125. The details of Tom
Delmer's recruitment into the secret world come from *The Black Boomerang*
supported by the *PWE Official History*.

CHAPTER 8 – THE STARS FORETELL
The real story of what Louis de Wohl did for British Intelligence can now be
told thanks to the release of all relevant files in the National Archives: notably,
his Security Service files in KV2/2821; from Naval Intelligence, ADM 223/84
(a handful of pages amongst the more sober [and realistic] business of Naval
Intelligence); the Colonial Office, CO 875/910 'Propaganda: Use of Astrology';
for MI14, the SOE War Diary section on 'Louis de Wohl: SOE and Astrological
Propaganda', HS 7/216-223; while WO 208/4475 – 'The Orchestra of Hitler's

Death' – was an attempt by MI14 to assess 'the mind of Hitler' and contains various MI6 political reports, rumours and odd statements, culminating in the various prognostications of what is termed 'our friend'. Clearly, the de Wohl musings were a minor operation in the grander scheme and should be read as such; over the years, they have been exaggerated into something bigger, not least conflating with the arrival of Rudolf Hess (about which, oddly, de Wohl was uncharacteristically quiet). A useful summary is P.R.J. Winter's paper, 'Libra Rising, Hitler, Astrology and British Intelligence, 1940–1943', *Intelligence and National Security*, Vol. 21, No. 3 (June 2006), pp. 394–415, though he did not have the benefit of access to Louis de Wohl's MI5 files which were released two years later.

For background on Admiral Godfrey's unusual interests, see: 'the paradoxes and contradictions', Beesley, p. xix; 'enjoyed greatly the company of scholars', *The Times* obituary, 'An outstanding Director of Naval Intelligence', 31 August 1971; 'under circumstances', Beesley, pp. 185–6; 'It had occurred to that ingenious', Montagu, *Beyond Top Secret U*, p. 29.

The general outline of what Louis de Wohl did in the summer and autumn of 1940 may be found in his autobiography (with obvious reservations) though some assertions are supported by the MI5 files. The quote 'careful and tactful' is from KV 2/2821, 117a 8. April 1941; contemporary reports on the Harrogate astrologers' conference include: 'he would scarcely have made war', *Daily Mail*, 26 March 1940; 'bad until November', *Orchestra of Hitler's Death*, p. 3, WO 208/4475.

The culmination of de Wohl's time that autumn may be found in TNA ADM 223/84 – 'Memo by J.H. Godfrey – 'The Astrological Tendencies of Herr Hitler's horoscope' report by Louis de Wohl, dated 14 September 1940; details on his appearance come from Jay article, 'dressed in a splendid officer's uniform'; Leo Marks on Sir Charles Hambro, *Between Silk And Cyanide: A Codebreaker's War* (HarperCollins, 2000) from p. 26; employed personally by Hambro, KV 2/2821, note 15 October 1942.

The demise of Knight's career is discussed in Miller, Masters and the files on the Ben Greene case which prompted it, which may be found in KV 4/227.

The Tilea article 'Hitler as Napoleon', *The Times*, 27 June 1941. Lennox background, Andrew, p. 235, MI5 history; his chart, KV 2/2821, 21 February 1942; desire not to add him to the blacklist is from letter dated 22 September 1940; further details from 4 November 1940, 114b, and 'Highland Dress' from 103a, 21 September 1940, as is 'idle hands' comment.

Louis de Wohl's work for MI14 is discussed by Noel Annan and Kenneth Strong in their respective memoirs, *Changing Enemies* (1995) and *Intelligence At The Top* (1968). 'You need three British battalions' from Annan, p. 4, and especially Chapter 2; *Smoky Joe*, p. 19 and p. 69, note 2. See Strong's own recollections from his own book, particularly Chapter 4.

The uses of astrology by politicians may be found in: Hugh Dowding, *Dark Star*, 1951; 'Mystic Mitterand and astrologer who called the Gulf War Shots', *The Sunday Times*, 4 May 1997; Joan Quigley, *Washington Post*, 4 May 1988, and her obituary in the same paper, 26 October 2014; 'Stars Over Big Business', *Baltimore Sun*, 17 July 1966; Sir Peter Tennant, *The Times* obituary, 17 January 1997.

Woodrow Wyatt, 'The Stars and Me', *The Times*, 21 May 1988; Copeland and Tennant's letters to *The Times*, 21 May 1988. An amusing analysis is Michael Kinsley, 'Just Ask Nancy', *The Times*, 7 May 1988. The full background to other political figures from Hotchkiss, *Baltimore Sun*, 1 November 1959; see also *Los Angeles Times*, 3 March 1974, 'How your horoscope can bring you wealth, love, success and happiness'.

Background details on Louis de Wohl's work in early 1941 are taken from his MI5 and War Office files: 'I don't like decisions', KV2/2821, 18 March 1941, 114b, as well as the note in the same folio on swastika and films. 'Invasion in May' story, *The Observer*, 13 April 1941.

For Dusko Popov's time in England, see his KV files as well as *Spy/Counterspy*, pp. 58–9, Russell Miller, p. 7. Cross-referenced material about Friedl Gartner, KV 2/1280 8, and hostess comment, 2/1276. The recollections of Dusko's handler Ewen Montagu are taken from *Beyond Top Secret U* (1977). 'You got yourself the most beautiful', Russell Miller, p. 67; 'fell under spell', from Foreword by Montagu to *Spy/Counterspy*; 'As the war progressed', Montagu, p. 54; 'sorry I thought you understood', Montagu, p. 105. The quote on astrology and dangers, from the Liddell diaries; *The Observer*, 14 May 2000, 'Whitehall kept watch on fortune tellers of war'. The quote 'under an atmosphere of great secrecy', KV 2/2281 114a 10 March 1941.

The astrologers' conference in Harrogate in March 1941 was covered by all newspapers. The quote 'the men who dare' came from the previous year's conference, *Daily Mail*, March 26 1940; 'Astrologers are unanimous', 26 March 1941; 'one thing is certain', 24 March 1941; 'end of actual fighting', 15 April 1941. 'Momentous historical event', Howe, p. 204. With regard to prediction concerning 11 May, see *Daily Mail*, 14 April 1941.

The Ouverture of Death is covered in WO 208/4475: 'we are up against a formidable adversary', p. 1; 'the successful result that Hitler's astrologer himself', p. 6; 'From all parts of the world', p. 2; 'By then the orchestra', p. 6.

Dennis Wheatley in early 1941 is covered in: 'since proposals and magic', Baker, p. 479; 'Rock has already lost', Cabell, p. 99; 'and perhaps my most satisfying', review of *Strange Conflict*, *Daily Express*, 18 April 1941.

'Sherry' Sheridan's work is covered in CO 875/910: his friendship with Dennis Wheatley discussed by Baker and see also his obituary, *The Times*, 28 January 1964. 'According to the stars', *The Observer*, 13 April 1941. 'There is no real mystery', MI6 history by Jeffery, p. 756.

CHAPTER 9 – MAGICAL MYSTERY TOUR

Ellic Howe's *The Black Game* is as good a starting point as any on the weird and wonderful world in which the Political Warfare Executive operated. Robert Harling's obituary of Howe was in the 8 October 1991 issue of *The Guardian*, 'Impish imprint of a printer's devil'. As with Tom Delmer, Howe was too modest to note his own crucial contribution to the subject though, amusingly, he notes on p. 6 of *The Black Game*, 'The 545 messy files which are available at the TNA (PRO) survived more by chance than by any scientific archival policy. A brisk gallop through his work is contained on pp. 191–92 of the *Official PWE History*.

As well as Tom Delmer's recollections in *Black Boomerang*, his nemesis Sir Hugh Carleton Greene's *The Third Floor Front: A View Of Broadcasting In The Sixties* (Bodley Head) deals with his view of broadcast propaganda from pp. 17–30. An excellent introduction to the Political Warfare Executive may be found in Andrew Roberts's intro to the *Official PWE History* by David Garnett, from which the quote 'two combative ministers' is taken from page xi.

Other quotes are: 'a gigantic waste of time', Giuseppe Martelli, letter to *The Times*, 4 June 1973; 'the nearest thing to a genius', Howe, *Black Game*, p. 95; 'If the Department's Installation', Howe, *Black Game*, p. 44; Crossman details and quotes from his biographer, Tony Howard; 'For deception purposes', Carleton Greene, p. 25 and other quotes from pp. 21–25; 'Delmer had an unusual', Howe, *Black Game*, p. 19; 'indefatigable', Garnett, p. 47; 'was able to speak Berlin slang', Howard, Crossman biography, p. 87.

The story of the Double XX – or Twenty Club – operations has been told many times before, but perhaps the most lapidary version is that from John C. Masterman himself. *The Double Cross System of 1939–1945* – and, indeed his own autobiography, *On The Chariot Wheel* – are standard texts. Two recent academic papers tell the background and subsequent history of Masterman's contribution to the secret war. See E.D.R. Harrison, 'J.C. Masterman and The Security Service, 1940–1972', Intelligence and National Security, 24:6 (2009), pp. 769–804; and also John P. Campbell, 'A Retrospective on John Masterman's The Double Cross System', *International Journal of Intelligence and Counter-Intelligence*, 18 (2005), pp. 320–53 (2005).

The quotes are: 'Dimly, very dimly', Masterman, p. 85; 'club cricket', Masterman, p. 90; 'The Abwehr in the field', p. 6 KV 3/8 131c 31 October 1944; 'The really valuable stuff', p. 4 KV 3/8 131c; 'There are signs the German', KV 3/172 116x 15 June 43; 'The whole organisation', Holt, *The Deceivers*, p. 105.

The various investigations of the secret agencies into Louis de Wohl and his wife, Alexandra, are contained in KV 2/2821. The quotes are: 'We know all about him', 109b January 1941; 'one of the other funny people', 109a 20.1.41; 'hard up for money', folio 108b; 'To the best of my knowledge', 109b; 'via the Bank of England', 109a; Colonel Hope reference from note on 12 May 1941; 'mystery woman', folio B24, 8 April 1941; 'German harlots', folio 105a 3 October 1940; 'I have never liked', note on 17 February 1942. The story of Aspidistra is told in the PWE history and *Black Boomerang*; 'atmosphere of club chat', Howard, p. 86.

Ken Benton's paper is a useful guide to how Section V operated in Iberia. The quotes are: 'By the end of the war', *Life of Greene*, p. 172; 'These views caused friction', Montagu, ISO, 25 Sept 1945, quoted in Holt, *The Deceivers*. Much of Philby, Bristow and Benton's various correspondence may be found in KV 3/170–2, each laboriously dealing with suspects. Kim Philby's *My Silent War*, though mordantly funny, is remarkable for what it left out. A useful guide is Robert Cecil's 'Philby's Spurious War', *Intelligence & National Security*, Vol. 9, No. 4 (October 1994), pp. 764–68, which sets everything into perspective. A useful popular guide is 'The Lisbon Operation', Chapter 3 of *Within Two Cloaks – Missions with SIS and SOE* by Philip Johns (Kimber, 1979). The quotes are: 'we were six officers', Sherry, Greene biography Vol. 2, p. 167; 'I am a royal parrot', Bristow, p. 18.

Dennis Wheatley in 1941 is discussed by Cabell and Baker; *Deceivers*, p. 168. 'After the Battle', p. 164 of Cabell for the paper.

As regards Philby's role, there are two broad camps in analysis: either mischief-making or severe criticisms. In the former are all his own writings, Kerr paper: 'A few home truths about Philby's Silent War' Cecil, *The Times*, 2 February 1978; for which his *INS* paper is important – 'Philby's Spurious War', Vol. 9, No. 4 (October 1994), pp. 761–68. More Thoughts on Kim Philby's My Silent War', *INS*, Vol. 10, No. 3 (January 1995), pp. 514–25, where he roundly criticises SIS and Menzies. Bristow, *A Game of Moles*, Chapter 2, 'Spain to St Albans with Philby' provides much useful background to the real work of Section V.

CHAPTER 10 – SKY FALL

Never in the field of publishing have so many conspiracies been aired by so many writers and fanned by so many flames over the Internet. From the outset, I consulted two level-headed volumes which provided the best insight into what happened in May 1941: *Grand Delusion* by Gabriel Gorodetsky (Yale, 1999) and *Flight From Reality* (Pimlico, 2001), edited by David Stafford, based on a conference at Edinburgh University. Both books provide the all important context to an often wilfully misunderstood story which has generated a vast literature, which veers from the sublime to the ridiculous. The release in 1999 of the relevant MI5 file (KV 2/38), far from laying ghosts to rest has merely inflamed the situation. On its first page, the Hess file shows that seventy-nine pages have been held back, which are fully expected to be released in 2017.

Alan Clark's article, 'A reputation ripe for revision', 2 January 1993, *The Times*. The sections from *Flying Visit* are: 'English men and women!', p. 77; 'Sweetie Pie', p. 81. The work of the PWE, Sefton Delmer and the propagandists on both sides of the fighting in the subsequent months has, for the first time, been examined in an exemplary academic paper. Dr Jo Fox's 'Propaganda and the Flight of Rudolf Hess', *Journal of Modern History* (March 2011), pp. 78–110, is an exhaustive guide. That same year, to coincide with the 70th anniversary of Hess's flight, Stephen McGinty's *Camp Z* showed for the first time how Hess was treated after his imprisonment. It is without a doubt one of the better over-all chronicles of the whole story. Peter Padfield's *Hess, Hitler and Churchill: The Real Turning Point of World War Two – A Secret History* (Icon, 2011) contains much useful, though in places circumstantial, evidence. See also Jasper Copping's story in the 26 September 2013 issue of the *Daily Telegraph*.

'It seems incredible,' Gorodetsky, p. 249; notes from C may be found in FO 1093.10 folios; 'for a moment, I thought she was joking', Ranfurly diaries, p. 5; 'had staggered the world', *The Times* editorial, 14 May 1941; 'Horoscope "lured" Hess to Britain', *The Times*, 15 September 1969; see also 'Book Says False Horoscope Lured Hess to Scotland', *Baltimore Sun*, 29 September 1969.

For the reaction of the Gestapo, see the chapter in Howe, *The Aktion Hess*. 'Top Nazi's Crash Landing in Scotland Remains A Mystery After Seventy Years', *Daily Record*, 13 April 2011. 'Records unlock secrets behind Hess Mission,' by Mike Evans, *The Times*, 11 June 1992. See also *Daily Express*, 14 May 1941, 'Hess has given us the chance of a lifetime'.

Hitler's reactions are taken from Speer, Goebbels's diary and Halder Diaries, pp. 386–87: see also the Duke of Hamilton's letter to *The Times*, 6 October 1969; essay by James Douglas-Hamilton, 'Hess and the Haushofers', in Stafford, *Flight From Reality*; 'and increasingly took refuge', *Daily Mail*, 14 May 1941.

Gabriel Gorodetsky details reactions in the Soviet Union, as does the chapter 'Rudolf Hess, A Post-Soviet Postscript', in Stafford, op cit. See also PREM 3/434/7 and FO 800/414 for all relevant original material. The reference to 18,000 pages, Gorodetsky, p. 247.

Anthony Masters, in his biography of Maxwell Knight, *The Man Who Was M – The Life of Maxwell Knight* (Blackwell, 1984), has a slightly different ver-sion, of Crowley and Knight concocting 'The Link' and Knight to circumvent Admiral Godfrey, (see, in particular, p. 127 of Chapter 7, 'Professional and Private Intrigue'). Further details about Aleister Crowley's role – which was to say the least tangential – may be found in Churton, p. 286.

The quote from Allan Hepburn is taken from p. 11 of his splendid, soci-ological study of the impact of espionage, *Intrigue – Espionage & Culture* (Yale, 2005). The quote 'He towers above all others', from *Baltimore Sun*, 7 August 1941.

Chapter 11 – Across The Water

Much misinformation about the role of William Stephenson appears in print and this has skewed – and often still does – the story of why Admiral Godfrey visited the United States in the summer of 1941 with Ian Fleming. The paper by Bradley F. Smith, 'Admiral Godfrey's Mission to America, June, July 1941' in *INS*, Vol. 1, issue 3, 1986 was the first to show the reality of what occurred. As noted in the text, William Stevenson's *A Man Called Intrepid* (1975) and Harford Montgomery Hyde's *The Quiet Canadian: The Secret Service Story of Sir William Stephenson* (1963) created many myths about his role. Along with Anthony Cave Brown's *Bodyguard of Lies*, the former was published in the seventies to great sales and critical derision. It has taken the more scholarly work of Gill Bennett, Keith Jeffery and others to unpick the true story of the BSC in America, not least with the publication of the official BSC history itself (St Ermins, 2001).

A spirited telling of the story of the arrival of Godfrey and Fleming in the US may be found in the first few pages of Mark Riebling, *Wedge: From Pearl Harbor to 9/11 – How the Secret War Between the FBI and CIA Has Endangered National Security* (New York, Simon & Schuster, 2002). The quotes are as follows: 'I have appointed', Bennett, p. 254; 'to organise the American public', Jeffery, p. 440; 'Fact is a figure', Bennett, p. 253.

For the role of Noel Coward, see note 2, p. 364; also p. 177, Dalton Diaries. The quote 'reached its forte fortissimo', is from p. 6, WO 208/4475; for more on Roald Dahl's work, see *The Irregulars: Roald Dahl and the British Spy Ring in Wartime Washington* by Jeanne Conant (Simon & Schuster, 2003) which, understandably, has only a cursory reference to Louis de Wohl.

The barest bones of the astrologer's visit to the United States were also discussed by Ellic Howe, who did not have access to any files: the quotes 'at fairly frequent intervals' is from Howe, p. 212. Those files, alas, are fragmentary, comprising: 'SOE War Diary: survey of Global activities' HS 7/216 – HS 7/223, from May to December 1941; the section 'Propaganda By The Stars', pp. 102–04 of the official BSC history (as noted in the text). Contemporary US newspaper clippings are: 'Hitler's star is setting', *New York Sun*, 22 June 1941; 'It was planned', BSC history, p. 102; see also the Hotchkiss story, *Baltimore Sun*, 1 November 1959.

For Dusko Popov's time in the United States, see his KV files and also his biographies. 'I didn't think could tell you', from Miller, p. 104; mikropunkt details from KV 2/848; 'vigorously protest', Hoover memo, newspapers in December 2014; On Miami Beach, 'I'll take her to South America', from Miller, p. 102. A level-headed discussion of Hoover's mishandling of the Tricycle affair may be found in Thomas Troy, 'The British Assault on J. Edgar Hoover', *International Journal of Intelligence and Counter-Intelligence*, 3, No. 2, (1989), pp. 169–209.

Later Louis de Wohl newspaper coverage is: 'Hitler's move on Russia', *AP* Cleveland, 6 August 1941; 'Hitler will die soon, Stars Inform Visiting Astrologer', *Los Angeles Times*, 9 September 1941; 'Hitler's astrologer sees heavenly stop light', *NY Sunday News*, 27 July 1941; 'Hitler and the astrologer', *Baltimore Sun*, 7 August 1941. The quotes are: 'After all, here is a prophet', *BSC History*, p. 103; 'Few European Notables' from part two, KV 2/2821; and the reference to Lindbergh is on p. 104 of the *BSC History*. 'I know from SOE', KV 2/2821 101 25.4.45.

For Dennis Wheatley at start of 1941, see Cabell, p. 181 and his various recollections of *The Deception Planners*. Louis de Wohl's return to the UK is covered in: 'I didn't expect to be met', 135a KV 2/2821 4 March 1942; 'not so inexpensive flat', 135a KV 2/2821; further details from note 201B, 14 January 1942; the phrase 'complete scoundrel' and reference to Tom Delmer is a later note dated 22 July 1942.

CHAPTER 12 – ZENITH
Sefton Delmer's memories and those of the PWE history coincide: while the history of the U-boats comes from various histories, especially *Dönitz and the Wolf Packs* by Bernard Edwards (1999) and the biography by Peter Padfield published by Harper Collins in 1985. Agnes Bernelle's *The Fun Palace* has a remarkable flavour of Weimar Germany; p. 39, has the description of Hitler; for details on Desmond Leslie, see his obituary in the *Independent*, 10 March 2001; the brandishing quote is pp. 94–95; description of her time see also pp. 84–86; *Atlantik Sender* is discussed by Delmer and the various Fleming biographers.

Johnny Bevan, from Dennis Wheatley, *The Deception Planners*, Chapter 5, 'Colonel Bevan Takes Over', pp. 59–65; Chapter 6, 'We Move To The Basement', pp. 66–76. The quote 'close liaison with PWE' is from Holt, p. 201. The details of Delmer, De Wohl and Zenit are from later files in KV 2/2821. The fate of the Abwehr in 1943 is discussed in Höhne, Brissaud and Philby papers by Cecil and Harrison. The link with Madame Szymanskà from MI6, p. 381; the final work of de Wohl is from KV2/2821 138a; the discussion of astrology in the House of Commons and newspapers is taken from the Hansard record of 4 June 1942.

EPILOGUE
Wilhelm Wulff wrote about his experiences in *Zodiac and Swastika* (Baker, 1975); Felix Kersten's role is discussed by John H. Waller in *The Devil's Doctor; Felix Kersten and The Last Plot to Turn Himmler Against Hitler* (Wiley, 2001). Further information from Kersten obituary, *The Guardian*, 21 April 1960. Details about the meeting of the clans is from Dennis Wheatley's *The Deception Planners*, Chapter 8, 'Torch', pp. 88–101.

The saga of Louis de Wohl and his ration card are taken from KV 2/2821 15 October 1942; the details on close surveillance, from same file 24 September 1942;

Ian Fleming's later war work has been discussed by Nicholas Rankin's _Ian Fleming's Commandos: The Story of 30 Assault Unit in World War II_ (Faber and Faber, 2013).

The final discussions of Louis De Wohl include MI6 material in CX/22699/616 in KV 2/2821 272a from 16 December 1943; the White Hawk Circle is discussed on 20 April 1943; Schellenberg's role at the end of the war is discussed in KV 2/94 p. 6 42a and his interrogation is from the PRO book on Camp 020, where he was held immediately after the end of the fighting.

For Louis de Wohl's career after the war, see stories as follows: _Los Angeles Times_, 29 March 1954; 'Star gazer de Wohl Gives Up The Stars', _Daily Mail_, 21 March 1960; obituary, _The Sunday Times_, 4 June 1961.

Acknowledgements

I would like to record my appreciation to many people who have – in recent months, and, indeed, over the years – provided much needed advice, insights and splendid help on a variety of curious, yet endlessly fascinating, subjects. My own 'occult' education has been aided by conversations with Professor Deborah Harkness, Dr Stephen Clucas and the late Dr Nicholas Goodrick-Clarke, founding director of the Centre for the Study of Esotericism at Exeter University. It is the writer's privilege to be able to consult the experts in the field. I am very grateful to Dr Roger Moorhouse for his advice and knowledge about Georg Elser and the incidents surrounding the explosion at the Bürgerbraükeller, and Sir Sidney Aster with regard to the Tilea Affair. A number of experts on the intelligence world have freely given of their time and help over the years: David Stafford, Nigel West, Gill Bennett, Eunan O'Halpin and Dr Jo Fox. Any errors of interpretation or fact, I should point out, are my own.

Phil Baker, the author of an exemplary biography of Dennis Wheatley, was fantastically helpful, not least in picking up some elementary errors. So, too, was Charles Beck, keeper of the remarkable Wheatley archive and the website denniswheatley.info, who also helped in innumerable ways. A couple of other collectors – who wish to remain anonymous – also helped provide some illustrations and background information. Dominic Wheatley, grandson of the great writer, was also very helpful and allowed me to quote extensively from much of Dennis's later writings.

Paul Busby, biographer of the Second Viscount Tredegar, was incredibly generous with his reading of the manuscript and advice concerning the convoluted life of Evan Morgan. Andrew Macklin, who runs the splendid Agnesbernelle.net site, was very helpful about the remarkable activities of 'Vicky' during the wartime years; at the Romanian Cultural Centre in London, I would also like to thank Carmen Campaneau for her help with regard to V.V. Tilea and the Ratiu family archive; Peter Fleming's daughters, Kate and Lucy, were very helpful.

The staff at Manchester University Library and the Manchester Central Library were very helpful in guiding me to find sometimes obscure references. So, too, were Oksana Newman and her cheerful colleagues at Cheshire East Libraries – for their help, professionalism and forebearance, I am once again in their debt. At a time when libraries are seriously under-funded and facing extinction, it is a reminder of the great service that they provide.

I would also like to thank librarians and archivists at a number of institutions; Hannah Brown at the Wellcome Trust; Dr Philip Young at the Warburg Institute; Erica New at the National Museum of Royal Navy, Portsmouth; and Li Wei Yang at the Huntington in Pasadena.

I also owe a particular debt of gratitude to Dr Peter Burt, Commodore and Honorary Historian at the Royal Motor Yacht Club in Sandbanks for helping find the portrait of Mansfield Cumming. It was painted in 1918 by H.F. Crowther Smith and believed to have been initialled by C himself; Tim Worner, the current owner, graciously allowed for it to be reproduced on these pages. Gillian Barnes-Riding at the Surrey Heath County Museum, was also very helpful in arranging for me to use the image of Max Knight which formed part of an exhibition on his life and (local) times.

I would like to thank the staff of The National Archive – particularly, Howard Davies in his earlier role – as well as Jane Rosen, James Taylor and Geoffrey Spender at the Imperial War Museum.

Friends, family and others read the manuscript. I am grateful for all their help, not least from the shared knowledge and advice of Jeremy Duns and Guy Walters, who know a thing or two about the subject. Thanks also to Dr David Whitehouse, for his friendship, encouragement and good advice. Thanks also to the denizens of Pussycat Alley –V and 3A (codenames as their real identities remain highly classified). Sadly, I should record the unfortunate circumstance of the passing of two friends, Ric Wickham and John Davies, whose companionship I appreciated at different times of my life. It was Ric who became a fellow observer of the heavens in my youth; and John, whose wise counsel is now sorely missed. I think they would have liked this book.

I also wish to thank my own agent (literary, not secret), Humfrey Hunter, dedicated handler (who commissioned the book) Mark Beynon, as well as the not exactly clandestine services of not really forged documentation but splendidly designed ones at The History Press: Naomi Reynolds, Caitlin Kirkman and Katie Beard.

All throughout this time, I have been helped (some of the time) by a black cat and (at all times and in all places) a truly bewitching, shining figure. As ever, without Sarah, my wife, the writing of this book would simply not have been possible. Her help, love and care in so many ways gave me the strength of purpose to head towards my desk. I should also thank her for not putting a hex on me as our workroom teetered with both esoterica and an equally esoteric failing – the loud playing of John Barry 007 soundtracks ('in the name of research', obviously). Thanks also to Tilly, who reminded me to have lunch (his own, mainly) by sticking his claws into my leg on innumerable occasions. To Sarah, thank you, love – it wouldn't have been possible without you. And now, the back room can be reclaimed from the ghosts (spectres, natch) and the cat can be fed.

Nicholas Booth
June, 2016

Permissions

All MI5 and official government files are Crown Copyright and reproduced here courtesy of the UK National Archive and permission of the Controller of HMSO.

All material quoted from the James Bond novels appears here with permission of Curtis Brown, as follows: p. 8, 'the whites of the eyes', from p. 77, *Casino Royale*, (c) 1953; p. 10, 'all just the stuff', from p. 100, *On Her Majesty's Secret Service*, (c) 1963; p. 100, 'Isn't that chap Sefton Delmer?' from p. 15, *Diamonds are Forever*, (c) 1955.

This book has not been authorised by any official James Bond publication or property. Various views in this book do not reflect the policies or are endorsed by the various individuals, institutions or, indeed, copyright holders.

A number of private collectors were very helpful in finding obscure images who did not wish to be publicly identified. Grateful acknowledgement is made to the following for permission to reproduce photographs shown here in the plate section.

Dr John Dee, courtesy of the Wellcome Foundation; the image of V.V. Tilea, courtesy of the Romanian Culture Centre in London (c) Ratiu Family Foundation, England 2016. All rights reserved. www.ratiu.com; the 'Modern Nostradamus' image of Louis de Wohl is from his MI5 file in KV2/2821 p. 11 of Part 2; Mansfield Cumming courtesy of Tim Worner and the Royal Motor Yacht Club; the image of Admiral Wilhelm Canaris comes from the Gedenkstaette Deutscher Widerstand in Berlin. The image of Max Knight (and friend) reproduced by the kind permission of Surrey Heath Museum, Knoll Road, Camberley; Evan Morgan (and his own friends at a tea party in 1935) courtesy of Tredegar House Archives, National Trust; Walter Schellenberg courtesy of the United States Holocaust Memorial Museum Reproductions Department, originally supplied by Gerald (Gred) Schwab, 1946. The image of Georg Elser is courtesy of the Gedenkstaette Deutscher Widerstand in Berlin). The image of Agnes Bernelle, provided by Andrew Macklin and public domain; the image of Dennis Wheatley, courtesy of Dominic Wheatley; the note about de Wohl's uniform is from TNA KV2/2821 113a; the dedication in the Crowley image from a frontispiece of a book given to Dennis Wheatley, now in private hands.

Every effort has been made to trace copyright holders and to obtain their permission for the use of copyright material. We apologise for any errors or omissions and would be grateful if notified of any corrections that should be incorporated in future reprints or editions of this book.

BIBLIOGRAPHY

Andrew, Christopher, *Her Majesty's Secret Service: The Making of the British Intelligence Community* (Hodder & Stoughton, 1986).

Andrew, Christopher, Defence *of the Realm: The Authorised History of MI5* (Penguin, 2010).

Aster, Sidney, *1939: The Making of the Second World War* (André Deutsch, 1973).

Balfour, Michael, *Propaganda In The War 1939–1945* (Routledge, 1979).

Baker, Phil, *The Devil is a Gentleman: The Life And Times of Dennis Wheatley* (Dedalus, 2005).

Bassett, Richard, *Hitler's Spy Chief: The Canaris Mystery* (Orion, 2005).

Beesley, Patrick, *Very Special Admiral: Biography of Admiral John H. Godfrey* (Hamish Hamilton, 1980).

Beevor, Jack, *SOE: Recollections and Reflections (1940–1945)* (The Bodley Head, 1981).

Bennett, Gillian, Churchill's *Man of Mystery: Desmond Morton And The World Of Intelligence* (Routledge, 2007).

Bennett, Gillian, *A Most Extraordinary and Mysterious Business: The Zinoviev Letter of 1924* (History Notes series of the Foreign and Commonwealth Office, 1999).

Bernelle, Agnes, *The Fun Palace* (Liliput Press, Dublin, 1986).

Best, Sigismund Payne, *The Venlo Incident* (Hutchinson, 1950).

Bloch, Michael, *Operation Willi: The Nazi Plot To Kidnap The Duke of Windsor* (Weidenfield & Nicolson, 1986).

Booth, Martin, *A Magick Life: A Biography of Aleister Crowley* (Simon and Schuster, 2001).

Brissaud, André, *Canaris* (Weidenfield & Nicolson, 1973).

British Security Coordination: The Secret History of British Intelligence in the Americas, 1940–1945 (St Ermin's, 1998).

Brouder, George C., *Foundation of the Nazi Police State* (University of Kentucky Press, 1990).

Bullock, Alan, *Hitler and Stalin: Parallel Lives* (Harper Collins, 1991).

Burleigh, Michael, The *Third Reich: A New History* (Pan, 2001).

Busby, Paul, *Hush Hush: The Peculiar Career of Lord Tredegar* (Little Knowledge, 2013)

Cabell, Craig, *Dennis Wheatley: Churchill's Storyteller* (Spellmount, 2005).

Cave Brown, Anthony, *The Secret Servant: The Life of Sir Stewart Menzies, Churchill's Spymaster* (Michael Joseph, 1988).

Churton, Tobias, *Aleister Crowley, the Biography* (Watkins, 2012).

Churton, Tobias, *The Beast In Berlin: Art, Sex and Magick in the Weimar Republic* (Inner Traditions, 2014).

Cradock, Percy, *Know Your Enemy: How The Joint Intelligence Committee Saw The World* (John Murray, 2001).

Cross, J.A., *Sir Samuel Hoare: A Political Biography* (Cape, 1977).

Crowley, Aleister, *The Confessions of Aleister Crowley* (Arkhan, 1989).

Crowley, Aleister, *The Diary of a Drug Fiend* (Webster, 2010).

Crowley, Amado, *The Secrets of Aleister Crowley* (Diamond, 1991).

Crowley, Amado, *The Riddles of Aleister Crowley* (Diamond, 1992).

Crowley, Amado, *The Wrath of Aleister Crowley* (Diamond, 1994).

Cruickshank, Charles, *Deception In World War II* (Oxford, 1981).

Curry, Jack, *The Security Service: 1909–1945* (Public Record Office, 1999).

Deacon, Richard, *A History of the British Secret Service* (Müller, 1969).

Delmer, Sefton, *Black Boomerang* (Secker, 1962).

Doerries, Reinhard (ed.), *Hitler's Last Chief of Foreign Intelligence: Allied Interrogations of Walter Schellenberg* (Routledge, 2007).

Elliott, Nicholas, *Never judge a man by his umbrella* (Michael Russell, 1991).

Fleming, Peter, *Operation Sea Lion* (Hart-Davis, 1957).

Foot, M.R.D., *Resistance* (Metheun, 1974).

Foot, M.R.D., *Special Operations Executive: Outline History of the SOE, 1940–1946* (Mandarin, 1990).

Garnett, David, The *Secret History of the PWE: The Political Warfare Executive, 1939–1945* (St Ermin's, 2002).

Gerson, Stephane, *Nostradamus: How an Obscure Renaissance Astrologer Became the Modern Prophet of Doom* (St Martin's, 2013).

Goodrick-Clarke, Nicholas, *Black Sun: Aryan Cults, Esoteric Nazism and the Politics of Identity* (NYUP, 2002).

Goodrick-Clarke, Nicholas, *Helena Blavatsky* (North Atlantic Books, 2004).

Gordon, Mel, *Erik Jan Hanussen: Hitler's Jewish Clairvoyant* (Feral House, 2001).

Gorodetsky, Gabriel, *Grand Delusion: Stalin and the German Invasion of Russia* (Yale 2001).

Hart-Davis, Duff, *Peter Fleming, A Biography* (Cape, 1974).

Hart-Davis, Duff, *Man of War: The Secret Life of Captain Alan Hillgarth, Officer, Adventurer, Agent* (Century, 2012).

Hinsley, F.H., *British Intelligence in the Second World War: Its Influence on Strategy and Operations Volume One* (HMSO, 1986).

Hinsley, F.H., *British Intelligence in the Second World War: Its Influence on Strategy and Operations (History of the Second World War)* (abridged paperback, HMSO, 1993).

Höhne, Heinz, *Canaris* (Secker & Warburg, 1979).

Hopkirk, Peter, *The Great Game: On Secret Service In High Asia* (OUP, 1991).

Howe, Ellic, *Magicians of The Golden Dawn* (Routledge, 1972).

Howe, Ellic, *Astrology And The Third Reich* (Aquarian Press, 1984).

Howe, Ellic, *The Black Game* (Queen Anne Press, 1988).

Hutchinson, Roger, *The Beast Demystified* (Mainstream, 1998).

Judd, Alan, *The Quest For C: Mansfield Cumming and the founding of the Secret Service* (Harper Collins, 2000).

Kahn, David, *Hitler's Spies* (Macmillan, 1978).

Knightley, Philip, *The Second Oldest Profession: The Spy as Bureaucrat, Patriot, Fantasist and Whore* (Deutsch, 1986).

Lampe, David, *The Last Ditch: The Secrets of the Nationwide British Resistance Organization and the Nazi Plans for the Occupation of Britain 1940–1944* (Cassell, 1968).

Linebarger, Jerry, *Psychological Warfare* (Infantry Journal Press, 1948).

Masters, Anthony, *The Man Who Was M: The Life of Charles Henry Maxwell Knight* (HarperCollins, 1986).

Masters, Anthony, *Literary Agents: The Novelist As Spy* (Blackwell, 1987).

McCormick, Donald, *17F: The Life Of Ian Fleming* (Peter Owen, 1993).

Miller, Joan, *One Girl's War, Personal Exploits In MI5's Most Secret Station* (Brandon, Kerry, 1986).

Miller, Russell, *Codename Tricycle* (Random House, 2004).

Milne, Tim, *Kim Philby, The Unknown Story of The KGB's Master Spy* (Biteback, 2014).

McLachlan, Donald, *Room 39: Naval Intelligence in action 1939–45* (W&N, 1968).

Minshall, Merlin, *Gilt-Edged* (Bachman & Turner, 1975).

Montagu, Ewen, *Beyond Top Secret U* (Peter Owen, 1977).

Moorhouse, Roger, *Killing Hitler: The Third Reich and the plots against the Führer* (Cape, 2006).

Muggeridge, Malcolm, *Chronicle of Wasted Time* (Collins, 1973).

Magida, Arthur J., *The Nazi Séance: The Strange Story of the Jewish Psychic in Hitler's Circle* (Palgrave, 2011).

Messinger, Gary, *Propaganda And The State In The First World War* (Manchester University Press, 1992).

Popov, Dusko, *Spy/Counterspy* (W&N, 1974).

Read, Anthony, and Fisher, David, *Colonel Z: The Life and Times of a Master of Spies* (Hodder & Stoughton, 1984).

Schellenberg, Walter, *Labyrinth, The: Memoirs of Walter Schellenberg, Hitler's Chief of Counterintelligence* (Deutsch, 1956).

Sisman, Adam, *Hugh Trevor-Roper, The Biography* (Weidenfield, 2012).

Spence, Richard, *Secret Agent 666: Aleister Crowley, British Intelligence and the Occult* (Feral House, 2008).

Stafford, David, *Churchill and Secret Service* (Murray, 1997).

Tilea, Viorel Virgil, *Envoy Extraordinary – Memoirs of A Romanian Diplomat* (Haggerston, 1998).

West, Nigel, *MI6* (Weidenfield, 1983).

West, Nigel, *Counterfeit Spies* (Little Brown, 1989).

Winder, Simon, *The Man Who Saved Britain* (Picador, 2006).

Watt, Donald Cameron, *How War Came: The Immediate Origins of the Second World War* (Heinemann, 1989).

Wheatley, Dennis, *The Deception Planners* (Hutchinson, 1981).

Winterbotham, Frederick, *The Nazi Connection* (W&N, 1978).

Winterbotham, Frederick, *The Ultra Secret* (Futura, 1985).

Wighton, Charles, and Peis, Gunter, *Hitler's Spies and Saboteurs, Based on the German Secret Service War Diary of General Lahousen* (Henry Holt 1958).

De Wohl, Louis, *The Stars of War and Peace* (Rider, 1952).

INDEX